To my respected
colleague and departmental
neighbor John Post

Henry

The Development of Plato's Metaphysics

The Development
of
Plato's
Metaphysics

Henry Teloh

The Pennsylvania State University Press

University Park and London

Vanderbilt University provided assistance
in the publication of this book.

Portions of the following chapters of this book
were published, in somewhat different form, in the
following journals: Chapter 1, *Southern Journal of
Philosophy*; Chapters 1, 3, and 4, *Apeiron*; Chapters 2
and 4, *The Journal of the History of Philosophy*; Chapter
4, *Phronesis*.

Library of Congress Cataloging in Publication Data

Teloh, Henry, 1944–
    The development of Plato's metaphysics.

    Includes index and bibliography.
    1. Plato—Metaphysics.   2. Metaphysics.
I. Title.
B398.M4T44   184   80-17160
ISBN 0-271-00268-9

Designed by Glenn Ruby
Composition by Asco Trade Typesetting Limited, Hong Kong
Printed in the United States of America

FOR MARY,
SALLY, and ELIZABETH

Contents

Contents   *ix*

Preface

In this book I argue that Plato modifies and even changes his basic metaphysical positions. The focus of the early dialogues is the *psyche* and its states; the middle dialogues employ at least two distinct theories of separate Forms; and the *Sophist* and *Philebus* use kinds not Forms to solve their respective problems. There is already a massive amount of literature on Plato; nevertheless, I hope that the broad scope of this essay, as well as its detailed exegesis and argument, will recommend it to students of Plato.

For clarity of exposition I state my positions in a forceful and categorical manner. But I do not want my systematic presentation to mislead the reader. While the apex of Plato's philosophy is his metaphysics, Plato does not present his metaphysical beliefs in anything like a systematic treatise. Plato writes about metaphysics usually in the dialectical context of other problems, for example, the education of the potential philosopher-kings in the *Republic*, the nature of *eros* in the *Symposium*, and the good life for man of the *Philebus*. Plato often leaves gaps and unclarities in his exposition, especially where to remove them would be neither dramatically appropriate, nor directly relevant to his task. Moreover, Plato does not have a unified and settled metaphysical system, even within a single dialogue period. Rather Plato develops and changes his metaphysics both in response to insights from his predecessors—the Eleatics, the Heracliteans, and others—and to the evolving and changing philosophical problems he faces. Finally, Plato does not metaspeculate to any great extent about his metaphysics; thus it is difficult to ascertain Plato's consciousness of his intellectual development. There are, then, reasons to be more hesitant and tentative than I am in attributing positions to Plato. Plato is not a rigid thinker who simply elaborates on a single theme—the separate Forms—from beginning to end.

I summarize in the introduction the conclusions of each chapter, and my summaries, for the most part, follow the order of my arguments in the book. The introduction provides, then, a useful synopsis of the entire book. I recommend that the reader reread the introduction after completing the book, so that the detailed exegesis of particular texts does not obscure my overarching theories about Plato's development.

Frequently I criticize other commentators. The scholars whom I criticize the most are invariably those from whom I have learned the most. I do not offer my critical comments in a rancorous spirit, but rather from a desire to understand what Plato means. The positions I attack are usually those that I find most attractive. The remarkable advancements in Platonic scholarship of the last half century are in part the result of the frankness, honesty, and good will with which *logoi* are given and received.

I have accumulated numerous intellectual and personal debts that I am very pleased to acknowledge. The reader should not assume that any of the persons mentioned below would endorse either a part or the whole of this manuscript. We cannot, however, exonerate our teachers from all responsibility, any more than Gorgias is blameless for how his pupils use rhetoric! Being good Platonists we should also believe that if the result is admirable, then the cause or father is good.

First I would like to thank my teachers of Greek and Ancient Philosophy at the University of Wisconsin—Madison: James Duerlinger, Jon Moline, W. H. Hay, Paul Plass, and Frederick Solmsen. I owe a special debt to Bill Hay, who supervised my dissertation on the *Hippias Major* and whose constant encouragement and good will are most welcome. I am also grateful to my colleagues in the Philosophy Department at Vanderbilt. One could not desire a more stimulating, diverse, yet congenial group of friends. The Vanderbilt Philosophy Department has achieved the rare status of a community. Numerous graduate students at Vanderbilt have also contributed to a superb academic environment; I have learned as much in seminars and independent studies on Ancient Philosophy as I have taught.

David Louzecky and I coauthored an article on the third man argument that continues to influence my views on the *Parmenides*. David's enduring friendship is a debt that I can never repay. David Pomerantz and I coauthored an essay that is an early ancestor of the first part of Chapter 1. Some of David's views about the virtues and self-predication are preserved in the present work, and my debt to Professor Pomerantz is immense. Yukio Katchi stimulated my views about different ontological strata in the middle dialogues through a paper he read, and I commented on, at the Pacific Division of the American Philosophical Association. Richard Patterson influenced my views on the *Timaeus* by his comments on a paper of mine at the Western Division.

This book incorporates revised parts of several previously published articles. I thank the following journals for permission to include material that originally appeared in them: *The Journal of the History of Philosophy* for "Parmenides and Plato's *Parmenides* 131a–132c"; *Apeiron* for "Self-Predication or Anaxagorean Causation in Plato," and "The Isolation and Connection of the Forms in Plato's Middle Dialogues"; *Phronesis* for

"Plato's Third Man Argument" (with D. Louzecky); and *The Southern Journal of Philosophy* for "A Vulgar and a Philosophical Test for Justice in Plato's *Republic*."

Graduate School Dean Ernest Campbell, the Vanderbilt Graduate School, and the University Research Council have generously supported this book at several stages: summer stipends for research, a manuscript-preparation grant, and a subvention grant for publication. I gratefully acknowledge the generosity of the Vanderbilt Graduate School.

John Pickering of The Pennsylvania State University Press is a most cordial and humane editor. His enthusiasm and support for this book is the *sine qua non*. William H. Leue of the State University of New York at Albany read the manuscript for the Press, and wrote detailed comments on it. Professor Leue's comments both helped to improve the structure of the book and stimulated me to think anew about some issues. W. L. Parker did an excellent job of editing the manuscript, and I am indebted to him for many useful suggestions.

Sheila Mitchell produced a clear typescript from my atrocious hand-writing. Sheila did most of this typing concurrent with her duties as department secretary. Lesser people than Sheila would have perished, and my debt to her is immense. Jim Smeal helped in the arduous task of preparing the Greek, for which I am grateful.

My greatest debt is to my family: my wife Mary and daughters Sally and Elizabeth. Their interests were often denied to permit me time to work on the manuscript. My parents, Henry and Martha, made it possible for me to attend college and graduate school, and they set an admirable example for all parents by allowing their son to experiment and find his own interests in life.

Introduction

Some of the most influential scholars of our century argue for a unitarian account of Plato's dialogues. They include Paul Shorey, Harold Cherniss, Paul Friedländer, and most recently R. E. Allen.[1]* For convenience let us call them the unitarians, and call their thesis the unitarian thesis. And though the unitarians do not agree on every point in the dialogues, there is a readily identifiable essence to their thesis: the cornerstone of Plato's thought from the earliest "Socratic" dialogue to his last work, the *Laws*, is the theory of separate Forms. The separate Forms are atemporal, aspatial paradigms, and they are ontologically prior to their instances; that is, a Form can exist uninstantiated, although no instance of that Form can exist without it. There are also three corollaries to the main thesis: (1) Plato does not have a "mundane" Socratic ontology even though he employs, in the early dialogues, Socrates' techniques of refutation. (2) The *Parmenides* is not a work of self-criticism; rather, its arguments either are not directed against the middle-period Forms or are known by Plato to be unsound. (3) The *Timaeus* is a late dialogue, and separate Forms have an important role in its cosmology. The unitarians basically see Plato as a consistent thinker who modified, developed, and elaborated new insights about the same cornerstone, the separate Forms. To support their thesis they appeal, among other things, to the fact that key terms in Plato's metaphysics—such as nature or essence (οὐσία); form, shape, or appearance (εἶδος, ἰδεα); pattern, example, or paradigm (παράδειγμα), and the like—occur in all dialogue periods.

Platonic studies is one of the most intensely trod scholarly areas, and it is foolhardy to claim that a position or argument traverses ground that is unplowed. Hence I do not claim that all the theses I will argue for are altogether novel; nevertheless, the combined influence and authority of the unitarians is so great that commentators are reticent to state and defend developmental hypotheses which deny that Plato always believes in separate Forms, and to assert that Plato changes his central philosophical concerns. This monograph attempts to fill this lacuna.

W. D. Ross, in Chapter 1 of *Plato's Theory of Ideas*, argues for a

*Numbered notes are assembled on pages 227–241, following the Supplementary Bibliography.

chronology of Plato's dialogues. I generally agree with Professor Ross's conclusions. However, following the sound advice of H. Cherniss,[2] I will not presuppose that within the three major periods—early, middle, and late—an accurate chronology is possible. Among the dialogues I will refer to, the *Gorgias, Euthyphro, Meno, Protagoras, Lysis, Laches, Republic* 1, *Charmides, Apology, Crito, Euthydemus,* and *Hippias Major* are early; the *Phaedrus, Phaedo, Symposium, Republic* 2–10, and *Parmenides* are middle; and the *Timaeus, Laws, Sophist, Theaetetus, Politicus,* and *Philebus* are late. I have mentioned the dialogues in random order within each period.

I have divided this essay into five chapters. In this introduction I will outline the major conclusions of each chapter. Thus this section is both an introduction to each chapter as well as a handy summary of the positions argued for in this book.

Summation of the Argument

The first chapter is about the early dialogues, and I am concerned in it with two major questions: (1) What is the ontological status of the virtues—justice, piety, courage, temperance, wisdom—that is, how and where do they exist? (2) What is virtue or a virtue? Plato never explicitly asks the first question, while the second dominates the early works. In order to answer the first question I extrapolate three necessary conditions for a virtue from Plato's practice of dialectic. If something is the virtue Φ, then it is (a) that *by which* all Φ acts are Φ, or are done Φ-ly; (b) it is *in* all and in only Φ acts; and (c) it is the epistemic paradigm by which we judge whether or not an act is a Φ act. For example, if something is the pious, then it is that by which all pious acts are pious; it is in all and in only pious acts; and it is the epistemic paradigm by which we judge whether or not an act is pious. These conditions are obviously open to a number of different interpretations, and hence they are consistent with different accounts of the ontological status of the virtues. A correct account of the ontological status of the virtues should also help us to explain and understand other early Socratic motifs, for example, Plato's denial of *akrasia* ("weakness of will"), his emphasis on care for the *psyche*, and the so-called self-predications in the *Protagoras*: "Justice is just," "Holiness is holy," and the like.

Using the above conditions and motifs, I will argue on both philosophical and exegetical grounds that the virtues are neither characteristics of acts, nor separate essences or Forms. The virtues are not characteristics of acts because the Socratic revolution in ethics is a turn inward to the *psyche*, and a concern for the conditions of the *psyche* with respect to virtue and vice. In the early dialogues Plato rejects descriptions of the virtues that mark out classes of actions, because if such descriptions are of sufficient generality, then they are always susceptible to counterexample. For example, if justice is the characteristic of "paying back one's debts," it will turn out that some such acts are just and others unjust. Thus this characteristic, and others like it, cannot be an epistemic paradigm because it marks out a class of actions that includes both just and unjust acts. But the paradigm of *F*-ness must be purely *F*; it cannot be *F* and not-*F*, or include *F*-acts and not-*F* acts.[3] Hence Plato rejects characteristics of acts as accounts of the virtues.

Harold Cherniss and R. E. Allen, among others, believe that the virtues are separate essences or Forms. They also claim that the separate essences are paradigms, but they deny that the paradigms are self-predicated. Justice, for example, is that by which we can tell whether or not acts are just, but justice itself is not just or, for that matter, unjust. The apparently self-predicational assertions are in fact, Allen and Cherniss believe, identity claims.[4] I will argue that self-predication is a necessary condition for epistemic paradigmatism; moreover, I will show from a careful analysis of the texts that Plato self-predicates the virtues. But are the virtues separate essences or Forms? I will argue on the basis of the above necessary conditions and motifs that the virtues are not Forms. The evidence in the early dialogues is that we are to look inward to the *psyche* for the paradigmatic virtues. When Plato says at *Euthyphro* 6e[5] that we are to look at the paradigm of piety, his language is consistent with the interpretation that we are to look inward at a psychic paradigm; and the evidence in the other texts that are close in date of composition to the *Euthyphro* shows that this is the best interpretation.

I argue that the virtues are psychic states. In early as well as late dialogues, the *psyche*[6] is the source or principle of motion. Thus psychic states cause or move a person to act. But the *psyche* is also, to use Socrates' nutritional metaphor, fed by *logoi*; hence it is intentionally and intelligently directed towards ends. Psychic states are, then, not only the moving causes of action, but also the reasons for action. That Socrates, in the early dialogues, does not distinguish reasons from causes explains his intellectualized views on education.

Justice, for example, is a necessary condition for a just act because it is *manifest in* every just act; it is a sufficient condition because it is the psychic cause *by which* all just acts are just. Socrates wants an interlocutor to look into his *psyche* at what produces virtuous behavior. A virtue is at first simply the cause of the appropriate type of behavior. When Socrates is able to say what a virtue is, then the acts it produces are focally and parasitically called after the virtue. For example, if we posit the claim that piety is wisdom, then we can parasitically call all pious acts wise acts. Virtuous actions are focally named after their psychic causes, and hence these psychic causes are paradigms.

I will also argue that the virtues are self-predicated because Plato employs the causal principle (CP). The causal principle is that a cause must have the quality that it produces (or in the case of formal and final causation, explains) in something else. The virtues are, to some extent, modeled on the Pre-Socratic power-elements—earth, air, fire, and water—that have what they transmit. Water makes things moist, for example, because it has moistness in it; justice makes actions and men just because it, itself, is just. The major conclusion of the first chapter is that the center of gravity for the early dialogues is the *psyche*, and not the separate Forms.

If the virtues were separate Forms or characteristics of acts, then the most that Plato could claim is that they are coinstantiated.[7] But as psychic states the virtues can be literally identical, and I will argue that they are. Each virtue is wisdom or the knowledge of good and evil, and hence justice = temperance = courage, and so on. In the early dialogues I show that the following argument occurs again and again:

> (1) Only knowledge (of good and evil) is really beneficial.
> (2) A virtue, Φ, is really beneficial.
> ∴ (3) Φ is the knowledge of good and evil.

Plato, I argue, believes that this argument is sound, but for pedagogical reasons he overtly rejects it with intentionally contrived and spurious claims.

To support my contentions about Plato's educational intent, I will investigate, in detail, the dramatic structures of the early dialogues, and early Socratic pedagogical technique. I show that dialectic *psychagoga* (*psyche*-guiding) is not simply negative refutation (*elenchus*), but also the positive leading of the *psyche* by suggestion, innuendo, paradox, or the like. Socratic education never consists, and for good reason, in the direct telling or transmitting of information. The early dialogues are not simply a series of refutations as some commentators believe.[8] *Aporia* (perplexity) administers the sharp shock of defeat, and opens the *psyche* to the possibility of truth, but then positive *psychagoga* is necessary for education; yet *e-duco* must continue to mean "lead out from within," and hence Socrates uses indirect means of communication.

I conclude the first chapter with a couple of criticisms of the early Socratic ethical enterprise; in particular, I argue that Socrates is caught in an uninformative circle of namings: actions are called after the psychic state that produces them, and psychic states are called after the actions they produce.

In the second chapter I discuss the beautiful in the *Hippias Major* and The Beautiful in the *Symposium*. I believe that the *Hippias Major* is a genuine Platonic dialogue, and that it is early in date of composition;[9] the

Symposium is a middle-period work. Thus this chapter is a bridge between my discussions of the early and the middle dialogues. The overarching purpose of this chapter is to show that the beautiful and The Beautiful[10] are very different sorts of beings, and in what ways they differ.

Beauty for Plato has a much broader meaning than it does for us; beauty is found not only in the fine arts but also in the mechanical; and Plato does not succumb to the later tendency to deny aesthetic value to the mechanical arts. Beauty is simply excellence in general, and excellence can be found in natural bodies, *psyches*, political states, artifacts, and the like.

In the *Hippias Major* I first discuss Hippias' three accounts of the beautiful. These accounts fail because they turn up what is both beautiful and not beautiful; a beautiful maiden is ugly when compared to Aphrodite, gold in some contexts is less appropriate and hence less beautiful than fig wood, and the conventionally noble life is not desirable for a god or hero. Thus a sensible particular, a mass object (gold), and a set of events are shown not to be the beautiful. Plato constantly reminds Hippias that the beautiful is that *by which* all beautiful things are beautiful, and hence the beautiful is itself always beautiful (292e). I show that the *Hippias Major* also presupposes that a cause must have the quality that it explains in something else, but unlike the virtues, the beautiful is not an efficient cause.

Next I discuss Socrates' three accounts of the beautiful. The latter two give important effects of the beautiful: the beautiful produces benefit and pleasure to sight and hearing. Plato designs these accounts so that they lead the *psyche* to the common source of real benefit and pleasure. But, as I will show, since they only state effects of the beautiful and not its nature, Plato, with intentionally startling and consciously contrived paradoxes, destroys the accounts in order to prod Hippias to investigate beauty for himself. In the *Gorgias* at 503e ff. Plato states a clear account of his early theory of excellence or beauty. The beautiful is the κόσμος (harmony) of a phenomenal object's elements, that explains why it is beneficial and pleasant to hearing and sight. I show that the same view is hinted at in the *Hippias Major*,[11] and when applied to that dialogue it helps us to explain Socrates' three accounts. Since the beautiful is the harmony or proportion within something, it is not a separate essence. I also remove several objections to this interpretation. The ontology of the *Hippias Major* is as "mundane" as that found in other early dialogues.

In the middle dialogues there is a striking μετάβασις εἰς ἄλλο γένος "a change into another kind."[12] While Plato earlier sought phenomenal excellence, in the middle works he receives a new vision of Being. The change is so drastic and so firmly announced that we must literally suppose that at this point in his development Plato reads "father"

Parmenides and accepts the Parmenidean criteria for Being. If something "is," then it must be ungenerated, indestructible, indivisible, unchanging, pure or uniform, and the like. The predicates applied to the Forms are the direct descendents of the "signposts" for Being in Parmenides' poem (cf. esp. DK 28 B8).[13] But Plato is also very much in the tradition of the Pre-Socratic philosophers, Democritus, Empedocles, Anaxagoras, and the others, who both believe Parmenides' account of Being and try to save the phenomena. Being must explain appearance. Plato turns to this task with originality and insight.

In the *Symposium* I concentrate on Diotima's ladder of assent. I show that the beautiful of the *Hippias Major* and *Gorgias* belongs on the lower rungs of the ascent prior to the appearance of "that marvelous, beautiful nature," The Beautiful. The beautiful is found *in* bodies, *psyches*, laws, institutions, and the like. But as soon as we turn away from the beauty of phenomena, and to the "great sea of The Beautiful," we encounter an object quite unlike anything found in the early dialogues. I show that this new kind of object, The Beautiful, is described in much the same way that Parmenides' Being is; of course there are important differences because Plato believes in a plurality of Forms as well as phenomena, while for Parmenides there is only Being. The Beautiful always is, it is neither generated nor destroyed, it is unchanging; The Beautiful is always and in every way beautiful so that it can appear to be pure beauty. The Beautiful is isolated and separate; it is not in things like the beautiful. Finally, while The Beautiful remains unchanging, beautiful phenomena, which are generated and destroyed, participate in it.

The middle dialogues introduce a contrast that is nowhere found in the early ones. The Beautiful always exists and is unchanging, while phenomena come to be and are destroyed, and also change in other ways. The gulf between the changeless and mutable, the really real and the deficiently real, is not found in the early works. In the early dialogues justice and the beautiful, when they exist, are always respectively just and beautiful. But neither a virtue nor the beautiful always exist because they are generated in things; in the *Laches* the question is how to add courage to the *psyche*, and in the *Gorgias* how to create excellence in a *psyche*. But a Form is not the sort of thing that is created or generated. I also show on other grounds that the ontologies of the early and middle dialogues are very different.

In the third chapter I argue that in the middle period Plato has two models for knowledge and that they imply incompatible accounts of what a Form is. In the *Symposium, Phaedo, Republic,* and *Phaedrus* there are two necessary and jointly sufficient conditions for the possession of knowledge: first, the intellectual sight of or grasp of a Form; and second, the ability to give an account. These conditions are usually complementary; giving an account helps the philosopher to achieve the sight of the Forms, and this sight generates further *logoi* (statements). Plato, however, often treats these two conditions as distinct models for knowledge: the first where he emphasizes the sight of the Forms and deemphasizes giving an account, the second where he stresses giving an account and minimizes the sight of the Forms.

These models depend upon incompatible accounts of what a Form is. When Plato emphasizes the visual model he begins with an unmitigated Parmenidean/Heraclitean juxtaposition: The Forms are a plurality of Parmenidean Beings, and they explain the contrary characteristics of phenomena, the famous "identity of opposites" of Heraclitus. Phenomena are not fully real, both because they are generated and destroyed and because they suffer contrary predicates. For example, a Georgia beauty queen is beautiful when compared with a monkey, but ugly when compared with Aphrodite (see *Symposium* 211a); Simmias is *one* man, and yet he has *many* parts (see *Parmenides* 129c–d). Since phenomena are temporally limited in existence and suffer contrary attributive, relational, and incomplete predicates, they are not completely real beings; moreover, they cannot be epistemic paradigms because they are impure; that is, they have mixtures of contrary predicates.

Plato introduces the Forms to explain the contrary predicates, and hence to "save the phenomena." Simmias is large by partaking in Largeness, and small by partaking in Smallness; he is one man among many because he partakes in Unity, and yet he has many parts because he partakes in Multiplicity (see *Parmenides* 129a ff., *Republic* 525a ff.). When Plato introduces the Forms to save the phenomena, he operates with a Parmenidean account of them: each Form is incomposite; that is, it does not have either physical or conceptual parts, and thus it is eternal, immutable, and separate from the physical flux. The Forms are unchanging monads, and thus real Beings. Each Form is, moreover, isolated both from phenomena and from the other Forms, and isolation is a necessary condition for a Form to be pure (καθαρόν, ἄμικτον, εἰλικρινές, *Symposium* 211e) and uniform (μονοειδές, *Symposium* 211b, *Phaedo* 78d). Purity and uniformity are identical, and they imply that a Form has only the following predicates: (1) the metapredicates had necessarily by all of the Forms, such as unchanging, pure, beautiful, divine, and the like; and (2) the definite descriptive predicate of a specific Form, for example, Equality is always equal, Justice is always just, and the like. The isolation of a Form, moreover, guarantees that it does not have the contrary relational predicates of phenomena, and hence it is the sort of entity that can both save the phenomena and act as an epistemic paradigm.

With the visual model for knowledge, I will also discuss two topics central to Plato's Forms: self-predication and degrees of reality. I will argue that Plato is committed to self-predication in the middle dialogues; that is, the definite descriptive predicate of a specific Form is said univocally of that Form and of the phenomena that partake in it. But why are the Forms self-predicated? I will show that self-predication is a necessary condition for epistemic paradigmatism; it explains why a Form always *appears* purely and uniformly *F*. Moreover, self-predication is a necessary condition for a Form to be the explanation of the relevant characteristic in phenomena. We can explain key self-predicational passages if we attribute to Plato an unconscious legacy from the Pre-Socratics: an explanatory entity must have the characteristic that it explains. Plato's Forms combine both Parmenides' criteria for Being and the Pre-Socratic philosophers' conception of an elementary substance-power, although the Forms are only formal and final causes.

I will also show that a Form is a real Being if and only if: (1) it is temporally unlimited in existence, (2) it has all of its predicates necessarily, and (3) it has no contrary predicates. A phenomenal object, x, is deficient with respect to a predicate F if: (1) x is contingently F, or (2) x is F and not-F, or (3) x is temporally limited in existence. Since all phenomenal objects satisfy condition (3), they are altogether deficient because they are temporally limited in existence. Hence different strata of reality in Plato result both from existential and from predicational considerations. I will also explain why Plato holds these conditions for real and deficient beings.

When Plato emphasizes the discursive model for knowledge, he produces a different account of what a Form is. Although he denies in the *Cratylus* that every "name" pictures or imitates its meaning, he assumes in the middle dialogues that the Forms connect just as names correctly connect in noncontingent *logoi*, and these *logoi* noncontingently connect with each other. Thus through examining *logoi* a philosopher can come to see the Forms and how they connect. On this conception a Form is a reified meaning.

Discursive knowledge has two distinct phases: (1) the definitions of particular Forms, and (2) the dialectical interweaving of *logoi* in order to gain a synoptic view of the Form-world. I will argue that the definitions of some Forms imply that they are composite, complex entities; for example, since the definition of Justice is "each part doing its proper work," the Form Justice is a meta-Form: Plato views it as the harmonious functioning of all the Forms. Furthermore, the interweaving of *logoi* implies that the Forms connect together, and thus that they are not isolated. These connections will, I argue, destroy the paradigmatic nature of the Forms, and so they will no longer be pure standards for judgment.

My purpose is not, however, to hang Plato with an inconsistency. The diagnosis of the inconsistency reveals a change and development in his thought. I believe that both within middle-period dialogues, and perhaps even across them if indeed the *Symposium* was composed earlier than the others,[14] there is a tendency for Plato to move from the visual to the discursive model, and hence from the isolation of the Forms to their connection. This change is, of course, a gradual movement, and it is not without backslidings.

In the fourth chapter I show that the *Parmenides* represents a crisis in Plato's thought, but that the seeds for a solution to the perplexities are already present in the middle works. The *Parmenides* attacks an earlier notion of Form, that connected with the visual model for knowledge; the first part of the dialogue attempts to show that Forms have contrary predicates just like the phenomena. The second part of the dialogue is a dialectical training in the discursive analysis of the Forms; while it does not itself have a positive content, it is the sort of analysis that will ultimately explain—as in the *Sophist*—the different and even contrary predicates of the εἴδη.

Zeno purports to show that the members of any plurality are *F* and not-*F*, and hence that they are inconsistent and nonexistent. Zeno believes that he is paying back the proponents of plurality with even greater absurdities than they see in Parmenides' Being. His motive is to indirectly support Parmenides' thesis that, as Plato puts it, "all is one." Zeno, in fact, draws the implications of the Heraclitean "identity of opposites," just as the real Parmenides did against the Milesians. Some Milesians had a monistic account of nature—water, air, or the like—but they were also pluralists; air, for example, appears as fire when it is rarefied, and thus what is really air is also fire. But, Parmenides argues, something cannot be both *F* and not-*F* and continue to exist; the Milesian accounts of nature are thus incoherent, and Being must be a uniform whole. Just as the real Parmenides attacks Heraclitean paradox and Milesian pluralism, so too the dramatic character Parmenides attacks Plato's two-tiered pluralism of Forms and phenomena. And with an ironical twist, just as the real Zeno defends Parmenides, so too the dramatic character Parmenides defends Zeno. The Eleatic arguments, however, depend upon a failure to distinguish qualities from things qualified.

Socrates moves to block the inference to Parmenides' thesis by introducing the Forms to save the phenomena, a move familiar to us from the middle dialogues. An object is *F* because it partakes in *F*-ness, and it is not-*F* because it partakes in not-*F*-ness. Hence Plato introduces the Forms to explain the contrary characteristics of phenomena. But if the Forms are to save the phenomena, they cannot, themselves, suffer contrary characteristics. To preserve their purity, Plato makes two assumptions: (1) the Forms do not interconnect with each other, and are as much as possible isolated; and (2) each Form is self-predicated. The *Parmenides* scrutinizes the type of Form connected with the visual model for knowledge; thus it attacks an account of Form found in the middle dialogues.

Socrates thrice challenges Parmenides to show that the Forms suffer the same perplexities as phenomena, and this challenge is the key to understanding the *Parmenides*. In the first part of the dialogue Parmenides responds to this challenge by an analysis of participation. Forms suffer contrary predicates because phenomena participate in them. Since each pure Form is as isolated as possible from everything else, the only way Parmenides can get at them is through participation. Different attempts to explain participation fail because the Forms come to have F and not-F characteristics. Each Form is, by hypothesis, one; that is, it is incomposite and unique. But if a Form is *in* the different phenomena, either as a part or as a whole, then it is split into parts or multiplied in phenomena; and if a Form is *over* the multiplicity, as in the third man arguments, then its explanatory function as the one that explains the many, in conjunction with the purity of a Form—F-ness is always F—generates an infinite series of specifically identical Forms. Each Form, which must be one, is yet many; thus the Forms suffer contrary predicates like the phenomena; hence they cannot explain and save the phenomena because they themselves are as much in need of salvation. Parmenides shows that a two-tiered pluralism, Forms and phenomena, generates the Heraclitean "identity of opposites" at both levels, when one attempts to relate the tiers. Plato, with a certain bitter irony, turns his dramatic figure Parmenides loose against his Parmenidean Forms.

Nevertheless, Parmenides does not conclude that the Forms do not exist. Rather he states that only a man of considerable endurance and dialectical skill will believe that the Forms exist. Moreover, if discourse is to be possible, the Forms must exist (135b–d), because, presumably, they are the meanings of general terms. The second part of the *Parmenides* is, I believe, an exercise in the sort of dialectical training that is required to investigate the predicates of the Forms, and to explain their contrary predicates. This dialectical exercise treats the Forms—or at least some sort of entity—as the subjects of assertions; but there are, as far as I can see, no positive doctrinal lessons in the second part of the *Parmenides*. The second part, however, announces a renewed approach to the Forms through *logoi*, an approach that culminates in the arguments of the *Sophist*. Thus while the first part of the dialogue attacks the conception of Form implied by the visual model for knowledge, the second part acknowledges that dialectical training in *logoi* may resolve the difficulties.

In the last chapter I will primarily discuss the *Philebus*, *Sophist*, and *Timaeus*. There are, in broad terms, two major, incompatible interpretations of the late dialogues. The unitarians believe that Plato never gives up the theory of separate, paradigmatic Forms, and hence he does not give up the theory in the late dialogues. Let me divide the unitarian position into two claims: (1) The *Timaeus* is a late dialogue, and separate Forms occur in the *Timaeus*. (2) Even if the *Timaeus* is not a late dialogue, separate Forms occur in other late dialogues—the *Sophist*, the *Philebus*, and the like. Revisionists believe that Plato so significantly modifies the Forms that separate, paradigmatic Forms are not found in the late dialogues. Revisionists such as Owen also argue that the *Timaeus* is not a late dialogue; rather it antedates the *Parmenides* in composition.

My position on the late dialogues will be unacceptable to both partisan camps. Our best evidence, to date, is that the *Timaeus* is a late dialogue; and, as I will show, there is no doubt that separate Forms are found in the *Timaeus*. Hence for the present I must assume that the *Timaeus* is late; perhaps in the near future philologists will refine their methods and present us with more conclusive evidence one way or the other. Therefore, I tentatively reject one claim of the revisionists. But I will also argue that Forms are not found in the *Philebus* and *Sophist*; the εἴδη and γένη of these dialogues are kinds not Forms. Moreover, the *Sophist* and the *Philebus* do not presuppose, require, or imply Forms; both dialogues are about specific problems—the good life for man and how to speak about what is not the case—that do not need Forms for their solutions. Thus I reject a claim made by the unitarians, namely, that Forms occur in the *Sophist* and the *Philebus*.

For the *Philebus* I argue that the monads at 15b–c, as well as pleasure, knowledge, and even the good life, are kinds. A specific art uses division and collection on kinds as its basic method. The grammarian divides the genus letter into its specific types, and the musician divides sound into its types. At *Philebus* 16c–e Socrates states that the genus *is* one *and* many *and* an indefinite multitude. The genus is many, I argue, because it is in its species, and it is an indefinite multitude because the species are in their particular cases, and hence the genus, by transitivity, is also in those cases. The *Philebus* provides a solution to how the one can be many; one genus can have many species, and a species can be instanced in numerous cases. The *Philebus* also provides a solution to participation; a case of a genus or a species instances that genus or that species. Both solutions, however, are plausible only because the *Philebus* is concerned with kinds not Forms.

A philosopher, in contrast with a specific artisan, is concerned with the principles behind all art. These principles are limit, the unlimited, and the efficient cause of the application of limit to the unlimited. I show that all these principles are in the *Cosmos*, and hence that none of them can be identified with separate Form. The unlimited is a kind of generic substratum—temperature, size, motion, or the like. Limit is mathematical, quantitative, expressed for example in unit and number. When limit is applied to the unlimited the result is a specific—4 feet tall, 98°F., or the like—in contrast with unlimited size, unlimited temperature, or unlimited whatever. The application is brought about by intelligent *psyche* in the *Cosmos*.

Cherniss argues that *Philebus* 58a ff. introduces Forms.[15] This passage contrasts immutable being with generated becoming. But I show that this contrast is consistent with different interpretations. It could introduce kinds and their cases, or Forms and their participants. For kinds are always existing, just so long as they have cases, and Plato believes that the kinds are always instantiated. Moreover, kinds are like paradigms in that they have the standard, unchanging features of their instances; for example, the whale swims, eats plankton, bears its young alive. Therefore, *Philebus* 58a ff. does not prove that Forms are in the *Philebus*.

For the *Sophist* I argue, on numerous grounds, that both the divisions and collections and the communions of the greatest εἴδη are about kinds. I show that the interconnections between the greatest εἴδη cannot be read either as Form connections or as universally quantified statements. This is also true for the results of division and collection. The sophist is a hunter of young men. No Form is a hunter of young men; nor are all sophists such hunters, since some may be in prison or exile. Motion is definitely not at rest. The Form, Motion, however, is at rest, as are all the Forms; nor is it extensionally the case that each thing that is in motion also, in some respect, is at rest. The εἴδη and γένη of the *Sophist* can plausibly be read only as kinds, not as Forms. This is precisely what we should expect, since the greatest kinds are introduced to solve a problem that is common to *physiologoi*, gods, giants, and late learners—what are being and not-being? Only the gods embrace the theory of Forms, and hence the others would not believe a solution that requires Forms.

I will also discuss the Greek verb "to be" in the *Sophist*. I argue *contra* Owen that the puzzles of this dialogue are, in part, existential in nature. *Contra* Ackrill I show that Plato does not separate an existential sense of "to be." I will argue that "*x* partakes in being" allows us to add an undifferentiated "is" to *x*; "*x* is" is what Charles Kahn calls the veridical use of "to be," and existential, predicative, and identity uses are all special cases of the fundamental veridical use.[16] This conclusion about "to be" is similar to that found in Chapter 3, where I analyze "real Being" in the middle dialogues.

The *Timaeus*, on the other hand, has the most radical separation of any Platonic dialogue. I will argue for the following positions: (A) In the middle dialogues the Forms always are, but Plato does not claim that they are eternal; in the *Timaeus* the Forms are outside of space and time, they are eternal; and (B) In the middle dialogues there are primarily Forms for only attributive, relational, and incomplete characteristics, the *F* and not-*F* qualities of phenomena. But in the *Timaeus* there are Forms both for these characteristics and for sortals: for example, man, fish, dog, and the like. This increased extension of the Form theory is connected with a desubstantialization of phenomena. In the middle dialogues there tend not to be Forms for sortals because, for example, Simmias is in himself a man (cf. *Phaedo* 102 f.), and a finger is a perfectly good case of what it is to be a finger (cf. *Republic* 523 ff.); thus there are substantially characterized particulars in the middle dialogues. But in the *Timaeus* phenomena are *in toto* mere reflections of the Forms; phenomena are totally dependent on the Forms and the receptacle for their existence. The separation of the *Timaeus* is more radical than that found in any other dialogue.

After the *Parmenides* Plato is not a unified thinker. He experiments with different problems and employs different ontologies to solve them. The *Sophist* and the *Philebus* answer the perplexities of the *Parmenides*, but in an ontological context of kinds not Forms. Then in the cosmological and storylike context of the *Timaeus* radical separation of Forms appears. Does Plato also believe in Forms when he writes the *Sophist* and the *Philebus*? The evidence underdetermines any answer to this question.[17] I will speculate that Plato's belief in Forms is compartmentalized and ignored in the *Sophist* and the *Philebus* as he pursues problems in an intracosmic context.

Comments on Interpretation

I will complete this introduction with a number of brief comments on interpretation.

Philosophical plausibility or historical charity is one of the most widely applied, but seldom mentioned, canons of interpretation, especially among philosophers rather than classicists. The temptation is immense to make an historical figure an up-to-date and plausible thinker, smoothing out the inconsistencies and updating the strange views of being, causation, or the like. There are, of course, a number of legitimate applications of this criterion. If an historical figure holds two inconsistent views, one philosophically plausible and the other not, and if other things are equal—textual evidence, consistency with other claims, for example—then one may select the plausible view. Nevertheless, one should state the inconsistency, and see what ramifications it has, if any. Again, if a thinker has two views, one implied by other elements of his system, the other inconsistent with them, and if other things are equal, then one may apply historical charity. There are, of course, numerous other proper uses for this canon.

Historical charity also establishes the presumption that one should attempt to remove purported inconsistencies. But this presumption has its limits, and they are set by the textual evidence. Often it is better to try to understand why a philosopher is inconsistent than to doggedly attempt to remove the inconsistency.

There are numerous prevalent misuses of philosophical plausibility. One of the most common is to reject a view because it is incorrect, unintelligible—on some suitably rigorous theory of meaning—or unacceptable in one's philosophical milieu. Witness the difficulty Neoplatonic interpreters of Plato have in finding a forum for their material. It is not a popular view to maintain that aspatial, atemporal entities like the Forms have efficient causal efficacy. Another more subtle misuse is anachronism. Where Plato talks about psychic powers, commentators without explanation or justification discuss characteristics, attributes, and qualities;[18] and these are soon transformed into what I find to be the puzzling notion of an "immanent universal." [19] Whole interpretations of Plato often follow from this type of subtle modernizing that is tantamount to misunderstanding. Another example is the belief, common since the linguistic turn in philosophy, that the early dialogue question "What is *x*?" asks for the meaning of the term "*x*." This interpretation, which does not have strong textual support, would seem obviously correct to many philosophers influenced by the linguistic turn.

There are excellent methods for increasing one's awareness of anachronism and misplaced philosophical plausibility. If one is to study Plato, a modest acquaintance with ancient science and literature is important, and a better than modest knowledge of Pre-Socratic philosophy—its problems, thought patterns, and solutions—is mandatory. Also one is made aware of his own philosophical presuppositions by reading diverse commentators on Plato: Aristotle, Plotinus, Santayana, Vlastos, and others.

Plato's dialogues are divisible into three major periods: early, middle, and late. Within a particular period, I will frequently appeal to different dialogues to marshal evidence for a point. The rationale for doing this is, of course, that dialogues relatively close in date of composition are more likely to shed light on each other than are those separated by a greater period of years; for antecedently it is as plausible that Plato changes his concerns and develops new problems and solutions as that he is a unitarian thinker. This rationale does not preclude the possibility that within dialogues of the same period Plato holds different and even inconsistent views. For example, in the *Phaedo* appetitive desire may belong to the body, while in the *Republic* it is a function of the *psyche*. Nor should we be blind to the possibility that there could be tensions within the same dialogue: Are we given different pictures of dialectic in *Republic* VI and VII? Is the philosopher king less happy than he could be when he reenters the cave, or is he only fully satisfied when word and deed chime in harmony together?

I will refrain from a wholesale interpretation of the early dialogues by means of the middle, of the middle by the late, and the converse of these. There are, however, occasions when I do collect evidence from dialogues outside the period at issue. We must weigh such evidence with care, and with an eye judiciously fixed on the probabilities. For example, if we want to know what the word "paradigm" means at *Euthyphro* 6d–e, then it is relevant to this question to see how Plato uses the word in later contexts; also it is relevant to see how the word is used in ancient Greek literature, philosophy, and science. By these techniques we can at least establish a range of possible uses, although a suitable selection from this range depends upon contextual features in the *Euthyphro* and other early dialogues. Furthermore, we will occasionally be able to observe where Plato is going only by seeing where he has gone. The enigmatic statement in the early dialogues that "Temperate [supply any virtue adjective] things are done by temperance" can only be fully understood by seeing that in *Republic* IV Plato believes that actions are paronymously named from their causes, a view that he works out there in considerable detail. Of course, we cannot attribute the developed view to the early dialogues, but it does provide us with some evidence about how to interpret the earlier claim.

Frequently my arguments are about what some word means: "form," "nature," "one," "paradigm," for examples. We cannot assume that Plato uses a rigorous, regimented technical vocabulary; the odds are, and in several cases we have strong evidence, that the same word has different uses in different contexts. "Form" (εἶδος), for example, is used differently when talking about the *psyche*, the appearance of a body, and the Forms. In the first case εἶδος is used to refer to a psychic part, then to a visual appearance, and last to a transcendent entity. So when I investigate what some word means, I examine that word in a certain context.

As mentioned above, there are several sources to determine the range of uses that a word has: other occurrences of it in Plato, the Pre-Socratics, the medical writers, and the like. Moreover, there is always the dictionary. But when a range is established, we must then investigate what I have called "contextual features." Let us imagine that the word at issue is the general term "x". What, in the context, does Plato say about x's? What kinds of predicates do x's have? Where are we to look for x's? How are x's produced? Do x's have causal efficacy? What kind of causal efficacy do x's have? The answers to these kinds of questions form what I call the "logical grammar" of "x", and the logical grammar of "x" tells us what sorts of things x's are. Our answers, of course, are more or less reliable depending upon the amount of information available. There is, however, at least one problem with this procedure: we cannot assume that every occurrence of "x" refers to the same type of entity; so our selection of

passages is governed by the recurrence of items in the logical grammar.
Unfortunately, different types of entities may well have common items in
their logical grammars.

The textual evidence sometimes underdetermines the competing interpretations of the text. The textual evidence is then consistent with each
theory, and does not help adjudicate between them. We will meet this
situation most frequently in the late dialogues. For example, the claim
that man or ox is ungenerated and indestructible is compatible either with
a theory of separate Forms, or with a theory of kinds. For kinds also
always exist, just so long as they are instantiated, and Plato, like Aristotle,
probably believes that they always have instances. Conceivably the entire
Platonic corpus could underdetermine competing theories, but usually
underdetermination is isolated in a single statement or paragraph. The
contexts, examples, and related claims that Plato makes will usually
remove the underdetermination.

One of the most fruitful, exciting, and informative techniques in the
history of thought is to unearth the unconscious presuppositions of and
influences on a person's claims. But one view of interpretation would
utterly preclude such digging. Richard Robinson, in the introduction to
his *Plato's Earlier Dialectic*, argues for very stringent canons of exegesis.[20]
One of these is that if a thinker says S and S implies or even clearly (to us)
implies T, we may not impute T to that thinker unless he asserts T; for
the historical figure may not think that S implies T, or he may never even
think of T, T may not occur to him. To violate Robinson's canon from
the start, presumably he would hold the same view about S presupposes
T; for the same arguments would have equal force in this case as in the
former.

Indeed, Robinson's canons do remind us about what we can prove from
a text. But if we are to do more than simply restate or rearrange what
Plato said, we must also deal with the probabilities of interpretation.
Consider the following situation: Plato states S (the beautiful is beautiful),
and he states that S because of T (the beautiful makes things beautiful).
Suppose that we cannot find in Plato an explicit assertion for why S and T
are related; must this be the end of the matter? But suppose that in the
Pre-Socratics we find explicit statements of a principle, P, that links
statements like S and T (a cause must have the characteristic that it
produces in something else). Furthermore, imagine that Aristotle also
makes explicit assertions of P, and that P allows us to explain and
understand numerous, apparently unrelated, and perplexing claims in
Plato. We cannot conclude that Plato was well aware of P or that Plato
understood that he was committed to P; but it is reasonable to conclude
that P unconsciously influenced Plato. Moreover, the evidence for this
conclusion increases if we also show that Plato accepts other Pre-Socratic

views that imply *P* (the Forms are modeled on the Pre-Socratic power-elements); but, of course, the evidence immeasurably weakens if *P* is inconsistent with Plato's explicit assertions. I will frequently employ this technique of exegesis, and we must be careful to realize that historical interpretation is a subtle business of weighing and evaluating the probabilities.

I will close with some brief comments about my use of the literary aspects of the dialogues. The question is to what extent the dramatic features of a dialogue are relevant to an interpretation of its philosophical content. For the early Socratic dialogues—which use indirect communication and appear to end in utter perplexity—a literary analysis is essential. Hence I discuss at length the dramatic structures of these dialogues in Chapter 1, and that of the *Hippias Major* in Chapter 2. I will not, however, analyze interlocutors' characters and lives, not because this is unimportant, but because it is not directly relevant to my concern. I would be the first to admit that to understand, for example, Thrasymachus' *logoi* one should look at the behavior and character of Thrasymachus. But in the middle and late works Plato presents his metaphysics in lengthy expository passages. Socrates is usually the dramatic speaker, but he speaks for Plato. Even in the middle and late dialogues, however, one must be sensitive to literary factors. The context in which an interlocutor says something, and the dramatic characters who speak, are relevant to the philosophical content. This study attempts to be sensitive to such considerations.

In this brief section on interpretation I have attempted to state and justify some of my methods of procedure in this essay. For this reason the examples used are from the arguments that follow. I hope that the reader is in general agreement with me about the strategies used, even if we should disagree about their results. Let us now turn to the arguments.

I

Characters, Separate Essences, or Psychic States in the Early Dialogues

This first chapter is divided into four sections. In the first section I will investigate the ontological question about the virtues: How and where do they exist? In the second section I will discuss the "unity" of the virtues and the dramatic structures of the early dialogues. The evidence from dramatic structure will help support my position about the unity of the virtues. In the third section I discuss Socratic dialectic, that is, Socratic educational technique. The results of this section will support my analysis of the dramatic structures of the early works. Finally, I will conclude, in the fourth section, with some criticisms of the early Socratic ethical enterprise.

SECTION I: The Ontological Status of the Virtues

In this section we are interested in the ontological question about how and where the virtues in the early dialogues exist. I will draw evidence from most of the early dialogues, and my conclusions will have general application to those dialogues, but I will focus the discussion in Section I on *Euthyphro* 6e.[1]

> Teach me then what this form (ἰδέα) is, in order that I may look upon it (ἀποβλέπων), and use it as a pattern (παραδείγματι), and what is such as (τοιοῦτον) it, of the things either you or someone else does, I may say is holy, and what is not such as it, I may say is not.

In this passage Socrates appears to instruct Euthyphro about the question of interest to us. But the passage really does not tell us where to look for the paradigm, piety. Thus although considerable attention has been focused on *Euthyphro* 6e, there is disagreement about its import. The unitarian scholars claim that 6e is a persuasive passage, in fact the most persuasive passage for their thesis because, so they believe, it asserts that piety is a separate Form, apart from its instances.[2] Other scholars challenge the unitarian thesis as applied to the early dialogues, and deny that separate Forms occur in them, but they tend to ignore the *Euthyphro*, and concentrate on the *Laches, Charmides,* and *Protagoras.*[3] Let us focus directly on the strongest passage for our opponents' position, *Euthyphro* 6e. I will argue that 6e is compatible with the position that piety is a psychic state; moreover, our best evidence, which is from other early dialogues,[4] better supports the claim that piety, and the other virtues, are psychic states than that they are separate Forms, or characteristics of acts.

For some time, scholars have adamantly proffered incompatible accounts of the ontological status of the virtues in the early dialogues. We can, then, expect that the evidence is far from unambiguous. To do justice to the competing nuances of the textual evidence I will proceed as follows: First I will state and briefly discuss three necessary conditions for a virtue. Second, I will state several problems and motifs in the early dialogues that a satisfactory account of the virtues should help us to explain and understand. Then I will proffer three popular and plausible accounts of the ontological status of the virtues: the virtues are characteristics of acts, they are separate Forms, and they are psychic states. I will describe at length the first two positions and reject them. I will then argue for the third position. My arguments will also help explain such perplexities as self-predication, Socrates' denial of weakness of will, his emphasis on self-knowledge, and his urging that we care for our *psyches*.

Four Conditions for the Virtues

What kind of thing does Socrates seek when he asks his standard τί ἐστι question: "What is piety, courage, justice, and the like?" We can find three necessary conditions for a virtue in the early dialogues, and they partially regulate whether or not Socrates accepts an answer to a "What is it?" question.

Condition (1). If *x* is a virtue, then *x* is in (one and the same thing in) every *x* act (or act done *x*-ly). For example, if courage is a virtue, then courage is *in* every courageous act or act done courageously; if piety is a virtue, then piety is *in* every pious act.

Some texts for this condition are:

> Is not piety the same itself with itself in (ἐν) every action, and again is not impiety the opposite of complete piety, and is not impiety itself

like to itself, and everything that is to be impious has some single form (ἰδέαν)? (*Euthyphro* 5c–d)

Then all of these men are courageous, but some have acquired courage in (ἐν) pleasures, some in pains, some in desires, and some in fears, ... So try again and tell me first what is this thing, courage, that is the same (ταὐτόν) in (ἐν) all these cases. (*Laches* 191e, cf. 191d, 192b)

How should we interpret the "in" relation? Is *x* in acts as a characteristic of them? Is *x* manifest or displayed in actions as, for example, some Wittgensteinians claim that pain is in pain behavior? Or is *x*, a separate *eidos*, imaged in acts? The "in" requirement is far from unambiguous, and diverse accounts of the ontological status of the virtues interpret this condition differently.

Condition (2). If *x* is a virtue, then one may look upon and use *x* as an epistemic paradigm, and those acts that are such as *x* are *x* acts, and those that are not, are not. For example, if temperance is a virtue, then one may look upon and use temperance as an epistemic paradigm, and those acts that are such as temperance are temperate acts, and those that are not, are not.

The primary text for this condition is *Euthyphro* 6e, quoted in the introduction to this section. Other related texts are:

Now it is evident that if temperance is present (πάρεστι) to you, you will have some opinion concerning it. For being within (ἐνοῦσαν) you it must, if it is within you, provide some perception (αἴσθησιν), from which you can form an opinion concerning it, that is, concerning what temperance is and what sort of thing (ὁποῖόν τι) it is. (*Charmides* 158e–159a)

Again then, Charmides, pay attention and look into yourself (εἰς σεαυτὸν ἐμβλέψας); understand what sort of person temperance being present (παροῦσα) makes (ποιεῖ) you, and what sort of thing (ποία) it is that produces (ἀπεργάζοιτο) such an effect. (*Charmides* 160d)

This condition also is not clear. Are we to look away at a pattern that is outside space and time? Are we to look at a characteristic of acts? Or are we to introspect a paradigm in the *psyche*? Each of these interpretations has different implications for how we understand "paradigm," "look at," "form," and "such as" at *Euthyphro* 6e.

There is a purported problem with these first two conditions.[5] The objection is that condition (1) cannot be applied because you cannot know that some act is an *x* act until you know the epistemic paradigm for *x* acts. If condition (1) presupposes condition (2), then it cannot help establish (2); but Socrates, so it is said, often erroneously offers and accepts some acts as *x* acts before the paradigm for *x* acts is found.

Socrates frequently does not question "vulgar" judgments about acts. In fact he infrequently rejects acts as instances of a virtue, but often refuses them on other grounds: for example, they do not constitute a standard for some virtue. For standards are needed to adjudicate hard cases: Is Euthyphro's indictment of his father pious? Is fighting in heavy armor courageous? Socrates is, I believe, entitled to his method. It is legitimate to construct a theory based upon the best available evidence, in this case "vulgar" judgments about acts, and then after completing the theory, to reevaluate the earlier evidence in light of it. Because Socrates employs this method in the early dialogues, a tentative use of condition (1) does not presuppose an answer to condition (2).

Condition (3). If *x* is a virtue, then (a) *x* is that by which a person acts *x*-ly and is an *x* person, and (b) *x* is that by which all *x* acts are *x*. For example, if justice is a virtue, then (a) justice is that by which a person acts justly and is a just person, and (b) justice is that by which all just acts are just.

Some texts for this condition are:

> Remember then that I did not ask you this, to teach me one or two of the many holy acts, but this very form (αὐτὸ τὸ εἶδος), by which (ᾧ) all holy acts are holy; for doubtless you said that the unholy acts are unholy and the holy acts holy by one form (μιᾷ ἰδέᾳ). (*Euthyphro* 6d)

> Stranger from Elea, is it not by justice (δικαιοσύνη) that the just men are just? ... Then also the wise are wise by wisdom (σοφίᾳ), and all good things are good by the good (τῷ ἀγαθῷ)? ... Then these are something, for otherwise the others would not be such by them, if they were not something .... Then are not all beautiful things beautiful by the beautiful (τῷ καλῷ)? ... By the beautiful which is something? (*Hippias Major* 287c–d; also cf. *Protagoras* 332b f.)

How are we to interpret the dative of agency? Does it introduce, to use Aristotelian categories, formal, final, or efficient causation? Is a person, for example, just because after mentally seeing the separate Form of Justice he attempts, because of this knowledge, to imitate it? Does one strive for the formal/final cause, justice, and by so striving do just acts? Or does justice make one just because it is an efficient cause in his *psyche*? One would then be just by justice because justice moves him to do just acts. There is obvious disagreement about how to understand the instrumental dative, but any adequate account should explain both how acts and persons are *x* by some virtue *x*.

Conditions (1)–(3) are necessary conditions for a virtue. We must, however, at the outset distinguish two different questions: What type of thing is a virtue? What is the definition of a virtue? Examples of answers to the former question are: The virtues are characteristics of acts, separate Forms, or psychic states. Examples of answers to the second question are: "Justice is the knowledge of good and evil," or "Courage is staying steadfast at one's post." We cannot answer the second question, and define a virtue, until we know what type of thing we are trying to define. Socrates states conditions (1)–(3) overtly to regulate the definitional enterprise, but they also provide the best clues to the ontological status of the virtues.

Condition (4). An answer to the ontological question, as I shall call it, should also help us to explain and understand other Socratic motifs. I will list these items under condition (4), although they are obviously neither conjointly nor disjointly necessary conditions for a virtue.

(4a) Socrates denies "weakness of will." If one knows, for example, what justice is, then one will act justly. The knowledge of justice is a sufficient condition for just acts. Socrates alternatively claims that the possession of justice is a sufficient condition for its possessor being just.

(4b) Socrates believes that the *sine qua non* of the good life is self-knowledge. The aphoristic dictum is "know thyself."

(4c) Socrates repeatedly exhorts his interlocutors to care for their *psyches*. The true rhetorician or philosopher in the *Gorgias* improves the *psyches* of his listeners. In the *Charmides* (156e), Socrates states that every good and evil ultimately springs from the *psyche*.

(4d) The *logoi* of the virtuous person survive *elenchus*; Socrates, himself, always says the same things about the same things, and he is never tripped up in his arguments (*Gorgias* 509a). Moreover, the words and deeds of the virtuous man chime in harmony together—they are consistent (*Laches* 188c f.).

(4e) Justice is just, and holiness is holy (*Protagoras* 330c,e). Hopefully, an answer to the ontological question about virtue will help us to interpret and understand these "self-predications." Let us now turn to different answers to the ontological question.

The Characteristic Account
W. K. C. Guthrie argues that "No one reading the *Euthyphro* would suggest that when he [Socrates] asks 'What is the pious?' he has in mind anything but the characteristic common to all acts to which we give the name 'pious,' whose presence in them explains and justifies our applying the same epithet to all."[6] Guthrie also holds the same view for the other virtues.

Guthrie is not, however, clear about what counts as an instance of a characteristic *in* an act. Probably he means the sort of thing that is found throughout the early dialogues.[7] For example, Laches first defines courage as staying steadfast at one's post (190e); Polemarchus initially defines justice as "to render to each his due" (*Republic* I 331e); Charmides first defines temperance as "a kind of quietness in actions" (159b); and Euthyphro initially says that piety is "to do what I am now doing, to prosecute my father or any other wrongdoer" (5d–e). Each of these accounts gives a characteristic of a class of acts, and Guthrie presumably believes that this type of answer would be correct if and only if it contains all and only the virtuous acts at issue.

We can summarize the characteristic view as follows:[8]

> *x* is a virtue, if *x* is—
> (A) the characteristic *in* all and only *x* acts,
> (B) when recognized in act *a*, adequate evidence to confirm that act *a* is an *x* act,
> (C) the necessary and sufficient condition by which an act is *x*, and
> (D) manifest or recognizable as *x* without reference to either separate Forms or internal psychic states.

(A) purportedly satisfies condition (1), (B) condition (2), and (C) condition (3). (D) encapsulates both the denial that separate Forms occur in the early dialogues, and the claim that the pious is a characteristic of acts not agents.

The characteristic view interprets "in" as a metaphor. This metaphor is cashed in by descriptive-classification talk. Acts with descriptions $d_1 \ldots d_n$, which share in common description j_1, the just-making characteristic, are just acts. For example, paying back an educational loan, returning a borrowed submachinegun, and robbing a corporation may all be just acts because each instantiates, as Polemarchus claims, "rendering to each his due." "In" also indicates that characteristics are not separate from acts; that is, they cannot exist uninstantiated.

These characteristics are also paradigms that we are to look upon and use to adjudicate disputes. But "look upon" should not be taken literally because the moral-making features of acts are not literally visible. One does not see with the physical eye "to render to each his due," although one can see that an act instantiates this characteristic. We look upon the paradigm in the sense that we come to understand it through dialectic. The correct characteristic is a paradigm because it includes all and only the acts at issue; of course, the fundamental problem remains about how to determine that an act instantiates the paradigm, but Socrates never promises mechanical solutions. "Such as" at *Euthyphro* 6e is interpreted as a metaphor for instantiation.

The characteristic-virtue, *x*, is analogous to a formal cause because it is the necessary and sufficient definitory condition(s) for all and only *x* acts. Hence the characteristic is that *by which* all *x* acts are *x*, and thus the characteristic view explains the use of the instrumental dative.

How does this position handle conditions (4a)–(4f)? It admits that Socrates is mistaken to deny "weakness of will." A knowledge of the characteristic, *x*, is clearly not a sufficient condition for doing *x* acts. Self-knowledge is not an extraordinary knowledge about the self; it is the successful clarification and defense of one's most important beliefs. Thus self-knowledge is contrasted with opinion, exemplified in the testimony of the law courts, the vulgar views about justice, and the like. Care for the *psyche* is, moreover, a picturesque way of talking about doing dialectic. If care for the *psyche* is both a process and an achievement, then doing what Socrates does in the early dialogues is the process, and fastening one's beliefs with chains of steel is the achievement.

If the characteristic view were to interpret, for example, ἡ δικαιοσύνη ... δίκαιόν ἐστιν at *Protagoras* 330c as the predication "Justice is just," then it would impute absurdity to Plato. For a characteristic does not instance itself. The other alternative is to deny a predicative interpretation of such claims, usually in favor of an "identity" one: "Justice is justice," or "Justice is what it is to be just." Later I will discuss the merits of these alternatives.

Let us now turn to criticisms of the characteristic view. Its plausibility is initially weakened by the recognition of a certain pattern in the early dialogues. The first response to Socrates' "What is it?" question is usually some characteristic of acts, but Socrates immediately rejects these accounts. Guthrie might reply, however, that no general moral is to be drawn from these rejections. Interlocutors initially state characteristics that include too much or too little without ruling out the possibility that some other characteristic is correct.

But Socrates has deeper reasons for these rejections. Sometimes he claims that characteristic accounts are, in principle, too narrow. Here Socrates mistakenly believes that an account is of particular acts, act-tokens and not an act-type. Evidence that Socrates mistakes act-types for act-tokens is found, for example, at *Euthyphro* 6d (cf. *Laches* 190e f., and *Meno* 71e f.).[9] Although Euthyphro defines piety as the characteristic "prosecuting wrongdoers," Socrates replies that he did not ask for "one or two of the numerous acts that are pious...." Euthyphro states that piety is an act-type, but Socrates misinterprets his account to give act-tokens, and he rejects the account because he believes that it is in terms of act-tokens.

When, however, Socrates recognizes that a characteristic account states an act-type, he maintains that the act-type is too inclusive. The set of acts delineated will include some members that are *F* and some that are not-*F*.

But if the characteristic is to be an epistemic paradigm, then all of the acts that instantiate the characteristic must be *F*. An interesting example of this procedure is in *Republic* I (331c). Socrates distills from Cephalus' speech the following account:

> But speaking of this very thing, justice, are we to affirm then without qualification that it is truth-telling and paying back what one has received from anyone, or may these very actions sometimes be just and sometimes unjust?

Socrates immediately rejects this account with a counterexample: it is not just to return a weapon to someone who is not in his right mind. There is, moreover, no attempt to amend the account. The requirements of Socratic dialectic do not permit more than one simple specification of a class of actions. Conjunctions of characteristics prove not to be satisfactory (cf. *Hippias Major* 299b ff.), and qualifications (as that an account does not apply to insane persons) only show that the account is not correct. Thus sufficiently general characteristic accounts are invariably rejected; hence a satisfactory account of a virtue cannot be given in terms of behavior. A "What is it?" question cannot turn up what is, for example, pious and impious (*Euthyphro* 8a), or what is beautiful and ugly (*Hippias Major* 289a–b, 290d; cf. *Charmides* 160c, 161a–b). For a virtue is a paradigm, and a paradigm cannot mark out a set of *F* and not-*F* acts. Thus characteristic accounts of sufficient generality are rejected because they are susceptible to counterexamples. This is the main reason, I believe, for the Socratic revolution in ethics: the movement from behavior to the condition of the *psyche*.

Socrates is after a characteristic of men not acts (*Laches* 192a–c, *Charmides* 159b–160e, *Republic* I 332c–335e, 340c–343a, *Protagoras* 332a–333b). In the *Laches* he presents Laches with two analogies to help Laches define what courage is. The first (189e–190b) compares sight (ὄψις), the proper power (δύναμις, *Charmides* 168d–e) of the eye, with virtue which they desire to add to a *psyche* (ἀρετὴ παραγενομένη ταῖς ψυχαῖς, 190b). Just as one must know what sight is before an eye can be improved, so too one must know what virtue is before a *psyche* can be made excellent; and just as sight is the proper power of the eye, so too virtue is the excellence of a *psyche*. But Laches does not understand what sort of thing courage is when he defines it as "staying steadfast at one's post," and so Socrates instructs him with another analogy: courage is like swiftness, "the power (δύναμις) that gets a great deal done in a little time," whether it be *in* running, playing the lyre, speaking, or the like (192a–b). Socrates then asks Laches to state what courage is *in* all courageous acts (192a–c). Laches replies that courage is "a certain endurance of the *psyche*." Although Socrates does not think that this account picks out the correct psychic state, he implies that this is the sort of answer he seeks, and the remainder of the *Laches'* discussion is at the level of *psyche*. Most other early dialogues also display a movement away from behavior to the condition of the *psyche* (cf. *Gorgias* 504d f., *Meno* 87b f., *Charmides* 158e f., *Crito* 47d f.). The Socratic revolution in ethics occurs when Socrates leads an interlocutor away from external behavior to the internal condition of the—normally the interlocutor's—*psyche*.

Yet we do not find this dialectical movement in the dialogue of most concern to us, the *Euthyphro*. However, the dialectical development of a dialogue must, in part, be explained by the educational abilities and attainments of its interlocutors. For pure sluggishness of intellect we could not find a better candidate than "Straight-Thinker." He persistently looks to the Homeric divinities for the paradigm of piety, and even after "refutation," he continues to believe that man's relation to these "divinities" is a mercantile transaction (14e). Euthyphro, then, has not been stung by Socratic *elenchus*, and his dogmatic belief structure remains intact. Since Euthyphro is always looking up, Socrates cannot direct Euthyphro's vision into his own *psyche*.

Socrates both rejects behavioral characterizations of the virtues and moves dialectically inward to the *psyche*. Nevertheless, important Socratic motifs are verbally formulated at the behavioral level, but the meaning of these mere semblances is far removed from Socrates' true view. Part of Plato's great dramatic art is to take a vulgar or even amoralist position and infuse with deep moral significance what is verbally the same claim. A classic instance of such transmutation is in *Republic* I. Thrasymachus claims that justice is the interest of the stronger, and that the just are happy. Socrates would verbally agree with these claims; but he transforms the physical strength of Thrasymachus' just man into the psychic strength of his own, mere obedience to external authority into obedience to internal reason, and happiness as the acquisition of external goods into happiness as the internal control of desire. Both Socrates and Thrasymachus believe that the just are strong! The Socratic movement into the *psyche* is a deep transmutation of values.

Let us now see how the characteristic view fares with conditions (1)–(4). In the *Hippias Major* (297a f.) Socrates claims that a cause must be different from (ἄλλο ἐστίν) its effect; if the beautiful is that *by which* the good is produced, then the beautiful and the good must be distinct. The instrumental dative relates distinct things. But on the characteristic view a virtue is simply a feature of an act. This position appears plausible because it interprets "in" by different descriptions of the same act, and "by which" as a definitory-formal cause, but these claims may well be anachronistic; they certainly remind one of modern moral theorizing. Later I will argue that the instrumental dative has efficient causal import, and that there is a plausible and yet more literal interpretation of "in."

The characteristic view, moreover, fails to explain why persons act (for example) justly and are just by justice. For the instrumental dative also indicates that a virtue is a sufficient condition for action (cf. *Protagoras* 332b f.). But knowledge of a characteristic does not in itself produce action, and conformity to external rules does not even guarantee virtuous behavior because, as we have seen, the moral rules invariably admit of counterexamples. The characteristic view is, I believe, wrongheaded because it does not see that Socrates attempts to close the unfortunate gap between obedience to moral rules and happiness with a movement inward to the *psyche*. The virtuous man is happy not because his actions conform to external standards, but because he possesses a good *psyche* (*Gorgias* 493a ff., 504b ff.).

The characteristic view would instruct us to look, metaphorically, at the characteristics of acts. But the *Charmides* (158e–159a, 160d) passages, quoted above, are our best evidence, in the early dialogues, about where Socrates wants us to look. Charmides is told to look into himself, since if temperance is present to him and within him, it will provide some perception (αἴσθησιν) of itself. Thus Socrates instructs Charmides to look into himself, not at his acts.

Finally, the characteristic view is not very helpful with (4a)–(4e). Since this position conceives of knowledge as wholly propositional in nature, it does not explain why Plato denies weakness of will and asserts that knowledge is a sufficient condition for virtuous action. A propositional knowledge of characteristics does not have such a strong connection with the sources of behavior. The characteristic view must also admit that self-knowledge is not literally directed to the self any more than care for the *psyche* is directed to the *psyche*. I will argue below that the "self-predicational" assertions are predications, and if my arguments are correct, then the characteristic view must attribute to Plato the absurdity that a characteristic instances itself.

We have, then, a cogent accumulation of evidence to reject the characteristic view as the correct interpretation of the ontological status of the virtues.

The Separate-Form View

R. E. Allen defends the unitarian thesis with respect to the early dialogues; he believes that the virtues are separate εἴδη or essences.[10] Although Allen argues his thesis primarily for the *Euthyphro*, he intends also for it to apply to the other early dialogues.

Allen explains that essences are not, strictly speaking, meanings. It would be a better approximation to call them reified meanings, or as Allen claims (twisting Quine's phrase), "essence is what meaning becomes when it is divorced from the word and wedded to the object."[11] Allen also believes that essences are causal conditions; however, essences are not causal "in the sense commonly associated with the banging of billiard balls, but in a sense analogous to that in which Aristotle speaks of a formal cause."[12] Essences are, Allen claims, necessary conditions for the existence of their instances, although separate from them. If, for example, the essence of piety (the pious) did not exist, then there would be no pious acts; that is, the pious itself is "ontologically prior" to its instances, although as a matter of "economy in the universe" Plato may well have thought that all of the Forms are instantiated.[13] Allen also believes that Plato's early Forms are epistemic paradigms, but unlike those found in the middle dialogues, they are not more real than their instances. Finally, a crucial claim for Allen, and one that he shares with the unitarian scholar Harold Cherniss, is the denial of self-predication; the instances of a Form do not resemble that Form but rather are dependent resemblances of it.[14]

We can summarize the separate-essence view as follows:[15]

> x is a virtue, if x is—
> (A) a universal common to all and only x acts,
> (B) separate from but not more real than x acts,
> (C) a necessary condition for any x act, and
> (D) an epistemic paradigm—that is, by looking at x we can decide which acts are x and which are not.

The separate-Form view intends for (A) and (B) to satisfy condition (1); Allen explains that when Socrates asks for "the same thing in every pious act" he seeks a separate paradigmatic universal common to all and only pious acts.[16] (C) purportedly satisfies condition (3) by interpreting the instrumental dative as a request for a separate, necessary condition, and (D) is meant to capture condition (2).

The separate-Form view denies the apparent implications of "in." The virtues are not in any literal sense in their instances; in fact, they are apart from them. Allen also denies that Ross's claim that Forms are "immanent" in the early dialogues makes any sense.[17] Indeed, Ross is unclear about what he means by "immanent," but I believe he holds the characteristic view, and I deem that view intelligible. For Allen the claim that, for example, justice is in all just acts really means that it is a universal, separate from but common to those acts.

The separate essences are not efficient causes, and thus the instrumental dative only introduces a formal necessary condition; justice, for example, is the necessary formal cause by which just acts are just, but, of course, an efficient cause of motion is needed for just action. Essences are not moving causes. Perhaps Allen would argue that while persons are not courageous by courage, the knowledge of courage makes them so. Finally, the paradigm we are to look upon and use to adjudicate disputes is an aspatial, atemporal, separate essence. The exemplifications of a paradigm, however, do not resemble it, but rather are dependent resemblances of it, and this is how Allen interprets "such as" at *Euthyphro* 6e.

How does the separate-Form view handle conditions (4a)–(4e)? "Knowledge of oneself" and "care for the *psyche*" are as in the middle dialogues a turning of the *psyche* away from the phenomenal world and to the supersensible essences. The *logoi* of the virtuous man are consistent, stable, and irrefutable because they are about the stable essences. The knowledge of these essences is sufficient for the appropriate behavior because of the unique character of its objects. The intensity of mental vision, and the stability of the *logoi* about the essences is more potent than our more mundane beliefs. Finally, the so-called self-predications "Justice is just," and "Holiness is holy," are really to be interpreted as the identity claims, "Justice is justice," and "Holiness is holiness," or as claims about the paradigmatic nature of a Form, "Justice is what it is to be just," and "Holiness is what it is to be holy." On the other hand, the derivative predications of phenomena, "Socrates is just" and the like, are relational dependency claims. Socrates' justness is a dependent resemblance, one that does not resemble the paradigm.[18]

Let us now turn to criticisms of the separate-essence view. First I will argue on textual grounds, *contra* Cherniss and Allen, that the "self-predicational" statements are predications. If my interpretation is correct, then Vlastos' Pauline interpretation is also mistaken.[19] Later I will explain why Plato self-predicates the virtues. Then I will examine certain philosophical arguments for and against self-predication, and I will decide in favor of the former. The upshot of these sections is that paradigmatism requires self-predication. Finally I will investigate whether the separate-essence view, with self-predication, provides an adequate account of the virtues, and I will show that it does not.

The Early Self-Predications

A crucial test for any interpretation of "self-predication" is whether it can be substituted *mutatis mutandis* where Socrates makes purportedly "self-predicational" assertions, and provide a coherent interpretation for the passages at issue. Let us test Allen's view for the "star instances of self-predication"[20] in the argument at *Protagoras* 329c–331e. This passage is a good test because the purported self-predications have a central role in an extensive argument. To be as sympathetic as possible to Allen, let us interpret his view as a disjunction: ἡ δικαιοσύνη ... δίκαιόν ἐστιν, for example, means either that "Justice is justice," "Justice is what justice really is," or that "Justice is what it is to be just."[21]

Socrates takes the position that the virtues are all names for one and the same thing (329c–d), and Protagoras rejoins that the virtues, just like the parts of the face, are unlike each other both in themselves and in their powers (330b). Socrates does not attempt to support his thesis, whatever it may be, in this argument; rather he tries to refute Protagoras' claim as is clear from his conclusion: "Either justice is the same as holiness, or they are very like each other, but above all (μάλιστα πάντων), justice is like (οἷον) holiness and holiness is like justice" (331b). Socrates attempts to show that justice and holiness are similar. Moreover, Protagoras' reply confirms this interpretation, and goes right to the heart of the matter: "It is not fair to call those things like (ὅμοια) which have only some likeness (ὅμοιόν τι)" (331e). Socrates attempts to show that justice and holiness are alike, and Protagoras replies that they are not sufficiently similar to be alike.[22]

To gain his conclusion, Socrates elicits Protagoras' assent to the premises "Justice is just" (ἡ δικαιοσύνη ... δίκαιόν ἐστιν, 330c), "Piety is pious" (330e), "Justice is pious" (τὴν δικαιοσύνην ὅσιον εἶναι, 331a–b), and "Piety is just" (331a–b); since piety and justice are both pious and just, they are like each other. But if any version of Allen's view is substituted for the premises of the argument, the passage becomes unintelligible. For all four premises have the same form; we must read them all in one and the same manner. But if we read them as Allen suggests, Socrates would be arguing the absurdity that since "Justice is identical with piety," or "Justice is what piety really is," therefore justice and piety are similar. Moreover, on Allen's interpretation, two of the premises, "Justice is justice," and "Holiness is holiness," play no role whatsoever in the argument. The conclusion that justice and piety are similar is plausible only if the premises are read as predications. But it is this conclusion that Socrates seeks, and it is this conclusion that Protagoras' whole reply is aimed against. Therefore, in this key *Protagoras* passage Plato commits the "self-predications" "Justice is just [and holy]," and "Holiness is holy [and just]." In the next section I will consider why Socrates would find it unobjectionable to say that justice is just and holy.[23]

Let us now consider philosophical problems with self-predication. The primary difficulty with the essence view is to understand the relation that must obtain between an essence and its instances so that the essence is an epistemic paradigm. Consider, for example, standards for measure, a clothing manufacturer's cloth samples, or paradigms of paint color in a hardware store. These are frequently thought to be similar to what Socrates seeks "to look upon and use as a paradigm" at *Euthyphro* 6e. Now I would argue that p is a paradigm for some predicate "is F" if and only if:

> (A) S can look at p and if some individual, x, resembles p in the relevant respects, then S is justified in asserting that x is F, and

(B) If x does not resemble p in the relevant respects, then S is justified in denying that x is F.

To be a paradigm, then, is to be designated a special example, and to be an example requires univocal predication of some predicate both to example and to what it exemplifies.[24] A swatch from a clothing manufacturer's sample is a paradigm of a certain material and pattern only if, for example, "is woolen herringbone" is univocally predicated of it and the cloth it exemplifies.

An objection to the above might be based upon Wittgenstein's claim that of the standard meter in Paris "one can say neither that it is one meter long nor that it is not one meter long" (*Philosophical Investigations* §50). If we justify our descriptions of meter sticks as one meter long by comparing them to the standard meter, we cannot justify, in this way, describing the standard meter as one meter long. But this does not imply that we cannot be justified in some other way. The standard meter is precisely 39.37 inches long; and if something is 39.37 inches long, then it is one meter long; hence the standard meter is one meter long. This inference justifies our claim that the standard meter is one meter long.[25] Moreover, there is no general principle that will allow us to correctly infer from different justifications for the application of a predicate to the equivocal use of that predicate.[26]

Yet Allen asserts that essences are paradigms, while at the same time he denies that they resemble their instances.[27] But how is this possible? In an article purporting to explain the middle-period Forms, Allen provides an analogy: instances are dependent reflections of essences just as mirror images of hands or red scarves are related to hands or red scarves. Since the mirror image of a hand is not a hand, nor is the mirror image of a red scarf, Allen claims, either red or a scarf, instances do not share univocal predicates with their essences.[28]

As applied to the early dialogues, there are serious objections to Allen's analogy. Allen is correct that hands and mirror images of hands are not both univocally hands; for the mirror image of a hand is not a hand at all. But this move does not help us with the early theory of Forms, because there is no evidence for Forms of sortal characteristics in the early dialogues. Nowhere in the early works does Plato posit Forms for hands or scarves, but he does—if we are to believe that Forms occur at all in the early dialogues—posit Forms for the virtues, beauty, and colors (cf. *Lysis* 217c).[29] So if there is to be an analogy, Allen's example must work with respect to the predicate "is red." But it is clear that a red scarf and an image of a red scarf are both red.[30]

What would a mirror image of a virtue be like? It would, I think, be a vulgar example of a virtue; vulgar virtue depends upon the judgments of the many. But, so far as I can see, vulgar instances of virtue are not dependent reflections of true virtue. There is another puzzling aspect of Allen's analogy. If we were to push the analogy further than Allen does, it implies that the Forms have the correct applications of the predicates, and that the phenomena do not have them at all; F-ness is F, but F phenomena are not in any way F, any more than an image of a hand is a hand. But Plato frequently asserts in the early dialogues that, for example, persons and their acts are just or unjust, courageous or cowardly, etc.

There is, I believe, a conclusive objection against Allen's position. If the essences and their instances do not resemble one another, and do not share an univocal predicate, then we cannot establish which paradigms instances are causally dependent upon. Recall that "is F" is predicated of phenomena, according to Allen, in virtue of a formal causal dependence on the essence of F. But if no particular shares univocally "is F" with its essence, then for all we can tell, that particular is dependent on any or no essence. Our decision is quite arbitrary. Moreover, dependency alone is not sufficient to establish an epistemic relation. Some sort of relation, besides mere dependency, is required to establish that an instance is either causally or epistemically dependent upon a specific paradigm.

Thus I reject Allen's denial of "self-predication" for both exegetical and philosophical reasons. What remains, then, is a separate-essence view where essences can be epistemic paradigms; that is, they and their instances resemble one another. Is this view to be found in the early dialogues?

Return to the Separate-Form View

The unitarian theorists Cherniss, Shorey, Friedländer, and Allen,[31] appeal primarily to *Euthyphro* 6e to support the claim that separate Forms occur in the early dialogues. A key element in this passage is that holy acts are said to be "such as" (τοιοῦτον), the paradigm of holiness. In this context, "such as" implies that a paradigm and its instances resemble one another, and Allen's objections to the implication fail, as we have seen. Moreover, there is no grammatical objection to so interpreting "such as."[32] But how can an act resemble a separate essence? To claim that the pious and a pious act are both pious is not to explain how they resemble each other, and have in common an univocal predicate.

Middle-period Forms have in common the following metapredicates: "unique," "incomposite," "invisible," "divine," "ungenerated," "intelligible," "immutable," and the like. Acts do not have these predicates in the same sense that Forms do because these metapredicates delineate the type of Being that Forms are, and acts—inasmuch as they are events—are a very different type of being. Plato, moreover, rejects characteristics in acts as accounts of a virtue; so how could an act and a Form have the relevant description in common? But even if, for example, courage were "staying steadfast at one's post," no Form could have this characteristic. If a paradigm does not resemble what is causally and epistemically dependent upon it, then we cannot establish such dependencies; yet I do not see how paradigms *as separate essences* can share an univocal predicate with their instances, at least when those instances are actions. Below I will argue for a very different understanding of paradigmatism, one that does permit derivative univocal predication. This philosophical objection to Allen's interpretation is obviously not sufficient to reject the position, but it does show that if Plato believes in separate paradigmatic essences and believes that acts are their primary instances, then he faces serious difficulties.

Let us now turn to how the separate-essence view fares with conditions (1)–(4). While Socrates states that a virtue is *in* acts, Allen makes a virtue separate from and ontologically prior to its instances. But this is an unacceptable interpretation of Socrates' "in" locution; he means to stress the close connection between a virtue and an act. While there is doubt about the precise interpretation of "in," the use of this term is not compatible with the separation or ontological priority of a virtue.

The separate-essence view has us look with "the mind's eye" away at the aspatial, atemporal essences. There is no doubt that such mental vision is a leitmotif of the middle works, but we cannot uncritically read later views into the early dialogues. Moreover, a similarity of terminology is not a reliable guide to an identity of doctrine without a close analysis of contexts and related philosophical content. Our best evidence for where to look for the paradigm at *Euthyphro* 6e would come either from the *Euthyphro* itself or, in the absence of evidence in the *Euthyphro*, from another early dialogue. The *Charmides* has two such passages (158e–159a, 160d). Charmides is to look into himself, and if temperance is in him, it will provide a perception of itself. Socrates' instructions are clear and unambiguous about where to search for temperance. Moreover, Socrates' instructions are integrated with the dialectical movement from behavior to the *psyche*. So while Socrates in the *Charmides* emphasizes looking inward at one's *psyche*, the separate-essence view has us look away at the paradigms.

Allen argues that the instrumental dative introduces only a necessary condition that is analogous to an Aristotelian formal cause. But Socrates' use of the dative does not even hint that any further condition is needed (cf. *Euthyphro* 6e, *Protagoras* 332b f., *Hippias Major* 287c–d). Piety, for example, is a sufficient condition for both pious persons and pious acts.

In the *Charmides* (158e–159a, 160d) Socrates states that temperance is present to (πάρεστι) and within (ἔνεστιν) Charmides. In the *Meno* virtue is one of the beings concerning the *psyche* (περὶ τὴν ψυχήν, *Meno* 87b); in the

Gorgias true rhetoric engenders justice in the *psyche* (504e); and the *Laches'* question is how to join or add (παραγενομένη) courage to the *psyche* just as sight is created in the eyes (*Laches* 189e–190b). These "entities" are the topics of their respective dialogues, but they are not ontologically prior to the *psyche*. For even talk about adding *x* to *y* does not presuppose the previous separate existence of *x*; at *Republic* 609a Plato, for example, refers to adding (προσεγένετο) rust to iron and mildew to grain. The *psyche* can exist without virtue, but a virtue cannot exist without a *psyche*. A virtue in the early dialogues is to be created, produced, or engendered in the *psyche* by true rhetoric or philosophy; but the separate essences are immutable, they are not subject to human creation. Finally, nowhere in the early dialogues does Socrates say that a virtue is ungenerated, indestructible, immutable, and the like, although these would be important characteristics of separate essences.

On the separate-essence view Socrates' denial of weakness of will is implausible. Neither the mental sight of essences nor the discursive grasp of them guarantees correct behavior. Moreover, I do not see how Allen adequately explains either knowledge of oneself or care for the *psyche*. On his view it is important to know the separate essences, not oneself; these essences, and not the *psyche* should be the ultimate objects of concern. But the early dialogues emphasize a primary concern for the *psyche* and our treatment of it (*Gorgias* 504d–e, 523d–e, *Crito* 47d–e, *Laches* 185d–e, *Charmides* 156e f.).

If the above arguments are correct, we must reject the separate-essence view.

The Psychic-State View

I will argue that a virtue is a psychic state or power (δύναμις).[33] A psychic state causes and explains behavior. Psychic states move one to act because the *psyche* is the source of motion. Commentators frequently note that in the late dialogues the *psyche* is the source of motion, but the same is also true for the early and middle dialogues. The virtues as psychic powers impel their possessors to act in a certain manner. A virtue not only motivates behavior but also is rational. As Socrates' nutritional metaphors state it: *logoi* feed the *psyche* either for better or for worse. A psychic power, then, both moves and directs behavior. Hence a psychic state motivates or causes behavior, and provides a reason for that behavior. Nowhere does Socrates, in the early dialogues, distinguish the reasons for action from the causes of behavior.

A psychic state is also an internal paradigm. An interlocutor is to look into his *psyche* to see what sort of thing causes virtuous action. Psychic powers are not paradigms in the same way that the middle-period Forms are. A Form must resemble its instances and share an univocal predicate with them, or we cannot use the Form to judge its instances. But psychic paradigms do not initially operate in this manner. An interlocutor should look inward at his *psyche*, and see what sort of thing produces just or pious action. A psychic state is first a causal paradigm for action. Then actions, as well as customs, laws, and institutions, are focally named after either the psychic states they tend to produce or tend to be produced by. Actions are also parasitically describable once we define what a virtuous condition of the *psyche* is. I will also argue that Plato self-predicates the psychic states because he models them, to some extent, after the Pre-Socratic power-elements. Fire produces heat because it is hot, and justice produces just acts and persons because it is just.

Socrates' procedure in the early dialogues is basically the following: He starts with some conventionally virtuous actions, and then moves inward by means of a series of refutations to the psychic cause of virtuous acts. After Socrates establishes the proper account of the psychic cause, he redraws the conventional lines between virtuous and vicious actions. Thus Socrates begins with conventional beliefs, but these beliefs are modified significantly after they are grounded in a defensible theory about the cause of virtuous behavior.

Socrates does not make the distinction between a disposition and a state. But there is good reason to impute an interest in the latter to him. Dispositions are usually individuated by behavior. Socrates, however, conflates conventionally distinct types of virtuous behavior (cf. *Gorgias* 507a–c, *Laches* 191d–e). Thus the virtues could not be distinct dispositions for him. Furthermore, I will argue that Socrates believes that a single state, the knowledge of good and evil, grounds and explains all of the virtue dispositions. Thus if a person is in this state, he is disposed toward all virtuous activity. The notion of a state requires *both* an analysis of the state that is independent of the behavior that it explains, *and* a procedure for determining the presence or absence of the state that is autonomous of behavior. Plato identifies virtue as the knowledge of good and evil, but he has no test for its presence over and above behavior. Hence, as I will show, the early dialogues have an epistemically uninformative circle; virtue is identified by the actions it produces, and these actions are focally called after their psychic cause. In short Socrates treats a state as if it were a disposition.

We may summarize the psychic-state view as follows:

x is a virtue, if *x* is—

(A) the necessary and sufficient psychic causal power to do all and only *x* acts,

(B) a psychic paradigm, and hence adequate evidence that an act produced by it is *x*, and

(C) that after which *x* acts are named.

(A) satisfies conditions (1) and (3). Since a virtue is a necessary causal condition for *x* acts, it is displayed or manifest *in* every *x* act. Because it is sufficient, it is that *by which* all *x* acts are *x*. Finally, since psychic states are internal paradigms, and acts are called after their causal relations to these paradigms, (B) and (C) satisfy condition (2).

The psychic-state view interprets Socrates' "in" locution in a straightforward manner; a psychic state results in or is manifest in action, much as a pain is manifest in pain behavior. An important difference, of course, is that while we may suppress pain behavior and still have a pain, we may not fail to do virtuous acts and still have a virtue. A virtue is such a strong motivational force that it cannot be overpowered by another desire, and this provides us with a clear interpretation of Socrates' use of the instrumental dative. For example, all just acts are just *by* justice because justice is the sufficient psychic cause of them. Just acts are, then, paronymously named from the psychic cause, justice. Moreover, a person is just because he does just acts, and he does just acts because he has psychic justice; or, what amounts to the same thing, a person is paronymously called after the condition of his *psyche*. Socrates instructs Euthyphro at 6e to look inward at himself, and to understand what produces pious or impious actions. If Euthyphro could understand this, then he would have a standard in virtue of which he could judge whether or not prosecuting his father is pious.

How does the psychic-state view handle conditions (4a)–(4e)? Socrates denies "weakness of will" because if one has the appropriate psychic state, then one has the sufficient cause of correct action. Self-knowledge is, literally, to know the condition of ones' own *psyche*. Self-knowledge is knowledge of the self because a person is or is primarily *psyche*. Care for the *psyche* is to be taken literally, and such care is important because the *psyche* is the source of motion. Because Socrates does not distinguish the reasons for action from the causes of behavior, he believes that a psychic state is a power with cognitive features. Hence the *logoi* of the true rhetorician or sophist can develop the δυνάμεις or focus them in one direction or another. The words and deeds of the virtuous man would, then, "chime in harmony together" because such a person is motivated to act in accordance with his *logoi*. Finally, the psychic-state view helps us to interpret and understand the early self-predications because the virtues are psychic powers. The psychic powers are like the Pre-Socratic power-elements in that they have the characteristics they produce. For example, justice is just because it has the power to produce just acts, and holiness is holy because it has the power to produce holy acts.

Let us now turn to evidence for the psychic-state position. The mere mention of παράδειγμα at *Euthyphro* 6e immediately reminds some commentators of the middle-period separate paradigms. This impression is further fostered by the fact that we are to look at this paradigm and use it to adjudicate disputes; for vision of the Forms is a leitmotif of the middle dialogues. Hence there is a similarity in terminology between 6e and passages about the Forms in later works. But need there also be the same theory? Παράδειγμα is, of course, used for separate paradigms in the *Republic* (592b), and the *Timaeus* (28a); however, in its core meaning of "example" or "standard" this term does not imply any particular ontological status. For example, at *Republic* 472e Plato describes the *Republic* as "a paradigm made in speech of the good city" (παράδειγμα ἐποιοῦμεν λόγῳ ἀγαθῆς πόλεως); the paradigm here is an incomplete but ideal verbal description of the good city. An ideal description traces the Form-world, and thus is a philosophical and truly artistic creation. Moreover, earlier in the *Republic* Plato discusses the nature of a good judge (409a–d). The noblest judges are late learners of injustice, and for this reason they seem to be "simple-minded" in youth and easily deceived by the wicked, since they do not have within themselves patterns (οὐκ ἔχοντες ἐν ἑαυτοῖς παραδείγματα) like the affections of the wicked (409a–b). Later in the same discussion Plato says (409c–d):

> But that cunning fellow quick to suspect evil, and who has done himself many unjust acts and who thinks himself a smart trickster, when he associates with his like does appear to be cleverer, being on his guard and fixing his eyes on the patterns within himself (πρὸς τὰ ἐν αὑτῷ παραδείγματα ἀποσκοπῶν). But when the time comes for him to mingle with the good and his elders, then on the contrary he appears stupid. He is unseasonably distrustful and he cannot recognize a sound character (ἦθος) because he has no such pattern (παράδειγμα) in himself.

The pattern mentioned three times at *Republic* 409 is a man's internal character (cf. *Republic* 484c). This character is within him and it is something he can look inward at—note that ἀποσκοπῶν has the same prefix as ἀποβλέπων at *Euthyphro* 6e—and recognize. Presumably in the *Republic* psychic harmony or justice constitutes a good character, and disorder an evil one.

Thus παράδειγμα even in the *Republic* has a fluid use; it can be used to refer to a separate Form, to a verbal description, or to states of character. Hence a major obstacle to the psychic-state view is disarmed: that is, that whenever Plato in a philosophical context uses παράδειγμα, he refers to a separate Form.[34] To determine exactly what "pattern" refers to at 6e we must turn to Plato's other statements about the virtues.

The paradigm at 6e is something we can "look at" (ἀποβλέπων). Visual insight of the separate Forms is, indeed, found in the middle dialogues, but we cannot safely read later views back into the earlier, unless the evidence from the early dialogues at least permits this interpretation. But in this case it does not. The passages at *Charmides* 158e–159a and 160d provide the only clear, extensive explanations of Socrates' early use of visual motifs, and hence our safest method is to interpret the *Euthyphro* in light of them. I will requote the *Charmides* passages given their decided importance:

> Now it is evident that if temperance is present (πάρεστι) to you, you will have some opinion concerning it. For being within (ἐνοῦσαν) you, it must, if it is within you, provide some perception (αἴσθησιν) from which you can form an opinion concerning it, that is, concerning what temperance is and what sort of thing (ὁποῖόν τι) it is.

> Again then, Charmides, pay attention and look into yourself (εἰς σεαυτὸν ἐμβλέψας); understand what sort of person temperance being present (παροῦσα) makes (ποιεῖ) you, and what sort of thing (ποία) it is, that produces (ἀπεργάζοιτο) such an effect.

We learn from these passages: (1) that Charmides must introspect temperance by looking into himself, (2) that temperance, if it is present, will provide a perception of itself, (3) that temperance is present to and within Charmides, if, indeed, Charmides is temperate, (4) that Charmides must declare what sort of thing temperance is, and (5) that temperance must be of such a sort that it makes and produces a temperate person. The temperance referred to at 158e–159a, and 160d, is the topic of the *Charmides*, and there is no evidence that any other type of object is sought. Nor is there any reason to believe that temperance in the *Charmides* is of a different ontological type than courage in the *Laches*, piety in the *Euthyphro*, etc. Socrates, moreover, replaces the neutral notion of presence (πάρεστι) with "being in" (ἐνοῦσαν), and in conjunction with his instructions to Charmides to look into himself, we can infer that temperance is the type of thing that is in Charmides. Given that Socrates has just emphasized that all good things *spring* from the *psyche* (156e), and that they are to seek charms for the *psyche*, there is no doubt that temperance is a psychic state.

"Look at," then, at *Euthyphro* 6e not only is compatible with the introspection of a psychic paradigm—and at *Republic* 591e Plato uses ἀποβλέπων for just this purpose—but our best evidence, that is closest in date of composition to the *Euthyphro*, requires this reading. Thus "pattern" at 6e also refers to the psychic state, piety. But this conclusion is still tentative until we explain other items in the logical grammar of "pattern."

How are we to interpret "such as" at *Euthyphro* 6e? We must be able to judge that acts are pious if they are such as (τοιοῦτον) piety, and impious if they are not. Allen argues that τοιοῦτον does not imply that the pious and a pious act resemble one another. How, then, could the pious be a paradigm? This puzzle will remain unsolved until we engage a theory of predication that is only adumbrated in the early dialogues, but is fully developed in *Republic* IV. At the risk of anachronism, then, let us turn to *Republic* IV.

Acts in the *Republic* are correctly called "just" if (1) they produce or tend to produce justice in the *psyche*, or (2) they are produced by or tend to be produced by a just *psyche*.[35] Just acts, laws, and institutions receive their predicates in a "focal" manner. In *Republic* III certain types of music and gymnastics are noble and just components of the educational system because they tend to produce harmonious *psyches*, and the lying tales of the poets are excluded from the ideal state because they tend to unbalance the *psyche*. More specifically, Socrates states at 443e–444a that we should "name the just and honorable action to be that which preserves and helps to produce this condition of *psyche* [psychic harmony] ... and to name the unjust action that which ever tends to overthrow this spiritual consti-tution" (also cf. 444c–d, 589b, 590b–c). Furthermore, psychic justice is more important and fundamental than behavioral justice since a person is, essentially, *psyche* (443c–d), and since psychic justice, reason ruling over spirit and appetite, is the cause (αἴτιον) of just acts (443b). For this reason Socrates claims that just behavior is an image (εἴδωλον) of psychic justice (443c). Just acts, then, are either produced by psychic justice or produce it, and are focally named in accord with these causal relations.

Just acts image psychic justice for two reasons: (1) they are causally dependent on it, and (2) they parasitically receive a description from it. Just acts consist in a person's minding his own business, and hence doing and having what it is proper for him to do or have (434d–e), while psychic justice is each part of the *psyche* minding its own business, and thus having the desires proper to it. Therefore just acts resemble psychic justice, and hence Socrates gives a characterization of just behavior, *but this characterization depends upon and is called after a psychic state.*

Plato's procedure in the *Republic* and the *Charmides* is the same. First he tries to determine what it is in the *psyche* that produces temperate behavior, and when he has a characterization of this, he then classifies and describes acts by their causal relation to this state. Thus we see him ask in the *Charmides* for the sort of thing (ποία) temperance must be, if it is to produce (ἀπεργάζοιτο) the required effect (160d). However, there are two major differences between the *Republic* and the early dialogues: (a) the notion of a multipartite *psyche* as found in *Republic* IV does not appear until the *Gorgias* (504d), which is probably a late/early dialogue,[36] and (b) the just *psyche* in the *Republic* is an image of the harmonious Form-world, whereas there is no evidence for this position in the early dialogues. For example, at *Republic* 500b–c Plato states that the man who truly fixes his gaze upon the eternal and unchanging order, and who sees that the Forms neither wrong nor are wronged by one another, but "all abide in harmony as reason bids," "endeavors to imitate them ... and to fashion himself in their likeness...." It is interesting to note that the closest the early dialogues come to this position is at *Gorgias* 507e–508a, where the just *psyche* is a microcosm of the visible *Cosmos* as a whole. In the *Republic*, then, acts are focally called after psychic states, and psychic justice is an image of the Forms.

We cannot, of course, read this developed *Republic* view *in toto* back into the early dialogues. Nevertheless, the early works display a prototype of this view. In the *Gorgias*, for example, just punishment benefits the *psyche* (477a), and wicked acts harm it (469b). *Gorgias* 504d–e succinctly summarizes the function of the true rhetorician or philosopher:

> Then it is this that our orator, the man of art and virtue, will have in view, when he applies to our *psyches* the words that he speaks, and also in all his actions ... how justice may be engendered in the *psyches* of his fellow-citizens, and how injustice may be removed....

Just acts, in this case *logoi*, produce justice in the *psyche*, and at 508c the just man is he who does just things. The types of acts one does flow from the sort of person one is. These scattered claims adumbrate the theory of predication detailed in the *Republic*. Acts are, for example, called just if: (1) they produce a just *psyche*, or (2) they are produced by (a person with) a just *psyche*.

We are now in a position to understand "such as" at *Euthyphro* 6e. The paradigm Socrates seeks is in the *psyche*, and once one determines what it is, then one can "see" whether or not it is present. The paradigm is, initially, simply the cause of behavior. But if Socrates were to actually define a virtue and answer the "What is it?" question concerning it, then actions could be paronymously described after the virtue, and would be, in a sense, similar to it. Let us hypothesize the weak thesis that wisdom is a necessary condition for virtue. Virtuous acts would then have at least a single characteristic in common: being wise acts. We do not, however, determine this characteristic by looking at the acts themselves but instead by examining their psychic causes. The characteristic and separate-essence positions fail because they look in the wrong direction.

Republic I provides an interesting example of this procedure. There the excellence of a *psyche* is justice, and justice is identified as the good management, rule, and deliberation by the *psyche* (353d f.). Good management, rule, and deliberation also constitute wisdom (350d), and wisdom is closely connected with a moderation in desire. But, then, the just man does wise things and he does not overreach the mean (349b f.). The behavior of the just man is described after the condition of his *psyche*. Plato does not extensively discuss moral rules in the early dialogues because he employs this theory of focal predication.

In the middle and late dialogues *psyche* is the source of motion (cf. *Phaedrus* 245c–246a).[37] This same view is also found in the early dialogues because the *psyche* is the real person, the body is simply a tool that the *psyche* uses (cf. the possibly spurious *Alcibiades* I 129e–130d); or, more pessimistically, the body is a tomb that snares and entraps the *psyche* (*Gorgias* 493a). We are urged to care for the *psyche* because it is the real person and the source of motion.

The virtues in the early dialogues are states of the *psyche*. In the *Charmides*, as we have seen, temperance is present to and within Charmides. The start of the hypothetical investigation of virtue in the *Meno* (87d) posits that virtue is "one of the beings concerning the *psyche*." We have also seen that the true rhetorician in the *Gorgias* engenders justice in the *psyches* of his listeners (504e). Finally, we also have the analogy in the *Laches* (189e–190b) that courage is added to the *psyche* just as sight is to the eyes, and there is no more indication that courage exists prior to its addition than that sight does. Courage is also said to be a power (δύναμις) that is in all courageous acts (191e f.). A virtue is in acts, and common to them, in that it results in or is manifest in those acts. I conclude that with respect to their ontological status the virtues in the early dialogues are states of the *psyche* that result in action.

One might object to my analysis that Forms are found in the early dialogues, and that they explain the predicates of both psychic states and acts. The objector could go on to claim that the passages I discuss are simply not the ones where the Forms are mentioned. There is no conclusive way to refute such an objection. In my judgment I have selected passages about the entities at issue in the early dialogues. My claim is the very strong one that all references to the virtues in the early dialogues are best explained as about psychic states, not about Forms. The burden of proof is on the objector to produce a passage that is not best explained by my theory.

When we remember that the *psyche* is the real person and the source of motion, we can understand how the psychic powers function. In the *Charmides* Plato even attributes to them acts: sight *sees* (ὁρᾶ ... ὄψις) itself, hearing *hears* itself, and perhaps knowledge *knows* itself (167c–169a). In the middle dialogues we find equally striking action language about the δυνάμεις: Love *loves* (Ἔρως ἔρως ἐστίν, *Symposium* 199e) its objects, knowledge *knows* real being and opinion *opines* what is between being and not being (*Republic* 478a). Socrates' more usual position is to attribute force and power terminology to the psychic states. Temperance in the *Charmides* *makes* and *produces* a temperate person (160d), and earlier in the same dialogue Socrates emphatically states that all good things *spring* (ὡρμῆσθαι) from a healthy *psyche* (156e). In a most important passage to assay the motivational strength of a psychic state, Protagoras and Socrates agree that the knowledge within (ἐνούσης, 352b) a person is "something noble and able to govern man, and whoever learns what is good and bad will never be *overpowered* (κρατηθῆναι) by anything to act other than as knowledge *bids* (κελεύῃ)" (352c).

The strength and command terminology is technically captured by the frequent use of the instrumental dative, and the dative indicates how the virtues function: "Men are temperate by temperance" (σωφροσύνῃ σωφρονοῦσιν, *Protagoras* 332b), "things done temperately are done by temperance" (*Protagoras* 332b), "Piety is that by which (ᾧ) actions are pious" (*Euthyphro* 6d, cf. *Gorgias* 520d, *Hippias Major* 287c). The dative does not introduce just a necessary or an enabling condition, because nowhere in the contexts of these passages does Socrates even suggest that anything further is required. A virtue is a sufficient cause for action, and it is an efficient cause because it is a state of the *psyche*.

The Causal Principle

Let us now turn to the "self-predications" in the early dialogues.[38] A common condition for causation, prior to Hume, is that a cause must have what it transmits or produces (the causal principle, hereafter referred to as [CP]).[39] In the Pre-Socratics the power-elements earth, air, fire, and water produce the elementary qualities hot, cold, moist, and dry. The Pre-Socratics, of course, do not distinguish a substance and its qualities, but rather think of the latter as mixed in the former; moistness, for example, is mixed in water. Since moistness is in water, water can make other things moist.

In Anaxagoras we find this view of causation developed to an extreme to accommodate Parmenides' strictures against nonbeing. Anaxagoras' statement, "In everything there is a portion of everything" (DK 59 B11,12) is the answer to the question, "How could hair come from what is not hair or flesh from what is not flesh?" (B10, also cf. Aristotle's *Physics* 187a23 f.).[40] Aristotle also employs the (CP), but he uses it with the distinction between a substance and its qualities firmly in his grasp: "That thing in virtue of which a quality belongs to other things has that quality to the highest degree. For example, fire is the hottest of things; for it is the cause of the heat of all other things" (*Metaphysics* 933b25, also cf. *Posterior Analytics* 72a29).[41]

Can we find the (CP) in Plato's early dialogues? I will show that a number of passages presuppose this view. Plato never explicitly asserts the (CP), and no one passage provides strong evidence that he employs it. There are, nevertheless, a number of passages where our awareness of the

(CP) explains what are otherwise very puzzling texts, and this explanatory power, in conjunction with the number of passages at issue, strengthens the evidence that Plato is unconsciously influenced by the (CP).

First let us look at *Euthydemus* 300e–301c. Dionysodorus asks Socrates whether beautiful things are different from the beautiful (τὸ καλόν) or the same as it, an apparently exhaustive dichotomy (300e–301a). Socrates, grasping both alternatives at once, answers that they are different from the beautiful, although some beauty (κάλλος τι) is present to each of them. Then Dionysodorus jumps upon the notion of presence and rides it to a comical conclusion: "So if an ox is present (παραγένηται) to you, you are an ox, and if I am present to you (πάρειμι), you are Dionysodorus?" (301a). As I will show in the next chapter, the language of "presence" or "coming to be at" is typical of Plato's early views about the beautiful; the beautiful is the harmony (κόσμος) of an object, its excellence (ἀρετή), that explains why the object is both useful, as well as pleasant to hearing and sight (see *Gorgias* 474d, 506d–e). The *Euthydemus*, moreover, is full of "crude," comical misinterpretations and verbal equivocations on Socrates' claims; but Socrates attempts, within the brief moments of respite given him by the juggling sophists, to explain and clarify his positions. Let us see what Socrates does in this case.

After Socrates disclaims the horrible consequences of Dionysodorus' interpretation of presence, Dionysodorus presents him with a crucial question: "In what way can one thing, by having a different thing present to it, be itself different (᾿Αλλὰ τίνα τρόπον, ἔφη, ἑτέρου ἑτέρῳ παραγενομένου τὸ ἕτερον ἕτερον ἂν εἴη)?" (301a–b). Socrates' answer is not what we would expect: "Is not the beautiful beautiful (τὸ καλὸν καλόν ἐστι) and the base base (τὸ αἰσχρὸν αἰσχρόν)? . . . Is not the same same and the different different?" (301b). At this point, unfortunately, the topic is abruptly dropped, and the participants go on to another comical interchange.

R. K. Sprague takes the question here to be, "How can the different be different?" and its answer to be, "Self-predication." [42] There is, however, a less truncated interpretation for these lines. Dionysodorus' question is how *A*, being different from *B*, can by its presence make *B* different. I suggest that Socrates answers this puzzle about causal efficacy with an application of the (CP): generally the answer is, "The Different (*A*) is different, and hence it can make that to which it is present (*B*) different"; and more specifically, "The beautiful is beautiful, and so it can make that to which it is present beautiful."

This interpretation gains support from passages in the *Hippias Major*. In the next chapter I show that Hippias' three attempts to state what the beautiful is fail because they propose what is (1) beautiful in relation to one thing, but not in relation to another, (2) beautiful in one context, but not in another, and (3) beautiful for the lives of some people but not for others. (1), (2), and (3) are each sufficient to reject an account of the beautiful because the beautiful is that *by which* all beautiful things are beautiful (288b, 289d, 292d, 294b), and this causal claim requires that the beautiful be always—in every relation, respect, and for every life—beautiful (cf. 292e). We can explain why the causal claim has this requirement by an application of the (CP); the beautiful is that by which *all* beautiful things are beautiful, because the beautiful is in every relation, context, and for all lives beautiful.

At *Charmides* 160d Socrates instructs Charmides to "pay attention and look into yourself; understand what sort of person (ὁποῖόν τινα) temperance, when it is present, makes you, and what sort of thing (ποία τις) produces such an effect." Charmides answers that "Temperance makes men ashamed or bashful and it is the same as modesty" (160e). Socrates' refutation of this account is relevant to our investigation. After establishing that modesty is both good and not good, he goes on to say, "Yet temperance is good if its presence makes men good and not bad (Σωφροσύνη δέ γε ἀγαθόν, εἴπερ ἀγαθοὺς ποιεῖ οἷς ἂν παρῇ, κακοὺς δὲ μή)" (161a). "Makes" indicates a causal connection between temperance and the person to whom it is present; moreover, we are told that temperance itself must be like the effect it produces, that is, good.

Similar assertions occur in other dialogues. The demiurge of the *Timaeus* must bring order into the discordant and disorderly motions because he thinks that order is better than disorder, and because "for him who is best it neither was nor is permissible to perform any action except what is most fair" (30a). At 29e, the demiurge "was good, and in him who is good no envy arises about anything, so that since he is devoid of envy he wanted everything to be as much as possible like (παραπλήσια) himself." Plato makes the same point while chastising the false poets at *Republic* 379a–c: God (ὁ θεός), because he is good, can be the cause only of good things, not of bad, contrary to what the poets assert. One might consider these statements merely as a type of ethical judgment, involving the view that what produces good must itself be judged good. In *Republic* I (335d–e), however, a similar ethical assertion is modeled on instances of physical causation: just men do not by justice make other men unjust, and good men do not by virtue make other men bad, for (γάρ) it is not the function (ἔργον) of heat to chill but of cold, and it is not the function of dryness to moisten but of moistness. We may well imagine that the function of heat is to make things hot because heat itself is hot, and that the function of dryness is to make things dry because dryness itself is dry (see *Phaedo* 103c ff.). In other words, these paradigm examples of physical causation

employ the (CP), as well as do the examples of virtue transmission that
are modeled upon them. I believe that other important ethical assertions
can be profitably interpreted as modeled upon paradigm examples of
physical causation: for example, a motif of the *Gorgias* that the true
rhetorician, who produces justice in the *psyches* of his listeners, must himself
be just (508c, 504d–e).

Another use of the (CP) is found in the *Lysis*. At 217c Socrates
distinguishes between (1) things which are such as (τοιαῦτα) or the same as
(αὐτά) what is present to them, and (2) things which are not. An example
of (2) is things which are dyed, or hair tinged with white lead. The hair
appears white when tinged, but though whiteness is present to it, it is no
more white than black (217d). So what is dyed is not similar in color
(τοιοῦτον τὴν χρόαν ... οἷον) to what is added (217c). The implication
here is that whiteness is white, although it fails to produce its proper effect
of white color due to the absence of other necessary conditions.

An example of (1) is the white color of hair which comes with old age:
here the hair becomes similar to (οἷονπερ) what is present to it, white by
the presence of whiteness (λευκοῦ παρουσίᾳ λευκαί, 217e). Οἷονπερ emphasizes the similarity between white hair and whiteness, while παρουσίᾳ
indicates a causal connection between whiteness and the white of the hair,
and also suggests that the cause is "right at" the effect.

Even the "star instances of self-predication" at *Protagoras* 330c,e are
readily intelligible as instances of the (CP). As I earlier argued, Socrates
attempts to show in this argument that Protagoras' claim that the parts of
virtue, just like the parts of the face, are unlike (οὐκ ... οἷον) each other
both in themselves and in their powers (οὔτε αὐτὸ οὔτε ἡ δύναμις αὐτοῦ,
330a–b) is false. To this end Socrates forces Protagoras to assent to the
premises that "Justice is just" (330c), "Holiness is holy" (330e), "Holiness
is just" (331b), and "Justice is holy" (330e). But why do Socrates and
Protagoras assent to these premises? David Savan has correctly seen a
connection between these premises and the virtues having powers, but he
makes this connection too tight when he says, "These apparently self-
predicative assertions affirm that the δύναμις of justice is just action, the
δύναμις of holiness is holy action."[43] The text does not show that "Justice
is just" means that "Justice has the power to make men just"; rather, the
former statement is a conclusion from the latter. Socrates moves directly
from talking about justice and holiness having powers (δύναμιν αὐτὸν
ἕκαστον ἰδίαν ἔχει, 330a,b) to gaining assent from Protagoras that justice
is a thing (πρᾶγμα, 330c), and a just thing at that. We can explain this
transition by an application of the (CP): since justice has the power to
make men just, it is itself just; since holiness has the power to make men
holy, it is itself holy. Finally, since justice and holiness are both just and

holy, they can be like each other both in themselves and in their powers. I conclude that the early self-predications of the virtues are best understood as instances of the (CP).[44]

Let us summarize this section with reference to *Euthyphro* 6e. Euthyphro is to look inward at a psychic paradigm. This paradigm causes pious action. If Euthyphro could state what this paradigm is (for instance, wisdom), then he could derivatively describe pious acts (for instance, wise acts). These acts would then be "such as" the paradigm. Euthyphro cannot say what the paradigm is; hence he does not know what condition his *psyche* should be in. This is both a lack of self-knowledge as well as a failure to care for the *psyche*.

I conclude that the center of gravity for the early dialogues is the *psyche*. I believe that all the passages in the early dialogues, that are thought to refer to separate Forms, can readily be interpreted on the model I have presented. Of course, space does not permit a discussion of all such passages.

SECTION II: The Identity of the Virtues and the Dramatic
Structures of the Early Dialogues

Let us now turn to Socrates' typical τί ἐστι... question: "What is justice, courage, temperance, or the like?" The arguments in this section are somewhat shorter than those in the previous one because a rigorous defense of the identity position by Professor Terry Penner ("The Unity of Virtue," *Philosophical Review*, 82 [1973]) has already appeared in print. I strongly urge the reader to study this essay. Penner argues that for the *Charmides*, *Laches*, and *Protagoras*, courage = temperance = justice = holiness = wisdom. To reduplicate Penner's arguments as little as possible, I will analyze the *Meno*, a sample argument from the *Protagoras*, and the dramatic structures of the *Charmides*, *Laches*, and *Euthyphro*. I will argue that each of these dialogues either implies or suggests that a virtue is identical with (=) the knowledge of good and evil (wisdom); furthermore, Socrates in each case either turns from this conclusion at the last moment, or after arguing for it so that it seems to be inescapable, overturns and rejects the identity for intentionally spurious and contrived reasons. Of course it is not easy to prove that Plato produces intentionally fallacious arguments, and evidence from the dramatic structure of a dialogue is often highly controversial. But I believe I can show that for pedagogical reasons Plato ends the early dialogues with contrived fallacies and invented paradoxes the answers to which are found in those dialogues.

If the virtues were separate essences or reified meanings, then it would be difficult to argue that they are identical.[45] For presumably "justice," "temperance," "holiness," and so on mean different things; so if the virtues are reified meanings, then they are distinct. Moreover, if the virtues were characteristics of acts, then on either an intentional or extensional interpretation of "characteristic," they would not be identical. For the meaning of justice $\neq$ the meaning of holiness $\neq$ the meaning of temperance; and the class of just acts $\neq$ the class of holy acts $\neq$ the class of temperate acts, and so on. The identity of the virtues is improbable: on the essence view because it purportedly conflicts with Plato's referential theory of meaning; and on the characteristic view because Plato purportedly distinguishes different classes of virtuous acts.

But if we shift the focus of our investigation to the substantial question—that is, to the real question of the early dialogues—about what it is in a man's *psyche* that makes him just, temperate, holy, and the like, then it is perfectly possible to give the same explanation for all of these. I will show that wisdom or knowledge of good and evil is the explanation for why a person possesses any virtue, and that each virtue = wisdom. Hence a single psychic state explains all of the virtues. For this reason the only essential characteristic common to virtuous behavior is that it is wise behavior, and Socrates only accidentally distinguishes different types of virtuous behavior. Wise behavior is paronymously named from wisdom. The "vulgar" criteria that Socrates uses to distinguish different types of virtuous behavior are accidental, contextual features irrelevant to the real nature of virtue.

The *Meno*

Let us now turn to the arguments. Meno will not wait for an answer to "What is virtue?" but wants to know immediately whether or not it can be taught. Socrates, in his typical posture of following the answerer wherever he wants to go, yields to Meno, and agrees to investigate the question whether or not virtue is teachable by means of an hypothesis: If virtue is one of those beings concerning the *psyche* (περὶ τὴν ψυχήν, 87b) that is a kind of knowledge, then it is teachable, and if it is not, then it is not teachable (87c). In outline the argument from *Meno* 87b to the end of the dialogue is as follows:

(a) If virtue is a kind of knowledge then it is teachable (διδακτόν 87c).

(b) Virtue is a kind of knowledge (87d–89b).

∴ (c) Virtue is teachable.

   (d) Neither sophists nor Athenian gentlemen teach virtue (89e–96b).

∴ (e) There are no teachers of virtue (96b).

   (f) If virtue is teachable (διδακτόν), there must be teachers and learners of it.

∴ (g) Virtue is not teachable (96c).

∴ (h) Virtue is not a kind of knowledge.

   (i) If there are good men, then they are good because of true opinion that is divinely instilled (96d–100b).

Statements (a), (b), and (c) constitute, I believe, Socrates' real view. Statement (d) is a true premise, but (e) does not follow from (d); nor do I think that Socrates believes that (e) follows from (d), because in the *Gorgias* he asserts that (e) is false. Statement (f) is false because of an equivocation on διδακτόν: it can mean either "is taught" or "is teachable." Only with the former meaning is (f) true. But the equivocation on διδακτόν is so clear, and so persistently repeated, that we would need clear, cogent evidence to impute this equivocation to Socrates. On my interpretation there is no such evidence. Statement (g), then, is not the conclusion of a sound argument from premises (e) and (f) because both premises are false. Statement (h), finally, is not the conclusion of a sound argument from (a) and (g), because (g) is false. Statement (i) is perplexing, but there is clear evidence at the end of the *Meno* that a man whose correct actions are explained only by true opinions is at best a pale shade of the really virtuous man.

Why does Socrates claim that virtue is a kind of knowledge? The argument at 87d–89b is, as I will show, repeated again and again in the early dialogues, and it, as much as any other argument in those works, is referred to when Socrates states (*Gorgias* 508c–509a):

> All this, which has been made evident on the lines I have stated some way back in our foregoing discussion, is held firm and fastened—if I may put it rather bluntly—with reasons of steel and adamant (so it would seem, at least, on the face of it) which you [Callicles] or somebody more gallant than yourself must undo, or else find you cannot make a right statement in terms other than those I now use. For my story is ever the same, that I cannot tell how the matter stands, and yet of all whom I have encountered, before as now, no one has been able to state it otherwise without making himself ridiculous.

Socrates' arguments are held "firm and fastened" with "reasons of steel and adamant," and yet he "cannot tell how the matter stands"! Socrates' humility, at least in this passage, must be interpreted as the assertion of his nondogmatic *credo*: that any argument, no matter how firmly fastened, can always be reopened (see *Crito* 49d–e). In any case, Socrates gives arguments and is not simply the perpetrator of destructive dialectic.[46] Let us return to the *Meno* argument.

We can outline the argument that virtue is a kind of knowledge as follows:

(1) Virtue is necessarily a benefit to its possessor.
(2) Only wisdom is necessarily beneficial.
∴ (3) Virtue is (a kind of) wisdom.

The most important texts for (1)–(3) are as follows:

> Then if virtue is something that is in the *psyche*, and it is necessary (ἀναγκαῖον) for it to be beneficial, then it must be wisdom, since all the other properties of the *psyche* are in themselves neither profitable nor harmful, but are made either one or the other by the addition of wisdom or folly; and hence, by this argument, virtue being profitable must be a sort of wisdom (φρόνησιν). (88c–d)

> Then may we assert this as a universal rule, that in man all other things depend upon the *psyche*, while the things of the *psyche* herself depend upon wisdom, if they are to be good; and so by this account the profitable will be wisdom, and virtue, we say, is profitable? (88e–89a)

> Hence we conclude that virtue is (εἶναι) either wholly or partly wisdom. (89a)

(I) The claim that virtue is necessarily good and hence necessarily beneficial is simply gotten by assent from Meno (87d–e). Likewise, Charmides readily assents that temperance is noble and thus good (*Charmides* 160e), and Laches is eager to agree that courage is a noble and good thing (*Laches* 192c–d).

(II) Socrates claims that neither the "goods" of the body (he mentions health, strength, beauty, and wealth) nor the "goods" of the *psyche* (temperance, justice, courage, intelligence, memory, and the like) are good in themselves; rather sometimes they profit a person and sometimes they harm him (87e–88b). One might object that health is the good of the body and justice the excellence of a *psyche*. But while health may be the good of a body, it need not be a benefit to the whole person. I may, for example, use my robust health to accomplish vile ends. In the case of a virtue, if wisdom is detached from that virtue, then it is only a false imitation of its former self. Courage without wisdom, for example, is "only

a sort of boldness" (88b), and boldness can be harmful as well as beneficial. Therefore none of the so-called "goods" of the *psyche* or the body is
necessarily beneficial *in the absence of* wisdom.

(III) Someone might object, on the basis of the claim emphasized in
(II), that this argument does not show that virtue *is* a kind of wisdom, but
rather that wisdom is a necessary condition for virtue.[47] This is, indeed, a
potent objection and one frequently made to the identity interpretation of
the passage. But the objection ignores the metaphysics presupposed by the
argument. Socrates is trying to discover what it is in the *psyche* that
produces beneficial results. Now suppose that there are two psychic
entities, virtue that always is beneficial because (by agreement) it
produces beneficial results, and wisdom that turns out to have the very
same function. "Wisdom" and "virtue" would then turn out to be names
for one and the same thing (see *Protagoras* 329c–d); for while we earlier
agreed upon the power of virtue, we now know what it is in the *psyche* that
has this power. Since there is no point in having two psychic entities with
the very same power and function, virtue is unmasked as wisdom and then
identified with wisdom.

(IV) Another objection to an identity interpretation of the argument is
that virtue cannot be wisdom because a virtuous man acts virtuously, but
a wise man does not always act as he knows he should. Again this
objection fails to take account of the metaphysical psychology involved.
Wisdom, as a psychic state, moves a person as much as virtue does. At 88c
Socrates says:

> And, in brief, all the undertakings and endurances of the *psyche*, when
> guided by wisdom, end in happiness, but when folly guides, in the
> opposite.

Socrates here uses the moderate terminology of guidance, but earlier he
also uses the instrumental dative (87d) and following the *Charmides* we
could even say that beneficial results "spring" from wisdom.

(V) We should also notice in this argument the Greek tendency to
think in terms of polar opposites. Virtue is wisdom, and vice is folly (see,
for example, 88c,e); virtue and vice, wisdom and folly, are two pairs of
polar opposites. Socrates could easily develop an argument that vice is
folly or ignorance, starting with the premise that vice is necessarily
harmful.

(VI) The conclusion to the argument is clearly cast in terms of an
identity claim, "Hence we say that virtue is wisdom, either all of wisdom
or a part of it," and it would be outright mistranslation to render the
conclusion an equivalence or anything other than an identity.

(VII) However, we do not learn in the *Meno* what kind of wisdom virtue is, although we do know that it must be the part of wisdom that makes all other things beneficial.

I conclude that the argument at 87d–89b attempts to show that virtue is a kind of wisdom.

Socrates believes that neither Athenian gentlemen nor sophists teach virtue (see *Gorgias* 515e ff., 520a ff.). But does it follow from this that there are no teachers of virtue? Of course not, and Socrates knows that it does not follow. For at *Gorgias* 521d–e Socrates, in a rather uncharacteristic statement, claims:[48]

> I think I am one of few, not to say the only one, in Athens who attempts the true art of statesmanship (τῇ ὡς ἀληϑῶς πολιτικῇ τέχνῃ), and the only man of the present time who manages affairs of state; hence as the speeches I make from time to time are not aimed at gratification, but at what is best instead of most pleasant, and as I do not care to deal in "these pretty toys" that you recommend, I shall have not a word to say at the bar.

Are we to suppose that in the *Meno* Socrates denies that there are teachers of virtue, and then in the *Gorgias* stumbles across one such teacher, himself? Socrates knows precisely what a teacher of virtue must do: aim his *logoi* not at the gratification of desire but at the improvement of the *psyche*. While we may disagree with Socrates about the *logoi* and pedagogical techniques he uses, there is no doubt that his purpose in the greater part of the early works is the improvement of the interlocutors' *psyches* (for Nicias' recognition of this see *Laches* 187e–188c).

Since Socrates believes that "(e) There are no teachers of virtue" is false, the arguments for "(g) Virtue is not teachable," and for "(h) Virtue is not a kind of knowledge" collapse because they are unsound. But why does Socrates state "(f) If virtue is teachable (διδακτόν), then there must be teachers and learners of it"? There appears to be an equivocation on διδακτόν which means either "is taught" or "is teachable." On the former, (f) is a truism, on the latter false. Socrates has no magic talisman against error, but this mistake is of a rather glorious magnitude. I believe that Socrates is trying to get Meno *to see for himself*[49] that there is a very great gap between what can be taught and the purported teachers of it. The sophists, including Meno's mentor Gorgias, and (as Protagoras and Anytus would have it) any well-bred Athenian citizen only purport to teach virtue. Only if Meno could see this would he free himself from vulgar conceptions and debates about virtue, and turn seriously to the question "What is virtue?" In any case, since Socrates believes that (e) is false, he also believes that the argument against "Virtue is knowledge" is unsound.

But does Socrates deny that virtue is wisdom because he sees at the end of the *Meno* that true opinion also produces correct action? I do not think so. A virtuous man is one whose words and deeds not only "chime in harmony together" (*Laches* 188d), but also his *logoi* are fastened in the *psyche* (*Gorgias* 508e–509a, *Meno* 98a) by chains of steel. But true opinion lacks such chains that are characteristic of rationality, and thus opinions may come through just about any source, and as easily again leave the *psyche*. For this reason Socrates likens the man of opinion to a "flitting shade" (100a) as compared with the true statesman who is able to make another such as himself. We do not yet see in the *Meno* the position of the *Republic* where true opinion can be tied down in the *psyche* by habit formation produced by gymnastics and music. Therefore Socrates believes in the *Meno* that the only virtue worthy of the name is wisdom.

The *Protagoras*

We have already analyzed the argument in the *Protagoras* about justice and holiness. This argument is only a preliminary skirmish between Protagoras and Socrates because it neither defends Socrates' claim that "justice," "temperance," and "holiness' are all names for one and the same thing (πάντα ὀνόματα τοῦ αὐτοῦ ἑνὸς ὄντος, 329c–d), nor attacks Protagoras' belief that the virtues are parts of virtue. Rather the argument is concerned with Protagoras' second claim that the virtues are unlike each other both in themselves and in their powers (330a–b). Socrates attempts to show that justice and holiness are alike because they are similar in two respects, and Protagoras rejoins that such similarity is not sufficient to show them alike. But even if Protagoras were to lose this argument, justice, holiness, courage, and the like could still be parts of virtue, since the parts of a thing certainly can resemble one another; and even if Socrates were to win the argument, he still would not show that "justice," "holiness," and the like are names for one and the same thing, for a resemblance does not prove an identity.

The next argument, however, goes right to the heart of the matter.[50] Starting at 332a ff. Socrates attempts to show that wisdom and temperance are identical. In outline the argument is as follows:

(1) Wisdom and folly are opposites (332a).
(2) What is done temperately is done by temperance (332a–b).
(3) Behaving foolishly is opposite to behaving temperately (332b).
(4) What is done foolishly is done by folly (332b).
(5) Opposite types of behavior are done by opposites (332c).
(6) Each thing has but one opposite (332c–d).
∴ (7) Folly and temperance are opposites (332e).

∴ (8) Either we must reject (6) or admit that temperance and wisdom are identical (333a).

This argument is a classic example of Socrates' wiry, strung out refutations; Protagoras assents to the premises in an order that makes it difficult for him to see where Socrates is going; and there is the pause, at the end of the argument, where Socrates says that they should reckon up their admissions, and then the trap closes. Statement (7) follows from (2), (3), (4), and (5); while the disjunction in (8) is forced by (1), (6), and (7). Statement (8) could disjunctively include any or all of the premises, but presumably Socrates picks (6) and the identity "temperance is wisdom" either because they are the most dubious statements, or because he is trying to force Protagoras' assent to the identity, and (6) has a strong claim to be true. Rarely does Socrates see that the conclusion to a refutation should be put in the form of a disjunction (you give up either *P* or *Q* or *R* or another), but here he seems to have a partial awareness of this.

Let me turn now to comments on the argument.

(I) The constant use of the instrumental dative and ὑπό followed by the genitive introduces sufficient causes. Temperance, for example, is the sufficient psychic cause of temperate behavior.

(II) The notion of an opposite here is that of a polar opposite and not of a logical contrary (see Aristotle's *Metaphysics* 1055a3 ff.). "Man" and "monkey" are logical contraries, but they are not polar opposites. Logical contraries cannot both be true of a subject, but they both can be false. "Like" and "unlike," "one" and "many," "just" and "unjust" are polar opposites. They cannot both be true, in the same respect, relation, or the like of an object; but one of them, so the ancient Greeks sometimes seem to believe, must be true of that subject. Thus when Protagoras, in the argument over justice and holiness, is asked whether justice is holy or unholy and holiness is just or unjust, he is obliged to answer one way or the other. Polar opposition is an example of the Greek tendency to think in terms of polarities.

(III) The argument clearly attempts to establish that what it is in the *psyche* that explains temperate behavior *is* what it is in the *psyche* that explains wise behavior; temperance is the former, wisdom the latter, and thus they are identical. The argument also presupposes that the only characteristic common to all instances of temperate behavior is that it is wise behavior, although the converse is not required. Socrates could also show, *mutatis mutandis*, that what it is in the *psyche* that produces intemperate behavior *is* what it is in the *psyche* that produces foolish behavior; since intemperance is the former and folly the latter, they would be identical. This argument would presuppose that all instances of intem-

perate behavior are also instances of foolish behavior, but not the converse.
(IV) The conclusion to the argument is (333a–b):

> Then which, Protogoras, of our propositions are we to reject—the
> statement that one thing has but one opposite; or the other, that
> wisdom is different from temperance, and each is a part of virtue ...
> and that the two are unlike both in themselves and in their powers as
> are the parts of the face? [Socrates, with a rhetorical flourish, reasserts
> that an opposite can have only one opposite and Protagoras, against
> his will, admits to the claim that:] Then temperance and wisdom
> would be one thing (οὐκοῦν ἓν ἂν εἴη ἡ σωφροσύνη καὶ ἡ σοφία).

Since "temperance" and "wisdom" are names for psychic states, the
conclusion can only be correctly translated as an identity. Therefore
wisdom and temperance are not parts of virtue nor are they unlike each
other in themselves and in their powers, for in a degenerate sense of
"resemble" one and the same thing resembles itself. Hence both of
Protagoras' theses are overturned with respect to temperance and wisdom.
And to say that temperance and wisdom have the very same power is to
imply that they both are causally responsible for the same behavior. We
can, then, stop referring to temperance and temperate behavior, and talk
about what they are revealed to be: wisdom, and wise behavior.

The *Charmides*

The discussion of temperance in the *Charmides* becomes bogged down, and
so at 172c–d Socrates says:

> For suppose, if you please, we concede that there may possibly be a
> science of science, and let us grant, and not withdraw, our original
> proposition that temperance is the knowledge of what one knows and
> does not know; granting all this, let us still more thoroughly inquire
> whether on these terms it will be of any profit to us. For our
> suggestion just now, that temperance of that sort, as our guide in
> ordering house or state, must be a great boon, was not, to my
> thinking, Critias, a proper admission.

It was earlier admitted, on all sides, that temperance is beneficial, but is
the knowledge of what one knows and does not know beneficial? This
strange sort of knowledge is here identified with a knowledge or lack
thereof of the arts—doctoring, piloting, shoemaking, and the like.
Socrates then sketches an extraordinary picture of a life, and presumably
a city-state, where the arts are completely in control (173a–d); the real
doctor practices medicine, the true pilot guides the ship, and even the
charlatans of prophecy are banished so that true prophets are enthroned

as the prognosticators of the future. This city is a technological marvel, and thus equipped, the citizens live and act according to knowledge, and are immediately able to identify and expel the false pretenders to any art.

But, Socrates points out, is it "by acting according to [this sort of] knowledge that we do well and are happy; this point we are not yet able to make out ... " (173d). Here enters the crucial Socratic distinction that is found in many dialogues. The particular arts, indeed, aim at the good of their subject matters—medicine engenders health in the body, cobbling produces the best shoes for the feet, piloting guides the ship to its proper destination (see *Gorgias* 462b ff. on true art)—but where in all of this is the human good, that is, the knowledge that makes us *live well* and *be happy*? This sort of master knowledge is not found among the other arts, not even the art of prophecy that knows all that was, is, and will be (173e–174b).

Suddenly Critias is nudged to see the sort of master art that is required (174b–c):

> And that science to which I refer as the most likely, I went on, gives him knowledge of what? Of good, he [Critias] replied, and of evil. Vile creature! I said, you have all this time been dragging me round and round, while concealing the fact that the life according to knowledge does not make us do well and be happy, not even if it be knowledge of all the other knowledges together, but only if it is of this single one concerning good and evil.

Socrates and Critias seem to have at last discovered what temperance is. But then the dialogue takes a strange, aporetic turn (174d):

> And that science [of good and evil], it seems, is not temperance, but one whose business is to benefit us; for it is not a science of sciences and lack of sciences, but of good and evil; so that if this is beneficial, temperance must be something else to us.

Thus Socrates and Critias are "worsted every way, and cannot discover what thing it can possibly be to which the lawgiver gave this name, temperance" (175b); they, of course, resolve to continue the search, and Charmides turns himself over to Socrates to be charmed by him for the rest of his life.

If we were to continue the search for temperance, what could we glean from this *aporia*? Socrates repeatedly, in his closing speech, hammers home the point that temperance is a noble, great good (175a, 175e, 176a); he says to Charmides, "For temperance I hold to be a great good, and you to be highly blessed, if you actually have it." Nowhere in the dialogue is the admission that temperance is a benefit to its possessor overturned, and even after temperance is said not to be the knowledge of good and evil, this key admission is repeated. We may assume, then, that temperance is a benefit to its possessor. Why does Socrates deny that temperance is the knowledge of good and evil? Instead of following the interlocutor wherever his answer leads (see *Euthyphro* 14c), when Critias says that only the knowledge of good and evil is really beneficial, Socrates drops the matter. Moreover, he rejects the claim that temperance is the knowledge of good and evil because they earlier agreed that temperance is the knowledge of what one knows and does not know. But this rejection is certainly odd, for they have just shown that temperance is not the knowledge of what one knows and does not know, for none of the subordinate arts produces happiness, only the master art of good and evil. I conclude, then, that Socrates means for us to see, for ourselves, that temperance is the knowledge of good and evil, and his argument for this is, *mutatis mutandis*, the very one found in the *Meno*:

(1) Temperance is necessarily beneficial.
(2) Only the knowledge of good and evil is necessarily beneficial.
∴ (3) Temperance is the knowledge of good and evil.

Unlike the *Meno*, however, where wisdom is simply said to be that part of knowledge that makes things beneficial, in the *Charmides* the wisdom at issue is shown to be the knowledge of good and evil.

The *Laches*

In the *Laches*, Laches offers the account that courage is an endurance of the *psyche* (καρτερία τις εἶναι τῆς ψυχῆς, 192b). Socrates immediately gains Laches' assent that courage is a noble and beneficial thing (192c–d), and on the basis of this forces him to amend his account, so that only wise endurance is courage. Thereupon follow a number of examples designed to show that wise endurance is not courage. Commentators often claim that these examples display the contextual features for brave acts,[51] but I believe that they have a very different point: wisdom is not the simple exercise of a τέχνη. Socrates' first example is of a man who endures wisely in spending money knowing that he will thereby gain more (192e); his second example is of a doctor, who when his son is suffering from inflammation of the lungs and begs for something to drink or eat, wisely endures in refusing (192e).

We may be tempted to say that the first case is not an example of courage, because the context is not the sort of situation in which courage is required. Socrates, moreover, suggests this interpretation when he prefaces the examples with the question: "Now let us see in what it [endurance] is wise. In all things both great and small?" But Socrates means to make the same point with both examples, and certainly a doctor could be courageous, in the face of his son's pleas for help, when he refrains from administering a food or drink that will prove harmful. What, then, is common to both examples? In a striking passage, later in the dialogue, that is put into the mouth of Nicias—who has often heard some such remarks from Socrates (194d)—we receive a valuable clue (195c–d):

> Because he [Laches] thinks [incorrectly] that doctors know something more, in treating sick persons, then how to tell what is healthy and what diseased? This, I imagine, is all that they know: but to tell whether health itself is to be dreaded by anyone rather than sickness,—do you suppose, Laches, that this is within a doctor's knowledge? Do you not think that for many it is better that they should never arise from their bed of sickness? Pray tell me, do you say that in every case it is better to live? Is it not often preferable to be dead?

What is common to both cases is that they display the mere exercise of a subordinate art: the money maker makes money, and the doctor attempts to heal. But courage does not involve this sort of wisdom, and thus courage cannot be wise endurance, where the wisdom is that of a special craft. Laches has no grasp of the master knowledge Nicias talks about, and Nicias is not much better off since he only repeats formulae previously heard from Socrates.

Socrates, then, gives a number of cases that have the perplexing consequence that the man who foolishly endures is more courageous than he who wisely endures. For example, the man who endures in war knowing that others will come to his aid, that the forces against him are fewer and feebler, and that he has the advantage of position, is less courageous than the man in the opposing army who is willing to stand up against him and endure (193a). But what are we to make of this case? The man who wisely endures has the wisdom of the military expert who knows where the advantage is in battle. His opponent is clearly foolish in this respect; but why, then, does Socrates judge that the foolish man is more courageous? Socrates does not tell us the reason for his decision, but we can easily provide a suitable one. The man in the inferior military position could be fighting for a noble cause, in which case, he is indeed brave. But without this sort of reason, he simply has foolish boldness. Courage, then, requires, whatever the odds are, the possession of a master art, wisdom.

Laches, however, does not have the slightest inkling how to overturn Socrates' examples, and thus he proves deficient in wisdom. But he and Socrates agree to endure in the search for courage. The conversation then turns to Nicias, who has often heard Socrates say "that every man is good in that wherein he is wise, and bad in that wherein he is unlearned" (194d). Socrates interprets this remark to mean that courage is some sort of wisdom (σοφίαν τινὰ τὴν ἀνδρείαν [εἶναι], 194d), and Laches, who thinks the claim to be quite outlandish, blurts out "Why, surely, wisdom and courage are distinct (χωρίς)" (195a). A considerable portion of the remainder of the dialogue is spent in trying to yank out of Nicias a statement about who has this knowledge: not the doctor (195b–d), nor the seer (195e–196a), nor does any animal have it (196d–197b); pretty soon it is clear that Nicias neither knows who possesses this knowledge, nor what the knowledge is.

Socrates then takes over the dialogue and forces Nicias' assent to the following premises:

(1) Courage, temperance, justice, and the like are—as we earlier agreed in the discussion—parts of virtue (198a).

(2) Courage is the knowledge of what is to be dreaded and dared. (This was earlier asserted by Nicias at 194e–195a.)

(3) Things that are dreaded are those that cause fear, and things to be dared are those that do not (198b).

(4) Fear is of expected evils and things to be dared are good things (198b–c).

∴ (5) Courage is the knowledge of good and evil things (198c).

(6) There is a single knowledge of past, present, and future goods and evils (198d–199a).

∴ (7) Courage is the knowledge of all goods and evils, past, present, or future (199b–c).

(8) The man who knows all good and evil things, whether in the past, present, or future, has the whole of virtue (199d).

∴ (9) We have not discovered what courage is (199e).

Statement (5) purportedly follows from (2), (3), and (4); (7) from (5) and (6); and (9) from (1), (7), and (8). But is it really the case that they have not discovered what courage is, or have they discovered that courage is the whole of virtue? If we accept the former alternative, then something has gone wrong with the argument between (2) and (7) inclusive; but there is no indication in the text of a misfire here.[52] If we accept the latter alternative, then we need only discard premise (1). But why do Socrates, Nicias, and Laches agree upon (1)? The only reason given is that to inquire about courage, rather than the whole of virtue, will make their task easier (190c–d), and this is not a very compelling reason, especially given the dramatic effect (1) has at the end.

Still we do not have good evidence that Socrates would throw out (1). But there still remains in the *Laches* an unanswered argument: all of the interlocutors agree that: (A) courage is a noble and beneficial possession. Furthermore, Socrates' criticisms of Laches, and Nicias' fumbling attempts to recount what Socrates says (as in the passage on the doctor quoted earlier) imply that: (B) only the knowledge of good and evil is really beneficial. We have, then, *mutatis mutandis*, the same argument found in the *Meno* and *Charmides*:

(A) Courage is really beneficial to its possessor.
(B) Only the knowledge of good and evil is really beneficial.
∴ (C) Courage is the knowledge of good and evil.

I believe that it is more plausible to take (C) as the real conclusion of the *Laches* than (9).

The *Euthyphro*

In the *Euthyphro*, moreover, there are important hints at the same conclusion.[53] At 14b–c Socrates says:

> You might, if you wished, Euthyphro, have answered much more briefly the chief part of my question. But it is plain that you do not care to instruct me. For now, when you were close upon it, you turned aside; and if you had answered it, I should have obtained from you all the instruction I need about piety.

It is Euthyphro's claim that piety is service (ὑπηρετική) to the gods that almost attains the status of a correct account. But Euthyphro cannot say what end we help the gods to accomplish. Socrates implies, however, that the gods are good;[54] first he rejects the Homeric conception of morally pernicious divinities (6a–b), and then he asserts that the gods love piety because of what it is (10a ff.). The gods love piety because they are, themselves, good; and being good the gods only do good things (see *Republic* 379c, *Timaeus* 30a). What, then, would our service to the gods be? Our service is clearly to do the same type of act, and if this is the case, piety is not distinct from the rest of the virtues; for piety is simply to care for the *psyche*.[55] Moreover, it is clearly implied throughout the *Euthyphro* that Euthyphro's moral failure is an intellectual one, and we may have the barest of hints at 14c that knowledge is what is required when Socrates recasts Euthyphro's fumbling comments about piety into a "knowledge (ἐπιστήμη) of sacrificing and praying." But for Euthyphro such a knowledge is no better than one of the special arts, and he immediately interprets it to be a barter between gods and men (14e).

The most, then, that we learn from the *Euthyphro* is that we have a general requirement to imitate the gods by also doing good things, and that Euthyphro fails in this because he is deficient in knowledge. Two consequences of this interpretation are (1) that the gods love us when we are pious (see *Republic* 612e–613b, *Alcibiades* I 134d, and *Philebus* 39e), and

(2) that the requirements of piety are not distinct from those of justice. Consequence (2) explains why piety has little or no role in later dialogues as a distinct virtue. We do not, then, learn from the *Euthyphro* that piety is wisdom, but we see that Euthyphro is deficient in wisdom, and that piety collapses into the general requirement to do good things. Our service to the gods is to help them accomplish "many fine things" (τῶν πολλῶν καὶ καλῶν, 14a). Is it not obvious what sort of knowledge this requires?

Why is the *Euthyphro* less explicit than most other early dialogues? We do not find in it the dialectical movement, as for example in the *Laches*, from external behavior to the *psyche*. But the dialectical development of a dialogue must, in part, be explained by the educational attainment of its interlocutors. For pure sluggishness of intellect we could not find a better candidate than "Straight Thinker." He persistently looks to the Homeric divinities for the paradigm of piety, and even after the process of "refutation," he continues to believe that man's relation to these "divinities" is a mercantile transaction (14e). Euthyphro, then, has not been stung by Socrates and his dogmatic belief structure remains intact. Since Euthyphro is always looking up, Socrates cannot direct his vision to his own *psyche*. Furthermore, Euthyphro knows nothing about the role of Socratic knowledge in virtuous behavior. Thus to leave Euthyphro with the account that "piety is a service to the gods because the pious man knowingly does good things," would be, at best, educationally detrimental. Euthyphro would simply assimilate this account to his Homeric belief system, and continue to study the gods' behavior for "knowledge" about right and wrong.

I conclude that the *Meno*, *Protagoras*, *Charmides*, and *Laches* imply that the virtues = wisdom or knowledge of good and evil. The *Euthyphro* does not have this implication, but it suggests that Euthyphro's failure of piety is an intellectual one, and that the requirements of piety are not distinct from those of the other virtues.

What is the Socratic knowledge of good and evil? From an ontological perspective such knowledge is a state of the *psyche*. Hence it produces and explains behavior. From a dialectical perspective the best example of an approach to the knowledge of good and evil is the *Crito*. In the *Crito* Socrates defends staying in prison and drinking the hemlock; this is, on the whole, the best course of action. On the one hand the knowledge of good and evil is a regulative ideal; it is the completely certain and defensible account. On the other hand Socrates is aware in the *Crito* that the dialectical defense of a position is never closed; it should be reopened whenever there is question about a premise. Socrates does not act on a subjective whim, but on the considered results of dialectical activity, even though such results are open to change and growth.

SECTION III: Socratic Teaching

We must explain why the early dialogues end in such a paradoxical and suggestive manner. Thus I will briefly discuss dialectic. Early Socratic dialectic consists in two complementary activities: the first is negative *elenchus* which, by the destruction of dogmatically held opinions, makes possible the reception of true beliefs; the second is *psychagoga*, the drawing out of true beliefs by argument, suggestion, innuendo, and informal paradox.

Imagine that the *psyche* is a web of beliefs, some of them, the more empirical ones, at the periphery, and those connected with one's ideology—one's whole outlook on life—at the center of the web. These beliefs are also intimately connected with action. I believe this to be one of Socrates' early pictures of the *psyche*, and his concern is about the core beliefs. Thus the topics of conversation in the early dialogues are an interlocutor's core beliefs: Euthyphro's whole life is guided by the study of the Homeric divinities; Charmides most prides himself on his quiet, modest behavior; Laches believes that the paradigm behavior for a general is to perish steadfast at his post; and Nicias constantly looks for the wise expert: unfortunately in the Sicilian campaign he trusted himself and his men to a seer, and the end was disaster. The intent of Socrates' negative dialectic is, with uncharacteristic insight, described by Nicias (*Laches* 187e–188a):

> You strike me as not being aware that, whoever comes into close contact with Socrates and has any talk with him face to face, is bound to be drawn round and round by him in the course of the argument—though it may have started at first on a quite different theme—and cannot stop until he is led into giving an account of himself, of the manner in which he now spends his days, and of the kind of life he has lived hitherto; and when one has been led into that, Socrates will never let him go until he has thoroughly and properly put all his ways to the test.

People do not voluntarily render an account of their lives and the beliefs that guide them. The resistance against digging to the core of one's *psyche* is immense, and to overcome this resistance Socrates engages in irony.[56] Constantly he defaces himself and builds the confidence of his interlocutor: in the *Laches* he persuades the generals to first give their opinions about fighting in heavy arms (181d):

> It seems to me, however, most proper that I, being so much younger and less experienced than you and your friends, should first hear what they have to say, and learn from them; . . .

And later when the question turns to the proper treatment of the *psyche* Socrates says (186c):

> But I should not be surprised if Nicias or Laches has discovered or learned it: for they have more means at their command to enable them to learn from others; and they are also older, and have had time to discover it.

Again in the *Euthyphro* Socrates props up Euthyphro's purported claims to knowledge at his own expense, and even offers to become Euthyphro's pupil in matters of piety (4e–5a):

> But, in the name of Zeus, Euthyphro, do you think your knowledge about divine laws and holiness and unholiness is so exact that, when the facts are as you say, you are not afraid of doing something unholy yourself in prosecuting your father for murder? [Euthyphro] I should be of no use, Socrates, and Euthyphro would be in no way different from other men, if I did not have exact knowledge about all such things.

Socrates' irony is not unjustified (also see *Republic* I 337e–338a, *Charmides* 166c–d, 167a). Some such tactic is needed to overcome the resistance to "rendering an account of one's life and ways." This is especially true because the nature of negative dialectic is *ad hominem*. It searches out, attacks, and destroys an answerer's core beliefs, those that form the very center of his psychic integration. That Socrates intends to do this is clear from the *Gorgias*, where he states numerous rules for the operation of *elenchus*. For example, at *Gorgias* 454b–c Socrates says to Gorgias:

> For, as I say, I ask my questions with a view to an orderly completion of our argument—I am not aiming at you, but am only anxious that we do not fall into a habit of snatching at each other's words with a hasty guess, and that you may complete your own statement in your own way, as the premises may allow.

Socrates' denial that he is aiming at Gorgias is either deep self-deception or outright insincerity. Sometimes Socrates tries to detach the *logoi* from their makers (see *Euthyphro* 11c), and to give them a life of their own, but such attempts fail; for the answerers often see that it is their lives that are at stake (*Laches* 187e–188a). Gorgias must complete his own statement in his own way so that *he* is committed to it, and to its downfall. Socrates admits as much at *Gorgias* 474a–b:

> For I know how to produce one witness in support of my statements, and that is the man himself with whom I find myself arguing: the many I dismiss: there is also one whose vote I know how to take, whilst to the multitude I have not a word to say.

While negative dialectic coerces the answerers' assent, and directly attacks his beliefs, positive dialectic or *psychagoga* (*psyche* leading) is noncoercive and benign. *Psychagoga* is the drawing out of true beliefs by argument, suggestion, innuendo, and paradox. Socratic education is never the filling of blank tablets, but rather the activation of innate human capacities.[57] At *Republic* 578d Socrates states about dialectic:

> Of this very thing, then, I said, there might be an art, an art of the speediest and most effective shifting or conversion of the *psyche*, not an art of producing vision in it, but on the assumption that it possesses vision but does not look where it should, an art of bringing this about.

Although this passage is from a middle dialogue, and the correct vision there is of the separate Forms, it also is a remarkable description of Plato's earlier beliefs. But in the early dialogues the gaze of the *psyche* should be turned away from conventional beliefs, the judgments of the many, and the decisions of law courts to the condition of one's own *psyche*. How does one stand with respect to temperance, justice, and ultimately wisdom? Socrates thinks of the *psyche* not only as the source of motion and as an object open to introspection, but also as a system of beliefs. Care for the *psyche*, on the latter conception, is a testing, evaluating, and defending of one's beliefs. The object is to turn mere belief into knowledge; this is done by evaluating the belief from different perspectives, turning over and over the arguments, and finally fastening the belief in the *psyche* with chains of steel and adamant (*Meno* 85c–d, 98a, *Gorgias* 508e–509a). The difference between true belief and knowledge is not that they are about different objects, as in *Republic V*, but that the latter transcends the former in its bonds (*Meno* 98a). We are not, then, faced with two worlds in the early dialogues, but with one world that is cognized in different ways.

But why doesn't Socrates simply tell Euthyphro about the only piety that is really beneficial; why doesn't he directly save Charmides from his false pretense of temperance, and from his later misery as one of the thirty tyrants? Why, if my interpretation of the dialogues is correct, does Socrates hide his real view, and end every dialogue in *aporia* ("perplexity")? Would it not be so much simpler to teach Meno the truth? But Socrates denies that he teaches anything! And here lies the key to his method. Traditional teaching as telling cannot produce knowledge. The man who has been told the way to Larissa only has true opinion, but he who has walked there and led others knows the route (*Meno* 97a–b). Telling someone the truth can only produce belief. But why doesn't Socrates at least attempt to produce true belief in hopeless souls like Euthyphro? His answer to this is twofold: (1) perplexity is the impetus to further investigation; to fill a blank tablet with another's beliefs is to invite the conceit of false knowledge; (2) Socrates, unlike Plato, thinks it within the purview of most men—which is why he questions the craftsmen, poets, and politicians in the *Apology*—to investigate virtue and excellence, and he believes it necessary for wisdom that this investigation be an autonomous one.[58]

Thus Socrates employs *psychagoga* in the early dialogues. He argues for his position, gives reasons to support it, and implies it; all of this draws the *psyche* to the truth. But then there must be a shock, a reversal, a paradox, to engage the autonomous resources of the answerer. Therefore, my analysis of Socrates' educational techniques requires that the dialogues have a dramatic structure like that I argued for earlier.

SECTION IV: Two Criticisms of the Early Dialogues

In this section I will briefly develop two criticisms of the early dialogues.

There are two distinct models for the *psyche* in the early dialogues. Socrates' dialectical method presupposes that the *psyche* is like a web of belief. For to test a person's beliefs is to test the condition of his *psyche*. The more empirical beliefs are at the periphery, and those connected with one's ideology, one's whole outlook on life, are towards the center of the web. The topics of conversation invariably turn to an interlocutor's core beliefs: Euthyphro's whole life is guided by the study of the Homeric divinities; Charmides most prides himself on his quiet, modest behavior; and Laches believes that a courageous general, such as himself, should perish steadfast at his post. Socrates believes that refutation and then *psychagoga*, the leading of the *psyche* to true beliefs, *a fortiori* establishes a motive force for action. At this point the model of the *psyche* as a source of motion enters.

Socrates not only has two models for the *psyche*, but also deems a psychic power to be a combination of propositional knowledge and motivational force. Courage, for example, includes a propositional understanding of good and evil, as well as a motive force to act in accord with this knowledge.[59] Because of this dual nature of a psychic power, Socrates denies that "weakness of will" is possible, and asserts that virtue is knowledge. He who knows what is best has both a reason to act and a sufficient cause of that act. Thus a psychic power is both a reason and a cause of action.

The *Republic*, however, criticizes the assimilation of the two models. In *Republic* IV spirit and appetite cause behavior, but they are irrational (ἀλόγιστος, *Republic* 439d, 441c); at best they only intend a generic object (for instance, drink), but there is no guarantee that this object is thought to be good (*Republic* 438a ff.). Thus not all desire is rational calculation for the good.[60] Hence spirit and appetite can overthrow reason, just as the military and artisans can refuse to obey the guardians. In the *Republic* weakness of will is possible. Reason, however, in the *Republic* still maintains an impetus for action; it is not passionless, but neither is it a sufficient condition for action since it must compete with spirit and appetite.

The different psychology of the *Republic* requires an expanded view of education. Music and gymnastics form the correct habits; they train spirit and appetite. Dialectic is not, even for the philosopher kings, a sufficient tool for education; for everyone in the republic must have the basic training in music and gymnastics (443e, 425c–e). Moreover, dialectical skill is no longer even a necessary condition for virtue, since the artisans and military have psychic and civic virtue,[61] but they do not study dialectic. Plato, himself, in the *Republic* separates the reasons from the causes of action, and thus he anticipates and accepts my first criticism.

The second criticism, however, is effective against both the early and the middle-period ethical psychology. We can formulate this criticism for the early dialogues by recalling two claims: (A) On the (CP) a virtue is F because it produces F acts, and (B) F acts are paronymously called after their psychic causes or the psychic states they produce. There is, then, an uninformative circle of namings; psychic states are called after what they produce, and the acts they produce are called after them. We do not know what sort of thing a virtue is until we see its effects, and we do not know how to properly describe these effects until we discern their cause. In the *Charmides* (158e–159a, 160d) Socrates might be interpreted as trying to break the circle by direct introspection of a psychic state. But the perception of a psychic state at 160d is inextricably tied to what the psychic state produces. Moreover, in the early dialogues we are never given any clear directions for introspection, nor are we really ever told what such an inward glance would yield. Thus Socrates treats states as dispositions because he does not identify them apart from the behavior they produce.

As Frankena puts it, turning Kant's phrase, "virtues without principles are blind, and principles without virtues are impotent."[62] Socrates looks for the virtues, but he presents little analysis of the principles for virtuous behavior. The latter defect destroys the former search. Socrates could avoid vacuity if he were to give independent principles of action. But Socrates, as we have seen, rejects the characteristic view because it is always possible to give a counterexample to a principle of action. For Socrates a *prima facie* principle is no principle at all, and this is his fundamental mistake.

Someone might object that the early dialogues are open to this criticism only because I interpret self-predication on the basis of the (CP). But the same problem can be formulated for the *Republic*[63] without condition (A)

above. I have argued that in *Republic* IV acts are correctly called just if:
(1) they produce or tend to produce psychic justice, or (2) they tend to be
or are produced by psychic justice. But at *Republic* 477c–d Plato tackles
the important question of how to individuate and identify different psychic
powers:

> Shall we say that the powers (δυνάμεις) are a certain kind of being by
> which we and all other things are able to do what we or they are
> able to do? I mean, for example, that both sight and hearing are
> powers.... Now, in a power I cannot see any color, shape or similar
> mark such as those upon which I might look in discriminating for
> myself one thing from another. But in the case of a power I look to
> these things only—that to which it is related and which it affects, and
> it is with reference to these that I come to call each of them [sight and
> hearing] a power, and that which is related to the same thing, I call
> the same power, and that to another I call other.

Psychic powers, in and of themselves, are not directly observable because
they do not provide criteria for their own identification and individuation.
This rejects the introspection of the *Charmides*. Therefore, psychic powers
must be identified by what they *relate to* or *produce*. In the case of belief and
knowledge there is no problem, for the former relates to what is "between Being and not-being," while the latter relates to "real Being." But
in the case of the virtues there is an uninformative circle of namings: we
cannot identify just acts without reference to psychic justice, and we
cannot identify psychic justice without reference to just acts. Hence
Socrates attempts to escape from the circle with the famous "vulgar
account" of the virtues (*Republic* 442c–443b)—to refrain from murder,
theft, sacrilege, and the like.[64] But the vulgar test is objectionable for
several reasons: (1) Socrates, himself, states in the *Euthyphro* (8b–d) that
nobody denies that murder is wrong—the question is whether some act is
an instance of murder; thus the vulgar test is vacuous. (2) The vulgar test
will not help in hard cases such as Euthyphro's indictment of his father;
thus the vulgar test cannot be a paradigm for correct behavior. (3) The
vulgar test depends upon the beliefs of the many, and the prevailing laws
of the city; but Plato certainly disagrees with many of these beliefs and
laws. Therefore, Socrates is caught in an uninformative circle in *Republic*
IV and V, and he cannot use vulgar beliefs about virtue to exonerate
himself from the circle.

2

The Beautiful in the *Hippias Major*, the *Gorgias*, and the *Symposium*

A half century ago G. M. A. Grube and Dorothy Tarrant debated the authenticity of the *Hippias Major*. Grube argued for Plato's authorship of the dialogue, while Tarrant believed that certain aspects of the dialogue "are best explained on the theory that it is the work of a young student of the Academy writing in Plato's lifetime."[1] Grube, in the opinion of many scholars, won the debate, and an increasing number of them treat the *Hippias Major* as a genuine creation of Plato's.[2] I too believe that the *Hippias Major* is authentic.

I will defend the thesis that the *Hippias Major* is a "Socratic" not a "Platonic" dialogue. While most of the other early works search for human excellence, the *Hippias Major* has the broader task of investigating aesthetic and utilitarian excellence (ἀρετή) in general. The dialogue has in common with the other early works two important, and unmistakably early, characteristics: (1) an aporetic dramatic structure, and (2) a "mundane" Socratic ontology.

The investigation of the *Hippias Major* not only will complement and complete our earlier discussion, but also it will support previous points. First I will investigate Hippias' three accounts of the beautiful. His candidates fail because they turn out to be beautiful and not beautiful, and thus they cannot be that *by which* all beautiful things are beautiful. I will then show that the beautiful must be always beautiful because it is that *by which* all beautiful things are beautiful. Second I will investigate Socrates' three accounts of the beautiful. I will show that these accounts have an aporetic dramatic structure similar to that found in other early dialogues; even though they do not state the nature of beauty, Socrates rejects them with intentional fallacies. Socrates' accounts, moreover, give us valuable clues to the beautiful; that is, they lead the *psyche* to it without directly telling what it is. From passages in the *Gorgias* we will see that the beautiful is the orderly and harmonious arrangement of a particular's elements.[3] This arrangement produces both utility and aesthetic pleasure. Third I will show that the beautiful is not a transcendent entity. Socrates' use of the instrumental dative, his use of the noncausal terms and constructions that relate the beautiful to beautiful things, and his use of vision terms, do not imply that the beautiful is a separate entity, and the latter two suggest, as I will argue, that it is an "immanent" one. Finally I will show that the beautiful of the *Hippias Major* is not The Beautiful of the *Symposium*;[4] rather it is found on the rungs of the ladder of ascent in the *Symposium*. The beautiful of the *Hippias Major* is in things as the harmonious arrangement of their elements, and hence it is the source of their excellence, both human and otherwise. Since it is in things, the beautiful is not a separate εἶδος like that found in the *Symposium*, and thus there is a major development in Plato's metaphysics between the *Hippias Major* and the *Symposium*. I will locate the source of this development in Eleaticism.

Hippias' Three Accounts

Hippias attempts three accounts of the beautiful, but each of them fails for the same type of reason. First he says that the beautiful is a beautiful woman, because he is unable to distinguish two questions that Socrates asks: "What is the beautiful (τὸ καλόν)?" and "What is beautiful (καλόν)?" (287d–e). Socrates seeks the former, but Hippias answers the latter, and although a beautiful woman is beautiful, Socrates shows that a beautiful woman is not the beautiful, because in comparison with (πρός) the race of gods a beautiful woman is ugly (289b). Then Hippias says that the beautiful is gold (289e). Socrates elicits this response from Hippias by how he phrases his request for an answer: He asks Hippias to tell him what it is that, being added to something, adorns it (κοσμεῖται) and makes it appear beautiful (289d). The use of "adorns" suggests to Hippias the process of gilding, and gold thus becomes a likely candidate for the beautiful. But, a figwood spoon is more appropriate than a gold one for ladling soup, so gold is no more beautiful than figwood (291c). Hippias' last account is that "for everyone it is most beautiful to be rich, healthy, honored by the Greeks, to reach old age, and after providing a beautiful funeral for one's deceased parents, to be beautifully and splendidly buried by one's own offspring" (291d–e). This account results from an apparent insight Hippias has into the beautiful. After the failure of his second account he says to Socrates, "You seem to me to seek to be told that the beautiful is some such thing that never appears ugly anywhere to anyone." Socrates' reply is ironic, "Certainly, Hippias, now you understand beautifully (καλῶς)" (291d). Hippias attempts to capture what everyone thinks is beautiful everywhere, but he fails; for it is not beautiful either for the gods or the heroes to be splendidly buried by their offspring.

So this account suffers a fate similar to the other two: the events are beautiful for some (τοῖς) but not for others (τοῖς, 293c). Therefore three types of things—a particular, a mass object (gold), and a group of events—are not the beautiful because they are in one relation, or context, or for some lives beautiful, and yet in others not beautiful.

The problem with particulars, mass objects, and events is that they are not beautiful in all contexts. Because they fail in this, they cannot be that *by which* all beautiful things are beautiful; for Socrates constantly contrasts their deficiency with the requirement that the beautiful *makes* all beautiful things beautiful (288a, 289d, 290b, 290d, 292c–d). The beautiful, on the other hand, is always (ἀεί, 292e) beautiful, because whenever it is added, it makes that to which it is present beautiful. Particulars are not deficient in that they are less beautiful, less real copies of the beautiful, as a run-of-the-mill coed is less beautiful than a Georgia beauty queen; for Socrates uses a phrase that mitigates against this type of deficiency: "all the really (τῷ ὄντι) beautiful uses and pursuits" (294c).[5] In the *Hippias Major* really beautiful uses and pursuits are deficient because in other contexts they are not beautiful. Therefore, the contrast between the beautiful and beautiful things is that the former is in every way beautiful, while the latter are not. Moreover, Socrates does not assert that the beautiful always exists, like a middle-period Form; the most that we learn is that, whenever the beautiful is present to something, the beautiful is beautiful.[6]

I have already implied that 292e should be read as the predication, "Doubtless the beautiful is always beautiful."[7] From Socrates' rejection of Hippias' three accounts, it is clear that phenomena cannot have the causal function of the beautiful because they are beautiful and not beautiful. Moreover, Socrates' first account implies that to be always beautiful is a necessary condition for the causal function of the beautiful since the beautiful is that which makes all beautiful things be but not appear beautiful. In outline Socrates' first account is:

(1) Suggested account: "The beautiful is the appropriate" (293e).
∴ (2) "The appropriate is beautiful (καλόν)" (293e).
(3) The appropriate only makes things *appear* beautiful, and does not make them *be* beautiful (294e).
(4) The beautiful only makes things *be* beautiful, and does not make them *appear* beautiful (294e).
∴ (5) "The appropriate is not a beautiful thing (τὸ πρέπον ἄλλο τι ἐφάνη ὂν ἢ καλόν)" (294e).
∴ (6) The appropriate is not the beautiful.

(2) follows from (1) in conjunction with the earlier claim, "Doubtless the beautiful is always beautiful" (292e). Hippias and Socrates agree upon (3) and (4). (5) follows from (3) and the suppressed premise that only what

makes something be, but not appear, beautiful is beautiful; and (6) follows from (5), and the earlier claim at 292e. Why does Socrates not immediately conclude from (3) and (4) that the appropriate is not the beautiful? The reason is that a key assumption, both earlier in the refutation of Hippias' views, and in this argument, is that if something is that *by which* all beautiful things are beautiful, then it is always (that is, in every respect and relation) beautiful. Since to be always beautiful is a necessary condition for the causal function of the beautiful, we may establish that something is not the beautiful by showing that, in any way, it is not beautiful.

But why does Socrates believe that to be always beautiful is a necessary condition for that *by which* all beautiful things are beautiful? The reason, as I showed earlier,[8] is that a cause must have the quality that it produces in something else. In the case of the beautiful, if it is the harmonious constitution of a particular's elements, then whenever it is present, the harmonious constitution must be beautiful, and must transmit its beauty to the particular. A particular would not be beautiful in every respect, but would be so in that respect in which the beautiful is present to it; moreover, a particular would not be beautiful in every comparison, even when compared with objects of the same type, because harmony admits of degrees. Finally, the harmonious constitution of a particular is not identical with that particular because, for example, one and the same *psyche* can be at time t_1 temperate and at time t_2 intemperate; and one and the same house can be at t_1 well constructed, and at t_2, after a hurricane, a shambles.[9] But is the beautiful the harmonious constitution of a particular's elements? Let us turn to Socrates' three accounts of the beautiful.

Socrates' Three Accounts

Hippias, a wise and noble (καλός) sophist (281a), fails to give a beautiful and well-composed (παγκάλως ... διακείμενος, 286a) speech about the beautiful,[10] and so Socrates, disguised as his own intimate friend,[11] offers to help Hippias; there is no doubt that Socrates' attempts will be closer to the mark. He offers three accounts of the beautiful, and from each of them we learn something about it. After we gather up these hints, I will show that we can explain and understand them from passages in the *Gorgias*. For in the *Gorgias* Socrates states that the excellence of something is the harmonious arrangement of its elements.

Socrates first suggests that the beautiful is the appropriate (τὸ πρέπον, 293e). This account is most appropriate because earlier in the dialogue Socrates and Hippias agreed that when appropriate something is beautiful (290d). The earlier examples of Pheidias' statue—gold, ivory, and stone—reveal that they think of the appropriate as a fitness that produces an aesthetically pleasant whole (290b–c); the examples of the figwood and gold spoons show that they also think of the appropriate as a fitness that produces a useful result (290e–291d). Thus the appropriate has both an aesthetic and an utilitarian function.

Hippias is asked whether the appropriate makes things be or appear beautiful, and he chooses the latter (294a). When Hippias mentions as paradigm examples of the appropriate, clothes and shoes that fit (294a), we see that he has much too crude a notion of "fitness." Beautiful clothes do not make a beautiful person. But Socrates does not directly attack Hippias' crude claim; rather, he says that if the appropriate makes someone appear more beautiful than he is, then it would be a deceit in respect to the beautiful (294a). What is logically remarkable about Socrates' rejection of this account is that he completely ignores the aesthetic and utilitarian notions of the appropriate mentioned earlier in the dialogue; he simply does not attempt to invest the appropriate with any more meaning than Hippias gives it.

Socrates has a limited objective in the first account. He and Hippias agree that the appropriate is not the beautiful because it makes things only *appear* but not be beautiful, while the beautiful makes them *be* but not appear so. Earlier in the dialogue Socrates shifted—to the discomfort of both Hippias and the reader—between *be* and *appear*. At 289d he asks for "that by which all other things are adorned and appear (φαίνεται) beautiful"; yet, at 292d, he wants to know "what it is that when added to something, makes that thing be (εἶναι) beautiful." The first account teaches us that Socrates is not interested in what people think is beautiful or what appears beautiful; rather, he is after what makes things be beautiful.

Moreover, the fate of the appropriate is not settled when Socrates rejects Hippias' interpretation of it. For the next two accounts are an aesthetic and an utilitarian, and so the first account reduces to the next two. Furthermore, we should note that when Socrates thinks of the appropriate as something other than a deceit in respect to the beautiful, he considers it a fitness or harmony of the elements in a thing (Pheidias' statue) or situation (a figwood spoon for eating soup), that produces aesthetic pleasure or utility.

The second account is that the beautiful is the useful (τὸ χρήσιμον, 295c). A group of objects is given for which the account is most appropriate: eyes, the whole body, all the animals, all utensils, land vehicles, freight ships, ships of war, all instruments in music and the other arts, and even customs and pursuits (295c–d). Each of these is beautiful in the respect or way in which it is useful. Moreover, when Socrates states his third account, that the beautiful is the pleasant to hearing and sight, he gives a different group of objects for which that account is most appropriate. We would classify these under the fine arts, although Socrates does not distinguish the mechanical and the fine arts by denying excellence and beauty to the former. One reason for this is that "καλός" has a much broader meaning than the English word "beautiful." It can mean "beautiful," "noble," "honorable," "fine," "fair," and "good," to give only a few examples. Likewise, "αἰσχρός," the opposite of "καλός" has as many contrary meanings. Thus when Socrates says at 292d, "Everything to which the beautiful is added is made beautiful, a stone, wood, man, god, every action, and learning," we see that "καλός" is much broader in meaning than our notion of aesthetic beauty. The beautiful is more akin to a thing's excellence (ἀρετή), and different types of things can have different types of excellence. We should not be surprised, then, to see Socrates reject the second and third accounts because each is too narrow; each account focuses upon one type of excellence, and does not state the nature of the beautiful that is common to all excellence.

Socrates quickly amends the second account: only what is useful for something good is beautiful. On this view the beautiful is the cause (αἴτιον, 296e) or the father (ἐν πατρός τινος ἰδέᾳ, 297b) of the good, and since a cause is different (ἄλλο) from its effect, the beautiful is different from the good. So far everything is in order, but then Socrates makes the startling inference that since the beautiful and the good are different, "the beautiful (τὸ καλόν) is not good (ἀγαθόν), and the good (τὸ ἀγαθόν) is not beautiful (καλόν)" (297c). This conclusion is unacceptable, and they abandon the whole account.

The distinction between the beautiful and one of its effects, benefit, is correct, and we see Socrates reassert it in the *Gorgias* (474d–e). But what are we to make of the final and fatal inference? I believe that it is an intentional fallacy meant to stun Hippias and leave him in a state of bewilderment. Only then would Hippias begin to investigate, for himself, the real nature of beauty. Socrates knows that "the beautiful is the useful for something good" only states a mark of the beautiful and not its nature, and if he were to leave Hippias with this account, Hippias would simply incorporate it into the "beautiful" speech, the one he is to give to schoolchildren, about what pursuits are noble and beautiful. Moreover, Hippias has not the slightest idea what real benefit is; for him power in political affairs is most beautiful (295e–296a). Thus Socrates overturns everything in the vain hope that Hippias will postpone his speech until he discovers for himself the real nature of the beautiful. For Hippias really is a corrupter of the youth.

Nevertheless, since the good and the beautiful are closely connected in Plato's thought (see *Philebus* 65a), there may be a temptation to interpret the conclusion, not as a *non sequitur*, but as the simple denial of an identity,

"The beautiful is not the good, and the good is not the beautiful." But there are serious objections to this interpretation: (1) While it does not produce a *non sequitur*, it does make the conclusion a mere restatement of the premise from which it is derived: "The beautiful and the good are not identical, therefore, they are not identical." But Socrates clearly indicates that two different assertions are at issue. (2) Nowhere in the *Hippias Major* is it agreed that the beautiful is the good, so a denial of the identity would not be sufficient to reject the account that the beautiful produces good. (3) The denial of an identity would not have the same shocking result— emphasized by the exclamation Μά Δί four times—as the predication translation. (4) The same argument recurs at 303e–304a, where it is used to reject the account that the beautiful is beneficial pleasure, but here "then neither would the good be beautiful nor the beautiful good" is clearly a purported consequence of "if each is different from the other." (5) Only if the consequence is read as a predication is it sufficient to require that the account be abandoned; for to say that the beautiful is not a good thing is, indeed, shocking. I conclude that the consequence is the denial of a predication.

But does Socrates intentionally produce the fallacy at 297c? Does he have enough of an intuitive grasp of the difference between a predication and an identity to see that it is fallacious to infer that "the beautiful is not good" from "the beautiful is not the good?" G. M. A. Grube denies that he does:[12]

> The *Hippias Major* was written at an early stage in Plato's life before the use of the predicate, i.e. the difference between: "Beauty is good," and "Beauty is the good," was clearly understood. The question of the copula is dealt with in the *Sophist* after which the *Hippias Major* could not have been written.

Grube claims (and W. Sellars with him[13]) that in the early dialogues Plato confuses identity and predication assertions. Thus he was not aware of the fallacy at 297c. Both Grube and Sellars cite the "self-predications" at *Protagoras* 330c,e, as further examples of this confusion, but we may dismiss this evidence because I have already shown that the *Protagoras* statements must be read as predications.[14] Even if Plato does not explicitly distinguish predications and identities until the *Sophist*, and even there he does not do so by saying anything like "I distinguish this from that," he might still use the distinction correctly in earlier dialogues.

There is, moreover, a grammatical device in the *Hippias Major* that marks an important component of the distinction: καλόν with the article τό before it is the substantive, "the beautiful," and καλόν without the article is the adjective "is beautiful."[15] When the article is used with both the grammatical subject and object of a sentence, then the identity use of the verb occurs; and when it is used with the subject but not with the predicate adjective, then the predicative use occurs. At 287d–e Socrates, but not Hippias, is easily able to distinguish "What is the beautiful (τὸ καλόν)?" and "What is beautiful (καλόν)?" Thus Socrates explicitly uses the article to mark off the substantive from the adjective, although Hippias *never* sees the difference. Furthermore, Socrates formulates his three accounts as identities, again using the article to clarify matters: the appropriate (τὸ πρέπον) is the beautiful (τὸ καλόν, 293e), the useful (τὸ χρήσιμον) is not the beautiful (τὸ καλόν, 296d), and the pleasant (τὸ ... ἡδύ) to hearing and sight is the beautiful (τὸ καλόν, 298a). In the *Protagoras* Socrates employs the notion of identity (329c–d): "Pray now, proceed to deal with these in a more precise exposition, stating whether virtue is a single thing, of which justice, temperance, and holiness are parts, or whether the things I have just mentioned are all names (ὀνόματα) for one and the same thing." Socrates implies that an identity assertion consists of two or more names that are of one and the same thing. In the *Hippias Major* he employs this notion when he gives his accounts: for example "the appropriate" and "the beautiful" name the same thing, thus the appropriate = the beautiful. In what I believe to be the correct account τὸ καλόν and τὸ κόσμον have different senses, but the same reference. Since τὸ κόσμον has a different sense, it clarifies the referent of both words, and herein lies the gain that is found in successfully saying what the beautiful is.

Plato, however, sometimes leaves off the article where we may either supply or not supply it depending on the context. While this grammatical feature of Greek could cause confusion between predication and identity, there is no evidence in the early dialogues that it does. Moreover, in the *Hippias Major* Plato explicitly marks off the substantive from the adjective with the article, and this makes it plausible that he does see the *non sequitur* at 297c, and hence intentionally manufactured it. That Hippias does not spot the fallacy is no indication of how clear it is, for Hippias was unable to distinguish the substantive and the adjective at 287d–e. 297c is just the sort of sophistry Socrates would pull on a "wise and beautiful" sophist,[16] although his ultimate concern is, of course, care for the *psyche*.

The third account is that the beautiful is what is pleasant to hearing and sight (298a). Socrates directs this account to aesthetic objects: "Beautiful persons, all decorations, paintings, and works of sculpture which are beautiful delight us when we see them; beautiful sounds, music in general, speeches, and stories accomplish the same thing" (298a). However, τὸ ἡδύ is ambiguous; it refers either to the objects just listed ("what is pleasant") or to the pleasures they produce ("the pleasant"). Since the beautiful makes beautiful *things* beautiful (287c–d), we would expect Socrates to investigate what it is about these things that produces pleasure to hearing and sight. But in the space of a few lines there is a shift in questions from "What is it about objects that makes them produce aesthetic pleasure?" to "What is common (τὸ κοινόν, 300a) to pleasures through hearing and sight and both together, on account of which we say that they are beautiful?" The answer to the latter question is now thought to be the beautiful. By his own admission in the *Gorgias* (474d–e), Socrates turns away from the beautiful to one of its marks.

Attempts to answer the second question fail. That they are each and both pleasures will not do, for there are other pleasures that are not beautiful. That they are pleasures through sight and hearing is unacceptable because this belongs to both but not to each. That they are pleasures through sight or hearing is wrong, because each belongs to one but not to the other. So what is common to each pleasure and to both together? Socrates states that it seems to him necessary that they are beautiful because they are the most harmless and best of pleasures (303e).[17] This account appears to merit further attention, but Socrates abruptly rejects it with exactly the same sophistry he used in the previous one.

Why does Socrates do this? Clearly aesthetic pleasures are produced by beautiful things, but the beautiful makes these things beautiful, so that they can produce such pleasures. The inescapable conclusion is that the beautiful is a state of particulars that not only makes them beautiful, but also accounts for their producing aesthetic pleasure. To twist a classic phrase in the *Euthyphro*: "beautiful things are not beautiful because they produce aesthetic pleasure, but they produce aesthetic pleasure because they are beautiful." Thus aesthetic pleasure and benefit are πάθη of the beautiful, and not its nature; but Socrates cannot tell Hippias this, for it is not Socrates' style to teach by telling. Thus Socrates abruptly rejects the last two accounts and gives Hippias the shock of *aporia*.

The *Gorgias*

Let us now turn to the *Gorgias* where a number of passages explain Socrates' views about excellence and beauty. At 474d–e Socrates says:

> All fair (καλά) things, like bodies and colors and figures and sounds and observances—is it looking at nothing that you call these fair in each case? Thus in the first place, when you say that fair bodies are fair, it must be either in view of their use for some particular purpose that each may serve, or in respect of some pleasure arising when, in the act of beholding them, they cause delight to the beholder.

Socrates offers aesthetic pleasure and utility as two tests for beauty. They are πάθη of the beautiful, and thus do not give its nature (οὐσία). In the

Euthyphro Socrates asks a famous question that displays this distinction (10a): "Is the holy holy because the gods love it, or do they love it because it is holy?" Euthyphro has not said what the holy is, rather he gives a πάθος of it: "Euthyphro, when I asked you to say what the holy is, you did not want to reveal its nature (οὐσίαν) to me, but rather gave some characteristic (πάθος) of it, something which happens to the holy, that it is loved by all the gods" (11a–b). Socrates does not deny that πάθη can mark out—put a boundary around—objects (see *Euthyphro* 9c), but he does deny that they give the nature of these objects. On the correct account of divinity, if something is pious then it is loved by the gods, and if something is god-loved then it is pious; if something is beautiful then it either produces benefit or aesthetic pleasure, and if something produces benefit or aesthetic pleasure, then it is beautiful. Thus god-loved can be a test for pious objects, and benefit or aesthetic pleasure can be a test for beautiful things; but neither of them gives the nature of the pious or the beautiful respectively. Socrates at *Gorgias* 474d–e only wants to mark out the group of fair things in order to refute Polus; thus he uses aesthetic pleasure and benefit as πάθη of beautiful things.

But what is the nature of the beautiful? At *Gorgias* 503e ff. Socrates gives a lengthy analysis of artistic production:[18]

[503e] He [the true rhetorician] is just like any other craftsman, who having his own particular work (ἔργον) in view, selects the things he applies to that work of his, not at random, but with the purpose of giving a certain form (εἶδος) to whatever he is working upon. You have only to look, for example, at the painters, the builders, the shipwrights, or any of the other craftsmen, whichever you like, to see how each of them arranges everything according to a certain order, and forces one part to fit and agree

[504a] with another (καὶ προσαναγκάζει τὸ ἕτερον τῷ ἑτέρῳ πρέπον τε εἶναι καὶ ἁρμόττειν), until he has combined the whole into a regular (τεταγμένον) and well-ordered (κεκοσμημένον) production;... Then if regularity (τάξεως) and order (κόσμου) are found in a house, it will be a good one, and if irregularity, a bad one....

[504c] For it seems to me that any regularity of the body is called
[504d] healthiness, and this leads to health being produced in it, and general bodily excellence.... And the regular and orderly states of the soul are called lawfulness and law, whereby men are similarly made law-abiding and orderly; and these states are justice and temperance....

[506d] And is that thing pleasant by whose advent we are pleased, and
[506e] that thing good by whose presence we are good?... But further, both we and everything else that is good, are good by the advent

of some virtue (ἀρετῆς)?... Then the virtue of each thing is a matter of regular and orderly arrangement (τάξει ἄρα τεταγμένον καὶ κεκοσμημένον)?... Hence it is a certain order (κόσμος) proper to each existent thing that by its advent in each makes it good?

Similar statements occur in the late *Philebus* (26a–b), where measure is responsible for all the beautiful things. Moreover, those commentators who believe that the *Hippias Major* is genuine also tend to think that it is close in date of composition to the *Gorgias*. E. R. Dodds, for example, places the *Gorgias* just after the *Hippias Major*, and claims that the *Gorgias* presupposes the discussion of beauty in the *Hippias Major*.[19]

The account of production at 503e ff. applies to all craftsmen: painters, philosophers, and even boat builders.[20] We may describe the stages of τέχνη as follows: (1) The true rhetorician, when constructing a speech, looks at (503e, 504d,e) what he wants to produce in the *psyches* of his listeners, that is, justice and temperance. The other craftsmen also look at their tasks (ἔργα, 503e). These tasks are not simply the replication of already existing houses, ships, or the like, but rather the "ideal designs" for such things. (2) Then the craftsman gives a certain form (εἶδος) to the matter; he forces one part to fit and agree with another until the whole is a regular and well-ordered production. The form of an object emerges from within it as it is being produced, and it is present to it when it is finished. Moreover, an object is a noble production, if the craftsman is successful in embodying the form well.

But where in all this talk about craft production is the beautiful? The *Gorgias* quotations give a clear account of it. The beautiful is added by the right use of craft, or in the case of natural objects, by the unhampered operations of nature. When a craftsman forces one part to fit and agree with another, until he combines the whole into a regular (τεταγμένον) and ordered (κεκοσμημένον) thing, then it is well made, good, and excellent (504a). The beautiful is an object's excellence (ἀρετῆς, 506d), and the excellence is its proper order (κόσμος ... ὁ ἑκάστου οἰκεῖος, 506e). Therefore, the beautiful is order or harmony.[21] The beautiful is being added to something as it is being well made, and it is present to it when it is well made. The beautiful is not a particular; rather it is the harmony of a particular's elements; nor should the beautiful be identified with the material of art; rather it is the way in which the material is arranged. The *Gorgias* quotations, allowing for minor variations in language—ἀγαθόν at 506e is nearly synonymous with καλόν[22]—are a direct answer to the question at *Hippias Major* 292d: "What is the beautiful, itself, that when added to something, it belongs to that to be beautiful?"

The beautiful is not the type form of a product, although it is an εἶδος (see *Hippias Major* 289d). When the type form or nature (φύσιν) of an object is placed into that from which (εἰς ἐκεῖνο ἐξ οὗ) it is made, then a certain type of object results (see *Cratylus* 389b–c). But the beautiful is present only when an object is well made, and its nature excellent. A poorly made shuttle still has the form of shuttle, but it does not have the beautiful.[23]

Particulars are not beautiful *simpliciter*, but neither do they have order *simpliciter*. Order is something relative to an end. A shuttle designed for the weaving of wool cloth may be unsuitable for silk cloth. From Socrates' second account we see that there is a general limitation on our judgment: no object suited for a bad end is καλός, no matter how well suited for the end. Also objects may possess different degrees of order, and hence one woman may be more beautiful than another. A pot, finally, is less beautiful than a woman because it is suited for a less important end.

How does the identification of the beautiful with order unify Socrates' three accounts? We need only discuss the last two since the appropriate reduces to them. The harmonious constitution of a particular both makes it useful (in some respect), and/or produces pleasure through sight or hearing. Thus we can say what is common to pleasures through hearing and sight: they are both produced by the same cause. The Doric rhythm produces pleasure; a strident sound does not. Likewise, a speech whose elements are well organized is pleasant to hear (cf. *Phaedrus* 264c), one that is disorganized is not. A well-proportioned statue is pleasant to sight; a poorly figured one is not.

Let us now place our conclusion into a broader context. Since the beautiful is the harmonious constitution of a particular, the ontology of the *Hippias Major* is "Socratic" not "Platonic." While most of the other early dialogues are concerned with moral excellence, the *Hippias Major* discusses excellence in general, including human excellence. This excellence is located, quite Socratically, in the well-made product of skilled craftsmanship. It is found, for example, in a properly educated *psyche*, in a well-cared-for body, and in a properly designed house. Excellence in phenomena is ultimately a microcosm of the excellence found in the Κόσμος as a whole (cf. *Gorgias* 507e–508a).

Our conclusion also places us squarely into one of two camps in a long-standing debate. We substantially agree with W. D. Ross, G. M. A. Grube, and E. R. Dodds, among others, who argue that forms are not separate in the early dialogues.[24] We must disagree with Harold Cherniss when he says, "From among the earliest of the dialogues on through the last—and this means, then, to the very end of Plato's life—the doctrine of [transcendent] ideas is the cornerstone of his thought,"[25] and again when he claims, "Neither here nor elsewhere is there any evidence for supposing 'paradigmatism' to have superseded some earlier conception of 'participation' in Plato's development of his theory."[26] The beautiful is the order of the elements of a particular, and thus the order of a particular is not separate from it, nor order in general from the *Cosmos*.

Three Possible Objections

We must, however, remove three objections to this interpretation of the beautiful. The three objections are: (1) that the uses of the instrumental dative and other causal terms (for instance, the beautiful *makes* beautiful things beautiful) indicate the transcendence of the cause; (2) that the uses of προσγίγνομαι "be added to," and cognate terms, imply the prior existence of what is added; and (3) that the occurrences of visual terminology, as at *Gorgias* 503e, as well as the term "εἶδος," imply that a craftsman is to look away at a separate Form.

Commentators usually do not find any particular ontological commitment in the use of the instrumental dative and other causal terms.[27] R. E. Allen, however, is an exception. He claims that these terms and constructions indicate the transcendence of the cause.[28] If a Form is transcendent or ontologically prior, then it can exist uninstantiated, although no instance can exist without it. Allen's view is obviously incompatible with my interpretation of the beautiful.

At *Hippias Major* 287c–d, Socrates and Hippias agree upon the following:[29]

> (1) By justice (δικαιοσύνη) the just (οἱ δίκαιοι) are just.
> ∴ (2) Justice is something (τι).
> (3) By wisdom (σοφίᾳ) the wise (οἱ σοφοί) are wise, and by the good all good things (πάντα τἀγαθά) are good.
> ∴ (4) Wisdom and the good are something, otherwise the others would not be what they are.
> (5) By the beautiful (τῷ καλῷ) all beautiful things (τὰ καλὰ πάντα) are beautiful.
> ∴ (6) The beautiful is something.

These are the most striking and suggestive uses of causal terminology in the *Hippias Major*. The masculine plurals οἱ δίκαιοι and οἱ σοφοί imply that justice and wisdom are primarily restricted to persons in their influence. Persons are primarily said to be just and wise by justice and wisdom respectively. But does this use of the instrumental dative indicate that justice and wisdom are ontologically prior to their instances? As I have already shown, there is no such suggestion. Justice and wisdom are psychic states and hence the *psyche* is ontologically prior to them; that is, a *psyche* can exist without justice or wisdom, but they cannot exist without the *psyche*.

The use of the neuter plurals "all good things" and "all beautiful things" imply that the good and the beautiful make many different types of things good and beautiful. This is, of course, precisely what we would expect, since many different sorts of things possess order. We also learn other things from this passage. First, there is an argument for the existence of the good and the beautiful. Since they are that by which other things are good and beautiful, they are "something" (τι). Now to claim that the good and the beautiful are "something" does not imply that they are ontologically prior to their instances; at most it simply states that they somehow exist. But it does not tell how they exist: whether in things or apart from them. Second, we learn that the good and the beautiful are necessary conditions for the goodness and beauty of other things. But there is no evidence for the further claim that the good and the beautiful can exist uninstantiated. The causal terminology simply does not have this implication.

In Socrates' second and third accounts he employs the premise that a cause is different (ἄλλο) from its effect. If the beautiful produces the good, then the beautiful and the good are distinct. Does this premise support Allen's claim that the beautiful is separate from its instances? I do not think so for the following reasons: (1) We are not sure that Socrates would apply the "distinctness condition" to all types of causation; in particular we do not know if the beautiful produces the good in the same way that it makes things beautiful. (2) To claim that two beings are distinct does not show anything about their ontological relationships. We should not, moreover, be misled by "being." In the passage quoted from the *Hippias Major*, above, the beautiful and the good are simply said to be something (that is, to exist), but this does not imply that they exist independently; they could be states of other things. (3) My interpretation of the beautiful accounts for the difference condition. For the harmonious constitution of a particular is not identical with that particular; for example, a house at time t_1 is well constructed, and at time t_2, after a hurricane, the *very same* house is a shambles. Therefore, the house itself is distinct from its excellence or lack thereof; of course there is a point where, if the house loses all of its order, it is no longer a house. Moreover, both the house and its order are "something." I conclude that the premise that a cause must be distinct from its effect neither implies the ontological priority of the cause, nor that the cause must be separate and apart from its effect.

At *Euthydemus* 300e–301e, beautiful things are said to be different (ἕτερα) from the beautiful, although some beauty (κάλλος τι) is present to each of them. The *Euthydemus* is generally thought to be a late/early dialogue. But what does this passage imply? Does it imply a tripartite ontology like that found in the *Phaedo* (102a ff.): the separate Form of Beauty, the immanent characteristic of beauty in particulars, and those particulars? Or does it imply the view that I have argued for the *Gorgias* and *Hippias Major*? I do not believe that this passage gives us enough information to tell what Socrates has in mind; in fact, it is consistent with either interpretation. For example, on my view, the beautiful is different from beautiful things since it is the harmony that makes them beautiful; also, an instance of harmony is present to each beautiful thing. Therefore, Allen can neither appeal to the difference condition, nor to this *Euthydemus* passage, to support the claim that the beautiful is separate from and ontologically prior to beautiful things.

At *Hippias Major* 289d Socrates says:

> Does it still seem to you that the beautiful itself, by which all other things are adorned and appear beautiful, that when this form is added to something (τῷ προσγένηται ἐκεῖνο τὸ εἶδος), that it is a woman, or mare, or lyre?

Of special interest is the word προσγίγνομαι, "be added to." This is the most common term used in the *Hippias Major* to describe the relation between the beautiful and beautiful things. This term and its cognates (παραγίγνομαι, πρόσειμι, πάρειμι, and the like) tell us how the cause is related to its effects, and thus they might impart information about the ontological status of the beautiful. W. D. Ross states that these terms "imply or suggest immanence," [30] and R. E. Allen attempts to neutralize Ross's view by arguing that they imply no particular ontological commitment. [31]

Let us begin with προσγίγνομαι. The prefix πρός indicates motion, and when it occurs with the dative case, completed motion. Liddell and Scott give as meanings for πρός with the dative: "abiding at a place," "hard by," "near," "at," "on," and "in." An almost paradigmatic use of προσγίγνομαι is that the reinforcements are "added to" or "come up to" the army. Παραγίγνομαι and πάρειμι have less of an association with motion than προσγίγνομαι and πρόσειμι, and they emphasize that one thing is present to another (cf. *Euthydemus* 301a, *Charmides* 159a, *Laches* 189e–190a).

All of these terms strongly suggest, when talking about particulars, spatial occurrences or relationships. Since, as we learn in the *Timaeus* (52a–c), the separate Forms do not enter into space, these terms would be inappropriate to underscore the aspatial nature of the Forms. When Plato uses such terms in the middle dialogues, he invariably refers to the immanent characteristics of phenomena. For example, he says in the *Phaedo* (100d): "Nothing else makes something beautiful but the presence (παρουσία) or communion (κοινωνία)—or whatever one calls it—of the beautiful, in whatever way it is added (προσγενομένη)." While there are separate Forms in the *Phaedo*, Plato here refers to the immanent aspect of the Form that later in the dialogue becomes an immanent characteristic different from the Form (cf. 102d, 103b).³² Thus I agree with Ross that these terms imply immanence.

The spatial reference of such terms, in conjunction with the paradigmatic use of προσγίγνομαι cited above, might lead one to believe that if *A* is added to *B*, then *A* exists independent of *B* prior to the addition. Hippias certainly holds this belief when he says that the beautiful is gold, and that when gold is added, it makes that to which it is present beautiful. This, however, is inconsistent with my interpretation of the beautiful; the beautiful, as the harmonious constitution of a particular's elements, is something (τι), but it is not a physical object, nor does it exist independently.

What we need is a clear case where when *A* is added to *B*, *A* is neither a physical object, nor does it exist independent of *B*. The *Republic* has such a case (608e–609a): "Do you say that there is for everything its special good and evil, for example, for the eyes ophthalmia, for the entire body disease, for grain mildew, rotting for wood, rust for bronze and iron ... and whenever one of these evils comes to (προσγένηται) anything, does it not make that to which it is added (ᾧ προσεγένετο) bad, and finally disintegrate and destroy it?" Ophthalmia, disease, mildew, rot, and rust are not independently existing physical objects; Plato probably thinks of them as disattunements of bodies (cf. *Gorgias* 504c). A second passage is in the *Laches* (189e–190a): Here Plato implies that virtue is joined (παραγίγνομαι) to the *psyche*, just as sight to the eyes (ὄψις παραγενομένη ὀφθαλμοῖς). Nowhere does Socrates suggest that sight can exist without an eye, or virtue without a *psyche*; yet he naturally speaks of them as being added. In fact, the analogy between sight and virtue is apt because sight is the power of the eye, and virtue a power of the *psyche*. I conclude that Plato's terminology is consistent with the claim that the beautiful is the harmony of a particular.

A final objection to my interpretation is that in the *Gorgias* a craftsman is said to look at (βλέπων) his task, and then place a form into the material (*Gorgias* 503e, 504d). While the task is not called an εἶδος, the inference seems clear that a craftsman looks at an εἶδος. But this claim resembles that made in the *Republic* (596b) where a craftsman makes a bed looking at the Form of Bed (πρὸς τὴν ἰδέαν βλέπων), and this Form is separate (cf. 597b). In the *Gorgias*, moreover, a craftsman does not look at already existing defective items, but rather at ideals that he is to embody. Thus, according to this objection, there are separate paradigmatic Forms in the early dialogues.³³

Does the vision terminology have this implication? In the *Cratylus* there is a striking passage where, in the context of craft production, verbs of vision are used five times, and their objects are either the form (εἶδος) of shuttle, or the form of name. The date of composition of the *Cratylus*, unfortunately, is in dispute.[34] I do believe, however, that separate Forms appear at the end of the dialogue (439c–440d), but in a very rough and rudimentary manner, which indicates that Plato has just started to think about them. Socrates often dreams (ὀνειρώττω) about whether there is Beauty itself, Good itself, and other such things (439c–d, 440b). That Socrates dreams about ethical Forms at the end of the *Cratylus*, does not show that the forms of shuttle and name, mentioned considerably earlier in the dialogue, are separate.

Let us look closely at *Cratylus* 389a ff. The generic and specific forms of shuttle and name are distinct. The differentia for the distinction is in terms of function. The generic form of shuttle is "what is naturally suited for weaving [*simpliciter*]" (389a), "what is the shuttle itself" (389b). The specific form is variously described as "the nature (φύσις) which is best for each type of weaving" (389b–c), "the instrument suited for each purpose" (389c), "the shuttle fitted by nature for each type of weaving" (389c), and "the proper form (τὸ προσῆκον εἶδος) of shuttle" (390b). The generic form of name is "what is the name itself" (390b), and the specific form of name is "the name naturally suited for each object" (389d), "the proper form of name for each thing" (390a), and "the name suited by nature for each thing" (390e). Clearly this is a start at the distinction between genus and species.

Brian Calvert believes that there is an ontological difference between the generic and specific forms: "Plato also seems to characterize the [generic] Form as that which is contemplated, and, I am inclined to think, separate and disembodied, as opposed to the Proper Form which can be, and is embodied."[35] Calvert's comment, however, will not withstand a close examination of the passage. Both the generic and specific forms are: (1) called εἴδη, (2) looked at, and (3) embodied. The craftsman looks at the generic form of shuttle (389a), and every shuttle must have (ἔχειν) that form (389b); the namemaker looks at the name itself, which he then places into (εἰς … τίθησιν) the syllables (389d). The artisan must discover (ἐξευρόντα) the specific instrument suited by nature for each purpose, and must place it into that from which he makes the product (389c); the namemaker looks at the name suited by nature for each object, and places its form into the letters and syllables (390e). The very same form, either generic or specific, that a craftsman looks at, he also embodies.

What are we to make of this εἶδος that is both viewed and embodied? Plato says that the form is αὐτό "itself," as in "the shuttle itself" (389b); but while αὐτό is often a sign for a Form in the middle dialogues, it is also used simply to add emphasis (cf. *Hippias Major* 289c, *Euthyphro* 5d).[36] Moreover, none of the predicates of the middle-period Forms—one, unchanging, divine, pure, and the like—occur in the passage, and Plato even suggests that a craftsman invents the εἶδος (389c).

A common Pre–Socratic use of εἶδος provides the solution. Both Gillespie and Baldry have shown that a prevalent meaning of εἶδος is "appearance" or "visual image."[37] I suggest that a craftsman looks at the appearance or visual image of what he wants to produce; and, of course, such images can be invented.[38] Undoubtedly, Plato was gifted with vivid visual imagery, so this would not be an unnatural view for him.[39] Moreover, it is a plausible account of craft production, at least more so than looking at a separate Form. We can also explain why the same form is viewed and embodied; when the form is embodied, the material takes on a certain appearance. This appearance is the same "in form" as the visual image, if the product is successfully completed. Thus while we admit visual images or appearances into the ontology of the *Gorgias* and the *Cratylus*, this does not force us to revise any of our previous conclusions; for that *by which* something is beautiful is not the image of order, but the order itself in a thing.

Summary of Socrates' View

I will first summarize my conclusions about the beautiful, and then compare it with The Beautiful in the *Symposium*. This comparison is part of a broader argument where I will show that the metaphysics of the middle dialogues takes a new and unforeseen turn; Plato posits a realm of separate Forms. The separate Forms are the result of a distinct Eleatic influence on Plato's thought. Plato's descriptions of the Forms are similar both in meaning and even in language to Parmenides' "signposts" for Being (B8). In the next chapter I will explain the philosophical reasons for Parmenides' influence on Plato. Here I only wish to show there is a μετάβασις εἰς ἄλλο γένος, a "change to another kind" in Plato's thought.

The beautiful in the *Gorgias* and *Hippias Major* is the order, in respect to some end, of the elements of a thing. The beautiful is how well something is made or naturally formed for some end. The beautiful emerges within a product as it is being well made, and it is present to it when it is well made.

The beautiful makes beautiful things beautiful, and this causal function does not imply the separation of the beautiful. The beautiful, as the harmonious organization of elements, transmits its beauty to whatever has it. Such transmission requires that the beautiful is always beautiful, so that it can transmit its beauty. We cannot infer from this, however, that the beautiful always exists. Nowhere in the early dialogues does Plato claim that either a virtue or the beautiful is eternal or temporally unlimited in existence. The most we learn is that, whenever ἀρετή is present, it makes things noble, good, and beautiful. This is what we should expect, since the topic of many early dialogues is how to *produce* virtue in the *psyche*;

furthermore, the beautiful is *created* by craft production or natural generation. Thus excellence is generated, and also lost.

The beautiful is always beautiful so that it is that *by which* all beautiful things are beautiful. The beautiful is always beautiful in every context, relation, and for every life. Beautiful things are not beautiful in some context, relation, or for some life. Thus we can see that the beautiful is different from beautiful things, because it is always beautiful while they are not. Particulars in the *Hippias Major*, when beautiful, really are (τῷ ὄντι, 294c) so, and Plato does not contrast them with the beautiful on the model of pale red and deep red; particulars are not pale imitations, images, or copies of the beautiful. The beautiful is not a separate and more real paradigmatic formal cause for beautiful things, although it is an immanent epistemic paradigm, since we must know what the beautiful is before we can clearly discern what pursuits or things are beautiful (*Hippias Major* 286c–e). We do not learn from the text of the *Hippias Major*, but we may reasonably infer, that the beautiful is always beautiful so that it can be an epistemic paradigm. Hence "self-predication" is a necessary condition for both the causal and the epistemic function of the beautiful.

Nowhere in the early works are the entities at issue said to be ungenerated, indestructible, incomposite, and always existing. Nor does Plato contrast immutable Justice with its changing instances, or eternal Beauty with its temporally limited participants. Such contrasts are utterly foreign to the early dialogues.

Weak Unitarian Theses

The strong unitarian thesis of Cherniss, Shorey, and Friedländer, among others, is false. There are no separate, immutable Forms in the early dialogues, although they do occur in the middle ones. Likewise, Allen's weaker thesis, that Forms are separate in both periods, although in the early dialogues they are not more real than their instances, is false. There is, however, a more subtle view, which grants that forms are not separate in the early works, and yet holds that the early view has traces of the middle and paves the way to it. John Malcolm defends this view:[40]

> We may grant that in the *Hippias Major* it is not explicitly stated that the Beautiful is truly beautiful and more beautiful than the particulars, but this seems implied by the statements that a beautiful maiden is no more beautiful than ugly (289c) and that the Beautiful is something that will never appear ugly anywhere to anyone (291d). Let us consider this in conjunction with the *Phaedo*. Socrates gets Simmias to admit that particular equals (stones or logs) may appear equal to one person and unequal to another (74b). They are con-

trasted with Equality itself which is never unequal (74c). On this basis, to be found already in the *Hippias* [*Major*], Plato moves to the doctrine that the particulars are striving to be like the Form Equality, but fall short and are deficiently equal (74d–e). They are copies of the standard or model. This is another example of how the *Hippias* leads us into the Middle Dialogues.

I will argue that Malcolm is misled at several points by a mere similarity in terminology, but not meaning, between the two dialogue periods.[41] The resemblance between the beautiful and a later Form is minimal, and their ontological differences are immense.

Gregory Vlastos claims that both the early virtues and the Forms are abstract qualities or characters.[42] He finds the "star instances of self-predication" in the early *Protagoras*, which self-predications, he says, are implied by the "degrees of reality" view in the middle works.[43] One may well wonder how Vlastos makes such an easy transition between the two periods when he seems to believe that separate Forms occur only in the middle and late dialogues. The reason is that Vlastos thinks of the virtues as abstract qualities or characters, which are then simply separated in the middle works. Separate or immanent, we are still dealing with qualities or characters, and self-predication is of a character;[44] thus instances of self-predication are found in dialogues of both periods. Vlastos inadvertently becomes a type of unitarian when he thinks that abstract qualities or characters are at issue in both periods. "Abstract quality" and "character" are modern philosophical jargon, and while it is practically impossible to avoid such language, great care must be taken to preserve Plato's meaning. Neither the virtues nor the beautiful are, in the modern meaning of such terms, "abstract qualities" or "characters," for the virtues are psychic powers and the beautiful is harmony *in rebus*; nor are the separate Forms such things because they are, as I will show, individuals. Thus the variant of unitarianism, implied by some of Vlastos' statements, results from anachronism.

The Early and Middle Dialogues

Let us begin our analysis with the words "one," "same," and "common" in the early works, and the predicate "one" in the middle ones. I will show that these words have very different implications in the two dialogue periods. In the early dialogues they regulate what a proper answer to a "What is it?" question is, but they do not, of themselves, have any transcendent ontological import. In the middle dialogues the predicate "one" implies that a Form is incomposite, and hence that it is removed from the world of generation and destruction.

In the *Laches* Socrates asks Laches to state "what this courage is which is the same (ταὐτόν) in all situations" (191e). The courage here referred to is a power of the *psyche* (192b), and is later identified with the knowledge of good and evil (194d, 199d–e). "Same" plays an important regulative role in dialectic; Socrates wants to know the same power that is exhibited in all the different situations mentioned. "Same" indicates that Socrates is after a type of universal, but not the type commonly supposed; he seeks the same power that produces all courageous acts. But we do not learn what type of universal Socrates seeks from his use of "same"; it is only when he says that courage is a power that we are able to fit the pieces together.

In the *Meno* Socrates carefully explains to Meno what he is after: "So also for the virtues, although they are many and diverse, they all have some one and the same nature (ἐν γέ τι εἶδος ταὐτὸν ἅπασαι ἔχουσι) on account of which they are virtues, and upon which it would be well to look when one answers the question about what virtue is" (72c–d). "One" and "same" are almost synonymous, and they again play a regulative role in question and answer. Perhaps "one" more than "same" connotes that a single object is sought, while "same" more than "one" suggests that this object is a common nature. Later in the *Meno* we learn that this nature is wisdom (87b–89a). Again "one" and "same" do not have, themselves, any transcendent ontological implications. At *Hippias Major* 300a–b Hippias is told to give that same thing (τι τὸ αὐτό), that common thing (τὸ κοινόν) that belongs to pleasures through sight, and those through hearing, and both together. The use of these phrases neither tells us how what is common is common, nor how it exists.

These notions primarily regulate the sort of answer that Socrates accepts to a "What is it?" question. An acceptable answer must state what is common or the same in all the cases considered, so that the answer is impervious to counterexample. Beyond this we do not learn anything else from the use of these words; we do not learn how the universal exists, or that it has any special sort of being. For this reason interlocutors initially pick out the wrong sorts of things in their answers, such as characteristics of acts.

This is not the case in the middle dialogues. Here "one" is one of the most important predicates of a Form, and it implies a special ontological status for the Forms. In many places Plato introduces the Forms as "each being one." In the *Cratylus* Socrates asks (439c–d): "Should we say there is Beauty itself and Good itself, and each of the Beings is thus one (ἓν ἕκαστον τῶν ὄντων οὕτω)." Immediately afterwards Plato claims that while beautiful phenomena are always in flux, The Beautiful, "is always such as it is (τὸ καλὸν τοιοῦτον ἀεί ἐστιν οἷόν ἐστιν)" (439d), and "always holds the same and is the same (ἀεί ὡσαύτως ἔχει καὶ τὸ αὐτό ἐστι)" (439e).[45] There is some sort of connection between being "one" and "always holding the same," but Plato does not here spell it out.

When we turn to the *Republic*, we find that the Forms are introduced on at least four occasions as "each being one" (476a, 479a, 507b–c, and 596a). I will quote only two of these passages:

[479a]   [The lover of appearances] does not think that there is Beauty itself and a certain Form of Beauty itself, which always remains unchanged, but he thinks that there are many beautiful things, and he cannot endure someone saying that The Beautiful is one (ἓν τὸ καλόν) ... for shall we say that there is any one of the beautiful things which will not appear ugly, and of the just which will not appear unjust?

[507b–c]   And there is Beauty itself and Good itself, and so for all of those things which we posited as a multiplicity, we turn about and posit one Form for each, which Form is one being (κατ' ἰδέαν μίαν ἑκάστου ὡς μιᾶς οὔσης) ... and those things [the phenomena] we say are seen but not thought, while the Forms are thought but not seen.

Plato does not directly tell us what he means by "one," but the contexts provide some information. All four passages contrast the one Form with the many phenomena, or, in the case of 476a, the one Form with its many manifestations. For example, while there are many couches, there is only one unique Form of Couch; and while there are many beautiful things, there is only one unique Form of Beauty. At *Republic* 597b ff. Plato provides conclusive evidence that part of what he means by "one" is "unique": "God, whether because he so willed or some necessity was placed upon him not to make more than one Couch itself in nature, thus only made one (μίαν μόνον), that which is the Couch itself."

Plato, however, must mean something more by "one" than "unique." For in the *Cratylus* and at 479a not only are the Forms said to be changeless, but also the oneness of each Form is contrasted with the mutability and flux of phenomena, that is, with their taking on contrary predicates; and at 507b–d the Forms are said to be invisible, although the connection, if any, between this quality and "one" is not given. But it is clear that the uniqueness of a Form neither implies its immutability nor its invisibility. At *Phaedo* 78b ff., however, Socrates explicitly connects immutability and invisibility with incompositeness. There, he and Cebes agree that what is incomposite (ἀξύνθετον) is least likely to be dissolved (διαιρεθῆναι) and most likely to be unchanging (78c). After admitting Forms into the class of changeless entities, Socrates connects uniformity, independence, and invisibility (ἀειδῆ) with changelessness (79a). So if "one" also means incompositeness at *Republic* 479a, 507c, and *Cratylus* 439c–d, we can bridge the gap between the oneness of a Form and its immutability and invisibility (for the connection between generation and composition see *Republic* 533b, 611b). We can also see why "one" is an important predicate of the Forms: if a Form is incomposite, then it is removed from the world of Heraclitean flux into the invisible, intelligible place (*Republic* 509d). When I discuss types of reality in the next chapter I will show why real Beings must be ungenerated, indestructible, and immutable with respect to all of their predicates; they have these predicates necessarily. We have further evidence that Plato partly means by "one" "incomposite" when in the argument (to be analyzed later) at *Parmenides* 131a f. Parmenides tries to show that each Form is not one because it is composite; that is, it is divided into many parts, or into many wholes that are the same in kind. I conclude that Plato predicates "one" of the Forms with the two meanings of "unique," and "incomposite," or "indivisible."

The objects of investigation in the early dialogues are unique in the weak sense that there is a single nature for the virtues and another for the beautiful. But many men could presumably have wisdom, and many things can have harmony. This nature can, then, be found in many places. The Forms are unique in the strong sense that there is only one Form of a kind: one and only one Form of Justice, one and only one Form of Beauty, and the like. Each Form can, of course, have many participants, but the real nature of *x*, unlike its nature in the early dialogues, is found only in the unique Form.

The other sense of "one" introduces a whole new ontology to the middle works. Nowhere in the early dialogues are the virtues or the beautiful said to be incomposite, indissoluble, ungenerated, indestructible, and unchanging. And it is hard to see how such predicates could be applied to the psychic powers and the beautiful. For the beautiful is tied to composition since it is a harmony of elements and such a harmony can easily be torn asunder; likewise, knowledge and wisdom are acquired by learning and are not beings *simpliciter*. On the other hand the Forms "are" (*Timaeus* 37e–38a); they are the really real Beings (*Republic* 477a ff., *Phaedrus* 247c). Plato contrasts the ungenerated and indestructible Forms with the phenomena that are generated and destroyed (*Symposium* 211 a–b, *Timaeus* 27d–28a, *Phaedo* 78d–79a). This contrast, that is so important to the type difference between Forms and phenomena, is nowhere found in the early dialogues. I conclude that there is a "change into another kind" in the middle works.

The Eleatic Influence

But why does Plato, who earlier searches for the excellence and virtue in things, in the middle dialogues embark on a most unusual metaphysics of transcendence? The historical source of Plato's Forms is clear: it is found in the Eleatic theory of Being.[46] In this chapter we will see just how closely Plato models the Forms on Parmenides' Being, both with respect to the predicate "one"and with respect to what he says about The Beautiful in the *Symposium*. In the next chapter we will analyze the philosophical reasons for this choice.

In the *Way of Truth* Parmenides gives the indications of or "signposts" to Being (DK 28 B8.4–6); it is ungenerated, imperishable, whole, unique,[47] immovable, complete, one, and continuous. We see that the predicate "one" (ἕν) takes its place among the other signposts, and that it occurs in the phrase "since it [Being] is now altogether, one, and continuous" (8.5–6). There is an obvious connection between "one," "altogether," and "continuous" or "cohesive" in 8.6 and "whole" in 8.4, and these predicates appear to indicate that Being is indivisible. This suspicion is verified at 8.22–25, where the homogeneity, fullness, and continuity of Being are given as the reasons why it is indivisible (οὐδὲ διαίρετόν ἐστιν). Therefore Parmenides uses ἕν explicitly to indicate indivisibility.

There is, however, another meaning for "one" in Parmenides' poem. Being is unique (μουνογενές, 8.4) not because it is the only member of a class, but because "there neither is nor will be anything else besides [outside of] Being" (8.36–37). Being is not unique in that it is different from anything else, rather it is all there is. The uniqueness of Being is contrasted with the two forms (μορφὰς ... δύο), light and dark, which mortals mistakenly name, failing to realize that there is only Being (8.38–39, 53). So the predicate μουνογενές means "unique," and it functions as another use of "one" in Parmenides' poem.[48]

In Melissus, "one" becomes the principle predicate of Being, and there is even a tendency on his part to assimilate it to Being when he talks about "the one" (τὸ ἕν, DK 30 B8.2, 6).[49] Simplicius preserves two fragments that unambiguously state Melissus' uses of "one":

[B6]   For if it were infinite it would be one (ἕν); for if it were two (δύο), they could not be infinite, but would have limits in respect to one another.

[B9]   If it is, it must be one (ἕν); being one, it must not have a body. For if it had thickness, it would have parts, and would no longer be one.

In B6 "one" means unique in Parmenides' strong sense of the term, and in B9 "one" means indivisible in that what is one cannot have, and hence cannot be divided into, parts. Melissus and Parmenides, then, use "one" to mean both "unique" and "indivisible."

Both Parmenides and Melissus, moreover, use the predicate "one" to "prove" that Being is ungenerated, indestructible, and homogeneous. But when we turn to Plato we find that he too uses these senses of "one," suitably modified to fit a plurality of Forms. Plato also introduces the Forms with this predicate, and connects it with the immutable nature of the Forms. But we have so far only circumstantial evidence that Plato adopts the Eleatic predicate "one."

There are, however, other reasons for believing in such an adoption. Friedländer has shown that *Republic* 476e ff. is a variation on a strictly Parmenidean theme,[50] while Hackforth has documented that *Phaedo* 78b ff. is cast in distinctly Parmenidean language;[51] and although neither commentator mentions the predicate "one," we do know that Plato thought this predicate to be the primary attribute of Eleatic Being. For at *Parmenides* 128a–b and *Sophist* 242d he attributes to Parmenides the thesis that "all is one" (ἓν ... τὸ πᾶν). Plato elevates the predicate "one" to such a prominent position in Eleatic thought that it even ingests its subject, Being. Since Plato applies, as I will show, many of the "lesser" Eleatic predicates to the Forms, and they imply and are implied by "one," it is reasonable to believe that he also adopts "one."

The *Symposium*

Let us now turn to *Symposium* 209e–212a, the apex of Diotima's speech, where there is a happy mixture of the old and the new. I will show that the beautiful of the *Hippias Major* occurs on the lower rungs of the ascent; the position here is like that found in the early dialogues. When we turn from the things of this world to that "marvelous, beautiful, nature" that is not in anything, we see a genuinely separate entity. The transcendence of this entity is certified by the more sober comments Socrates makes about it, and these statements have a distinctly Eleatic origin. I will also compare The Beautiful of the *Symposium* with the beautiful of the *Hippias Major*, and show exactly how they differ.

The passage at 209e–212a is an ascent ending with a revelation (τέλεα καὶ ἐποπτικά, 210a),[52] and vision is the dominant motif. As we proceed upward the language becomes more rhythmic, culminating in the revelatory nature of The Beautiful. But the beautiful of the *Hippias Major* is not at all like the final object of enchantment in the *Symposium*; rather it belongs on the lower rungs of the ascent. Some phrases that describe lower instances of beauty are: (1) the beauty of a body is akin (ἀδελφόν) to that of other bodies, and the beauty of all bodies is one and the same (ἕν τε καὶ ταὐτόν, 210b); (2) beauty is at or near (ἐπί) bodies; we should honor the beauty in (ἐν) *psyches* more than that in (ἐν) bodies; beauty also is seen in (ἐν) observances and laws (210b–c); and (3) all of beauty is akin itself to itself (πᾶν αὐτὸ αὑτῷ συγγενές, 210c). These phrases resemble claims found in the *Hippias Major* and the *Gorgias*. The beautiful is in or at (attached to) beautiful things, and this is similar in meaning to "be present to," and "be added to" in the early works. Beauty is in things, and there is no suggestion at this level that it is a separate entity. The beautiful is in things, presumably, in the manner described at *Gorgias* 506d–e: the beauty of *psyches* is their proper order (κόσμος), and that of bodies is their harmonious organization.

The uses of ἐν, ταὐτόν, and ἀδελφόν recall "one," "same," and "common" in the early dialogues. The beautiful is common to a number of different things, because all of them exhibit order, but such a kinship does not imply separation. The phrase "akin itself to itself," while resembling αὐτὸ καθ' αὐτό, "itself in itself," in the middle dialogues, does not, I believe, have the same emphasis. In, for example the *Phaedo*, αὐτὸ καθ' αὐτό is applied both to the *psyche* and to the Forms (66a, 66e–67a, 78d). This phrase means that something is drawn "itself into itself," so that it is removed from other things; when a *psyche* is "itself in itself" then it is removed from the body (66a), and a Form is such because it is drawn into itself, and removed from other things (78d). Such isolation, I will show, is a necessary condition for a Form to be pure and uniform (*Phaedo* 78d, *Symposium* 211b). But in earlier dialogues verbally similar phrases do not have the same implications; rather they emphasize what the word "same" alone means, or they stress the *per se* identity of the universal more than "same" alone can. In the *Euthyphro* (5d) Socrates asks: "Is not holiness the same itself with itself (ταὐτόν ... αὐτὸ αὑτῷ) in every action, and unholiness the complete opposite of holiness, is it not itself like to itself (αὐτὸ δὲ αὑτῷ ὅμοιον)?" These phrases are emphatic assertions of the identity of the universal, but again they do not imply that it is separate.

When Socrates states that the whole of beauty is akin (πᾶν ... συγγενές, *Symposium* 210c), he implies no more than the harmony and friendship of all good and noble things in the Κόσμος that is mentioned in the *Gorgias* (507e–508a): "And wise men tell us, Callicles, that heaven and earth and gods and men are held together by communion and friendship, by orderliness, temperance, and justice; and that is the reason, my friend, why they call the whole of this world by the name of order, not of disorder or dissoluteness." Plato's early theory of excellence and nobility is, as is also the case in many Pre-Socratic systems, a microcosm of the greater harmony seen in the movements of the planets, the regular and orderly changes of the seasons, and the unending but harmonious successions of days and nights. As Anaximander says in his only surviving fragment (DK 12 B1): "They [the elements] pay reparation to each other for their injustice according to the ordinance of time." This fragment beautifully captures the harmony and justice the Greeks found in all regular and orderly changes, where the ascendency of one element is followed by the ascendency of another in an unending balance. From the end of the *Gorgias* through *Republic* IV, and even afterwards, this cosmic view is instantiated in psychic justice, and in the early dialogues it grounds a theory of general excellence, that is applied to the *Cosmos* as a whole as well as to the things within it. I conclude that in the lower stages of the ascent, we find the object of investigation in the *Hippias Major*; yet, while the beautiful is fully incorporated into the ontology of the *Symposium*, it is only of preliminary interest, an essential way station traversed on an entirely new search.

Perhaps as early as *Symposium* 210d, starting with the words "turning towards the great sea (πέλαγος) of The Beautiful and looking at it," we start the final stage of the revelation. It is not a mere form of abstraction from beautiful phenomena, but the turning about of the whole *psyche* to an entirely new type of knowledge (210d), and the sudden revelation (ἐξαίφνης κατόψεται) of a different kind of Being that this knowledge is about (210e). Although the language at this point is dithyrambic, Platonic madness has a highly articulate and intellectual content; The Beautiful is not an indescribable sight. Diotima has several carefully planned things to say about it, and it has recently been argued that her descriptions have a clear Parmenidean heritage.[53] Plato, relating Diotima's words, states (211a–b):

> First of all it [The Beautiful] always is (ἀεὶ ὄν), it neither comes to be (γιγνόμενον) nor is destroyed (ἀπολλύμενον), it neither increases (αὐξανόμενον) nor decreases; next, it is not beautiful in part and in part ugly, nor is it beautiful at one time and not at another, in one respect beautiful and in another ugly, nor is it beautiful here and ugly there, so that it is beautiful to some and ugly to others. Nor again does The Beautiful appear (φαντασθήσεται) to the initiate as a face or hands, or any other bodily thing, nor as a particular statement (λόγος) or piece of knowledge, nor as being somewhere in any other thing, such as in (ἐν) an animal or the earth or the heavens (ἐν οὐρανῷ) or in any other thing, but itself in itself always being uniform with itself (αὐτὸ καθ᾽ αὑτὸ μεθ᾽ αὑτοῦ μονοειδὲς ἀεὶ ὄν), and all of the other beautiful things partake of it in such a manner, that while they come to be and are destroyed, it [The Beautiful] neither comes to be more nor less nor suffers anything.

Plato does not slavishly copy his predecessors, but there is a remarkable resemblance, sometimes in language, and certainly in meaning, between what Plato states about The Beautiful and Parmenides' predicates of Being.[54] One of the first "proofs" for Being is that it is ungenerated (ἀγένητον) and indestructible (ἀνώλεθρον, B8.3 ff.); accordingly Plato twice emphasizes in prose what Parmenides said in verse: The Beautiful is ungenerated and indestructible. We do not find in Parmenides the claim that Being "always is"; rather he states that "it neither was nor will be, since it is now altogether, one and continuous" (8.5–6). But in Melissus we find "always existing" clearly associated with Being (B 1–3), and thus this notion is incorporated into the Eleatic legacy. Plato's next predications of The Beautiful find half a counterpart in Parmenides when he asks: "How and whence did it grow (αὐξηθέν)?" (8.7). Parmenides does not, of course, have any comments about the predicate "is beautiful," but Plato's statement that The Beautiful is beautiful in every relation, time, respect, and place is, nevertheless, a variation on a Parmenidean theme; for Being is "continuous" (8.5), "indivisible" (8.22), and "all of it is alike (πᾶν ἐστιν ὁμοῖον)" (8.22). Being is all alike because there cannot be more of it here and less of it there, nor can there be any gaps in Being, that could keep it from clinging to itself. Plato uses the striking word μονοειδές to emphasize that The Beautiful is in every way uniformly beautiful. Moreover, if we allow for the fact that Plato isolates Beauty from other things, while for Parmenides Being is all there is, there is a striking resemblance between "The Beautiful is itself in itself always being uniform with itself" (αὐτὸ καθ᾽ αὐτὸ μεθ᾽ αὑτοῦ μονοειδὲς ἀεὶ ὄν, 211b) and Parmenides' "It remains the same in the same and lies in itself" (ταὐτόν τ᾽ ἐν ταὐτῷ τε μένον καθ᾽ ἑαυτό τε κεῖται, 8.29). Both passages emphasize, in similar language, the inward-drawn nature of their subjects. Finally, Plato's claim that The Beautiful does not suffer anything is reminiscent of the unmoved and unshaking nature of Being, as well as Parmenides' claim that "coming into being and perishing, to be and not to be, change of place and exchange of bright colors" are "the mere names of mortals" (8.38–41).

Parmenides' influence on Plato's Forms is unmistakable. The Forms are a plurality of Eleatic monads, and Plato takes a highly original place among those philosophers who both accept Parmenides' account of what it is to be, and yet try to save the visible phenomena from nonexistence. Unlike Parmenides, however, we will see that Plato posits different types of reality.

In a previous paragraph I claimed that Plato states that The Beautiful is in every way beautiful, although the passage quoted at 211a–b only claims that The Beautiful is not beautiful in one respect, in one relation, and at one time, and ugly in another. Surely this passage does not imply that The Beautiful is neither beautiful nor ugly *simpliciter*, and thus has neither quality, for the ladder of ascent is an advance through beautiful things, and an odd sort of asymmetry would occur if The Beautiful is not the most beautiful thing.[55] What lures our *eros* is that The

Beautiful is pure unadulterated beauty. Plato states that "When a man has been thus far tutored in the lore of love, passing from view to view of beautiful things (τὰ καλά), in the right and regular ascent, suddenly he will have revealed to him, as he draws to the close of his dealings in love, a marvelous beautiful nature" (τι θαυμαστὸν τὴν φύσιν καλόν, 210e). The Beautiful is a marvelous *beautiful* nature, and only if it has this characteristic can The Beautiful appear to the initiate as pure, unmixed beauty. If The Beautiful was not single-formed (μονοειδές), and was neither beautiful nor ugly, then it would not be the final vision (212a) in the ascent. "Self-predication," then, is a necessary condition for the teleological pull of Beauty and for its "visual" appearance. I will return to self-predication in the next chapter.

Numerous descriptions reveal this marvelous beautiful nature. The first six listed below are from Diotima's speech prior to the introduction of The Beautiful, but they are of the objects of wisdom and the beloved, and The Beautiful is the most important object of wisdom, and what is most beloved, in the context of the *Symposium*. The descriptions are: (1) [wisdom is of] the most beautiful things (τῶν καλλίστων, 204b), (2) all beautiful (πάγκαλος, 204c), (3) really beautiful (τῷ ὄντι καλόν, 204c), (4) splendid (ἀβρόν, 204c), (5) perfect (τέλεον, 204c), (6) blessed (μακαριστόν, 204c), (7) the great sea of the beautiful (210d), (8) a marvelous beautiful nature (210e), (9) uniform or single-form (211b, e), (10) pure (εἰλικρινές, 211e), (11) pure (καθαρόν, 211e), (12) unmixed (ἄμικτον, 211e), and (13) divine (αὐτὸ τὸ θεῖον, 211e).

There are two plausible interpretations of these descriptions: (A) The Beautiful is (1)–(13) because it is always, in every way, and to everyone who finally sees it, beautiful, while beautiful phenomena are ugly in at least some respect; and (B) The Beautiful is (1)–(13) because first it satisfies condition (A), and second it is qualitatively different in the type of Beauty it has; it is like bright red compared with pale red, or a Georgia beauty queen with a run-of-the-mill coed. The most that we can be certain of from the descriptions is (A), and this is especially true of other passages in the middle dialogues that contrast a Form and its participants (cf. *Phaedo* 74b–c, *Republic* 477a ff.).[56] A Form, *F*-ness, is always *F*, while its participants are *F* and not-*F*. I will later show that this is Plato's standard account of the purity and unmixed nature of a Form. But it is difficult to believe that in the *Symposium* Plato does not embrace (B), especially when he says that the Form of Beauty is splendid, blessed, and divine. The religious and erotic lure of The Beautiful would seem to require not just pure beauty but qualitatively more beauty. And even if we were to impute (B) to Plato, doing so would not imply equivocal predication; for a superbly *F* thing and a humdrumly *F* thing are still both *F*, because such adverbial qualifications do not change the meaning of the predicate *F*.[57] Nevertheless, we cannot be dogmatic about whether Plato intends (A) or (B), since the evidence in the *Symposium* is inconclusive on either side.

The Beautiful and the beautiful

Let us now compare and contrast the beautiful and The Beautiful. In the *Hippias Major* we learn that phenomena are not always beautiful, while the beautiful is always beautiful (292e). The latter is necessary for the beautiful to be both the cause of beauty and an epistemic paradigm of beauty. The unitarians, on the basis of these claims, believe that the beautiful in the *Hippias Major* and The Beautiful in the *Symposium* are one and the same thing. Furthermore, Malcolm argues the weaker position that these claims prepare the way for the later ontology.[58] But the comparisons in the two dialogues are quite different. The Beautiful in the *Symposium* always is, it is neither generated nor destroyed, it is without increase and decrease, and it is always beautiful. Its participants come to be and are destroyed (that is, they are temporally limited in existence), they suffer change, and they are beautiful and not beautiful. Generically the contrast in the *Symposium* is between the changeless Form and its mutable participants. This is, as I will show in the next chapter, both an existential and a predicative contrast: the Form always exists, the phenomena came to be and are destroyed; the Form is always and necessarily *F*, its participants are contingently *F* and contingently not-*F*.[59] There is no evidence in the *Symposium* that the Form transmits its beauty as an efficient cause; it is the final cause of human striving, and probably an epistemic paradigm or formal cause of what it is to be beautiful; that is, as the perfect example of beauty it provides the formal conditions for beauty. Nevertheless, all we can be certain of from the *Symposium* is that The Beautiful is a final cause, since it is the ultimate object of *eros*. Perhaps it is also qualitatively more beautiful than its participants.

The contrast between the changeless and the mutable is utterly foreign to the *Hippias Major*. The beautiful is always beautiful, but this does not imply that it always exists. The language of 211a–b is not found in early dialogues, nor are any of the descriptions (1)–(13) above. While in the *Symposium* only the Form is really beautiful, in the *Hippias Major* beautiful things are really beautiful (τῷ ὄντι χαλά, 294c) and this is possible precisely because what makes them beautiful is present to them (παρόντος γε τοῦ ποιοῦντος [although here in the context of making them appear so], 294c). The beautiful is always beautiful because whenever it is present or added to something, it is that thing's excellence or harmony, and thus it transmits its beauty to that thing. Finally, we should note that "participation" has superseded "being present to" and "being added to," and in the *Symposium* the participants and what they participate in are separate beings. I conclude that the contrasts in the *Hippias Major* and *Symposium* are very different, and that the beautiful and The Beautiful are different types of beings.

Symposium 211a–b is one of the most definite statements of transcendence. Some commentators deny this on the grounds that The Beautiful is only said not to appear or present itself as in anything, and the whole passage, whose content is attributed to Diotima, not Socrates, is highly religious and elevated in language, and thus not the sort of place to ascertain Plato's real metaphysical beliefs.[60] These are not, however, compelling reasons. That Plato has Socrates attribute the speech to Diotima shows that Socrates could be a graceful and tactful guest, and it may also show that the speech goes considerably beyond what the historical Socrates believed. The qualities of The Beautiful are carefully selected and presented, and they often recur in other middle dialogues (cf. *Phaedo* 78d, 79d, 80b). Moreover, we are not dependent upon this passage alone for evidence about the transcendence of the Forms.[61] We have already seen a connection between "incomposite," "ungenerated and indestructible," and "unchanging." Since the Forms have these characteristics, the second of which is stated at 210a, and the third of which is implied by the whole passage, they are not found among phenomena, nor are they spatial or temporally limited objects (cf. *Phaedo* 79a–b, *Republic* 486a). Forms are, then, separate or transcendent; they are not in things. The beauty of phenomena, however, is in (ἐν) them, and the clearest account Plato gives of its immanence is that it is the excellence of things, their harmony (*Gorgias* 506d–e). We have, then, a clear distinction between immanence and transcendence with only the former occurring in the early dialogues.

John Malcolm compares *Hippias Major* 291d, "I think you want to be told that some such thing as this is the beautiful, what never appears ugly anywhere to anyone," with *Phaedo* 74b–c, "Do not equal stones and pieces of wood, though they remain the same, appear equal to one person but not equal to another [whether τῷ means 'to some person,' or 'in some respect' is irrelevant for our purposes]? ... Well, then, did equal things themselves ever appear to you unequal [the puzzling plural τὰ ἴσα need not concern us] or Equality inequality?"[62] There is not, however, a similarity of meaning between the two passages. Hippias is concerned with what people think is beautiful, whether or not what they think is correct. This is clear from his third account where he tries to capture in a lengthy list of events all of the things people believe are beautiful for all lives. But Socrates brushes opinion aside; he seeks what is beautiful for all and always (292e). On the other hand, if we take φανεῖται and ἐφάνη in the *Phaedo* at face value, and we certainly are not licensed to substitute "is" for "appears," then Forms have a very special epistemic status: they always appear to be what they are, and not their opposite. I will return to this point in the next chapter.[63] No similar status is attributed to the beautiful, because in the *Hippias Major* really beautiful things may not appear so (cf. 294c). So the two passages are not similar in meaning, and thus they offer us no reason to think that "the *Hippias Major* leads us into the Middle Dialogues." [64] The only truth in Malcolm's claim, quoted above, is that in dialogues of both periods the highest objects of investigation are epistemic paradigms, although the ontological status of these paradigms is quite different.

In the middle dialogues there are two types of reality, Forms and phenomena. Such ontological differences are bound to be reflected in epistemological ones, and they are. In *Republic* V knowledge knows real Being, and opinion opines what is midway between Being and not-being (477a ff.). There is no knowledge of phenomenal reality in the middle works; knowledge is only of the Forms. But in the early dialogues Socrates does not distinguish belief from knowledge in this way. He does have epistemic priorities; for example, we must know what the beautiful is before we can know what pursuits are beautiful, and we must know what justice is before we can know what acts or persons are just; but the very same objects can be both believed and known. As we saw earlier, the *Meno* distinguishes belief from knowledge in that the latter transcends the former in its trammels; knowledge is tied down in the *psyche* with reasons (98a), while belief comes through many sources, including unreliable and irrational ones. We are justified in claiming to know something in the early works if and only if we can defend our claim against dialectical attack, but, of course, we can make the very same claim about the same object or event with an unevidenced conviction that is mere belief. Plato does not separate the objects of opinion and the objects of knowledge in his early works because he does not yet emphasize the distinction between the immutable and the always changing. But once this distinction becomes a dominant concern in the middle works, knowledge is only about the immutable Forms, and opinion must be only about the changing phenomena.

The conclusion of this chapter is that there is a "change in kind" between the ontology and epistemology of the early and that of the middle dialogues. In the former, Plato's concerns are firmly rooted within the visible Κόσμος, and he seeks for the excellence, especially human ἀρετή, of its various components. In the latter Plato's concern is with immutable, real Being, and such Being is not within the heavens (ἐν οὐρανῷ, *Symposium* 211b); it is aspatial and always existing. The differences between the two periods are so great that it is incorrect to claim that the former even lays much of a ground for the latter; the differences between the two periods

far outweigh their similarities. Plato's intellectual development has received a shock, a jolt, as harsh as any he administers in the early works.
Parmenides provides this jolt, although we should not minimize the effects
of Heraclitus and Anaxagoras. Once Plato becomes cognizant of their
beliefs about Being and the problem of "saving the phenomena" from the
Heraclitean "identity of opposites" his work would no longer be primarily
anthropocentric and intracosmic in focus. Plato's new-found admiration
for the Pre-Socratics tempers the influence of Socrates, and introduces a
new set of problems to which the Forms are the purported solution.

3

The Isolation and Connection
of the Forms in Plato's
Middle Dialogues

Plato emphasizes both a visual and a discursive grasp of the Forms. These diverse epistemic paths have often had different, and not always complementary, influences on later philosophers. Whole Neoplatonic systems are cast in metaphor, with visual and touch metaphors dominating, while recurring philosophical concerns with analyticity and necessary truth have their distant antecedents in Parmenides' "proofs," Zeno's "logic," and Plato's interweaving of the Forms.

First I will discuss the visual route to the Forms, and what a Form is by way of this route. Vision of the Forms requires that they have a particular type of nature, and I will examine in detail what this nature is. This investigation leads us to central topics in Platonic scholarship: the reasons for positing Forms, the contrast between Forms and phenomena, paradigmatism, self-predication, types of reality, and participation.

Then I will analyze the discursive path to the Forms. I will show that the Forms have a nature different from that encountered on the visual route. When Plato investigates Forms through *logoi*, the Forms are not the pure paradigms for vision; they interconnect with one another, just as the terms in noncontingent *logoi* interconnect. We come, then, to see how the Form-world is structured through an investigation of *logoi*.

The *Phaedo*, *Republic*, and *Phaedrus* begin with an emphasis on the visual route, and develop into a more synoptic understanding of the Form-world. Moreover, after the *aporia* of the *Parmenides* it is this later strain of Plato's thought that predominates and attempts to escape the perplexities. I believe, then, that there is a gradual development in Plato's thought: he moves from the visual to the discursive model for understanding the Forms, and concomitantly from their isolation to their connection.

Since my intent is to describe and explain Plato's ontological development, I will only select and discuss those passages relevant to this concern. Thus this chapter will, unlike the first chapter where Plato's metaphysics and ethics are intricately connected, largely ignore his ethical and political views.

The Visual Account of Knowledge

Although most of Plato's visual statements are highly metaphorical, an example being the description of how dialectic leads forth the "eye of the soul" that is "buried in the barbaric bog" (*Republic* 533c–d), nevertheless, Plato does think of knowledge as a sort of mental vision. Plato's visual statements are metaphorical in that they explain intellectual vision on the model of physical vision, but intellectual vision is not, itself, a model for some other nonvisual epistemological process. Intellectual vision, for example, cannot be reduced to discursive knowledge.[1] Visual statements, moreover, form a leitmotif of the middle dialogues. For example, at the beginning of Book VI of the *Republic* (484c–d) Plato says:

> Do you think that there is any difference between the blind and those who are really deprived of the knowledge of each Being, that is, those who do not have a vivid pattern in their souls (ἐναργὲς ἐν τῇ ψυχῇ ἔχοντες παράδειγμα) and are not able as painters to look (ἀπο-βλέποντες) upon what is most true, and always referring to that, and viewing (θεώμενοι) it as acutely as possible, to establish in this world also the laws about beautiful, just and good things . . . .

A number of themes are interwoven in this passage: (1) the ignorant man is "blind"; (2) the philosopher has a vivid pattern in his *psyche* of the laws of beauty, justice, and the like; (3) the philosopher is like an artist; (4) the true artist looks sharply at the real paradigms; and (5) such vision is a necessary condition for true political, ethical, and aesthetic crafting. This passage is typical in its varied use of vision terms, and I would speculate that Plato's talk about "clear patterns in the *psyche*" suggests that he was not just a man of vision, but also a man who had visions. Further support for this speculation will come below when I discuss the "incorrigible appearance" of a Form. If Plato were a man with heightened imagery, then we would be able to psychologically explain and understand passages like the above, especially his comment about "clear images in the *psyche*."

But vision is not the only metaphor for grasping a Form. Sexual metaphors of touching, seizing, and grasping also occur (490a–b).

> . . . it is the nature of the real lover of knowledge to strive emulously for true Being and he would not linger over the many particulars that are opined to be real, but would hold on his way, and the edge of his

passion would not be blunted nor would his desire fail till he came into touch with (ἄψασθαι) the nature of each thing in itself by that part of his soul to which it belongs to lay hold (ἐφάπτεσθαι) on that kind of reality—that part akin to it, namely, and through that approaching it, and consorting (μιγείς) with reality really, he would beget intelligence and truth, attain to knowledge and truly live and grow, and so find surcease from his travail of soul, but not before.

Vision is the dominant mode of grasping the Forms, but in this remarkable passage touch receives its due. There is no indication, however, of the later Neoplatonic position where subject and object are obliterated in an assimilation that in Plotinus may well be an identity. Plato does not believe that we desire either to return to or to be identical with our origin; approaching, consorting, and mingling with reality always preserves the subject-object distinction. For this reason visual and not touch metaphors predominate.

There are at least two reasons why Plato believes that we know the Forms through mental vision: (1) He sometimes distinguishes true opinion from knowledge by using analogies that reveal the important role of visual evidence, for the Greeks, in knowledge claims. He who has traveled the road to Larisa knows the way, whereas he who only has heard about the correct route, although he can describe it to others, only has true opinion (*Meno* 97a–b). Knowledge, then, is an acquaintance with some object, route, or state of affairs. (2) After both verbs of seeing and knowing (as well as verbs of thinking, willing, believing, and the like) the Greeks used not only propositional clauses, but also, and with frequency, simply direct objects. Parmenides is the first philosopher to give conscious expression to this phenomenon (DK 28 B8.34–36): "For it is the same to think (νοεῖν), and that for the sake of which there is thought, for you will not find thought without Being (τοῦ ἐόντος), in which it is expressed (ἐν ᾧ πεφατισμένον ἐστίν)." For Parmenides every thought must have an object; it is like an arrow, shot out into reality, that must land somewhere. Since we are at that point in the development of human thought prior to subtle speculations about such things as intentional objects, Parmenides believes that every thought must, if it is to avoid vacuity, be about Being. Hence he banishes as utterly obscure and barren those paths that are not about Being.

The grammatical structure of the direct object, in conjunction with an account of vision as a type of contact through the stream of sight with the perceived object (*Timaeus* 45b–c), partially caused an assimilation between the mechanisms of sight and those of knowledge; this is why Plato considers both knowledge and sight to be outward-directed powers (δυνάμεις, *Republic* 477b–c).[2] Therefore knowing *p* is having some sort of contact with *p*, and because of reason (1), the most likely candidate is some type of visual contact with *p*. Thus at *Republic* 478a ff. Plato states that knowledge knows (τὸ ὄν, "Being") and opinion opines (μεταξὺ κεῖσθαι τοῦ εἰλικρινῶς ὄντος τε καὶ τοῦ πάντως μὴ ὄντος, "what is halfway between pure Being and utter nonbeing"). Since intentional verbs often have things and not propositions as their objects, the question of how one can think what is not is problematic for the Greeks. A belief, thought, or statement must have something which "is" for an object or else it is utterly vacuous. A thorough resolution of this problem would require, among other things, an analysis of the "objects" of thought and speech and how they exist. Plato does not even begin such an analysis until the *Sophist*, and his solution there preserves the object requirement: one cannot think absolute nonbeing, but only *something* different from *what is* (also see *Euthydemus* 284c). The conjunction of reason (1) and reason (2) provides at best a partial explanation for why Plato believes that knowledge is a type of vision, and later we will see why the Forms are the only possible objects of knowledge.

Before I investigate the nature of the Forms, I will discuss two passages where vision has the dominant role. Plato opens the *Phaedo* discussion of recollection by giving an example of it (73a–b):

> When people are questioned, if you put the questions well, they answer correctly of themselves about everything; and yet if they had not within them some knowledge and right reason, they could not do this. And that this is so is shown most clearly if you take them to mathematical diagrams or anything of that sort.

This example of recollection is not primarily dependent upon perception. Although Socrates draws geometrical diagrams in the dust in order to instruct Meno's slave boy (*Meno* 82b ff.), it is his questions about these diagrams that lead the boy first to see that his initial answer is wrong, and then what the correct answer is. Dialectic is the correct method for eliciting knowledge, and Plato provides a cautious explanation that innate right reason (ὀρθὸς λόγος) accounts for the process.

The next example of recollection, however, is quite different (73d):

> Well, you know that a lover when he sees a lyre or a cloak or anything else that his beloved is wont to use, perceives the lyre and in his mind receives an image (ἐν τῇ διανοίᾳ ἔλαβον τὸ εἶδος) of the boy to whom the lyre belongs, do you not? But this is recollection, just as when one sees Simmias, one often remembers Cebes, and I could cite countless such examples.

This example of recollection is heavily dependent upon vision. The initial stimulus is the perception of some object, a lyre, cloak, or Simmias; and the recollected response is the calling-up of a visual image (εἶδος) in the understanding. Εἶδος here has a nontechnical meaning of visual appearance or shape,[3] and Plato commits himself to the erroneous but perennially popular account of memory as the having of a mental image that has a feeling of familiarity about it. This account of recollection provides the working model for the remainder of Plato's discussion. In recollecting the Forms the stimulus is the perception of, for example, equal sticks or stones, and the recollected response, which is derived from the perception (ἐκ τούτων, 74b),[4] is of Equality itself. We do not, however, simply understand (ἐνενοήσαμεν, 74b) what Equality is through comparing it with its deficient instances; we also *see* how it appears to us. Plato emphasizes the visual grasp of Equality when he uses the following argument purportedly to prove that Equality is not identical with any group of equal things (74b–c):

> (1) Equal stones and pieces of wood, although they remain the same, sometimes appear equal in one respect (to one person), and unequal in another (to another).[5]
>
> (2) Equality itself never appears unequal.
>
> ∴ (3) Equality itself is not identical with the equal sticks and stones.

Later I will discuss the importance of the appearance (φαίνεσθαι) terminology,[6] but here I only want to emphasize that recollected knowledge of the Forms is visual: the Forms appear or manifest themselves to us in complete purity. Only at the end of his discussion of recollection, almost as an afterthought, does Plato mention that the man who knows must be able to give an account of what he knows (76b).

In Diotima's speech about *eros* (*Symposium* 210a–212a) there is an emphasis upon visual knowledge, although Plato here better integrates it with giving an account than he does in the *Phaedo*. We may schematize the steps of the ascent as follows (210a–211b): (1) First, one must love a particular body, and (1a) engender beautiful *logoi* therein; (2) one must understand (κατανοῆσαι) that the beauty in one body is akin in appearance (ἐπ᾽ εἴδει) to that of another; (3) one must set a higher value on the beauty of *psyches*, and (3a) bring forth *logoi* in them; (4) one must see (θεάσασθαι) the beauty in observances and laws, and (4a) see (ἰδεῖν) that their beauty is akin; (5) one sees (ἴδη) the beauty of different branches of knowledge; (6) one must turn towards and contemplate (θεωρῶν) the great *pelagos* of the beautiful, and (6a) bring forth beautiful *logoi*; until (7) he sees (κατίδη) a certain sort of knowledge, that is of The Beautiful itself.

Plato accentuates the visual nature of the ascent by describing it as "the orderly and correct seeing (θεώμενος) of the beautiful things" (210e). This ascent is not only an ever more inclusive grasp of Beauty, but also at its termination a sight of pure, separate Beauty, and the final achievement is cast in the language of the mystery rites:[7] the initiate suddenly has revealed to him (ἐξαίφνης κατόψεται) a marvelous beautiful nature. Plato then describes in great detail how The Beautiful will appear or present itself (φαντασθήσεται) to the initiate: it shines forth in splendid purity, while the phenomena embrace the "identity of opposites" (211a–b, 211d). Although knowledge of The Beautiful generates true instances of virtue (212a), and presumably also true *logoi*, the knowledge, itself, is a vision of the Form.

Forms on the Visual Model

What, then, are the Forms on the visual model? The *Symposium*, *Phaedo*, *Phaedrus*, and *Republic* show a distinct Parmenidean influence. In the *Phaedo* Plato says (78d and 80a–b):

> Is the essence itself, which we in asking and answering questions call true Being, always the same, or is it liable to any change? Equality itself, Beauty itself, and each Being which is real, do they ever admit of any change whatsoever? Or does each of these real Beings, since it is uniform (μονοειδές) and in itself (αὐτὸ καθ᾽ αὐτό), remain the same and never in any way admit of any change?
>
> ... the *psyche* is most like the divine and immortal and intellectual and uniform and indissoluble (ἀδιαλύτῳ) and ever unchanging, and the body, on the contrary, most like the human and mortal and multiform and unintellectual and dissoluble and ever changing.

Each Form is incomposite (ἀξύνθετον, *Phaedo* 78b f.; also see *Timaeus* 35a) and indissoluble, and thus the Forms are removed from the spatial world of changing and temporally limited bodies. The incomposite nature of a Form also implies that it is unchanging (*Phaedo* 78d, *Symposium* 211a–b), always existing (*Phaedo* 78b, *Republic* 485b, 486a, *Symposium* 211a), isolated or aloof from all other things (*Symposium* 211b, *Phaedo* 78d), uniform and pure (*Symposium* 211b, *Phaedo* 78d, 80a–b), and invisible to the physical sight (*Phaedo* 78c–79a). Each Form is also unique (*Republic* 476a, 479a, 507b–c, 596a). These predicates, as well as the language in which they are cast, show the influence of Parmenides' fragment B8, where he gives the indications of or signposts to Being.[8] Plato's separate Forms, at least in their early stage of development,[9] are a plurality of Parmenidean Beings.

What, then, does Plato mean when he says that a Form is incomposite or indivisible? Part of what he means is that Forms are not physical objects, and since they are not composite, they cannot be broken into and destroyed by outside forces (*Phaedo* 78c, *Timaeus* 33a). Forms, then, are unchanging and indestructible. Furthermore, a Form lacks the sort of internal diversity seen in phenomena; a Form is all alike (μονοειδές, ὅμοιον, *Symposium* 211b, *Phaedo* 78d). Plato here echoes Parmenides' claim that since Being is all alike (ὁμοῖον), it is not divisible (οὐδὲ διαιρετόν), and neither could there be more of it here and less of it there, but all is full of Being (B8. 22–5).[10] Because the Forms are uniform and pure, they are the simple objects of intellectual vision.

What precisely does the uniformity and purity of a Form consist in? There are two necessary and jointly sufficient conditions for a Form to be a uniform and pure, real Being: (A) Each Form has in every respect, relation, context, and at every time a definite descriptive "self" predicate, such as "The Beautiful is always beautiful," "Equality is always equal," "Justice is always just," and the like. And (B) each Form has the meta-predicates that are applied to all of the Forms, such as "always being," "ungenerated," "indestructible," "unchanging," "pure," "divine," "incomposite," and the like. A Form is a *pure, real* Being if and only if (A) and (B). A definite descriptive predicate in (A) uniquely identifies a Form, and sets it apart from all other things. (A) carries most of the weight for a Form's purity and uniformity, but since, as I will show, a Form must be always *F* in a sense that implies that the Form always exists and is *F*, if it is to be an object of knowledge, (B) also is a necessary condition for uniformity and purity. (B) carries most of the weight for a Form's reality; the predicates in (B) mark out the type of reality that a Form has, and they distinguish the Forms from deficiently real phenomena. But (A) is also a necessary condition for a real Being, since part of a Form's unchanging nature is that it is always *F*.

Let us concentrate on condition (A), since it is primarily concerned with a Form's purity and uniformity. When I discuss types of reality, later in this chapter, we will focus on (B). The best way to examine the purity of a Form is to see how, in one way, Plato contrasts Forms and phenomena. In *Republic* VII he distinguishes those activities that do and those that do not lead to a contemplation of the Forms. Some perceptions have this function, but others do not. In the case of a finger (523c–d):

> Each one of them appears to be equally a finger [in looking at the fingers on a hand], and in this respect it makes no difference whether it is observed as intermediate or at either extreme, whether it is white or black, thick or thin, or of any other quality of this kind. For in none of these cases is the *psyche* of most men impelled to question the reason and to ask what in the world is a finger, since the faculty of sight never signifies to it at the same time that the finger is the opposite of a finger.

Let us apply the category "sortal predicates" to predicates like "is a finger," "is a bed," "is a man and animal." Sortal predicates tell us either specifically or generically what kind of thing something is; in Aristotle's system they describe items in the category of substance. An object *x* is not both a finger and not a finger; a finger does not have the logical contrary of a finger (a man, monkey, hand, or the like), nor does a finger *qua* finger have a polar opposite.[11] Fingers are the subjects for other predicates, and they are not, themselves, juxtaposed to contrary predicates. Moreover, while a finger can at one time appear to be, for example, a pencil, and at another time a finger, a finger does not appear at the same time, to the same percipient, to be both a finger and the contrary of a finger. For these reasons we are not led from a finger and the perception of a finger to ask "What really is finger, itself?"

Such is not the case with relational predicates (524a–b):

> ... is not this again a case where the *psyche* must be at a loss as to what significance for it the sensation of hardness has, if the sense reports the same thing as also soft? And, similarly, as to what the sensation of light and heavy means by light and heavy, if it reports the heavy as light and the light as heavy (εἰ τό τε βαρὺ κοῦφον καὶ τὸ κοῦφον βαρὺ σημαίνει).

Nor for incomplete predicates (525a):

> For we see the same thing at the same time as one (ἕν) and as an indefinite plurality (ἄπειρα τὸ πλῆθος).

An object, *x*, can be at one and the same time both heavy and light, large and small, one and many. Many relational and incomplete predicates are truly said of an object at the same time that their polar opposites are also true of that object. Moreover, the same object can appear to have polar opposites at one and the same time. For the clarification of this (524c):

> ... the intelligence is compelled to contemplate The Great and Small, not thus confounded but as distinct entities, in the opposite way from sensation.... And is it not in some such experience as this that the question first occurs to us, what in the world, then, is The Great and The Small? ... And this is the origin of the designation intelligible for the one, and visible for the other.

Plato does not argue in this passage to the existence of Forms, nor does he posit Forms to explain the characteristics "mixed" in phenomena. He does, however, do this in other passages I will discuss shortly. Rather, perception confuses the *psyche* by reporting to it the contrary predicates of a single object that are true of it at the same time, and this engages the intellect to investigate what, for example, intelligible Unity and Largeness are, in themselves.

In the *Phaedo* Socrates says (74b–c):

Do not equal stones and pieces of wood, though they remain the same, sometimes appear to us equal in one respect and unequal in another? Certainly. Well, then, did The Equals, themselves (αὐτὰ τὰ ἴσα), ever appear (ἐφάνη) to you unequal, or Equality (ἡ ἰσότης) inequality? No, Socrates, never. Then those equal things are not the same as Equality itself (αὐτὸ τὸ ἴσον)? Not at all, I should say, Socrates.

What happens when a relational or incomplete characteristic becomes αὐτὸ καθ᾽ αὐτό, "itself in itself"? It comes to have many of the logical features of a sortal predicate. A finger is, in itself, a finger, and the predicate "is a finger" is correctly said of it not because a finger is related to something else, nor because the predicate is incomplete and in need of further contextual specification, but simply because there is a perfectly good instance of "What it is to be a finger." Forms corresponding to relational and incomplete predicates are intellectually unproblematic for the same reasons that fingers are: Unity itself is not the unity of something, nor is it unity in some respect—it is perfect and complete Unity, a Unity that is always one; Largeness is not the largeness of something, nor is it largeness as compared with some group of objects—it is perfect and complete Largeness, a Largeness that is always large. Thus when Plato reifies relational and incomplete characteristics, he makes them non-relational and complete. At *Phaedo* 74b–c we see an interesting implication of this theme. Plato apparently[12] refers to Equality itself as the Equal Things themselves (αὐτὰ τὰ ἴσα). Here the Form of Equality consists in two or more perfectly equal things; these things are not equal at some time, or in some respect, or relation, rather they are equal *simpliciter* (also see *Parmenides* 129d, τὰ πολλὰ ὁμοιότητα). The Equal Things themselves are not composite, at least not in the senses we distinguished earlier, since they are uniformly and purely equal, and they cannot be broken into and dispersed like physical objects. Therefore Equality is always equal, Largeness is always large, and Unity is always one.

Plato also thinks that Forms are what I will call incorrigible *entities*. Usually philosophers argue that a claim is incorrigible because the claimant has a privileged position in respect to what his claim is about. First-person claims about mental events, for example, are thought to be incorrigible because the claimant has the sole direct access to the events. This, however, is not Plato's view. In the *Phaedo* Equality always appears, presents itself, or shines forth (φαίνεται) as equal, and in the *Symposium* (211a–b) The Beautiful always appears (φαντασθήσεται) beautiful to the philosophical initiate (cf. *Republic* 508d καταλάμπει, *Phaedrus* 250b λαμπρόν, 250c φάσματα, and also see 250d). Nevertheless, Forms are intersubjective entities in that they are accessible to whomever achieves philosophical vision. The frequent use of appearance terminology, which has gone unnoticed outside Heideggerian circles,[13] commits Plato to the view that a Form always appears to be *F*; by their very nature the Forms provide absolute epistemological certainty: a Form self-evidently appears to be what it is. The purity and uniformity of a Form, moreover, is a necessary condition for it to be an incorrigible entity; a Form always appears to be uniformly "self-predicated," because it is so. A Form cannot be in a context, respect, relation, or at a time where its true nature is deceptive. Therefore, *F*-ness is always *F* is a necessary condition for *F*-ness to always appear *F*.

The Forms have not only an epistemic but also an explanatory function. In the *Parmenides* Zeno denies that there are phenomena; for if there were many things, they would have contrary predicates (being like and unlike, one and many), which is impossible (127e; cf. *Phaedrus* 261d). Because Zeno does not distinguish qualities from things qualified, he thinks he has proved the phenomena to be inconsistent and hence nonexistent, and Plato depicts Zeno's argument as an indirect proof for Parmenides' thesis that "all is one" (128a–b). Socrates then introduces the separate Forms to explain the contrary predicates, and hence to save the phenomena (129a ff.). For example, something can be like by partaking of Likeness, and at the same time unlike by partaking of Unlikeness; Socrates can have many parts because he partakes of Plurality, and yet he is one person, among many, because he partakes of Unity (129c–d). Not only are the Forms, themselves, a plurality of Parmenidean monads, but also they make possible the many less real phenomena.

In the *Phaedo* the Forms have the same function (102a–c):

> . . . they had agreed that each of the Forms exist, and that the other things that participate in them get their names from the Forms, then Socrates asked: Now if you consent to this, do you not, when you say that Simmias is greater than Socrates and smaller than Phaedo, say that there is in Simmias greatness and smallness? Yes. But, said Socrates, you agree that the statement that Simmias is greater than Socrates is not true as stated in those words. For Simmias is not greater than Socrates by reason of being Simmias, but by reason of the greatness he happens to have; nor is he greater than Socrates because Socrates is Socrates, but because Socrates has smallness relatively to his greatness. True.

Plato's concern is again not with sortal predicates such as "Socrates is a man," but with relational and (as in the case of "is equal," earlier in the *Phaedo*) incomplete ones. Let us revert to the Pre-Socratics to understand the genesis and importance of this concern.

Many of Heraclitus' oracular utterances result from what he takes to be an "identity of opposites." The *Cosmos* and its contents are at war within themselves; each thing is pulled in opposite directions, and the resultant harmony is a strife of opposites. If seawater is healthy for fishes, but harmful for man, then seawater is healthy and harmful.[14] If seawater is healthy and harmful, then it is at strife with itself, and its health and harm pull in opposite directions. We cannot, however, really decide whether Heraclitus thinks that things are inconsistent; for his "paradoxes" occur precisely because he does not make distinctions that we find commonplace and "universal." Heraclitus does not distinguish a substance and its qualities, relations, or the like, but rather thinks of them all as element-powers or as mixtures of different element-powers. Thus seawater contains two warring element-powers. Concomitantly Heraclitus does not distinguish identity and predication. Thus he cannot formulate the question whether or not seawater is a contradictory entity. What we call the predication "x is F and not-F" Heraclitus analyzes as a strife between opposites that, nevertheless, maintains the integrity of an entity because "war and harmony are the same [and not the same]!"

Parmenides quite likely refers to Heraclitus (B6.4–9):

> ... mortals who know nothing wander, double-headed; for helplessness guides the wandering thought in their hearts. They are carried deaf and blind at the same time, amazed, a horde incapable of judgment, by whom to be and not to be are considered the same and yet not the same, and for whom the path of all things is backward-turning.

"By whom to be and not to be are considered the same and yet not the same" is the sort of riddle that immediately suggests Heraclitus. But there may yet be a broader opponent in Parmenides' sights: the Milesian physical philosophers, as well as Heraclitus, choose some one primary element as the nature of things, but they go on to claim that other things exist as well. For example, in Anaximenes air and breath are the nature of things, but the other elements also exist as air in different forms.

Parmenides does not make the distinction between predication and identity, but he has a good grasp of the dialectic of identity and difference. When applied to Anaximenes this dialectic yields the following results: if air is being, and fire is different from air, then fire is nonbeing, for either it is or it is not. But if fire is really air, and fire is nonbeing while air is being, then "to be and not to be are the same and not the same."

Plato depicts Zeno as making the same sorts of moves in the *Parmenides*. If, as we can describe it, "x is predicatively F and not-F," then x is impossible. Eleatic dialectic produces the conclusion in either of two ways: given that Zeno does not distinguish substances and qualities, x is immediately inconsistent and hence nonexistent: or if *F* is being, then since not-*F* is different from *F*, and either it is or it is not, not-*F* is not being. But then *x* is and is not, which is impossible. Thus problems with contrary qualities are at the root of the Eleatic attack on natural phenomena.

Plato's Forms are as much an answer to this problem as Aristotle's distinction between form, privation, and substratum in *Physics* I. The *Phaedo*, in particular, employs several distinctions that explain contrary qualities. The *Phaedo* contrasts particulars both with their immanent characteristics and with the Forms they participate in.[15] Simmias, Socrates, *psyches*, lumps of snow, and fire are substrata for characteristics (*Phaedo* 102b ff.). Socrates' largeness and Simmias' smallness are different from the Forms Largeness and Smallness; Largeness itself (αὐτὸ τὸ μέγεθος) is different from the largeness in us (τὸ ἐν ἡμῖν μέγεθος, 102d). Plato also employs the distinction between essential and accidental predicates.[16] Simmias is not greater than Socrates by reason of being Simmias, but because he has the immanent character greatness; nor is he greater than Socrates because of what Socrates is, but because Socrates has the immanent character smallness (102b-d). Greatness and smallness are accidental features of Simmias and Socrates. Socrates and Simmias essentially possess *psyches* and thus are alive, while certain lumps of matter are essentially fire and hot, snow and cold, fever- and sickness-engendering (*Phaedo* 103d, 105b–c, 105d f.).

Plato does not believe that phenomena are inconsistent. At *Republic* 436b and again at 436e–437a he states a principle that resembles the law of noncontradiction, except that it is stated in terms of contraries, and applies not to propositions but to entities, acts, and qualities:

> It is obvious that the same thing will never do or suffer opposites in the same respect in relation to the same thing and at the same time.

> No such remark then will disconcert us or any whit the more make us believe that it is ever possible for the same thing at the same time in the same respect and the same relation to suffer, be, or do opposites.

Contra the Eleatics, Plato is certain that phenomenal entities are not inconsistent. He is also very much aware that characteristics like largeness and smallness are relational; Simmias is "named" great and small when his largeness surpasses the smallness of another, and his smallness is exceeded by the largeness of a third person (102c–d). Ultimately it is not Simmias who stands in some relation, but the immanent characteristics in Simmias. What Plato must do, however, is to provide an analysis of relational and incomplete predicates. Participation, as we have already seen from the *Parmenides*, provides the solution. Phenomenal entities derive their nonsortal characteristics from the Forms they participate in (cf. *Phaedo* 100c, 102a–b). Simmias is large and has the immanent characteristic largeness because he participates in Largeness itself; Socrates is small and has the immanent characteristic smallness because he participates in Smallness itself.

There are, to say the least, a number of odd features to this analysis. Participation reduces all relational and incomplete predicates to a single type of relation, participation in a Form. Let us take the predicate "one." This predicate is incomplete because we must specify "one in what respect." "One" is not, however, relational, but participation makes it into a relational predicate; for example, Simmias is one man because he participates in the Form Unity or Oneness (cf. *Parmenides* 129c–d). Simmias is one man because he relates by participation to Unity itself. But Unity itself is one *simpliciter*, and this creates serious problems. For Simmias is one man, a fish is one fish, a cloud is one cloud, and a battle is one battle, all by participation in the same Form. However, we identify and individuate men, clouds, and battles in very different ways, but participation in Unity ignores this. Also there are different senses of "one," as in "one bank," "one bank account," and "one bank manager"; but all of these senses are collapsed in the Form that is one *simpliciter*. Since these senses are not distinct at the Form level, it is hard to see how participation in Unity explains them.

Simmias has the characteristic largeness by partaking in the Form Largeness. With this analysis Simmias' largeness no longer relates to someone else's smallness. Dyadic relations are thus resolved into two monadic entities: the immanent character and the Form, and the relation of participation. Since Simmias can be both large and small, he partakes in Largeness and Smallness. But since Largeness is large *simpliciter* and Smallness is small *simpliciter*, we would expect Simmias to be both large and small *simpliciter*; but certainly he is not, for example, both the tallest and the shortest of men. A problem with participation is that it ultimately ignores the relations between phenomena, and resolves them into the noncontingent connections between Forms. Participation in Largeness makes a thing large because Largeness is analytically larger than anything else. There is at most the slightest hint in the text that Plato would attempt to solve this problem by a "degrees of participation" theory; at *Parmenides* 129a he mentions that those who participate in Likeness become like, and those who participate in Unlikeness become unlike, and those who partake of both become both like and unlike "all in the manner and degree of their participation" (ταύτῃ τε καὶ κατὰ τοσοῦτον ὅσον ἂν μεταλαμβάνῃ) (H. N. Fowler's Loeb translation that I am far from sure is correct).

Since Plato is armed with the Forms in all their Parmenidean steadfastness, he need not fear the Heraclitean flux of this world; that is, the "identity" and war between opposites. It is absolutely essential to the Forms that they do not, themselves, suffer the same perplexities as phenomena; for if Forms have F and not-F predicates, then they could not save the phenomena, because they would be as much in need of salvation themselves. Plato is aware of this problem in the *Parmenides*, because he challenges Parmenides to prove: (1) Likeness is unlike, Unlikeness is like, Unity is many, and Plurality is one (129b–c, d); (2) the Forms, themselves, have opposite qualities (129c); and (3) the Forms suffer the same perplexities as visible objects (129e–130a). Challenges (1)–(3) are closely related; for if we assume that the Forms are self-predicated, then by (1) Parmenides must prove that Likeness, which is like, is also unlike; and Unity, which is one, is also many. Socrates also challenges Parmenides to show that the Forms can be mixed with and separated from each other (129d–e). Since Socrates makes this challenge just after enumerating a series of contrary Forms, I believe that it is similar to the other three challenges. If contrary Forms could mix with each other, then Likeness would be unlike, Unlikeness like, Unity many, and so on. Generically, Socrates challenges Parmenides to show that Forms have contrary predicates, and he thrice emphatically states that if Parmenides did this, he would be amazed (129b,c,e). And his amazement would be justified, for then the Forms would have the same problem Zeno purported to find with phenomena, and their explanatory value would be destroyed. In the next chapter we will see how Parmenides answers this challenge.

We have seen in the *Republic* (523 ff.) that only attributive, relational, and incomplete predicates stimulate *nous* to investigate separate entities: Largeness itself, One itself, and the like. Sortal predicates such as "is a finger" do not have this function. A finger is a finger in a complete way, and there is nothing cognitively unreliable about a finger *qua* finger. Therefore, a phenomenal finger is a perfectly good case of "What it is to be a finger." Moreover, in the *Phaedo* (102 ff.), Forms are introduced only to explain relational predicates; Simmias is large by partaking in Largeness and small by partaking in Smallness. At 102a–c Socrates implies that Simmias is by his own nature a man, but not large or small; Simmias is a perfectly good instance of "What it is to be a man." Likewise, certain lumps of stuff are perfectly good instances of fire or snow; these lumps are essentially fire or snow respectively. Hence the middle dialogues imply that there are many essentially characterized particulars, and sortal predicates describe their essential characteristics. Thus Plato primarily introduces Forms for attributive, relational, and incomplete predicates; there are probably not Forms corresponding to sortal predicates—at least until the *Phaedrus* and the *Parmenides*.

Two passages are sometimes thought to introduce Forms for sortals

(*Phaedo* 102 ff. and *Republic* 596 ff.) But A. Nehamas and F. C. White have cogently argued that the *Phaedo* passage does not introduce Forms of fire, snow, *psyche*, or three.[17] The point of this passage is that what is essentially fire—a particular lump of material—must also be hot, and what is essentially a group of three things must also be odd. Likewise, *psyche* must also be alive. There are not, they argue, analytic connections between the Forms Snow and Cold, Threeness and Odd, and so on, but rather there are such connections between what phenomena really are—their essential properties—and certain Forms they must participate in because of these properties.

The passage in *Republic* X is not a reliable source for information about the Forms. Cherniss has shown that the passage is an extensive analogy, and that Plato introduces the Form of Bed only as an analogue for the craftsman's bed and the painter's image of a bed.[18] Just as God creates the Form, so too the craftsman crafts the wooden bed, and the painter paints the thrice-deficient image. The painter copies the wooden bed, and the craftsman looks to the Form in his crafting. Notice that *Republic* X claims that God makes the Form of Bed; moreover, the craftsman looks at this Form in making phenomenal beds. But except for this passage, Plato consistently denies that God or a demiurge creates the Forms, and craftsmen are distinct from philosophers in the *Republic* because philosophers know Forms whereas craftsmen do not. I conclude that there is good reason to believe that neither the *Republic* nor the *Phaedo* introduce Forms for sortals. Hence there are probably only Forms for attributive, relational, and incomplete characteristics in the *Phaedo* and the *Republic*; but this is precisely what we should expect, since these are the characteristics that are cognitively unreliable.

In the *Phaedo*, we see that self-predication is intimately connected with a Form's explanatory role. At *Phaedo* 100c Socrates says:

> I think that if anything is beautiful (καλόν) besides The Beautiful itself (αὐτὸ τὸ καλόν) it is beautiful for no other reason than because it partakes of absolute Beauty; and this applies to everything.

This passage certainly implies that The Beautiful is beautiful just as we earlier saw in the *Symposium* that The Beautiful is a "marvelous beautiful nature." Later in the *Phaedo* Plato also states that the immanent characteristic, as well as the Form, has the characteristic it explains (102d–e):

> I think it is evident not only that Greatness itself (αὐτὸ τὸ μέγεθος) will never be great (μέγα) and also small, but that the greatness in us will never admit the small or allow itself to be exceeded.... But it will not receive and admit smallness, thereby becoming other than it was. So I have received and admitted smallness and am still the same

small person I was; but the greatness in me, being great (μέγα ὄν), has not suffered itself to become small. In the same way the smallness in us will never become or be great, nor will any other opposite which is still what it was ever become or be also its own opposite.

We have seen that the Forms have both an epistemic and an explanatory function. A necessary condition for the epistemic function is that a Form is purely and uniformly F; also a Form, as an incorrigible entity, must always appear purely and uniformly F. Thus a Form cannot be placed in a context, relation, and respect, or at a time when it is not and does not appear to be F. Moreover, a necessary condition for the explanatory function is that a Form is purely and uniformly F. If a Form were F and not-F, then it could not save the phenomena from the same deficiency. This requirement for the epistemic and explanatory functions of the Forms has important implications: if something is to be perfect and uniform, then it must exist in isolation from all other things.

Both Plato and Parmenides connect perfection with isolation. Plato states that The Beautiful presents itself as "itself in itself always being uniform with itself" (*Symposium* 211b), and in Parmenides there is the similar thought that Being "abides the same in the same place, resting in itself, and thus remains steadfast, where it is" (B8.29–30).[19] Both Plato and Parmenides believe that if something is perfect, then it must be self-sufficient and hence drawn into itself, aloof, and isolated.[20] Parmenides' Being is "single born" or "unique"[21] not in that it is the only member of a class, but because it is all there is; there is nothing outside of or beyond Being (8.4, 36–37). Plato's visible *Cosmos* is a perfect blessed divinity not only because it has a spherical shape like Parmenides' Being, but also because it includes within itself all of the visible stuff, and thus it cannot be attacked from without (*Timaeus* 32c ff.); it is, then, "one world alone, round and revolving in a circle, solitary but able by reason of its excellence to bear itself company, needing no other acquaintance or friend but sufficient to itself" (34b). The perfection of each Form requires that it be separate from the phenomena and unaffected by them (*Symposium* 211b), and that it be isolated from the other Forms. For a Form must be pure and unmixed (ἄμικτον, *Symposium* 211e) and thus it is αὐτὸ καθ᾽ αὑτό, just as the purified *psyche* in the *Phaedo* draws "itself into itself" and away from the body in order that it can look upon the Forms that are "themselves in themselves" (64c, 66a, 66d–e).

On the visual model a Form always is and appears uniformly and purely F. Isolation is a necessary condition for uniformity and purity, and they are a necessary condition for paradigmatism. Phenomena have a mixture of contrary predicates because (1) they are composite and hence destructible entities; (2) they are related to each other; and (3) they have a multiplicity of parts or elements. Simmias is at one time alive, and later dead; he is tall in comparison with Socrates, but short in comparison with Cebes; he is one man, and yet he has many parts, his right hand, left hand, face, and so on. If a Form is to avoid contrary predicates, then it must be (1) always existing, (2) isolated from all other entities, and (3) without physical parts. The Forms obviously satisfy (1) and (3), but (2) needs some comment. If Forms could be related to each other, then some of them would have contrary predicates. Likeness, for example, would be unlike other Forms, Difference would be different from Beauty, but the same as itself, and so on. Some of these examples, of course, resemble the dialectic of the *Sophist*, and in this dialogue the Eleatic Stranger investigates how certain εἴδη can have different and even contrary predicates. But with the visual model for knowledge, this is not possible; a Form must both be and appear uniformly *F*, and a necessary condition for the uniformity, purity, and unmixed nature of a Form is that it is isolated from all other things. For this reason Plato stresses, in the *Symposium*, *Phaedo*, and *Phaedrus*, that a Form is αὐτὸ καθ' αὐτό "itself in itself," and this phrase describes the inward-drawn and isolated nature of a Form.

Purity and uniformity are a necessary condition for paradigmatism. Plato frequently implies that his Forms are individuals; Equality is the perfectly equal thing(s), Beauty is the purely beautiful thing, and the like. Gregory Vlastos believes that Plato was not only the first philosopher to distinguish the universal and the particular, but also the first to conflate the distinction.[22] But this claim is not true for the middle dialogues; Plato's Forms are paradigmatic individuals, and there is no evidence that he distinguishes, as does Aristotle, what is "one in form" from what is "one in number." In Plato's middle-period universe everything is either an individual that is "one in number" or a particular, immanent, characteristic of some individual, and Aristotle's notion of a universal that is not "one in number" is utterly foreign to Plato's thought.[23] Because Plato believes that Forms are individuals, they must be separate from their instances and they are common to them only in the sense that many things can participate in one and the same Form. Plato does not develop the notion of an Aristotelian immanent universal because he does not have the further notion of what is "one in species" but not in number, and which yet exists. Elsewhere I have shown that Aristotle in *Metaphysics* Z 13 and 14 attacks Plato's "universals" on the ground that they are also individual.[24] Nothing individual is common to many things. Aristotle's attack has the dialectical twist that Plato's Forms must be the common essences *in* things, since the essence of *x* cannot exist apart from *x* (Z 6). The common essences in things, however, cannot be individuals, or else phenomena that have the same essence become numerically identical (Z 13 1038b13–16), which is absurd. Aristotle thus convicts Plato of the contradiction of making universals individual, but when he imputes to Plato the notion of his own universal *in rebus*, it is the result of a previous dialectical attack on separation. I conclude that in the middle dialogues Plato does not conflate the universal and individual because he has not achieved the notion of a nonindividual. Plato's middle-period Forms, at least in their early stages of development, are paradigmatic individuals.

Not only does Plato imply that his Forms are separate paradigms, but also he says that they are. At *Republic* 500e and 592b Plato says:

> But if the multitude become aware that what we are saying of the philosopher is true, will they still be harsh with philosophers, and will they distrust our statement that no city could ever be blessed unless its lineaments were drawn by artists who used the heavenly model (τῷ θείῳ παραδείγματι)?

> Well, said I, perhaps there is a pattern (παράδειγμα) of it [The Ideal City] laid up in heaven for him who wishes to contemplate it and so beholding it to constitute himself its citizen.

It is essential to a paradigm that one *can* look upon, behold, or contemplate it; a paradigm must be open to pure intellectual vision. When we look upon a paradigm, we may use it to make judgments (*Republic* 472b f.), and on the basis of these judgments, engage in social and political reform. If something sufficiently resembles a standard, then it can be correctly judged to be an instantiation of it, and if not, not. Uniformity is a necessary condition for paradigmatism. If a Form were to change its qualities or be destroyed, it would not be a perduring standard, and if a Form were to have irrelevant contingent predicates or contrary ones, it would not be a pure standard, but a confusing, chaotic one. Uniformity, then, is a necessary condition for epistemological paradigmatism, and isolation is a necessary condition for uniformity. Therefore, the visual model for knowledge implies that the paradigmatic Forms are isolated Parmenidean monads. I will argue later in this chapter that Plato quickly moves away from this view when he investigates through *logoi* how the Forms connect. These connections will destroy the paradigmatic nature of the Forms.

Immutable Knowledge and Its Unchanging Objects

Why does Plato believe that the objects of knowledge must be temporally unlimited in existence, and unchanging? Hintikka cogently argues that Greek philosophers, including Plato, believe that knowledge is only of unchanging objects (cf. *Republic* 485b, *Philebus* 59a–c, *Timaeus* 27d–28a, 29b–d) because (1) they tend to express knowledge claims in temporally indefinite sentences, and (2) they tend to think that knowledge is some sort of acquaintance with an object.[25] The same temporally indefinite sentence can be true in one utterance context and false in another; thus for one to be always true, it must be about an unchanging object. If, for example, I state that John is sitting in his chair at time t_1, and John is sitting in his chair, then my claim is true; if John should at some other time leave his chair, the statement I made at t_1 would still be true. But the ancient Greek philosophers tend not to view matters in this way; they do not temporally individuate statements. Thus the *very same* statement I made at t_1 would later become false, if John should leave his chair. For a statement to be always true, then, it must be about an unchanging object. Moreover, acquaintance claims about an object at t_1 are evidence that the object is the same at t_2 only if the object is unchanging. Grasping and seeing a Form is epistemically analogous to a temporally indefinite sentence; intellectual sight would not be veridical unless one and the same grasp was always correct. If at time t_1 I see some object x, but at t_2 x changes, then my vision of x at t_1 is no longer veridical. Thus a vision of x is veridical only if x does not change.

Aristotle explicitly states that knowledge is of unchanging objects (*Metaphysics* 1039b27–1040a7), and that "always true statements" must be about unchanging objects:

> Therefore as regards the class of things which admit of both contrary states [to be and not to be] *the same opinion or the same statement comes to be false and true*, and it is possible at one time to be right and at another wrong; but as regards things which cannot be otherwise the same opinion is not sometimes true and sometimes false, but the same opinions are always true or always false (1051b13–17, emphasis mine; also see the striking and important passage at *Categories* 4a22 ff.).

Since Aristotle believes that the same statement can be true at one time and false at another, for one to be always true it must be about an unchanging object.

In Plato there is also evidence for this position, although it is much less explicit. In the *Gorgias* (454d–e) Socrates distinguishes opinion and knowledge in that the former can be true or false, but the latter is always true. The implications of this distinction are not, however, put to any metaphysical use; rather Socrates separates art from empirical knack on the basis of the epistemic distinction. Sophistic rhetoric persuades of mere belief, but philosophical rhetoric produces knowledge. In the *Republic*, however, the epistemic distinction has important metaphysical import. At 477e–478a Socrates says:

But not long ago you agreed that knowledge and opinion are not identical. How could any rational man affirm the identity of the fallible and the infallible? Excellent, said I, and we are plainly agreed that opinion is a different thing from knowledge? Yes, different. Each of them, then, since it has a different power, is related to a different object? Of necessity. Knowledge, I presume, to that which is, to know the condition of that which is?

Plato now believes that the distinction between belief and knowledge implies that they are about different objects. Knowledge knows Being (τὸ ὄν, 477a,b, 478a,b,c, 479d), pure Being (477a, 478d, 479d), real and true Being (511d, 515c, *Phaedrus* 247c); opinion opines what "partakes of to be and not to be, and is correctly designated neither in purity" (477a). Knowledge knows the former because it is infallible, while opinion opines the latter because it is fallible. But Plato is not making the claim that S knows that *p* only if *p* is true; for him the infallibility or unerring (τὸ ἀναμάρτητον, 477e) nature of knowledge requires that it be about unchanging objects: S knows that *p* only if *p* is a real, immutable Being. We can make sense of this strong claim from what Hintikka says: knowledge consists in part in temporally indefinite sentences, and for such a sentence to be always true, it must be about an unchanging object.

Since knowledge is always true, it, itself, becomes immutable like its objects. Undoubtedly the principle that like is known by like is here operative in Plato's thought. From this analysis we can explain a number of strange things that Plato says about knowledge. In the *Symposium* the final stage of the ascent is not just a sight of pure, separate Beauty, but also a sight (κατίδη) of a new sort of knowledge connected with that Beauty (210d). In the *Phaedrus* (247d–e), when we travel with the gods beyond the rim of the universe, "In the revolution it [the *psyche*] beholds Justice itself, Temperance itself, and Knowledge (ἐπιστήμη) itself, not such knowledge as has a beginning and varies as it is associated with one or another of the things we call realities, but that which abides in the really real Beings...." In the *Parmenides* Plato often perplexes commentators when he distinguishes god's Knowledge, which is of the Forms, from its merely human counterpart (133b ff.). Knowledge is elevated to almost the status of a Form, because like the Forms it is immutable and unchanging, and it has this characteristic because it is about the immutable and unchanging.

Self-Predication and the Causal Principle

Throughout this chapter I have argued that the Forms are "self-predicated," *F*-ness is always *F*. It is essential to self-predication that a

Form have an univocal predicate with its participants. "Is beautiful," for example, has the same meaning when applied both to the Form of Beauty and to its participants. Beauty, however, is uniformly beautiful: it is beautiful in every respect, relation, context, *and* at every time; beautiful phenomena have an impure or mixed beauty: they are also not beautiful in some respect, relation, context, *or* at some time. But in those ways that phenomena are beautiful, they are beautiful with the same meaning of the predicate that is applied to the Form. First I will gather together the reasons for univocal self-predication; then I will remove certain philosophical objections to it.

The epistemic function of a Form implies univocal self-predication. The Forms are standards by which we judge the characteristics of phenomena. As standards the Forms must share a univocal predicate with their participants. Let us suppose that F_1 and F_2 are, for example, different meanings of the predicate "is beautiful." Let us further suppose that the Form is F_1 and its participants F_2. But by looking at F-ness that is F_1, how can we use it as a standard to judge of the presence or absence of F_2? If the only relation a participant has to a Form is that it is dependent upon that Form for some characteristic,[26] why is it dependent upon that Form for that characteristic? Equivocal predication splits Plato's two types of reality into nonrelating entities; it destroys paradigmatism and makes it impossible to determine what Form some sensible object partakes in.

Recollection also implies univocal predication. For we recollect the pure Form from the impure phenomena (cf. *Phaedo* 74b). Obviously this process is not direct and immediate, but rather requires an advance through F things and an integration of *logoi*, as in the ascent of the *Symposium*. Nevertheless, recollection begins from phenomena, and such a start would not be possible if the predicates of the phenomena were equivocal with those of the Forms. For example, if equal sticks and stones are not equal with the same meaning of the predicate that Equality has, then why should they start to recollect Equality to us rather than anything else? Equivocation between Forms and phenomena makes recollection an arbitrary affair. Finally, a Form must be self-predicated if it is to present the proper appearance. If a Form were neither F nor not-F,[27] then how could we see or grasp it; what would we see or grasp it as?

The explanatory function of a Form also implies univocal predication. A particular is F and not-F because it participates in F-ness and not-F-ness, where these are understood to be polar opposites. Thus Forms save phenomena from the Heraclitean war of opposites and the Eleatic charge of inconsistency. But the Forms must have the qualities they explain, or participation is a sham. For if Forms and phenomena do not share univocal predicates, then it is arbitrary what Form explains what characteristic; and this is tantamount to the position that no Form explains any characteristic. Hence ontological dependency is not enough; participation also requires that a Form have the same predicate that it explains. Only in this way can *x* be *F* by participating in *F*-ness.

E. N. Lee objects to this analysis as follows:[28] Participation is a striving and wanting to be like a Form (cf. *Phaedo* 74d–e). But, of course, phenomena are deficient, and thus they fall short of their desired end (cf. *Phaedo* 74d–e). For example, I may desire to be wealthy like a Rockefeller, but after having saved $432, I am hardly wealthy. Lee suggests that phenomena relate to Forms in this way: they depend upon Forms for their characteristics, strive to achieve them, but fall short and are deficient. I do not object to Lee's account of participation, although I will later state certain reservations about it. Furthermore, Lee's position implies that a Form has the quality that is desired; The Beautiful is the object of *eros* because it is beautiful. But how are phenomena deficient? The evidence indicates that a beautiful woman or equal sticks and stones are deficient because they are not always and in every way, respectively, beautiful and equal.[29]. The beauty of a woman fades with age, although she strives for and desires a temporally unlimited and context-free sort of beauty that is found only in the Form. But this, of course, does not imply that the sticks and stones are in no way equal, or that the woman is never beautiful. They are equal in some respects; she is beautiful in some comparisons. We should also note that Lee's account is inconsistent with the requirements of paradigmatism, recollection, and explanation. If phenomena fail to share univocal predicates with the Forms, then we could never tell what anything was striving for.

Another reason that Forms are self-predicated is that a cause ($\alpha\iota\tau\iota\alpha$) must have the quality that it explains. Below I will argue that the separate Forms are formal and final causes, while the immanent characteristics are more akin to the Pre-Socratic power-elements which are efficient causes. But the principle that a cause must have the quality that it explains applies to all three types of causes. A separate Form, which is a formal and final cause, must be *F*, if it is to explain why other things are *F* or strive to be *F*, and an immanent characteristic must be *F*, if it is to transmit that quality to something else.

At *Phaedo* 96c–d, Socrates, at the beginning of his autobiographical sketch, says that his youthful investigations into natural science made him forget what he previously thought that he knew: that people grow through eating and drinking, and that in this way "flesh is added to flesh and bones to bones." Although the forgotten view is not explicitly attributed to Anaxagoras, we do know that he held such a view.[30] When Anaxagoras is introduced at 97b ff. as the proponent of a *Nous* that arranges all things, Socrates justifiably complains that Anaxagoras did not make use of *Nous* to explain phenomena, but rather appealed to mechanical causes, and

Anaxagoras' mechanical causation operates on the principle that like produces like.

Socrates' youthful investigations into nature show, however, that mechanical causation is incompatible with the principle that like explains like. Thus he rejects mechanical causation on three grounds:

(1) The same cause can have contrary effects. (For example: "If you said that a man is greater or smaller than another by a head, you would, I think, be afraid of meeting with the reply that the greater is greater and the smaller is smaller by the same thing [a head]" [101a; see also 96d–e].)

(2) Contrary causes can have the same effect. (For example: "Both addition and division can produce two things" [96e–97b]. Plato is apparently thinking of mathematical operations in physical terms.)

(3) Something can be made large by what is small, which is absurd. (For example: A large man is large by a head that is small [101a–b].)

Grounds (1)–(3) imply that an adequate explanation must satisfy at least three conditions: (1) the same cause cannot have contrary effects, (2) contrary causes cannot have the same effect, and (3) a cause cannot have the quality contrary to that which it explains.

At 99c–d we learn that although Socrates wanted to explain the causation of phenomena by the action of *Nous*, neither was he able to find a teacher who knew its nature, nor was he able to discover it by himself. So he is forced to embark on a second voyage in quest of the answer. The second voyage introduces the Forms as causes (αἰτίαι, 100b), and at 100c Socrates gives an example of how the Forms operate as causes:

> I think that if anything is beautiful (καλόν) besides The Beautiful (αὐτὸ τὸ καλόν), it is beautiful for no other reason than because it partakes of (μετέχει) The Beautiful, and this applies in all cases.

This causal explanation is safe (ἀσφαλές, 100e), not only because it satisfies the above three conditions, but also because it meets three stronger ones: (A) The same cause cannot have different effects. (B) Different causes cannot have the same effect. And (C) a cause must have the quality that it explains in something else. Condition (A) is not present in the passage, but there is reason to believe that Plato would accept it. At *Republic* 476a, 479a, 507b–c, and 596a he introduces one Form to explain the occurrence of each distinct type of nonsortal quality. For example, The Beautiful is only responsible—in a nonaccidental way—for the presence of beauty. An instance of (B) is that *all* beautiful things are made (ποιεῖ) beautiful only by the presence or communion (εἴτε παρουσία εἴτε κοινωνία) of The Beautiful, and not by any other cause, such as their lovely color or shape (100c–d). Same cause, same effect. Vlastos has pointed out that 100c implies that The Beautiful is itself beautiful.[31] Furthermore, at 102d–e Socrates says that both Largeness itself and the immanent largeness are large, and that neither of them will admit the Small, that is itself small. But what is the point of the predications "The Beautiful is beautiful," and "Largeness is large"? Paradigmatism is not at issue in these passages; Socrates does say, however, that the Forms are αἰτίαι. Therefore, I believe that Plato assumes the principle that a cause must have the quality that it explains in something else. Just as phenomena receive their names from the Forms they partake in (*Phaedo* 102b, 103b), so too their qualities are explained by those Forms, and this is possible precisely because the Forms, themselves, have these qualities.

We have now seen that both the epistemic and explanatory functions of a Form require self-predication. Paradigmatism, recollection, and the uniform appearance of a Form each imply that F-ness is F. Participation and explanation imply the same view. Let us now turn to some purported philosophical objections to self-predication.

One might deny univocal predication because the predicates of Forms are predicated necessarily of them whereas the contrary predicates of phenomena are predicated contingently. The first claim, as I will show, is part of what Plato means by a real, unchanging Being that is an object of knowledge, and the second claim is plausible because Forms are primarily introduced, in the middle dialogues, to explain attributive, relational, and incomplete predicates;[32] if some phenomenon, x, participates in a Form corresponding to one of these predicates, then x can also cease to participate in that Form. The middle-period Forms primarily explain the contingent predicates of phenomena. Moreover, the distinction between "had necessarily" and "had contingently" also accounts for the usual self-predicational contexts; F-ness is always and necessarily F, while phenomena are contingently F and contingently not-F. Later I will show, however, that phenomena have some necessary predicates, and that we cannot distinguish Forms from phenomena solely on the basis of a modal difference.

But does this modal distinction entail a nonunivocal predicate? If we read modal operators as changing the meaning of a predicate, we must wreak havoc. For example, it implies that we equivocate when we conclude "I am contingently an unmarried adult" from "I am contingently a bachelor," and "Bachelors necessarily are unmarried adults." I conclude that even if the predicates of Forms are had necessarily, while those of phenomena, which are explained by participation in a Form, are had contingently, these predicates are still univocal: F-ness and F phenomena are univocally F.

Another defense of equivocal predication is that since a paradigm is superbly F, while its instances are humdrumly F, the predicate "F" is equivocally said of the Form and its participants. This account likens a Form to its participants on the model of deep red to pale red, or a Georgia beauty queen to a run-of-the-mill coed. *F*-ness is *F* in a much more brilliant way than the humdrum characteristics of phenomena. We have seen that this sort of contrast may occur in the *Symposium*; but Plato usually contrasts the Forms with their instances on the different ground that the Form is unqualifiedly *F*, *F* in all contexts, while a participant is qualifiedly *F* and not-*F*, *F* in some contexts but not-*F* in others. Thus the argument for equivocal predication is not well founded in the text. Furthermore, it is also philosophically implausible. What needs to be shown for this defense to be cogent is why such adverbial modifiers change the meaning of "*F*". I know of no general principle about the use of adverbs that implies such equivocation. Dull and bright red are still shades of red.

Some commentators[33] attempt to support at least nonunivocal predication by an appeal to Aristotle's notion of πρὸς ἓν καὶ μίαν τινὰ φύσιν λεγόμενον (*Metaphysics* 1003a33–4), or what Owen labels "focal meaning."[34] The source of their hope is Aristotle's claim that a term can be used in many senses without thereby being equivocal, if it is used with a single focus. Two Aristotelian examples are: healthy food produces bodily health, and a healthy complexion is caused by bodily health. The food and complexion are causally related to a single focal condition: the health of the body. Substance is being in an unqualified sense, while items in categories other than substance are being in a derivative sense. Derivative being ontologically depends on the focal entity, substance. Focal meaning thus explains our application of terms by means of causal, ontological, and other sorts of relations (cf. *Categories* I, 1a12–15). In the *Phaedo* (102b, 103e) Plato implies that the Forms are the primary bearers of predicates, and that those things that partake in the Forms come to have their predicates from the Forms; moreover, a Form, *F*-ness, must exist for any *F* thing to exist, and *F*-ness explains the presence of *F* characteristics in phenomena. Hence Plato employs a variant of Aristotle's notion of focal meaning, and we saw in Chapter 1 that in *Republic* IV just acts are focally called after psychic justice. Both Aristotle and Plato formulate their positions by an extensive use of focal predication.

But does focal predication imply the use of nonunivocal predicates? Focal predication explains the application of predicates by means of relations, but certainly this explanation is compatible with univocal, nonunivocal, or equivocal predication. We must "Look and see," and, at a deeper level, engage the theoretical requirements of the position at issue. In the first Aristotelian example, there does not appear to be any common characteristic corresponding to the term "healthy," but in the second example there are both primary and secondary beings or existents. And even if "being" is said in many different senses, this does not imply that many different meanings of the term "being" occur, for a difference in sense—which sometimes happens when, for example, a word is applied to different kinds of things—does not imply a difference of meaning. So even if Forms are the focal objects for derivative predications of phenomena, there can still be an univocal predicate; furthermore, there are theoretical requirements that necessitate an univocal predicate. For *F*-ness must be univocally *F* with its participants if it is to be an epistemic paradigm and an explanation for participation.

Types of Reality

Let us next examine types of reality in the middle works. Then I will terminate the discussion of what the Forms are, on the visual model, with a discussion of participation and causation. We will then turn to the discursive model for knowledge and the interconnections of the Forms.

Plato's metaphysical strata are the source of numerous metaphysical hierarchies, at least the source of inspiration for them; yet there is deep and repeated disagreement about how to interpret the following:

(1) Forms are Being (τὸ ὄν, *Republic* 477a,b, 478a,b,c, 479d), perfect or complete Being (477a, 597a), pure Being (477a, 478d, 479d), more Being [than phenomena] (515d), really real Being (οὐσία ὄντως οὖσα, *Phaedrus* 247c), true Being (511d, 515c); and finally, Forms are always *F*, *F* at every time, in every respect, in every relation, and to everyone (*Symposium* 211a, *Phaedo* 74b–d).

(2) Phenomena "partake of to be and not to be (εἶναί τε καὶ μὴ εἶναι), and are correctly designated neither in purity" (478e); they are "halfway between pure Being (τοῦ ... ὄντος, οὐσία) and absolute nonbeing (τοῦ αὖ μηδαμῇ ὄντος)" (477a, 479c); they fall short of Being (*Phaedo* 74d); are inferior to it (*Phaedo* 74e, 75b); also phenomena are *F* and not-*F*, at different times, or in different respects, or relations (*Republic* 436e–437a, 479a–b, 602c–d, *Phaedo* 74b–c).

(3) The lowest stratum is nonbeing (τὸ μὴ ὄν, 477a, 478b,c, 479c), nothing (μηδέν, 478b), pure nonbeing (479b), complete nonbeing (478d), and in no way being (477a).

Coordinate with the metaphysical strata are the epistemological claims: (A) Being is completely knowable (*Republic* 477a), the object of knowledge (477a–b), and knowledge is without missing or unerring (τὸ ἀναμάρτητον, 477e). (B) Phenomena are the objects of opinion (477b), opinion is not unerring (477e), and opinion is darker than knowledge but brighter than ignorance (478c). And (C) Nonbeing is entirely unknowable (477a).

We have already investigated the implications of the contrast between a Form that is purely and uniformly *F*, and phenomena that are *F* and not-*F*. We are now interested in the broader contrast between real and deficient being, although the epistemic and explanatory distinctions play an important role in the broader contrast. How, then, does Plato distinguish real and deficient being?

There are two commonly received but diametrically opposed interpretations of this distinction. R. C. Cross and A. D. Woozley claim that "the expressions 'exist,' 'is real,' occur as synonyms,"[35] and they attribute to Plato "two levels of reality or existence, that of Forms which are completely real or existent, and that of sensible particulars, which are semi-real, partly existent and partly non-existent."[36] They read εἶναι in the absolute construction as well as τὸ ὄν and οὐσία as existential in nature; so let us call their view "the existence interpretation." Gregory Vlastos argues that Forms are *more real* than phenomena, because Forms are cognitively reliable, and phenomena are not.[37] Forms are reliable because they have their predicates necessarily and are not adulterated with *F* and not-*F* predications; phenomena are deficient because they have their predicates contingently and suffer *F* and not-*F* predications. Vlastos interprets εἶναι in the absolute construction—especially in *Republic* V 477a ff.—as complement-hungry; it is to be completed by a predicate. Let us call Vlastos' view "the predication interpretation."

I will argue that the necessary conditions for a real Being or Form are both existential and predicative. These uses of "to be" are subordinate cases of what Charles Kahn calls the general fact-stating use of the Greek verb "to be."[38] Although Plato distinguishes the predicative and identity uses, he never explicitly separates the predicative and existential uses of "to be,"[39] and he frequently conflates them when he uses εἶναι in the absolute construction to mean "what is so," or "what is the case."[40] We have already seen that a Form is an epistemic paradigm only if it is uniformly *F*; moreover, a sensible particular cannot be the paradigm of *F*, because it is *F* and not-*F*. But existential conditions are also involved in both the reality and the cognitive reliability of Forms, as well as in the deficiency of phenomena. Specifically I will show: (1) that a Form is a reliable, real Being only if it is temporally unlimited in existence;[41] (2) that nonexistence is a necessary and a sufficient condition for nonbeing in *Republic* V;[42] and (3) that phenomena are *in toto* deficient—that is, with respect to all of their predicates: sortal, relational, attributive, and the like—if they are generated and destroyed; that is, if they are temporally limited in existence. My major criticism of the predication interpretation is that it does not show that phenomena are cognitively deficient and less real than Forms in respect to their sortal predicates; that is, to those types of predicates that describe what kind of thing either a natural entity or an artifact is. Vlastos also fails to show that phenomena are deficient in respect to those predicates that describe the type of deficient reality that all phenomena have—"visible," "corporeal," "mutable," and the like. For these predicates are neither had contingently nor are they juxtaposed with their respective polar opposites.

We can divide Vlastos' claims into positive and negative arguments. The negative argument successfully criticizes Cross and Woozley's existence interpretation. Plato's statement that phenomena "partake of to be and not to be" (*Republic* 478e) does not, as Cross and Woozley believe, mean that phenomena are "partly existent and partly non-existent." For as Vlastos conclusively shows, the notions of "degrees of existence" and "partial existence and non-existence" were no more intelligible to an ancient Greek than they are to us. If Plato were straining against his natural language to express these claims, then there would be signs of struggle in the text, but we do not find any.[43] Cross and Woozley's view, however, is not the plausible existence interpretation. For, as I will show, we do find in the text repeated assertions that phenomena "are generated and destroyed," that is, they are (exist at time t_1) and are not (do not exist at time t_2), while the Forms always are, that is, they are temporally unlimited in existence. This existential contrast plays an important role in different types of reality, but not to the exclusion of the predication interpretation.

Vlastos' positive argument is that one sense of "real" is "cognitively reliable."[44] He argues that Plato's claims about phenomena are not like the statement "Unicorns are not real," but rather like "These flowers are not real." For the former implies the nonexistence of unicorns, while the latter presupposes the existence of, for example, plastic flowers, and implies that they do not have the predicates of real flowers.[45] This is the only mention Vlastos makes of existence in his predication interpretation; statements about phenomena presuppose their existence. But Vlastos does not contrast the kind of existence phenomena have with that which the Forms have. Vlastos' analogy, moreover, only shows how a deficiently real thing can nevertheless exist; for he gives two tests, *which he treats as equivalent*, for distinguishing different strata of reality, and neither of them implies that phenomena lack predicates that the relevant Forms have. The first test is that "the sensibles are always, the Forms never, F and not-F."[46] Let us call this the "purity test." The purity test states that an object (either a Form or a sensible particular) is not deficient with respect to a predicate F if that object *is not* not-F in any respect, in any relation, at any time, and so on; and an object is deficient with respect to F if that object also *is* not-F in a different respect or relation, or at a different time, and so on. I will call a predicate of an object "pure" if that object is not deficient in respect to that predicate, and impure if it is. The second test is that "... nothing can qualify as a cognoscendum ... if it is cluttered up with contingent characteristics. All of its properties must stick to it with logical glue...."[47] Let us call this the "modal test." The modal test states that an object is not deficient with respect to F if it has F necessarily, and that it is deficient with respect to F if it has F contingently.

Vlastos believes that Forms have no impure predicates, since the Forms are pure, unmixed, uniform (*Phaedo* 67b, 78d, *Symposium* 211b,e, *Republic*

585b), and self-predicated; for example, "The Beautiful is always beautiful" (*Hippias Major* 292e, *Symposium* 210e–211a), "Equality is equal" (*Phaedo* 74b–c), and the like. Furthermore, Vlastos claims that Forms have all their predicates necessarily. Phenomena, so Vlastos believes, have all their predicates contingently, and each of their predicates is impure. For if some predicate of a sensible object is had necessarily, then on the modal test that object would not be deficient in respect to that predicate; and if some predicate of a phenomenal object is pure, then on the purity test that object would not be deficient in respect to that predicate. Vlastos, of course, believes that sensible objects are *in toto* cognitively deficient.[48]

The modal and purity tests, however, are not equivalent, although Vlastos treats them as such. Socrates is one man among many because he partakes in Unity (τοῦ ἑνός), but he has many parts because he partakes in Multiplicity (πλήθους, *Parmenides* 129c–d). Socrates does not satisfy the purity test in respect to "one and many," but he does satisfy the modal test since he has both of these predicates necessarily. For even if all other phenomena were destroyed, Socrates would still be *one* phenomenal being, and every such being is composite, and thus has many parts (*Phaedo* 78b–c, *Republic* 533b, 611b). Furthermore, predicates like "one," "many," "visible," "composite," "mutable," "generated," and "destructible," are had necessarily by all sensible objects; for beings on this level of reality are, by definition, mutable, composite, generated, and so on. Thus the modal account cannot be used to show that while Forms are *in toto* cognitively reliable, phenomena are *in toto* deficient.[49] The purity account has the same defect. For phenomena are, for example, by definition composite beings, and thus the predicate "composite" is pure.

The strongest revision of Vlastos' position that maintains the predicative interpretation is: (1) Forms are *in toto* cognitively reliable real Beings if and only if (A) they have no impure predicates, *and* (B) they have all their predicates necessarily. (A) is necessary for a Form to be a pure, unchaotic paradigm, and (B) is necessary since knowledge is of unchanging objects, and Plato, like other Greek philosophers, assumes that if some object *x* has *F* contingently, then at some time *x* will not be *F*.[50] (2) Phenomena are *in toto* cognitively deficient if for every predicate *F* of *x* (where *x* ranges over phenomenal objects), *F* is either impure, *or* *x* has *F* contingently.

Is the revised Vlastos position correct? I will argue that it does not prove that phenomena are deficient in respect to their sortal predicates. Plato, however, demotes phenomena *in toto* to the deficient world of opinion (*Republic* 476c, *Symposium* 211a–b, *Phaedo* 78d–79a). To develop this criticism let us investigate the extension of the Form theory, and Plato's explanation for the acquisition of characteristics.

I have already argued that the evidence in the middle dialogues strongly supports the position that there are primarily Forms for only attributive, relational, and incomplete predicates.[51] At *Republic* 523b ff. *Phaedo* 74b f., 102b f., and *Parmenides* 128e–130a, Plato investigates or posits Forms because the phenomena are *F* and not-*F*. These predicates are attributive (for example, "is just"), relational ("is large"), and incomplete ("is one"). None of these types of predicates describe the essential natures of their subjects. At *Republic* 507b–c Plato appears to use a one-over-many argument that would also generate Forms corresponding to sortal predicates, but his examples of contrary Forms, as instances of his general principle, again imply that Plato's target is to explain the contrary qualities of phenomena. Thus Plato primarily introduces Forms for the *F* and not-*F* characteristics of phenomena.

I have also argued that Plato believes in essentially characterized particulars in the middle dialogues. Since Forms primarily explain characters that have polar opposites, essential characters tend to be explained by their bearers. Simmias is, by his own nature, a man (*Phaedo* 102b f.), and some lumps of stuff are by their own natures, essentially fire and snow respectively. These particulars have a substantial existence in their own right, and Plato's distinction in the *Phaedo* between essential and accidental features makes this possible. Plato does not develop a theory of kinds in the middle dialogues, nor does he engage in the extensive divisions and collections of the late works, because he does not posit Forms for "man," "cow," or the like. In Chapter 5 I will show that the *Philebus* and *Sophist* are concerned only with kinds, not Forms, and that these dialogues are about kinds of phenomena. I believe that there are essentially characterized particulars in the middle dialogues because these entities are striving *psyches* (*Phaedo* 74b, 75b).[52] Since *psyche* explains the essential attributes of a particular, there is no reason to posit Forms for sortals.

Since sensible particulars are substantial bearers of contrary predicates, and have their own essential natures, they only depend on the Forms to explain their contrary characters. This account of the extension of the Form theory is inconsistent with a prominent model of how phenomena copy Forms. R. E. Allen argues that phenomena are *in toto* mere semblances of the Forms, and depend upon them both for their characters and for their existence.[53] Phenomena are like mirror images; their whole being is relational and dependent. But there is good reason, from the text, to deny that "the whole being" of a sensible particular is relational and dependent; for Plato depicts phenomena as substantial bearers of contrary predicates, and these subjects do not, in their essential natures, depend upon Forms for their existence.

Vlastos can explain, with this extension of the Form theory, why phenomena are deficient in respect to those predicates had by participation in a Form. Some of these predicates are had contingently, for example, "Simmias is not naturally taller than Socrates by reason of being Simmias" (*Phaedo* 102b–c), which implies that there is no logical connection between Simmias and his tallness. Moreover, predicates like "one," "tall," "heavy," "like," and "beautiful," are impure, because Plato believes that they are always found with a polar opposite.[54] Vlastos could also claim that "visible" and "generated," for which there are no corresponding Forms, are, nevertheless, impure since in some contexts phenomena are not visible, and all phenomena are generated and destroyed. However, I do not see how Vlastos could explain the deficiency of predicates like "composite," since sensible particulars have this predicate necessarily, and they are never incomposite, that is, without physical components. But Vlastos' account of deficient reality is in even more serious difficulty. Simmias' nature, encapsulated in the sortal predicate "man," is not afflicted with either infirmity: there is no polar opposite of man, and Simmias has the predicate "man" necessarily. Furthermore, as long as Simmias is Simmias, he does not have any logical contrary of man, such as duck, dog, goose. Thus on either of Vlastos' tests "Simmias is a man" is a cognitively reliable claim, and, of course, this result also follows for other sortal predicates. Plato, however, demotes phenomena *in toto* to a deficient reality (*Republic* 476c, *Symposium* 211a–b, *Phaedo* 78d–79a), and his grounds are the same in each passage: Forms always exist, while phenomena are generated and destroyed.

Vlastos is unable to prove that phenomena are deficient in respect to their sortal predicates. We must, then, provide another condition for their *in toto* deficiency. I will argue that this is an existential condition: temporal limitation in existence.

Hintikka, as we have seen, cogently argues that Greek philosophers, including Plato, believe that knowledge is only of unchanging objects (cf. *Republic* 485b, *Philebus* 59a–c, *Timaeus* 27d–28a, 29b–d). Hintikka's arguments imply that (1) if x is an object of knowledge, then x is temporally unlimited in existence, and does not change its predicates, and (2) if x is temporally limited in existence, then x cannot, in respect to any predicate, be an object of knowledge. For substantially coming to be and substantially ceasing to be change the truth value of a temporally indefinite sentence, no matter what sort of predicate it ascribes to a subject. Can we confirm these claims in the text?

Parmenides' fragment B8 is our best source for at least the philosophers' meaning of ἔστι.[55] Parmenides says (lines 1–6), "One story remains for telling, that it is (ὡς ἔστιν), and for this there are many signs [predicates]: that Being (τὸ ἐόν) is ungenerated and indestructible, it is (ἔστι) whole, unshaking, and complete; neither was it, nor will it be, since it exists (ἔστι) now, altogether, one, and continuous."[56] Being is ungenerated and indestructible, and it has its signs necessarily; moreover, Parmenides does not distinguish existential and predicative signs in the absolute construction ὡς ἔστιν. An examination of contexts shows, however, that "whole," "unshaking," "complete," "one," and "continuous" are predicates of Being, and "it exists now" is an existential claim. Moreover, Parmenides employs—to roughly characterize his manner of procedure—the same type of argument to establish both existential and predicative signs: since it is impossible to think or speak of nonbeing, Being could not grow or generate from nonbeing or dissipate to nonbeing; Being is whole, complete, one, continuous, and unshakable because unthinkable nonbeing cannot separate Being, and thus produce space for change.

Plato accepts, as much as possible, Parmenides' account of Being, but he contrasts the Forms with deficiently real phenomena:

> [The Beautiful] always is, it neither comes to be nor perishes, neither increases nor decreases, next it is not beautiful in part and in part ugly, beautiful at one time and not at another, beautiful in one relation but ugly in another, beautiful here but ugly there . . . and the other beautiful things partake of it so that while they come to be and perish (γιγνομένων . . . ἀπολλυμένων), it grows neither more or less, nor suffers anything (*Symposium* 210e–211b).

> Is Being (ἡ οὐσία), itself, about which in asking and answering we say that it is what is (τὸ εἶναι), always the same or is it in any way other? . . . does Being (τὸ ὄν) receive any change whatever? Or is each of them always what is (ὁ ἔστι), uniform, itself with itself, always holding the same, and never in any way receiving any change? . . . Are the many things . . . that have the names of the Forms, always the same, or since they are entirely opposed to the Forms, . . . are they never the same (*Phaedo* 78d–e)?

These passages intertwine *two* contrasts: (1) Forms always exist, they do not have generation and destruction; phenomena come to be and perish, they are temporally limited in existence (also see *Republic* 485b, 508d, 546a). (2) Forms are uniform and unchanging, they are always and in every way *F*, and do not have a temporal change of predicates; phenomena are *F* and not-*F*, and they have a temporal change of predicates (also see *Phaedo* 74b–c, *Republic* 479a–b, 602c–d). We emphasized the second contrast when discussing the epistemic and explanatory functions of the Forms, but evidently both contrasts are involved in the analysis of different types of reality.

Both contrasts are equally prominent in the context of the *Symposium* passage. The Beautiful is completely satisfactory both because it is pure, unmixed beauty (211e), and because it always exists, unlike the *mortal trash* encountered in the ascent (211e). However, the existential contrast dominates the *Phaedo*. In the *Phaedo*, Plato argues that the *psyche* is deathless since it is more like the incomposite, indestructible Forms than like the composite, dissolvable body (78b ff.). Therefore Forms are ungenerated and indestructible; hence they are existentially suited to be the objects of knowledge.

A Form, moreover, has all of its predicates necessarily and purely. Formal predicates are true of all the Forms:[57] "ungenerated," "indestructible," "uniform," "unchanging," "pure," "divine," "blessed," and the like; and each Form has a definite descriptive "self" predicate: "The Beautiful is always beautiful," "Justice is always just," and so on. Some predicates are had necessarily because of the existential status of Forms ("ungenerated," "always existing," and the like); others because of their religious status ("divine," "blessed," and the like); and the remainder because of their paradigmatic status ("pure," "uniform," "is beautiful," "is equal," and the like).[58]

A Form, then, is *in toto* a cognitively reliable real Being if and only if: (1) it is temporally unlimited in existence, (2) it has no impure predicates, and (3) it has all its predicates necessarily. If a Form were to cease to exist or to change a predicate—and Greek philosophers assume that if a predicate is had contingently, then it is temporally limited in its application— then it could not be the object of an always true temporally indefinite sentence; and if a Form were to have an impure predicate, then it could not be the paradigm of *F*-ness.

We have already seen that in the middle dialogues phenomena are generated and destroyed; only in this way are they deficient with respect to their sortal predicates, since these predicates "pass" the purity and modal tests. Thus in *Republic* V Plato compares phenomena to the contents of dreams, but a necessary component of their dreamlike status is that they are temporally limited in existence; just as dreams are generally less perduring than sensible particulars, so too sensible particulars are less perduring than the Forms.

I will first summarize my conclusions about the types of reality, and then apply them to *Republic* V.

(1) Some object *x* is *in toto* a cognitively reliable, real Being if and only if *x* is temporally unlimited in existence, and *x* has no *F* and not-*F* predicates, and *x* has all its predicates necessarily.

(2) *x* is cognitively deficient in respect to its sortal predicates if *x* is temporally limited in its existence.[59]

(3) *x* is cognitively deficient with respect to a predicate *F*, if *x* is *F* and not-*F*, or *x* is *F* contingently, or *x* is temporally limited in existence.

(4) Hence *x* is deficient *in toto* if *x* is temporally limited in existence.

Vlastos argues that an existential interpretation of Plato's statements—that phenomena are "halfway between Being and nonbeing" (*Republic* 477a, 479c), and "partake of to be and not to be" (478e)—is unintelligible because phenomena would then be "partly existent and partly non-existent." He reads these statements as ellipses for the *F* and not-*F* predications at 479a–b.[60] But 477a occurs two Stephanus pages before its unheralded explanation at 479a–b. I believe, applying Kahn's thesis, that we should interpret εἶναι and τὸ ὄν at 477a, 479e, and 478e as general fact assertions—that is, as "What is the case?"—with both existential and predicative claims as special cases. For the statements have a plausible existential interpretation: Forms always are, phenomena are (exist at t_1) and are not (do not exist at t_2), and nonbeing does not exist. Also Plato can justifiably infer that if some object x is F and not-F, then x is a temporally limited existent; and if x is a temporally limited existent, then x is F and not-F. For only phenomena are F and not-F, and all phenomena are F and not-F, since they are all "one and many," and "generated and destroyed."

Nonexistence is a necessary and a sufficient condition for nonbeing. Without it we make the ancient mistake of identifying nonbeing with the receptacle in the *Timaeus*. For the bottom stratum in *Republic* V, without nonexistence, would be as close to indescribable being as possible. And this is the receptacle of the *Timaeus* that is as devoid as possible of shape or form (50d), having only some traces of the elements before the demiurgic action (53b, 48b), baffling and obscure (49a), in a baffling way partaking of the intelligible (51a), and grasped by bastard reason (52b). But nonbeing is entirely unknowable (477a), because it is nothing (μηδέν, 478b); there is nothing out there, not even a nearly indescribable receptacle, for an intentional psychic state to focus upon (cf. *Cratylus* 420b–c, *Timaeus* 45b–d, and *Republic* 477c–d). Therefore nonbeing in *Republic* V is not the receptacle.

Forms as Formal and Final Causes and The Good

To conclude with the nature of the Forms, on the visual model, let us analyze how the Forms are causes (αἰτίαι), and the nature of participation. My conclusions about these notions are, to some extent, implicit in the preceding arguments, but they should be made explicit to avoid misunderstanding.

In the early dialogues the virtues are efficient causes of acts, but in the middle ones the Forms are not efficient causes; rather they are formal and final ones. It might seem anachronistic to discuss the Forms as *aitiai* in terms of Aristotelian distinctions. But the word αἰτία in Greek has a much

broader meaning than the English "cause," and is probably best translated as "reason" or "explanation."[61] Aristotle captures the diverse uses of
αἰτία, prevalent at his time, under his four "becauses" or answers to
"Why?" questions (cf. *Physics* II, Chapter iii, *Metaphysics* 983a ff.). Thus
we are reasonably justified in approaching the Forms with Aristotelian
terminology.

The Forms are final causes. In the *Symposium* The Beautiful is the lure
for the ascent; *eros* finds its complete fulfillment in perfect, always existing
Beauty, and other beautiful things are only way stations on the route of
ascent. In the *Republic* the Forms are again the true objects of love (485b,
475e ff.,); and when a philosophical nature turns its psychic energy into
the proper channel (485d–e), it "strives emulously for true Being ... and
the edge of its passion would not be blunted ... till it came into touch with
the nature of each thing in itself ..." (490a–b). The philosophical nature,
moreover, attempts to imitate the objects of its admiration and "to fashion
itself in their likeness, and assimilate itself to them" (500c–d). It is easy to
understand why and how the Forms are the ultimate objects of human
striving. Since they are unchanging and pure, the Forms provide a type of
satisfaction that is unavailable from any other source. Not only are we
unable to completely possess them, which fires our desire, but also they
endure, unlike lesser things that ultimately fall into nonbeing. The
children of our bodies and *psyches* will all too soon be beyond memory.
Moreover, what guides the human teleological orientation is one's epistemic condition. Plato posits Justice and Injustice, Good and Evil, Beauty
and Ugliness (476a), because people strive in varying degrees for one of
each opposite pair; what guides their striving is their epistemic state.

In the *Phaedo* and *Phaedrus* there is some evidence that Plato embraces a
universal teleology, although how it operates, in nonhuman contexts, he
does not say. In the *Phaedo* the equal sticks and stones aim (βούλεται) to be
like Equality itself, but fall short and are inferior to it (74d); they yearn
(προθυμεῖται) to be like Equality, but fall short (75b). Commentators
frequently dismiss these passages as mere metaphor, but they have a
serious and deeply engrained origin. For the ancient Greeks believe that
nature is alive, the whole of it; the reeds whisper and the rivers sing, and
this is not mere metaphor. We see hylozoism in the *Phaedrus* where ψυχὴ
πᾶσα (245c), and πᾶσα ἡ ψυχή (246b) refer as much to the whole (world?)
psyche as to individual *psyches*; and, of course, there is the world *psyche* of the
Timaeus that vivifies the whole *Cosmos*. In the *Phaedo* Socrates seeks for the
Good that causes things to be placed as it is best for them to be, and that
embraces and holds together all things (ἅπαντα, 99c). While the Good
may have its greatest influence among the fiery planets, Plato does not
limit its power to this realm alone; the Good embraces and holds together
all things. In its function of embracing and holding together, the Good is

like the animistic ἀρχαί of the Milesians; the *apeiron* of Anaximander steers and guides all things as does the ἀήρ of Anaximenes. The Good has a pervasive teleological influence.

Vlastos argues that the Forms are not teleological *aitiai*. He apparently has three reasons for this claim:[62] (1) teleological causes do not exist until they are achieved, but the Forms do not come into being; (2) teleology implies change or motion, hence it is the prerogative of mind or soul, and not the Forms, since they are absolutely immutable; and (3) the second best way in the *Phaedo* hypothesizes the existence of Forms after Socrates has already admitted that he cannot find the teleological causes; and since there is no mention of teleology in the last argument for the immortality of the *psyche*, we see that the Forms are not teleological causes.

The first two reasons misunderstand the nature of Plato's teleological causes. The Forms are final causes because they always exist. Only temporally unlimited and unchanging existents could be the final satisfactory reference points of aspiration. As final causes, the Forms are unmoved as is the object of desire in Aristotle; moreover, the Forms remain unchanged although they can move other things, just as the object of desire does. Thus the teleological nature of the Forms is not incompatible with their immutability. *Psyches* move teleologically, but that for the sake of which they act is some Form; thus the Forms are ends and teleological causes.

At *Phaedo* 99e ff. Plato only claims that he has not been able to discover, or to find out from another, what The Good is. The Good, of course, is that highest teleological principle and unhypothetical ἀρχή; but when Plato proceeds to posit the existence of the Forms, this does not imply that the Forms are not lower-level teleological ἀρχαί. That Plato does not mention the teleological nature of the Forms in the last argument for the immortality of the *psyche* only shows that he is not interested in this aspect of the Forms in that argument. I conclude that there is no cogent argument against the Forms being final causes.

We have already shown that the Forms are analogous to formal causes. As paradigms they resemble, to some extent, laws or formulas that specify the necessary and sufficient conditions for "being *F*." Of course Forms are not just laws or formulas because they exist and are in fact the really existent things. Perhaps it would be better to say that Forms are the primary instantiations of laws or formulas, but this is misleading; for it suggests that there are Forms as well as the laws they instantiate, but there are only Forms. Forms are the perfect patterns that embody, and yet do not state, the necessary and sufficient conditions for "being *F*."

Edward Zeller, and more recently the Neoplatonic philosopher J. N. Findlay, believe that Forms are efficient causes.[63] The evidence for this position is very thin. In the *Republic* The Good is said to beget (ἐγέννησεν,

508c) the power of knowing in the knower and truth in the objects known; not only is The Good a Form (τὴν τοῦ ἀγαθοῦ ἰδέαν, 508e), but also it has the power (δυνάμει, 509b; δύναμιν, *Phaedo* 99c) required for such generation. Earlier in the *Republic* Forms are said to appear (φαίνεσθαι, 476a) in phenomena, and this may suggest that they appear or emanate themselves. In the *Phaedo* beautiful things are made (ποιεῖ, 100d) beautiful by The Beautiful, and The Beautiful is that by which (τῷ καλῷ, 100e) beautiful things are beautiful. Later in the *Phaedo* the language of activity, force, and possession dominates; Forms possess (κατάσχῃ) particulars, compel (ἀναγκάζει) particulars to acquire certain qualities, bring with them other Forms, and repel yet others (*Phaedo* 104d).

It is highly debatable how The Good generates the power to know and be known. That it does this by some form of efficient emanation is much less plausible than a teleological interpretation. The Good in the *Republic* is a reified version of [the knowledge of] good and evil in earlier dialogues; thus nothing else is of benefit unless we know the end that is The Good (505b, 505e–506a). The Good, then, is the ultimate object of psychic striving (505e). I suggest the following interpretation: The Good makes things intelligible because it produces their ends or functions; the essence of something is its end or function (cf. *Republic* I 352e f.), and hence The Good creates the natures of things. We know what something is if and only if we know its end or function, and so The Good both makes things intelligible and produces intelligence. At *Republic* 509b there is a famous passage that is one of the founts for Neoplatonism:

> In like manner, then, you are to say that the objects of knowledge not only receive from the presence of The Good their being known, but their very existence (τὸ εἶναι) and nature (τὴν οὐσίαν) is derived to them from it, although The Good itself is not nature, but surpasses (ὑπερέχοντες) Being or Essence (τῆς οὐσίας) in dignity and power.

The fact that The Good surpasses Being or Essence in dignity and power, reminds us of the Plotinian One that is beyond Being. Unlike the Plotinian One, however, The Good is probably only a final cause. The Good surpasses Essence because it creates the ends or essences of things, but this creation is more like a lure and pull from a terminus than an emanation. The analogy with the sun, while of great beauty, does not provide much help in understanding The Good. For the sun only activates a medium, air, and in this way makes possible, as a necessary condition, visibility and sight. Furthermore, the sun only provides a necessary condition for growth and existence. But The Good creates Being, intelligence, and intelligibility. Something exists if and only if it has an end; its essence is its end; it is intelligible only in so far as it has an essence or end, and we know it when we know its essence or end. The Good creates subordinate ends, because it is the final end towards which all things strive, and it creates intelligence because we only know things in the strongest, unhypothetical manner when we know The Good. I conclude that The Good is a final and not an efficient cause.

When Plato says at *Republic* 476a that each Form appears everywhere as many phantasma (φανταζόμενα), we are, of course, reminded of the Plotinian language of emanation. Nevertheless, this is an isolated, unique passage, and it is susceptible to different interpretations. All Plato might mean is that the Form has many visible instantiations, but this does not tell us anything about how the Form is related to its instances. The "effects" of Beauty are found in many places, but this does not imply that Beauty is an efficient cause.

Likewise, in the *Phaedo* when Plato states that The Beautiful makes things beautiful, and is that by which (the instrumental dative) things are beautiful, there need not be efficient causation. For this terminology is compatible with formal, final, or efficient causation. The Beautiful makes things beautiful because it is the "formal" paradigm of Beauty or it is that towards which beautiful things strive *qua* beautiful. When Plato proceeds to say that forms possess phenomena and compel them to have certain characteristics, it is probable that he is talking about the immanent characteristics in things (cf. *Phaedo* 102d–e), and not the separate Forms. Plato does not analyze the nature of immanent characters, but rather describes the logical conditions under which they are present; x has the immanent character F if and only if x participates in the Form F-ness. But there is some suggestion that immanent characters are like the Pre-Socratic power-elements. Dyadic relational predicates, such as "is large" and "is small," are compressed into the monadic model—Simmias' largeness and Socrates' smallness—of the Pre-Socratic power-elements. Moreover, the immanent characters have the qualities they "transmit" to their possessors (*Phaedo* 102d–e). I conclude that the language of compulsion and possession fits with the model of immanent characters that transmit their qualities to what they possess. Thus while the immanent forms are similar to efficient causes, there is no evidence that the separate Forms are.

There is also a serious philosophical objection to the claim that the separate Forms are efficient causes. The separate Forms are immutable. Thus either they have the same causal efficacy (that is, they always and constantly make the very same things F), or they change in causal efficacy. The latter alternative is consistent with experience since phenomena come to be and cease to be, for example, beautiful, but it is incompatible with the immutable nature of a Form. The former alternative is consistent with the immutable nature of a Form, but it is incompatible with experience; the membership in the class of beautiful things changes. I conclude that Forms are final causes, are analogous to formal causes, and are not efficient causes.

Participation

Participation is one of the most frequently discussed problems in Plato, and yet, paradoxically, very little is said about why things participate in Forms. Debate centers about whether Forms share univocal, nonunivocal, or equivocal predicates with their participants, and whether participation is partaking, resembling, copying, being a resemblance of, or the like. I have already argued that Forms and their participants have univocal predicates. Only in this way are the two worlds unified; univocal predication is a necessary ingredient in coherent accounts of paradigmatism, recollection, participation, and formal or final causation. Plato's terminology of participation is fluid, although, as has recently been argued, there may be a development in his thought from simple partaking, to resembling, ultimately to copying or being a resemblance of a Form.[64] Univocal predication is essential to each of these accounts; and when we discuss the *Timaeus*, I will show that even if phenomena are resemblances of or copies of Forms, they also resemble those Forms. A successful resemblance resembles its original.

The overlooked question is why sensible particulars participate in, copy, or imitate the Forms. Very little attention is given to this question either by commentators (Lee and Turnbull are exceptions[65]), or by Plato. Since our evidence is very tentative, our conclusions also must be. "Participate," "resemble," "imitate," and "copy," are verbs that suggest agency on the part of what participates, copies, etc. Now while Plato frequently describes sensible particulars as imitations or copies, he also uses the verb forms and says that phenomena participate in, imitate, or copy (*Phaedo* 74e, 100c) the Forms. This suggests that the phenomena are active in the process of participation; they participate in, imitate, or copy. Earlier we discussed a passage in the *Phaedo* (74d f.) where equal things aim or desire to be *like* Equality but fall short and are deficient. Perhaps we are to see this as a general account of why phenomena participate, imitate, or copy the Forms; they strive to be like them but fall short and are deficient in that they never obtain the pure, context-free possession of a quality. *Psyche* is undoubtedly the source of motion in dialogues of all periods, but this is not an objection to this interpretation. For Plato's *Cosmos* is animated and vivified from center to periphery by *psyche*, and even the sticks and stones are in some sense alive.

I find this interpretation very attractive, but it has one great drawback: why do unintelligent forms of life strive to imitate some Forms but not others? This question admits of no more of an answer from Plato than how in the *Phaedrus* those *psyches* that have fallen into ants and hawks can reclaim themselves and escape from the wheel of rebirth. *Nous* cannot exist without *psyche*, but is all *psyche* somehow intelligent? In *Republic* IV appetitive *psyche* is "intentional," it is of thirst or sex; but I do not see how Plato can extend this to the sticks and stones that strive for Equality.

The Discursive Account of Knowledge

Let us now turn to the discursive account of knowledge, and its implications for the Forms. Besides the mental vision of the Forms, Plato has another method for investigating them: a philosopher can study the Forms through the use of *logoi*. This investigation presupposes a referential theory of meaning. Names (ὄνομα), a notion that in the middle dialogues covers general nouns and adjectives, must have fixed meanings, that is, the Forms (*Republic* 507b–c, 596a, *Parmenides* 135b–c), or otherwise discourse would be impossible. The major problem of the *Cratylus*, whether names are used to refer to their objects by natural imitation or by convention, presupposes a referential theory of meaning. Plato, moreover, extends his referential theory so that not only do names denote Forms, but also the Forms must interrelate just as the dialectician correctly connects names in noncontingent *logoi*, and the *logoi* noncontingently with each other. Even if names do not mirror or picture Forms, their correct connections in *logoi* do, and this is required if the dialectician is to investigate both the Forms and their connections through *logoi* (cf. *Phaedo* 100a ff.).

First I will discuss Plato's definitions of particular Forms and their implications for the Forms; then I will discuss dialectic and its implications. The tendencies described in this section culminate with greater force and vividness in the late dialogues, especially in the *Sophist*. I will show that as the Forms come to be seen through *logoi* they: (1) become internally complex—although they are not physical composites, they are no longer uniform; and (2) begin to take on contrary predicates, and thus they are no longer epistemic paradigms.

In the *Republic* Plato defines justice as "each part doing its proper work": a *psyche* is just when its components do their proper work, and a state is just when each of its citizens does his proper work, that is, engages in the correct moral and occupational behavior. Is, then, "each part doing its proper work" also a definition of the Form Justice, or does it only define the justice *in* a man and *in* a state? Plato admits that the method he uses to define a *psyche's* justice cannot produce an accurate (ἀκριβῶς) understanding (435d). Presumably this is because it relies on an incompletely tested hypothesis, in this case the hypothesis that "the same thing will never do or suffer opposites in the same respect, in relation to the same thing, and at the same time" (436b, 436e–437a). Plato removes certain superficial objections to this hypothesis, but it still needs a more thorough grounding. Would a better method yield a different definition, this time about the Form, Justice? In *Republic* VI (504d–505a), Plato states that the longer and better method makes use of knowledge of The Good, and that it produces accurate, unhypothetical understanding. He does not suggest, however, that the better method yields a different definition of Justice: rather it disarms objections to the hypothesis upon which the earlier one is based, and grounds that account in an unhypothetical first principle. The longer method gives a complete unhypothetical account of Justice, if only we knew The Good. Thus unless we are to believe that Plato never defines the Form Justice, it also must be "each part doing its proper work"; for no other account of Justice occurs in Plato's *Republic*. But what are the "parts" and what is the "whole" that this account presupposes even when it is applied to the Form Justice? Plato provides an answer to this in *Republic* VI (500b–c):

> The man whose mind is truly fixed on eternal realities fixes his gaze upon the things of the eternal and unchanging order, and seeing that they neither wrong [do injustice] nor are wronged [suffer injustice] by one another (οὔτ᾽ ἀδικοῦντα οὔτ᾽ ἀδικούμενα ὑπ᾽ ἀλλήλων) but all abide in harmony (κόσμῳ) as reason bids, he will endeavor to imitate them . . . and to fashion himself in their likeness. . . .

When Plato views Justice through its *logos*, it is a meta-Form; it is each of the other Forms doing its proper work, so that the Forms constitute a just and harmonious world. The paradigm of Justice is no longer the simple, uniform Form, but the whole Form-world, and the harmonious interrelations between its constituents. This conception of Justice is implied by Plato's definition, and Justice is clearly a complex Form, since its very nature is to be a *cosmos* of elements. Since the eternal Beings are in harmony, they connect with each other; and although Plato does not cash in his metaphor of harmony in this passage, harmony is the first stage in a development that ends with the "analytic" connections between Forms.

But Plato also believes in the *Republic* that Justice is an incomposite, atomistic paradigm. For the Forms are "one" (476a, 479a, 507b–c), and this implies that they are incomposite and ungenerated; moreover, the Forms are pure paradigms for mental vision, and this implies that they are uniform, which in turn implies that they are isolated. An isolated, pure paradigm, however, cannot be an object of definition, for a definition presupposes either external relations to other things or connections between internal components. Without some form of complexity and connection, definition is impossible. Thus the pure paradigms for mental vision are not what is seen through *logoi*, and Plato begins to develop diverse notions of the Form Justice, one corresponding to the visual and the other to the discursive route for knowledge. I do not believe that Plato was conscious of these diverse strains; for if he were, he would not claim, without serious modification, that there is one and only one Form for each type (*Republic* 597b ff.).

It is also interesting to note that the isolation and connection of the Forms is mirrored in diverse accounts of the *psyche*. In the *Phaedo*, *nous*, as pure intellect that is isolated from the body and its desires, imitates and grasps the isolated, incomposite Forms; but in the *Republic* the harmonious tripartite *psyche*, composed of reason, spirit, and appetite, imitates in its justice the Justice of the Form-world as a whole. Thus Plato employs Justice both as a pure paradigm and as a meta-Form, that is, as the harmonious connections between all of the Forms including first-order Justice.

Plato's definition of The Beautiful leads to a similar position. In dialogues of diverse periods Beauty is identified with *cosmos*,[66] and the instantiation of this characteristic in phenomena produces benefit and pleasure (cf. *Philebus* 26a–b, *Gorgias* 503e ff., 474d–e, and the *Hippias Major*). A beautiful *psyche* is an ordered one, a good and noble life exhibits order, and even the *Cosmos* is as perfect as possible because of its *cosmos* (*Gorgias* 507e–508a, *Timaeus* 29e–30a). Moreover, Plato assimilates several important Forms to a single highest principle of order; The Beautiful, The Good, Justice, Temperance, and even Truth are all *cosmos*, and hence, in this respect, identical with each other (cf. *Philebus* 65a, *Phaedo* 99c, *Republic* 430e, 486d). Each of these Forms, however, has a different emphasis: The Beautiful a visible and aesthetic (cf. *Phaedrus* 250d), The Good a value-oriented, utilitarian, and epistemological (cf. *Republic* 505b, 506a, 505e), Justice and Temperance an ethical, and the Truth an ontological and epistemological. Plato does not separate and compartmentalize these considerations into distinct subjects as we do today. If something is really beneficial (of utility), then it is noble (of aesthetic and ethical value), and what is really noble is real Being that is also the only possible object of knowledge. Thus the Forms are the objects of knowledge, aesthetic appreciation, ethical value, personal and political benefit, and ultimate satisfaction.

When seen through *logoi*, Beauty, Goodness, Truth, and the like are complex entities; they are a harmony of constituent elements. As such they are incompatible with the conception of the Forms as atomistic paradigms.[67] But we are forced to admit both of these conceptions of Beauty because Plato states the atomistic view at, for example, *Symposium* 210e–211a; although whenever he gives a *logos* of The Beautiful it is in terms of *cosmos*. Beauty as a harmony of Forms is Justice, but it emphasizes the aesthetic more than the moral nature of the whole Form-world.

Plato states that the *Republic* is an attempt to sketch in speech a paradigm of a good city (παράδειγμα ἐποιοῦμεν λόγῳ ἀγαθῆς πόλεως, 472e). Furthermore, he compares the philosophical activity of the *Republic* to artistic creation, and the philosopher to an artist, but unlike the justly reviled imitator of phenomena, the philosopher makes his sketch by looking at and using the Forms as models (500d, 501b).[68] Does the pictorial status of the *Republic* as an attempt to sketch in speech, mold, and define the Ideal City commit Plato to the existence of a very complex Form of the City? Perhaps Plato could explain this pictorial status by reference to a limited number of the other Forms, such as Justice, Temperance, The Good, and their interconnections. Nevertheless, at *Republic* IX (592a–b) he posits, with some hesitation, a Form of The Ideal City:

> ... in his [the philosopher's] own city he certainly will [partake in politics], yet perhaps not in the city of his birth .... You mean the city whose establishment we have described, the one that is posited in speech (τῇ ἐν λόγοις κειμένῃ) since it can be found nowhere on earth .... Perhaps there is a pattern of it laid up in the universe (ἐν οὐρανῷ ἴσως παράδειγμα ἀνάκειται) for him who wishes to see it and in seeing it to constitute himself its citizen.

Plato's tentative positing of this Form is an extreme application of his referential theory of meaning. Since the *Republic* is a presumably consistent and coherent set of *logoi* that define The Ideal City, it must picture how the Forms connect to make the complex Form of the City. This Form is at least as complex as the Animal itself that contains within itself the Forms of all other living things (*Timaeus* 30c–d, 39e–40a). We are now far removed from the conception of a Form as an atomistic, uniform, pure paradigm for intellectual vision. The Form of The Ideal City is a complex, multiform, composed from the interweaving of Justice, Courage, Goodness, and the like, and supplemented by, we might imagine, a knowledge of natural types: the lover of appetite, wisdom, and honor. Human nature must be correctly molded by a philosopher king who looks at the Forms for there to be an ideal city.

Two passages best exemplify the dialectical route (*Phaedo* 99d–100a, and *Republic* 537c):

> After this, then, said he, since I had given up investigating realities, I decided that I must be careful not to suffer the misfortune which happens to people who look at the sun and watch it during an eclipse. For some of them ruin their eyes unless they look at its image in water or something of the sort. I thought of that danger, and I was afraid my *psyche* would be blinded if I looked at things with my eyes and tried to grasp them with any of my senses. So I thought I must

have recourse to *logoi* and examine in them the truth of realities. Now perhaps my metaphor is not quite accurate; for I do not grant in the least that he who studies realities by means of *logoi* is looking at them in images any more than he who studies them in the facts of daily life. However, that is the way I began. I assume in each case some principle which I consider strongest, and whatever seems to me to agree with this, whether relating to cause or to anything else, I regard as true, and whatever disagrees with it, as untrue.

For he who can view things in their connection (συνοπτικός) is a dialectician; he who cannot, is not.

The interpretation of the *Phaedo* passage is far from clear. If we identify the investigation of realities in facts (ἔργοις) or deeds with recollection, then the point of the passage is more intelligible. To examine Forms, starting from phenomena, is no more real a route than to investigate them through *logoi*. To see Forms through *logoi* is not to use images any more than the visual ascent that begins from phenomena. Thus the *Phaedo* passage asserts an equal validity for both the visual and the discursive routes. Plato proceeds to hypothesize that there are Forms, and that Forms are explanations; he then draws certain consequences from these hypothetical starting points: Forms are safe or uninformative explanations; Forms also provide more refined, extended, and informative explanations because they connect with each other. The discursive route leads to an investigation of the connections between Forms, and in the *Republic* passage the dialectician is he who has a synoptic view of such connections.

Since dialectic is the weaving together of *logoi* in order to obtain a synoptic view, it implies that the Forms connect together; and such connections, I will argue, lead to their having contrary predicates. Plato uses διαλέγεσθαι to mean simply "discussion" or "discourse" and for this reason he applies the term to most types of philosophical discussion. He also states that there are different types of διαλέγεσθαι and that they should be fitted to different kinds of *psyches* (*Phaedrus* 271b ff.), a view that he exemplifies in the dialogues. Plato is not, at least in the middle dialogues, dogmatic about what the highest philosophical discourse is, but rather appears to experiment with different philosophical techniques. I will discuss two such techniques: the noetic ascent in the *Republic*, and division and collection in the *Phaedrus*, in order to see their implications for the Forms.

Plato's description of noetic ascent in the *Republic* is unfortunately brief and obscure (*Republic* 511b–c). Starting with an hypothesis, a dialectician proceeds up through hypotheses until an unhypothetical ἀρχή is reached; then he proceeds downward from the ἀρχή, using only annihilated or unhypothesized hypotheses, until the original or starting hypothesis is proven. Plato states that these movements are through both hypotheses and Forms, and the inclusion of Forms implies that they are structured similarly to the hypotheses. Plato does not, however, clarify how one hypothesis is "higher" or "lower" than another, although his analogies with mathematical procedure and his metaphors of "higher" and "lower" suggest that, as we can now state it, the higher hypotheses will entail the lower.[69] The ontological correlate of the noetic method would then be that the higher Forms contain the lower as, perhaps, a Leibnizian subject contains its predicates. In any case, the "higher" Forms must be rich enough in complexity that they "include" and "entail" the lower ones. If this interpretation is correct, the Forms are complex entities that "embrace" or "contain" other such entities; furthermore, some Forms are "higher" than others and "lower" than yet others. When Forms lose their isolation and begin to interconnect, the emergence of contrary predicates is inevitable.

This inclusion of contrariety would, we might speculate, be most evident at the level of The Good. For The Good not only is a Form (508e), but also it has, as the unhypothetical starting point, the function of unifying, containing, and making intelligible the whole Form-world. But Plato clearly posits Forms corresponding to contraries (for example, Justice and Injustice, Good and Evil, Beauty and Ugliness, *Republic* 476a); and thus The Good would have to contain such contraries. How such containment is possible Plato does not say, but it has definite adverse ramifications for the purity of some "higher" Forms, although we do not know whether or not Plato was aware of this.

Plato gives in the *Phaedrus*, perhaps for the first time, an *account* of division and collection dialectic.[70] The principles of discourse are (265d–e):

> That of perceiving and bringing together in one Form (ἰδέαν) the scattered particulars, that one may make clear by definition the particular thing that he wishes to explain; ... That of dividing things again by Forms (κατ' εἴδη), where the natural joints are, and not trying to break any part (μέρος), after the manner of a bad carver.

When Plato practices division and collection dialectic, the Forms cannot be incomposite monads. The Forms do not have physical parts, and thus they are not composite like phenomena; but they are internally complex, and hence they are no longer uniform. Forms now have natural joints and are probably arranged in genus/species hierarchies.[71] The nonspecific Forms, then, could not be pure because they contain incompatible differentiae. This conception of an εἶδος as seen through division and collection dialectic dominates the late dialogues and even the *Timaeus*, where The Animal itself is the container for the other genera and species. Aristotle also argues that paradigms cannot be genera (*Metaphysics* Z 14), for since paradigms are substances, that is, individuals, they cannot contain incompatible differentiae, whereas Aristotelian genera can because they are not individuals.

I do not claim that Plato is explicitly aware of the two strands of his thought. He frequently combines and interweaves both the visual and the discursive routes to knowledge and the different conceptions of Form that connect with these routes. Nevertheless, both routes are found in the text, and they represent different and incompatible components in Plato's middle-period thought.

What are the Forms on the discursive model? Certainly they remain separate and ontologically prior to their instances as do the pure paradigms; that is, a Form can exist uninstantiated, although no instance of a Form can exist without the Form, and the Forms are aspatial and temporally unlimited in existence. When Plato posits a Form for The Ideal City and claims that it can be found nowhere on earth (*Republic* 592a–b), he certainly suggests that not all Forms are instantiated. But we should not be dogmatic on this point. For at *Republic* 472b–c Plato states that we must be satisfied if men approximate as much as possible to the moral Forms, and he may believe that any or most cities contain some justice, and hence imperfectly instantiate the Form of The Ideal City. But Forms do not have the power to spawn, efficiently, earthly resemblances, and as formal and final causes there is no absurdity involved in the notion of an uninstantiated Form. Forms are separate from phenomena because they are aspatial, and they are aspatial because they lack physical composition. Thus both notions of Form share in common many characteristics.

On the discursive model, all the predicates of Forms are had necessarily. In those passages where Plato clearly discusses the connections between Forms, his examples are of what we would call noncontingent connections. Thus the Forms continue to be the objects of knowledge, because they are the proper objects described by temporally indefinite sentences. But on the discursive model the definite descriptive "self"-predicates of the Forms recede into the background; what is now of importance is those predicates that are had through the connections between the Forms. Plato begins to map out the Form-world by displaying, through *logoi*, the connections between its members.

In conclusion: Plato uses both intellectual vision and dialectic as models for knowledge. Moreover, these models connect with inconsistent conceptions of Form: on the former a Form is an isolated, incomposite, pure paradigm; on the latter it is internally complex, composite, impure, and interwoven with the other Forms. My intent is not to hang Plato with an inconsistency, for I believe that he tends towards a resolution of the inconsistency, although he probably was not explicitly aware of it, the different models for knowledge, or his development. In his early exuberance with the Forms he: (1) tends to rely on the visual model; (2) is concerned more with specific Forms than the Form-world; (3) juxtaposes the purity of the Forms with the impurity of phenomena; and (4) introduces the Forms to explain the contrary characteristics of phenomena. With maturity he: (A) tends to see the Forms through *logoi*; (B) is concerned with large segments of the Form-world rather than with specific Forms; (C) emphasizes the interweaving of the Forms; and (D) begins to rely on a general one-over-many argument to introduce the Forms. There is, then, a clear but gradual development in Plato's middle-period thought, although backslidings to the visual model frequently occur. This development occurs both within particular dialogues and across the middle dialogues. The *Phaedo* opens discussion of the Forms with their visual recollection, and concludes the investigation of immortality by seeing them through *logoi*; the *Phaedrus* first pictures us as seeing the Forms while traveling with the gods, but proceeds to discuss division and collection dialectic; the *Republic's* early concern with the moral Forms, and especially Justice, gives way to the synoptic view of the dialectician in Book VII. Furthermore, although *logoi* and vision are usually complementary, there is a clear distinction between the emphasis on vision in the middle works and the priority of philosophical method and *logoi* in the late ones.

The *Parmenides* (129a–130e), *Symposium* (210e–211a), *Phaedo* (74b–c, 102a ff.), and *Republic* (476a, 479a–c, 523b–524c, 507c) juxtapose the pure Forms with the impure phenomena, and some of these passages posit the Forms to explain the contrary characteristics of phenomena. But in the late middle dialogue *Phaedrus* (249b–c) Plato uses a general version of the one-over-many argument, that is, one where contrary Forms or characteristics are clearly not uppermost in his thought. This one-over-many argument is the backbone of division and collection, and the new reason for positing the Forms. In the *Philebus* Plato explicitly remarks on this development (14c–15c; also see *Sophist* 251a–c): the problem of how a particular can have contrary predicates is childish and worthy of disregard, but how an εἶδος can be one thing that is common to many is still very perplexing. There is, then, a shift in motivation for positing the Forms: Plato no longer contrasts their purity with the impurity of phenomena, but rather he posits them on the basis of the one-over-many argument. I will show in the last chapter that this new emphasis is connected with an ever-increasing interest, first visible in the *Phaedrus*, in kinds and their delineation through division and collection.

4

The Crisis of the *Parmenides*

Plato does not metaspeculate to any great extent about his philosophical concerns, and that he does not is a matter of regret to his readers. Plato never asks what is a Form, or what is participation, and where he comes closest to the latter question in the *Parmenides*, Plato does not inform us about his attitude toward the arguments. We do not know, at least from the *Parmenides*, whether Plato thinks that, for example, the third man arguments are sound or unsound. The best we can do, then, is to look at the arguments themselves. I will show that several arguments in the *Parmenides* are sound against the pure Forms of the visual model; that is, they successfully attack the purity and uniformity of a separate Form.

Although Plato's attitude toward the arguments of the *Parmenides* is unclear, he thrice expresses, with great emphasis, the same belief: he would be very surprised if the Forms have contrary predicates like phenomena. For if they do, then they could not save phenomena from the Heraclitean identity of opposites, and, moreover, they would not be pure paradigms for vision. Plato's emphasis on this problem implies that it is the key to understanding the *Parmenides*. I will argue that Parmenides, the dramatic figure, attempts to show that Forms suffer contrary predicates: they are one and many, one—unique and incomposite—in themselves, and many because of the implications of participation. The dramatic character Parmenides reenacts his historical predecessor's belief that any plurality, including a plurality of Forms, implies the identity of opposites, and hence the nonexistence of plurality.[1] Plato does not, however, retract his belief in Forms; Forms must exist, if discourse is to be possible. What is required to save the Forms is a dialectical study of their predicates, and their connections. In other words, a renewed emphasis on the discursive model for knowledge is needed. Such an investigation would show how F-ness can be both F and not-F. Ultimately, as I will argue, the *Sophist* takes up precisely this question; but whether transcendent Forms will emerge from an extensive investigation of form interconnections is a topic for the next chapter.

Parmenides and Zeno have come to Athens, and they are very close friends, both philosophically and otherwise (or so Plato claims). Zeno reads a treatise, of typical Eleatic style, that purports to pay back the proponents of the many with even greater absurdities than they believe are implied by the hypothesis that "all things are one" (128c–d). We have good reason to believe that the dramatic characters, Parmenides and Zeno, are not in every respect accurate proponents of their historical predecessors' positions. The real Parmenides anchored his philosophy about a theory of Being, while the dramatic Parmenides' fundamental view is the unitarian claim that "all things are one."[2] The latter claim, however, has increasing prominence in Eleatic thought after Parmenides, and is an important test for Being. Furthermore, the dramatic figures, Parmenides and Zeno, adequately represent Eleatic argumentation as to style, intent, and rigor, if not in detail and mere reduplication of historical arguments. For example, a major weapon of the Eleatics, the destructive dilemma, is used to great effect in the *Parmenides*.[3]

Plato, with his eye on the historical facts, gives them an ironical twist; we know that the real Zeno defends Parmenides, but in the *Parmenides* the dramatic character Parmenides defends Zeno, and thus indirectly supports his own thesis that "all is one." But with another twist, the dramatic Parmenides does not draw the expected conclusion, but instead claims that a defense of the Forms is most difficult, and will require a great dialectical effort (133b–c, 135a). Parmenides, who has just attacked his own contribution to the Forms, their oneness, in a startling turn of events, finds the hypothesis that there are Forms necessary for discourse and leads Socrates in a dialectical attempt to investigate them.[4]

Zeno claims that if existences (τὰ ὄντα) are many, then the same things are like and unlike, which is impossible (ἀδύνατον, 127e). The purpose of his treatise is to prove that there is no multiplicity (127e), and Zeno admits that he is saying very much the same thing as Parmenides, for he claims that there is no many, while Parmenides shows that all is one (128c–d). Zeno's attack on multiplicity is unrestricted in scope; any plurality, including a plurality of Forms, is susceptible to Zeno's argument. This is a clue about how the Eleatics will attack the Forms; for the Forms are like any other plurality whose members will suffer contrary predicates. But as I argued earlier, the objects of intellectual acquaintance are a plurality of isolated members. Isolation is a necessary condition for the purity and uniformity of a Form. Thus Parmenides cannot directly attack the Forms by displaying the implications of their mixture and separation. Parmenides cannot assume that Forms have connections like those mirrored among phenomena. Forms, moreover, are separate from phenomena, although phenomena participate in them. Since many sensible particulars participate in a single "isolated" Form, there is an Eleatic entry for attack into Plato's pluralism. If each Form were completely isolated, then it would be as immune as Parmenides' Being from the Heraclitean identity of opposites. But complete isolation is impossible, since the Forms must save the phenomena. Hence separation is not enough, since it is separation with participation, and this is a weakness in Plato's two–tiered pluralism of Forms and phenomena. For this reason Parmenides investigates participation rather than the direct connections between Forms, but his motive remains the same: to display the contrary predicates of the plurality.

Zeno believes that his arguments against the possibility of plurality are sound, but their cogency lies in his failure to distinguish predication and identity. To say that "what is *F* is not-*F*" is, the Eleatics believe, to claim that what has the nature *F* also has the nature not-*F*, which is impossible.[5] Zeno's arguments immediately introduce the crucial problem of the *Parmenides*: how can one thing be many or the many things one; or how can the one be many and the many one? Both Zeno and Plato favor the latter formulation. For the use of the article in τὸ ἕν, "the one" or "what is one," and in τὰ πολλά, "the many" or "what is many," suggests that it is the nature of the one to be one, and of the many to be many. In the case of phenomena, Zeno could then show that the one is many and the many are one (cf. *Phaedrus* 261d, where the Eleatic Palamedes is said to do just this), and these results appear to be contradictions since "what is [the nature of] one is also many" and the converse.[6]

Plato's Forms are set up, and legitimately so, for the same perplexity: for The One is purely one, its nature is to be one; and The Many is purely many, its nature is to be many. Thus if The One should be many, or The Many one, an impossible consequence follows; for a nature would have the contrary of that nature. I will show that this is precisely what happens to the Forms. A philosophical resolution to such perplexities requires a sorting out of the identity and predicative senses of "to be," as well as an account of how εἴδη can have contrary predicates. Both endeavors occur and interrelate in the *Sophist*, and the *Parmenides* ultimately points to the *Sophist* when it urges a dialectical investigation of the εἴδη.

At 129a Socrates introduces the Forms to escape the perplexity of Zeno's conclusion:

> But tell me, do you not believe there is a Form of Likeness itself, and another Form of Unlikeness, the opposite of the first, and that you and I and all things that we call many partake of these two? And that those which partake of Likeness become like, and those which partake of Unlikeness become unlike, and those which partake of both become both like and unlike, all in the manner and degree of their participation?

Plato introduces the Forms to explain the contrary characteristics of phenomena, and hence to save them from inconsistency. He explains relational and incomplete predicates by analyzing them all as the participation in a Form. The Forms, then, have a connection with phenomena because the latter participate in them, even though the Forms are separate.

At 129b f. Socrates specifically states that the Forms explain one/many problems among phenomena:

> [It is not at all strange] if he shows that all things are one by participation in Unity (τοῦ ἑνός) and that the same are also many by participation in The Many (τῷ πλήθους).... He will say, when he wishes to show that I am many, that there are my right parts and my left parts, my front parts and my back parts, likewise upper and lower, all different; for I do, I suppose, partake of Multitude; and when he wishes to show that I am one, he will say that we here are seven persons, of whom I am one, a man, partaking of Unity; and so he shows that both assertions are true.

Since the Forms explain one/many problems among phenomena, they cannot, themselves, suffer such problems. For if they did, they would stand in need of explanation as much as the phenomena do, and hence the Forms would not satisfactorily explain the one/many perplexities about phenomena.

As we have already seen, "is one" is a metapredicate of all the Forms, since each Form is incomposite and unique. Now while Parmenides does not directly attack The Many, it is open for him to claim that The Many is one, and such an assertion is a perfectly well-formed and theoretically necessary claim about a Form. Moreover, it raises one/many problems at the Form level, and if left unsolved such problems would obviously negate the explanatory and epistemic functions of at least some Forms. The One, on the other hand, is, in a sense, many because it has many participants; in fact all of the Forms that are incomposite and unique are also, as we will see, many because each has many participants. Parmenides follows this route of attack, and he attempts to force Plato to admit that each Form which must be one is yet, due to participation, many. As Plato, himself, says (129c):

> ... but if he shows that absolute Unity is also many, and the absolute Many again are one, then I shall be amazed. The same applies to all other things. If he shows that the kinds and Forms in themselves (ἐν αὐτοῖς) possess these opposite qualities, it is marvelous; but if he shows that I am both one and many, what marvel is there in that?

The Visual-Model Forms

In the *Parmenides* Plato reaffirms the essential characteristics of the middle-period Forms.[7] At 130b Parmenides asks:

Tell me, did you invent this distinction yourself, which separates (χωρίς) the Forms themselves from the things that partake in them? And do you think there is such a thing as Likeness itself apart from (χωρίς) the likeness that we possess (ἡμεῖς ὁμοιότητος ἔχομεν) and One and Many, and all of the things you hear Zeno speaking about just now?

Socrates answers this question affirmatively. This passage clearly asserts the separation of a Form from its participants, and for this it uses what for Plato is the rare term χωρίς. In this passage Plato distinguishes the Forms from the immanent characteristics that we possess, as he does earlier in the *Phaedo*.

Plato posits without question Forms for "the things Zeno was speaking about," and Zeno's arguments pivoted upon problems concerning relational and incomplete predicates. Thus the extension of the Form theory clearly covers these characteristics, as well as moral qualities, just as in the middle dialogues; but there is now some question in the *Parmenides* about whether there are also Forms corresponding to sortal characteristics (130b–d). The extension of the Form theory in the *Parmenides* thus at least includes that found in the middle dialogues. Later I will analyze the importance of 130b–d.

Plato posits Forms for the same reason in the *Parmenides*, the *Phaedo*, and the *Republic*: to explain the contrary characteristics of phenomena. Also at 130e–131a Plato describes the same theory of primary and derivative designation that is found in the *Phaedo*; the participants in the Forms are named after them (also cf. 133d). Forms in the *Parmenides* are also pure and uniform; the self-predication of a Form is, as I will show, a key premise in at least three of Parmenides' arguments against the Forms. Self-predication is a necessary condition both for the Forms to be the explanations for contrary characteristics, and for them to be the primary bearers of the predicates derivatively ascribed to phenomena. Plato also believes in the *Parmenides* that the Forms are in themselves (αὐτὰ καθ' αὑτά, 133a); and while this terminology is most frequently used to isolate the Forms from phenomena, Plato also intends to isolate the Forms "in themselves" (ἐν αὑτοῖς, 129c) from each other, so that they cannot have opposite characteristics. For this reason he denies that opposite Forms, and probably any Forms, can be mingled with and separated from each other (129e).

In Chapter II I argue that Plato's application of the predicate "one" to the Forms is an Eleatic legacy. Each Form is incomposite and unique, just as is Eleatic Being. Parmenides' arguments challenge the pure application of the predicate, and different arguments attack one or the other meaning of "one." Parmenides, himself, sums up the force of his arguments at 133a–b by saying that Socrates has not even yet grasped "the greatness of the difficulty involved in your assumption that each Form is one (ἓν εἶδος ἕκαστον), and separate from the other beings." The Forms in the *Parmenides* are, then, one, self-predicated, themselves in themselves, separate, and the explanations for the contrary characteristics of phenomena. The *Parmenides* thus analyzes the same conception of a Form that is found in the middle dialogues in conjunction with the visual model. A primary component of this theory is that a Form is purely self-predicated, and does not suffer *F* and not-*F* predicates, so that it can be a pure, unchaotic paradigm for visual acquaintance and judgment. Ironically, Parmenides attacks his own legacy to the Forms: the pure application of the predicate "one".

The Challenge to Parmenides

After introducing the Forms to save the phenomena, Socrates challenges Parmenides as follows:

(A) And even if all [sensible] things partake of both opposites, and are enabled by their participation to be both like and unlike themselves, what is there wonderful about that? But if anyone showed that the Like things themselves become unlike, or the Unlike things like, that would, in my opinion, be a wonder ... (129a–b, also cf. d).

(B) If he shows that the kinds and Forms in themselves possess these opposite qualities, it is marvelous (129c).

(C) If, however, as I was saying just now, he first distinguishes the Forms, themselves in themselves, such as Likeness and Unlikeness, Multitude and Unity, Rest and Motion, and the like, and then shows that they can be mingled and separated, I should, said he, be filled with amazement, Zeno (129d–e).

(D) ... as I say, I should be more amazed if anyone could show in the Forms in themselves ... this same multifarious and perplexing entanglement that you described in visible objects (129e–130a).

Challenges (A)–(D) are, I believe, related. The neuter plurals αὐτὰ τὰ ὅμοια ("the Like things themselves") and τὰ ἀνόμοια ("the Unlike things") at 129b are clear references to the Forms, and they imply self-predication. Plato refers to the Forms Likeness, Unlikeness, and Multiplicity with the neuter plurals because these Forms are self-predicated; for if, for example, the Many is many, then it is the perfect multiplicity, and hence the plural grammatical form is the correct way to refer to it.

When Plato challenges Parmenides in (A) to show that Likeness is unlike, Unlikeness like, The One many and The Many one (οὐ τὸ ἓν πολλὰ οὐδὲ τὰ πολλὰ ἕν, 129d), we should assume that each Form is self-predicated; thus Plato's challenge is for Parmenides to show that Likeness is like and unlike, and The One is one and many. Challenges (B) and (D) confirm this interpretation, and also suggest an extension of it. The Forms would possess opposite qualities and suffer the same perplexing entanglements as visible objects, if the contrary of their self-predicate, *or if any contrary predicates*, were said of them. For Zeno purports to prove that if phenomena are in any way *F* and not-*F*, then they are impossible and nonexistent. (C) suggests the more narrow challenge, since Socrates enumerates pairs of contrary Forms; if contrary Forms could mix with each other, then a Form would have a predicate contrary to its self-predicate; for example, Likeness would be unlike, and Rest would be in motion. Thus Socrates generically challenges Parmenides to show that Forms have contrary predicates, and specifically that they have a predicate contrary to their self-predicate. Parmenides takes up the former challenge through an investigation of participation, but he does not attempt the more specific challenge since he cannot assume *ab initio* that the Forms interconnect.

Commentators have almost completely ignored Socrates' challenge,[8] but it is implausible that a challenge, one that is elaborated with such care and repetition, would go unanswered by Parmenides. The interpretation I will present of 131a–c and of the third man arguments has the advantage of illuminating Parmenides' response to the challenge. Although Socrates firmly believes that the Forms are incomposite and unique, Parmenides shows that on any of the suggested accounts of participation, the Forms are either composite or not unique, that is, a multiplicity. Socrates not only is unable to give up the oneness of each Form, but also he cannot refute the dialectical results of Parmenides' arguments; hence each Form, which must be one, is yet many, and so the Forms have the same perplexities that Zeno attributes to phenomena.[9] The coexistence of contrary predicates in the Forms makes it impossible either for the Forms to save the phenomena, or by an application of Zeno's reasoning that Parmenides does not pursue, for them to exist themselves. We have then a complex dramatic situation where Parmenides defends his pupil Zeno—a reversal of the historical situation—against the Forms, and hence, by implication, supports his own thesis that "all is one."

Parmenides' Response

Let us now turn to the arguments seriatim. Parmenides first questions Socrates about the extension of the Form theory. Socrates readily admits that there are the Forms Likeness, One, Many, Justice, The Beautiful,

The Good, and "all such things," but he is troubled about whether there are Forms corresponding to the predicates "man," "fire," and "water," and he thinks it absurd to posit Forms for hair, mud, dirt, and any other vile and worthless thing (130b–d). Yet even in respect to the last case Socrates says that he is "... sometimes disturbed by the thought that perhaps what is true of one thing is true of all. Then when I have taken up this position, I run away for fear of falling into some abyss of nonsense and perishing; so when I come to those things which we were just saying do have Forms, I stay and busy myself with them" (130d).

This passage reflects, I believe, Plato's emerging uncertainty about the grounds for positing the Forms. Likeness, One, and Many are posited because phenomena have the corresponding characteristics impurely. The same consideration contributes to the belief in moral and aesthetic Forms since phenomena are just in one respect and unjust in another, beautiful in one comparison and ugly in another. Thus Plato also posits moral and aesthetic Forms on the ground that phenomena have such characteristics impurely. A similar reason, however, cannot be given for Forms corresponding to sortal predicates; phenomena have these predicates necessarily and purely.

But we may see Plato moving in the *Parmenides* (132a–b, 132d, 133a), to an argument that generates a Form for every general predicate, including hair, mud, and dirt. This is a completely general one-over-many argument: if many things are Φ, then there must be a single Form, Φ-ness, in virtue of which they all are Φ; or if things resemble one another in respect of Φ, then there must be a single Form, Φ-ness, in virtue of which they resemble one another in respect Φ. These types of one-over-many arguments generate Forms for all recurrent characteristics, and they certainly justify Socrates' fear that "what is true of one thing [one recurrent characteristic] is true of all."

Parmenides' remonstration to Socrates that it is because of his youth and reliance on others' opinions (130e) that he does not posit Forms for the less lovely things, may well mark a shift in Plato's reasons for believing in the Forms. While in the middle dialogues he is concerned with saving the phenomena of moral life, by positing absolute standards for value, and in saving the visible phenomena from inconsistency, in the late dialogues, as I will show, the εἴδη are primarily the semantic "meanings" of discourse, and the kinds of phenomena. The εἴδη must exist if there is to be intelligible speech, and because they are the εἴδη of all phenomena. The extension of the εἴδη theory is, then, much greater in the late dialogues than that found, with certainty, in the middle ones.[10]

Parmenides opens the next argument at 131a f. by presenting the horns of a typical Eleatic destructive dilemma;[11] a particular partakes either of the whole or a part of a Form (131a). As we shall see, there are at least three such destructive dilemmas in *Parmenides* 131a–132c: either a Form is in its instances or it is over them; if it is in them, then it is in them either as a whole or as a part; and either a Form is a thought or it is the object of thought. At 131a f. the Forms are treated as in things, and a very literal sense of "partaking" is at issue. To partake of a pie, for example, is to have either all or some of it. But we should hesitate to say that this argument is a blatant *ignoratio*, if for no other reason than that Plato does not give an explicit account of participation, and hence even such literal interpretations should be examined, if only to be rejected.

If Socrates chooses the first alternative, then a Form that is one and the same (ἓν ἄρα ὂν καὶ ταὐτόν), is as a whole in each of many separate particulars, and hence it becomes separated from itself (αὐτὸ αὑτοῦ χωρίς, 131b); and if he chooses the second, the unitary Form becomes divided into parts, and so it is no longer one (131c). Socrates concludes by admitting that he cannot see how particulars can partake of either the whole or the parts of a Form.

Parmenides twice, at each horn, reminds Socrates of the oneness of each Form (ἓν ὄν, τὸ ἓν εἶδος, and so on, 131a,c), which emphasizes Socrates' commitment to the predicate; and Parmenides interprets "partaking" (μετέχειν) as the Forms being in (ἐν, ἐνεῖναι) the phenomena. Because Socrates concludes by admitting that he does not know how partaking is possible on this model, there is no doubt that the argument is a critique of "being in" as an account of partaking. Nevertheless, what is seldom emphasized is that Socrates must defend the oneness of each Form against Parmenides' attacks, and the lack of such a defense dooms the "being in" interpretation. The thrust of Parmenides' argument is that, if Socrates chooses the first alternative, then the Form is no longer unique (one), because it is separated into many wholes that are the same in kind; and if he chooses the second alternative, then the Form is no longer incomposite (one), since it is divided into parts. Whichever alternative Socrates chooses, and there are only the two possibilities if Forms are in things (131a), each Form which must be one is yet many, and hence a part of the Eleatic heritage that is essential to the Forms is destroyed. Forms relate to phenomena, since phenomena participate in them, and this relationship, on the "in" interpretation, generates one/many problems at the level of the Forms themselves. The Forms, then, cannot explain similar problems concerning phenomena.

Commentators frequently claim that this argument is irrelevant to the middle-period theory of Forms, because it does not consider their separation. Indeed, Plato has resources to answer the objection, but there is still a plausible reason why Parmenides makes it. It is essential to Eleatic dialectic that both horns of a destructive dilemma lead to unacceptable results. The larger dilemma at issue is whether a Form is in its participants or whether it is over them as in both versions of the third man argument. For an orderly completion of the argument both horns must be rejected. Plato, with what must have been a certain bitter delight, turns one of the great achievements of Eleatic logic against the Forms.

This argument also rejects one possible interpretation of separation; Forms cannot be construed extensionally as classes of immanent characteristics. *F*-ness is not the class of *F* characteristics in F things. Since classes are usually individuated by their members, we could if we were Plato reject such an interpretation on the ground that a Form would change as its participants do. But there is no evidence, at least in the middle dialogues, that Plato understood the logic of classes: hence he would reject the possibility of such an "extensional" interpretation by showing that a Form would lack the proper sort of incomposite, unique oneness. A Form cannot be a class whose members are either "parts" or "wholes" of that Form.

In the *Parmenides* (130b) Plato clearly distinguishes *F*-ness itself from the *F*-ness that we possess. For example, Largeness itself is separate from (χωρίς) the largeness in us. With this distinction Plato can certainly answer Parmenides' argument. Immanent characteristics are individuated by their possessors: for example, Simmias' largeness depends for its existence on Simmias, and if Simmias did not exist, then his largeness could not exist. Nevertheless, immanent characteristics are not unique, since the same kind of largeness is (contingently) found in many sensible particulars. Thus the logic of immanent characteristics is different from that of the separate Forms; a Form is not dependent for its existence on any particular, nor is it individuated by a possessor. In the middle works Forms are individuated by their definite descriptive self-predicates. A Form is also unique whereas the immanent characteristics are not. Only the immanent characteristics are in phenomena.

Self-Predication and the Causal Principle

At *Parmenides* 131c–e Parmenides states three further consequences of the claim that only a part of a Form is in each of the Form's instances, and these conclusions are agreed to be absurd:

(A) A large thing is large by a part of Largeness that is smaller than Largeness itself.

(B) An equal thing is equal by a small part of Equality, which part is less than Equality itself.

(C) If we take away a part of Smallness, then Smallness will be larger than its part. But that to which the part is added will be smaller and not larger.

Why are these consequences absurd; and since (A)–(C) apparently illustrate a common absurdity, what is this common absurdity? According to Gregory Vlastos, (A)–(C) implicitly contain the problem of self-predication. He says, "To say that a 'part' of the Form, Largeness, is smaller than Largeness is most certainly to imply that Largeness is large."[12] Self-predication, however, cannot be an adequate, complete interpretation of these passages. While (A) implies that Largeness is larger than its part, by a parity of reasoning, (B) implies that Equality is not equal to its parts (ᾧ ἐλάττονι ὄντι αὐτοῦ τοῦ ἴσου, 131d), and (C) implies that Smallness is larger (αὐτὸ τὸ σμικρὸν μεῖζον ἔσται, 131d) than its parts. The last two are the contrary of self-predication since, for example, the adjective corresponding to Largeness is predicated of Smallness. I agree with Vlastos that Plato uses incomplete and relational predicates in such a way that if Equality is not equal to one of its parts, then we may infer that Equality is not equal, and if Smallness is larger than one of its parts, then Smallness is large.[13] Thus in (C) Smallness is large, and in (B) Equality is not equal, and (A)–(C) are not, without further explanation, direct evidence for self-predication.

Vlastos' account neither gives what is common to the three conclusions, nor takes into account the explanatory nature of Forms and their purported "parts." (A)–(C) are absurd precisely because a formal, final, or efficient cause must have the quality that it explains or produces in something else. In turn this explanatory principle implies self-predication. (A)–(C) all violate this explanatory principle. In (A), large phenomena are made large *by* a part of Largeness that is small (since it is smaller than Largeness), and in (B) equal things are made equal *by* a part of Equality that is not equal. In (C), small things are made small by Smallness that is large; in this example Smallness itself, which is large since it is larger than its parts, is contrasted with the phenomena that are made small by the parts of Smallness. Although the parts of Smallness are small, since they are smaller than Smallness, each larger part of Smallness would, presumably, make something smaller than a smaller part would, and herein lies the absurdity. The limiting case would be where Smallness that is larger than any of its parts makes something smaller than any of its smaller parts could make it.

Because Plato assumes the above explanatory principle, (A)–(C) are unacceptable. The parts of a Form do not stand in the proper sort of explanatory relation to the phenomena. Therefore, particulars do not have "parts" of a Form because these parts cannot account for the characteristics of phenomena. But an implication of the absurdities is that if the Forms are to be the explanations for characteristics, then they must be self–predicated; for example, Largeness is always large, and Equality is always equal. I conclude that the Forms under consideration in the *Par-*

menides are self-predicated, and as we will see self-predication is a key premise in both versions of the third man argument.

The Third Man Arguments

Next let us examine the perennially perplexing third man argument (132a–b, hereafter referred to as the T.M.A.). Plato juxtaposes the T.M.A. with the preceding argument because the account of partaking involved here has the Form *over* its participants. The T.M.A. is a type of *reductio* argument. Parmenides states the initial assumption (or first step) as follows:

> I fancy your reason for believing that each Form is one is something like this; when there is a number of things that seem to you to be large, you may think, as you look at them all, that there is one and the same Form concerning them, and hence you think that Largeness is one. That is true, he [Socrates] said.

The T.M.A. opens with Socrates assenting to the premise that "Each Form is one" (ἓν ἕκαστον εἶδος, 132a),[14] which is the same statement Plato introduces the Forms with in the *Republic* (476a, 479a, 507b–c, and 596a). A Form is one in that it is incomposite and unique, but incompositeness is not what is at issue in the T.M.A. Rather, Parmenides attempts to show that a one-over-many argument which generates a single, unique Form will, with repeated applications, generate more than one Form of each type. In the second step Parmenides states (132a):

> What then if in the same manner you look with the *psyche* at all of these, Largeness itself and the other large things, will not another single Largeness appear, by which all of these must appear to be large? So it seems.

Vlastos, as well as most of the commentators who have replied to him, think that "Plato's argument professes to be a deductive argument";[15] that is, the second step is deduced from the first. But since the second step is not a valid conclusion from the first, the problem of the T.M.A., according to Vlastos and most of his critics, is to discover "the simplest premises, not given in the present Argument, that would have to be added to its first step, to make (A₂) [the second step] a legitimate conclusion."[16] These are the premises Vlastos supplies:[17]

(A) *the self-predication assumption*: Any Form can be predicated of itself. Largeness is itself large. *F*-ness is itself *F*.

(B) *the nonidentity assumption*: If anything has a certain character, it cannot be identical ·with the Form in virtue of which we apprehend that character. If *x* is *F*, *x* cannot be identical with *F*-ness.

On Vlastos' interpretation the relationship between the first and second steps is that of a premise to a conclusion. But since the second step cannot validly be derived from the first, he supplies the most economical premises he can for the derivation.[18] But does Plato give any indication that he intends for the second step to be deduced from the first?

In the second step τί δ' ... ἐάν (what then if) could hardly be used by Plato to indicate that that step is a conclusion. Rather in the second step Parmenides is made to say that if the large things and Largeness are viewed ὡσαύτως (in the same manner as) the large phenomena were viewed in the first, then another Form appears. Plato does not indicate that in understanding the second step one needs concepts in addition to those used in the first. In fact, the terse manner in which Parmenides is made to state the second step suggests that once the reasoning used in the first step is understood, the second is simply an extension of this reasoning to a new set of things.[19] Likewise, in the third step (132b), which generates a third Form of Largeness, καί ... αὖ (and again) does not indicate that that step is a conclusion. What Plato says is that if we take the large things, Largeness$_1$ and Largeness$_2$, then over these there will be yet another Form of Largeness, Largeness$_3$.

The text of the *Parmenides* does not support the view that the second step is derived from the first. In reading the three stated steps of the T.M.A., one is not struck by any logical gap between these steps, but rather by their parallel structure. Each step employs the same reasoning, but this reasoning is employed about different sets. In order to explain this parallel structure, and the force of the *reductio*, it is necessary to formulate a general statement as a common ground from which all of the steps of the argument can be generated. I offer (T) as such a ground:

(T) If a number of things are *F*, there is a single Form in virtue of which we apprehend these things as *F*, and these things (either individually or in any combination) are not identical with this Form.[20]

(T) is a good ground for several reasons. First, the infinite number of steps can be generated from (T) by replacing "a number of things" in (T) by different sets. This preserves the parallel structure of the steps. Second, deriving all of the steps from (T) is more economical than deriving the second step from the first in conjunction with two suppressed premises: the self-predication and nonidentity assumptions. Third, (T) is a generalization of the first step. This accounts for the plausibility of the argument as a typical Eleatic *reductio*. For each succeeding step is an extension of the preceding to cover a higher-order set. Once one accepts the one-over-many argument in the first step, it is difficult to deny the succeeding steps because they result from a generalized one-over-many argument, and certain established beliefs about the Forms. Finally, (T) has two concepts that are the strongest concepts we need see as common to all of the steps. These concepts are: a concept of predication, "... is *F*," and a concept of nonidentity, "whatever is *F* cannot be identical with the Form in virtue of which it is *F*." One might object that the second and succeeding steps have not only a concept of predication in respect to phenomena but also a concept of self-predication in respect to the Forms. This is true, as long as we remember that self-predication results from an extension of the concept of predication to the Forms. In this way the parallel structure of the steps, as Plato lays them out, as well as the force of the *reductio*, remains intact.

As is typical with Eleatic *reductios*, the first step posits the contradictory of what is to be shown; the first step states that "each Form is one." The argument concludes with Parmenides claiming to prove that "each of the Forms will be for you no longer one, but an indefinite multitude" (καὶ οὐκέτι δὴ ἓν ἕκαστόν σοι τῶν εἰδῶν ἔσται, ἀλλὰ ἄπειρα τὸ πλῆθος, 132b). Parmenides does not attempt to prove that each Form has an unlimited number of parts, but rather that there is an indefinite multitude of each kind of Form—for example, many Largenesses, one for each of the newly emerging sets of large things. There is, then, more than one of each sort of Form, and the Forms are no longer unique; for example, there is no longer one and only one Largeness, one and only one Justice, and so on, but more than one of each.[21] Again Parmenides forces Socrates to deny an essential part of the Eleatic legacy; but this time his dialectical reasoning proceeds upon the assumption that the Form is over the phenomena.

But the point of the *reductio* is not just to generate an indefinite multitude of Forms of the same kind; it is also to answer Socrates' challenge. In the *Republic* Plato discusses certain puzzles about particulars that lead to the contemplation of true Being (523b–525a). One of these is that we see the same thing at the same time as one and as an indefinite multitude (ἅμα γὰρ ταὐτὸν ὡς ἕν τε ὁρῶμεν καὶ ὡς ἄπειρα τὸ πλῆθος, 525a). This passage suggests a group of one-many puzzles. On the one hand it could mean that a particular is one thing, but that it has an indefinite multitude of parts (cf. *Parmenides* 129b f.); on the other hand it could mean that this particular is one thing, but that there is an indefinite multitude of the same sort of particular. The first puzzle is similar to what occurs when a part of a Form is in each thing, and the second puzzle is similar to the whole of a Form being in each participant and the T.M.A. For in the T.M.A. each Form is one thing, but there is an indefinite multitude of the same kind of Form.

Plato is concerned with a group of puzzles about what is meant by "same," "one," and "indefinite multitude," in talking about particulars; especially he is concerned to explain contrary applications of such predicates. He introduces Forms to solve such puzzles and to save the phenomena: each man is one by participating in Unity, and yet he has many parts by participating in Plurality. But Plato's ingenuity has gone for naught, since Parmenides shows that similar puzzles arise about the Forms if they are one and separate from their participants (*Parmenides* 133b). Each Form which, by hypothesis, must be one, is shown by means of the *reductio* to be an indefinite multitude. Thus Parmenides succeeds in meeting Socrates' challenge; each Form appears to be one and many, and thus the Forms cannot save the phenomena from the same perplexity. The Forms are without value in explaining phenomena.

In a broader context, the purpose of the dramatic character Parmenides is to attack Plato's pluralistic modification of his historical predecessor's theory of Being. Plato cannot have a two-tiered pluralism, Forms and phenomena, because attempts to relate the tiers result in the destruction of each Form's oneness. The dramatic character Parmenides, moreover, reenacts his predecessor's belief that any plurality, including, we may surmise, a plurality of Forms, implies the "identity of opposites" (cf. DK 28 B6.8–9), and hence the illegitimacy of plurality. Parmenides cannot directly display the connections between Forms as Zeno did with the connections between phenomena, because Forms are themselves in themselves, and uniformly self-predicated. Thus he focuses upon the only clear connections Forms have, those with their participants. Forms are no more inconsistent entities (cf. *Republic* 436e–437a) than phenomena are; but the mere appearance of contrary predicates among the Forms, themselves, leaves Plato without an explanation for such predicates.[22]

Gregory Vlastos and Harold Cherniss believe that the T.M.A. contains an inconsistency, but they draw different conclusions from the analysis of the inconsistency. The inconsistency, according to Vlastos and Cherniss, is between the self-predication assumption (A) and the nonidentity assumption (B), both of which are stated above. Vlastos claims that although (A) and (B) are each necessary and jointly sufficient for the derivation of the second step from the first, they are sufficient in a vacuous manner. For (A) and (B), Vlastos claims, are mutually inconsistent. Hence the second step follows from the first in conjunction with (A) and (B) in a trivial manner.[23] Substituting F-ness for x in (B) yields the contradiction (C): If F-ness is F, F-ness cannot be identical with F-ness. Thus the self-predication and nonidentity assumptions are mutually inconsistent. Vlastos concludes from this inconsistency that the T.M.A. and the *Parmenides*, part I, are a record of "honest perplexity." Plato was not able to identify explicitly both suppressed premises, (A) and (B), of the T.M.A., and thus he was not aware of his commitment to self-predication; nevertheless, he knew something was wrong, and he manifests his perplexity by producing the infinite-series argument, the T.M.A.[24]

Cherniss believes that Plato is quite aware of the above-mentioned inconsistency, and he produces the T.M.A. to instruct us about it.[25]

Cherniss proceeds to argue that Plato does not self-predicate the Forms; apparently self-predicative assertions are, in fact, identity claims. Phenomena are copies or resemblances of the Forms, but they do not resemble the Forms because the Forms are not self-predicated. In the T.M.A. Plato intends for the reader to diagnose the self-predication assumption and to understand that he, Plato, is not committed to self-predication. Thus while both Vlastos and Cherniss purport to see an inconsistency in the premises of the T.M.A., they draw very different conclusions from this perceived inconsistency.

I do not believe that the premises of the T.M.A. are inconsistent; moreover, (T) is not an internally inconsistent principle, and it validly generates an infinite series with the proper substitutions. In fact I believe that the T.M.A. is a valid argument, and that on the visual model for knowledge, Plato is committed to the truth of its premises. In other words, the T.M.A. is a sound argument against the uniform, pure, paradigms. But why do Cherniss and Vlastos believe that (A) and (B) are inconsistent?

In an article with Professor David Louzecky,[26] I argue in detail that (A) and (B) are not inconsistent; here I will only summarize the claims. Vlastos states, "We may take it for granted that it cannot be true that x, y, z are seen as F in virtue of F-ness and also in virtue of a Form other than F-ness,"[27] and Cherniss makes precisely the same assumption.[28] What they mean is that large things cannot be or be apprehended as large by virtue of more than one Form. Since x, y, z are variables that can have either Forms or phenomena as values, Vlastos' statement implies that for every set of F things there must be one and only one Form in virtue of which the members of those sets are F. Thus in (B), "F-ness" is treated as the name of a single Form, and not a variable, and the substitution of F-ness for x in (B) results in an inconsistency.

Because Vlastos requires one and only one Form for every set of F things, he reads the first step of the T.M.A. (132a1) as requiring that "there is in every case a single Form" (ἓν ἕκαστον εἶδος) and the conclusion is an explicit contradiction of this, as is the second step. Thus the premises that are added to the first step to imply the second must be inconsistent.

There are a number of reasons why Vlastos, I believe, mistranslates the first step:

(1) ἕκαστον in the phrase ἓν ἕκαστον εἶδος refers only to sets of particulars, if we accept Vlastos' translation of the term, "in every case."

(2) πόλλ᾽ ἄττα μεγάλα, "many large things," in the first step, refers only to particulars,[29] for Plato speaks of seeing the many large things in the first step, but of seeing with the *psyche* the large things and Largeness

in the second step. The second step requires a reference to the *psyche* because Forms are understood by the reasoning power in the *psyche*, and thus Largeness is not introduced until the second step. Thus "many large things" in the first step does not refer to all of the sets of *F* things, but only those composed of phenomena. Hence the first step claims only that there is a single Form, Largeness, for every set of large sensible particulars.

(3) Vlastos claims that the first step of the T.M.A. states "the funda-mental thesis of the Theory of Forms or Ideas which is the target of the polemic in all of the objections raised by Parmenides in the first part of the dialogue."[30] Vlastos' claim is correct, but the theory of Forms for which Plato is famous is introduced to solve the apparent incoherence of phenomena, and hence it deals only with phenomena.

(4) ἕκαστον is more plausibly read as modifying εἶδος than as referring to sets of *F* things; and ἕν should be placed in the predicate position as is typical of Greek usage.[31] Thus ἓν ἕκαστον εἶδος should be translated "each Form is one," and not "there is in every case a single Form." If Plato were to say what Vlastos would have him say, then he would have used the genitive case ἑκάστου, or the adverb ἑκάστοτε, or perhaps περί and the accusative. [Textual evidence is provided in detail for (4) in our article.]

ἓν ἕκαστον εἶδος in the first step means "each Form is one," and not, as Vlastos and Cherniss believe, "there is in every case a single Form." Thus it is incorrect to transcribe, as Vlastos does, the first step as follows:[32]

(1) If a certain set of things share a given character then there exists a unique Form corresponding to that character; and each of those things has that character by participating in that Form.

By "a certain set of things" in (1) Vlastos means that there is one and only one Form for every set of *F* things, and, of course, the second step con-tradicts this claim because it posits a second Form, *F*-ness$_2$. But the first step claims only that there is a single Form for every set of *F* phenomena. By means of (T), in conjunction with the self-predication assumption, we can validly generate a second Form of *F*-ness, and so on for an infinite series of such Forms. While the one-over-many argument, as applied to phenomena, generates a unique Form for them, a generalization of such an argument, (T), in conjunction with the self-predication assumption, validly generates an indefinite number of the same kind of Form. For in (T), as well as in Vlastos' (B), "*F*-ness" in "the *F*-ness in virtue of which *F* things are *F*" is a variable name; it stands for whatever Form it is in virtue of which the members of the set *at issue* are *F*. Thus (A) and (B)—the self-predication and nonidentity assumptions—are consistent.

The T.M.A. is a sound argument against the self-predicated Forms, that is, against those Forms that are the objects of mental vision. (T), however, contains a weak separation assumption that a Form, *F*-ness, is not identical with its participants; but Plato certainly believes that his Forms are separate from phenomena because they are aspatial and incomposite entities. Separation implies that a Form is not identical with its participants either individually or in any combination, as well as the stronger claim that a Form is not within the οὐρανός (*Symposium* 211b). Plato also self-predicates the Forms. In the last chapter we saw that self-predication is a necessary condition for key elements in Plato's metaphysics: (1) the Forms as objects of visual acquaintance, (2) epistemic paradigmatism, (3) the incorrigible nature of the Forms, and (4) the explanatory nature of the Forms. We also saw that there is explicit textual evidence for self-predication. Plato's three commitments to separation, self-predication, and the one-over-many argument (at least as restricted to impure predicates), involve the Forms in the T.M.A. Thus the T.M.A. is a sound attack on the visual formulation of the middle-period Forms.

But does the T.M.A. also impugn the Forms as seen through *logoi*? Since Plato does not fully develop this view in the middle dialogues, we cannot definitely answer this question until we investigate the late dialogues in the next chapter. But some definite tendencies should be noted. When Plato investigates the Forms through *logoi*, self-predication, uniformity, and purity are not of primary concern. A Form is identified not by its pure, definite, descriptive "self"-predicate, but by its connections with other Forms. A further emphasis on this route to knowledge might disarm the objections of the *Parmenides*, for it would explain how Forms come to have their predicates, including contrary ones, by their connections with other Forms; and it would at least change the nature of self-predication, since any self-predicate of a Form would be explained by the Form's self-participation.[33] A Form would have a predicate *F* because it participates in *F*-ness, and it would have a self-predicate because it participates, for some reason, in itself. Self-participation denies the separation assumption at the level of Forms; a self-participant is not separate from itself. In this way the T.M.A. could be blocked. I will show that there are adequate hints in the *Parmenides* that a further dialectical investigation of the Forms, through *logoi*, is needed to save the theory. Whether Forms will emerge from this investigation as the same type of entity as those found in the middle dialogues, is an important and difficult question. In Chapter 5 I will show that, at least in the *Sophist* and the *Philebus*, they do not.

Harold Cherniss, among others, believes that the T.M.A. is an *ignoratio*.[34] Even in the middle period Plato is not propounding a theory of self-predicated Forms, and thus the T.M.A. attacks only a misunderstanding of the theory. Moreover, Cherniss claims that *Republic* 597c–d explicitly refutes the T.M.A., and shows it to be a misunderstanding of the theory of Forms:[35]

> ... if he [God] should make only two [Forms], there would again appear one (μία) of which they both would possess the form (τὸ εἶδος ἔχοιεν), and that would be what is the Couch (ὅ ἔστι κλίνη), but not the other two ... God, then, ... knowing this and wishing to be the real author of the real (ὄντως) Couch, and not of some particular couch, ... produced it in nature unique (μίαν).

Cherniss believes that the phrase ὅ ἔστι is sufficient to scuttle the T.M.A. The Form of Couch is what is the Couch, while only its participants have the character of being a couch. Hence the Form is the Couch, and is not self-predicated, while the participants have the character "couch." But in the *Phaedo* (78d), Plato in the same breath states that what is ὅ ἔστι is also uniform (μονοειδές), or single-form. The latter term certainly implies that a Form uniformly has some characteristic, and the obvious characteristic to impute to a Form is its self-predicate. The Form is what is *F* because it is purely and uniformly *F*. Thus ὅ ἔστι does not block the T.M.A. by a denial of self-predication. W. D. Ross is right on the mark when he states of 597c–d:[36]

> To show that if there were two Ideas of Bed there would have to be a third does nothing to disprove the contention that if there is one Idea of Bed, related to particulars as Plato supposes, there must be a second.

Republic 597c–d only gives Plato's initial reasons for believing in a single Form, but of itself, it does nothing to block either self-predication or an infinite series.

Socrates next makes a desperate attempt to maintain the oneness of each Form. He says, "Parmenides ... might not each Form be a thought (νόημα) that can exist nowhere else than in the *psyche*, and so each Form would be one (ἕν), and would no longer undergo the consequences you just talked about?" (132b). Parmenides replies to this idealistic escape attempt with a favorite doctrine of his historical predecessor: a thought must be a thought of something, and of something that is (cf. DK 28 B8.34–36); and in the *Republic* (477c–d) we have already seen that Plato individuates the psychic powers by what they relate to; knowledge is (intentionally) of true Being, while belief is of what is halfway between Being and nonbeing. In Socrates' case it must be a thought of the one Form (μίαν ἰδέαν, 132c) that is over the phenomena. We are, by this, thrown back to problems about partaking, and so the Eleatic legacy, the oneness of each Form, remains undefended. Parmenides diagnoses Socrates' problems as following from his assumption that each Form is one (ἓν εἶδος ἕκαστον), and something distinct from the phenomena (133b). The unity, and ultimately the purity, of each Form is in serious jeopardy unless Socrates can avoid the multiplicity implied by participation and can explain the contrary characteristics of Forms. As a parting shot, Parmenides hurls a final absurdity at the possibility that Forms are thoughts (132c): if Forms are thoughts, and things participate in Forms, then "either everything is made of thoughts, and all things think, or ... being thoughts, they are without thought."

The second version of the T.M.A. is no less successful against the visual Forms. Socrates describes the theory at issue as follows (132d):

> ... but Parmenides, I think the most likely view is, that these Forms exist in nature as paradigms, and the other things resemble (ἐοικέναι) them and are imitations (ὁμοιώματα) of them; the participation itself of the other things in the Forms is nothing other than a likening (εἰκασθῆναι) or imaging of the Forms.

On this model phenomena are resemblances, images, or copies of the Forms, and the Forms are originals and paradigms. But Parmenides proceeds to argue that a resemblance resembles its original, and since "resembles" is a symmetrical relation, the original or Form also resembles its images. This implies self-predication, and an infinite series results. For a Form is introduced to explain why phenomena resemble one another, but then if they also resemble the Form and the converse, a second Form must be posited to explain this community of character, and so on. Thus an indefinite multiplicity of Forms of the same type is generated, and each type of Form has no longer a unique instantiation, but is a multiplicity.

Plato, in his middle period, is clearly committed to the interpretations of the three premises of this argument. Starting with Book VI of the *Republic*, if not before, Forms are thought of as paradigms, and their participants are said to resemble and copy them. Plato also uses a one-over-many argument that begins with shared resemblances between phenomena, that is, with the respects in which they resemble one another, although in the *Phaedo* and the *Republic* this argument is probably restricted to nonsortal predicates. In fact, this variant of the one-over-many argument is simply a further explanation and description of how phenomena share characteristics. The largeness of Simmias and the largeness of Socrates resemble one another *qua* largeness. Plato also believes that a resemblance resembles its original; for, as we saw in the last chapter, if a resemblance did not resemble its original, then there would be no way to tell what original the resemblance is a resemblance of.[37] A resemblance must resemble its original to be a resemblance of that original. Plato also subscribes to the separation of the original from its copies, and hence he is committed to the three premises of the second version [where the generalization (T) is suitably modified to fit this version]. Plato has, as yet, no way of replying to Parmenides because the argument is a sound attack on the middle-period Forms.

Cherniss finds two defects in the argument.[38] It proves too much, since any resemblance that we attempt to explain ultimately generates an infinite series. This is correct, but it hardly provides a reason why Plato rejects the argument. Obviously the conclusion is unacceptable, but this does not imply that Plato has the resources to deny it. Cherniss also claims that the relationship between a copy and its original is asymmetrical: a copy is a copy of an original, but the original is not a copy of the copy; likewise an original is an original of a copy, but the copy is not an original of the original. This point is perfectly correct, but it does not imply that a copy and original cannot resemble one another. For their sharing a common characteristic is a different relation from the original-copy one. Even if an original resembles its copies, this certainly does not imply that the original is not an original of those copies. The debate between Cherniss and Allen on the one hand, and the self-predicationists on the other, is in the end whether or not the Forms are self-predicated. A denial of self-predication would render impotent the third man arguments, but at an unacceptable cost to Plato's metaphysics. For Forms cannot be explanatory and epistemic paradigms, unless their participants resemble them.

A Hint of Development

Only one argument remains in the first part of the *Parmenides*, and I will only sketch it in outline, since what is of greatest interest is a by-product of how Parmenides sets up the argument. Parmenides claims that it is very difficult to have knowledge of the Forms because they have their natures in relation to each other, while the phenomena are what they are in relation to themselves (133c–d). Purported further results of this claim— with of course the introduction of other premises—are that: (A) knowledge itself is only of the Forms; (B) human knowledge is only of phenomena; (C) only God possesses knowledge itself, and hence only God knows the Forms; (D) we possess only human knowledge, and thus know only phenomena; and (E) God does not then know human affairs. But (E) is clearly impious. This argument completely ignores recollection and dialectic as processes by which we come to know the Forms, and it makes the interesting distinction discussed in Chapter 3, between knowledge itself and merely human knowledge. There is no doubt that Plato has the philosophical resources to reply to this argument.

The text does not permit certainty about why Parmenides produces this extraordinary argument. But an interesting and novel treatment of certain Forms results from the claim that the Forms have their natures in relation to each other (αὐταὶ πρὸς αὑτὰς τὴν οὐσίαν ἔχουσιν, 133c). Parmenides provides a dialectical example concerning mastery and slavery (133d–134a). A human master is a master (δεσπότης) of a human slave, and a human slave is a slave (δοῦλος) of a human master; but Mastership itself is mastership (δεσποτεία) of Slavery itself, and Slavery itself is the slavery (δουλεία) of Mastership itself. This brief dialectical encounter has far-reaching implications, although we cannot yet be sure that Plato is aware of them. Only a human master is a master, and he is a master because he is a master of a slave; only a human slave is a slave, and he is a slave because he is a slave of a master. The predicates "is a master" and "is a slave" are applied only in respect to human masters and slaves. Mastership is not a master because it is not in relation to phenomena, and Slavery, likewise, is not a slave. Thus Parmenides' dialectic denies that Mastership and Slavery are self-predicated. Mastership is the mastership of (or in relation to) Slavery itself, and Slavery itself is the slavery of Mastership itself. Mastership and Slavery are what they are in relation to each other, and they are no longer self-predicated. We see in this passage an early attempt to analyze the predicates of the Forms, and an analysis similar to that later found in the *Sophist*. Furthermore, as we shall see in the next chapter, the interconnected εἴδη begin to be more like kinds than Forms.

Conclusion

What is Plato's attitude towards the Forms at the end of *Parmenides*, part I? Parmenides states the following immediately before and after the last argument (133b–c, 135a):

> If anyone should say that the Forms cannot even be known if they are such as we say they must be, no one could prove to him that he was wrong, unless he who argued that they could be known were a man of wide education and ability and were willing to follow the proof through many long and elaborate details. . . .

> Therefore he who hears such assertions [that the Forms exist and are in themselves] is confused in his mind and argues that the Forms do not exist, and even if they do exist cannot by any possibility be known by man; . . . Only a man of very great natural gifts will be able to understand that everything has a kind (γένος) and nature (οὐσία) itself in itself, . . . and find out all these facts and teach anyone else to analyze them properly and understand them.

Parmenides, speaking not as a monist but as a paradigm example of a rigorous thinker, does not deny that Forms exist, nor does he deny that they can be known. These passages clearly imply that what is required to exonerate the Forms from perplexity is a rigorous training and education, and 135c–d reveals that this training will be in dialectic:

> ... for you [Socrates] try too soon, before you are properly trained, to define The Beautiful, The Just, The Good, and all the other Forms.... Your impulse towards dialectic is noble and divine, you may be assured of that; but exercise and train yourself while you are still young in an art which seems to be useless and is called by most people mere loquacity; otherwise the truth will escape you.

Parmenides suggests as an example of this dialectical training an application of Zeno's method, which surely indicates the high esteem Plato has for Eleatic techniques of argument, even though he unremittingly parodies them in the *Euthydemus*. Eleatic arguments, for all their mistakes, when seriously pursued are paradigms of rationality.

Plato's refusal to stop believing in the Forms does not imply that they will be in the late dialogues the same type of entities that are encountered in the middle ones. We have already seen that even in the middle dialogues the separate Forms have two sorts of natures: one connected with the visual and the other with the discursive model for knowledge. We cannot state antecedently how Forms will exist, or even if they will be separate, until we investigate the later dialectical analysis of them. It is perfectly possible that what Plato labels "Forms" is not one and the same theory, but a group of theories that develop, change, and evolve. As Plato investigates the nature of the Forms through *logoi*, he may not even be aware that their natures change and evolve. The *logoi*, so to speak, have a life of their own. At 135b–c Parmenides states that he who denies the existence of Forms "in every way destroys the power of discourse (δια-λέγεσθαι)." This certainly suggests that the Forms are the meanings of names, and for this reason their connections can be investigated through *logoi*. I conclude that a likely approach to the problems of the *Parmenides*, especially that of the contrary predicates of the Forms, is an emphasis on the dialectical route to the Forms.

Does the second part of the *Parmenides* explicitly or implicitly answer the *aporia* of the first part? I do not see that it does. W. D. Ross makes, what I believe to be, telling criticisms of the most plausible positive interpretations of the second part, and he provides a cogent analysis of it.[39]

> The real clue to the interpretation is Parmenides' five-times-repeated description of the arguments as affording γυμνασία, training in argument. He nowhere suggests that they will directly enlighten Socrates on the difficulties Parmenides has pointed out in the theory of Ideas, or on any other philosophical problem.

and again:[40]

> What Parmenides promises Socrates from the study of the hypotheses
> is not direct development or emendation of his theory, but a gain in
> dialectical skill which may ultimately produce that result; and that, I
> believe, is the whole purpose of the "second part."

More specifically, I agree with Gilbert Ryle when he claims that the
second part investigates what happens when the Forms are the subjects of
predicates.[41] However, I do not see that positive results emerge, but rather
a training in techniques of argumentation. If dialectical training is about
the Forms as the subjects of predication, then such training will ultimately
lead to an analysis of why the Forms have the predicates they do have,
especially those predicates that are contraries.

5

Revisionism in the Late Dialogues

There are, to put the debate in broad terms, two major contradictory interpretations of the late dialogues. The unitarians argue that Plato never gives up the theory of separate, paradigmatic Forms, and hence he does not reject the theory in the late dialogues. Of course he may extend the theory, modify it, or further explicate it; examples are the extensive divisions and collections in the *Sophist* and the *Statesman*, and the communion of the greatest kinds in the *Sophist*. A key element in the unitarian position is that the *Timaeus* is a late dialogue,[1] for there is little doubt that separate, paradigmatic Forms are in the *Timaeus*. The revisionists believe that Plato so significantly modifies the Forms that separate, paradigmatic Forms are not found in the late dialogues.[2] In effect Plato changes his ontological commitments. The εἴδη and γένη of the *Philebus*, *Sophist*, and *Statesman* are kinds or classes, given some suitable interpretation of these notions. Kinds or classes are not Forms because, among other things, they are not separate from their instances. Plato changes his ontology, the revisionists usually claim, because of the serious criticisms of the Forms in the *Parmenides*.

The scope of this chapter is narrowly limited to a discussion of Plato's ontological commitments in the late dialogues, with one exception. The exception is that I will discuss, in some detail, the uses of the Greek verb "to be" in the *Sophist*. I will show that, just as in the middle dialogues "to be" has as its primary meaning the veridical "what is the case," or "what is so," and that existential and predicative uses are special cases of the primary meaning. Thus the problems in the *Sophist* about not-being are not just about negative predications.[3]

My position on the late dialogues will be unacceptable to both partisan camps. Moreover, I will not argue for a unified consistent Plato even within the late dialogues. This may well be disturbing to those philosophers who argue as if the principle of charity is the main consideration in correct exegesis. But one must be true to the primary evidence, and in Platonic studies that is the text.

I will argue that the *Sophist*, *Philebus*, and *Theaetetus* are not committed to separate Forms. The notions employed and analyzed in these dialogues are kinds, the principles in the *Cosmos* that generate and ground kinds, and the psychic categories that isomorphically map onto some of the most important kinds. In the *Philebus*, the monads mentioned at 15b–c, as well as pleasure, knowledge, and even the good life are kinds; each art employs as its method division and collection, and proper artistic method divides generic kinds into subgenera and species. Limit, unlimited, and *nous* are the principles, existing in the *Cosmos*, that generate kinds—the mixed class. These principles, as I will show, can also be interpreted as generating individuals. In the *Sophist* the divisions are again through kinds, and the five greatest γένη are also kinds. The interrelations between the greatest γένη, I will argue, cannot be read as being between separate, paradigmatic Forms, nor do they admit an extensional interpretation based on universally quantified statements. The greatest γένη, however, consistently and plausibly can be interpreted as kind interconnections; for example, "Motion is not what it is to be at rest," or "Motion is not the state of rest." Nevertheless, the late dialogues also contain a "Neo-Kantian" type of view that influenced several interpreters around the turn of the century.[4] In the *Sophist* the kinds are at one point said to be "in the *psyche*" (250b); the *Theaetetus* discusses in fascinating detail why the knowledge of, for example, being, sameness, difference, and even beauty comes from the *psyche*, itself in itself, and is brought to perception (184c–187a); and the *Timaeus* depicts the *psyche* as an intermediate mixture constructed from divisible and indivisible being, sameness, and difference, so that the *psyche* can cognize these notions either among eternal Beings or among those things that always come to be (35a, 37a–b). The *Theaetetus* passage provides the most extensive list of such psychic categories, and even includes beauty among them, although the *Phaedrus* emphasizes that beauty has the most luminous sensible manifestations of any Form (250b). But only being, sameness, and difference are included as psychic categories in all three dialogues. I believe that the logical grammar of these psychic categories is isomorphically identical with that of the corresponding kinds, and thus when Plato describes the communions of the μεγίστη τῶν γενῶν in the *Sophist*, he *a fortiori* maps the relations between the categories. It is not at all clear what kinds have corresponding categories, but it does not appear that kinds corresponding to sortals have them—for example, man, cow, fisherman, sophist, and the like.

Some unitarians argue that even in those passages of the *Sophist*, *Philebus*, and *Theaetetus* where they cannot prove that Forms are mentioned, Forms ground and explain the subsidiary entities employed there. For example, it might be claimed that Forms are the principles behind limits in the *Philebus*. Therefore Plato continues to believe in Forms even when he introduces other notions to explain specific problems, for example, the constitution of the good life in the *Philebus*. There is, of course, no decisive refutation of this sort of move; Plato may well have believed in separate Forms when he wrote the *Philebus*, even if such Forms are not mentioned in that dialogue. Plato may not have introduced Forms into the *Philebus* because that dialogue has a specific problem and a methodology to solve the problem that simply does not require the Forms. Nevertheless, I will argue that a textually warranted, plausible, and self-sufficient interpretation of the *Philebus* and *Sophist* can make do without the Forms. What Plato may have believed, beyond what he communicates in his written dialogues, is a fascinating topic; and I will briefly speculate about it, which is all that the evidence permits, when I discuss the *Timaeus*.

I will not attempt to chronologically order the *Timaeus*, although very important questions about Plato's development depend upon where it is placed. I will assume that the *Timaeus* is a late dialogue, perhaps one of Plato's very late creations, followed only by the *Laws* and possibly by the *Philebus*.[5]

Separate, paradigmatic Forms are found in the *Timaeus*. But, as I will show, the *Timaeus* does not have the same position as the *Phaedo*. In the *Phaedo* there are essentially characterized particulars; for example, Socrates is essentially a man, some lumps of stuff are snow, and the like, and Plato does not posit Forms for such natures. Socrates is, in himself, a perfectly complete and adequate example of a man. But in the *Timaeus* the receptacle is as close as possible to a bare substratum; it is uncharacterized in order that it may receive any type of character, and in its primordial state it only has "traces" of the elements earth, air, fire, and water. The *Timaeus*, unlike the *Phaedo*, has only one subject, the receptacle, and while that subject may be essentially a receiver and molding stuff, it is the only essentially characterized stratum in the *Cosmos*. Moreover, in the *Timaeus* for the first time Plato forges the distinctions between eternal, existing through all of time, and temporally limited in existence, where the latter two are the domain of becoming. The Forms are, eternally; the *Cosmos* and planets always will be; while particular phenomena are always becoming and ceasing to be in time.[6] These distinctions are more radical than the "always are" and the "are and are not" one found in the middle works. The *Timaeus* depicts a radical two-worlds separation: the eternal Forms do not enter the receptacle, and the receptacle does not contain any particulars that have natures, but only characters that "cling to existence as best they may" (52c). Nevertheless, there is no plausible mechanism by means of which Plato denies "self-predication" in the *Timaeus*. The characters in the receptacle are still ikons and images of the Forms, and in fact Plato's paradigm/copy terminology is better developed in the *Timaeus* than in any other dialogue.

The evidence compels me to admit that in the late dialogues Plato experiments with different ontologies and methodologies. This is precisely what we should expect from a highly creative philosopher, and it is also appropriate because Plato attacks a wide variety of philosophical problems—the generation of the animal *Cosmos*, the good life for man, how one can speak about not-being, etc. After the *Parmenides* Plato's faith and certainty in the Forms is shaken, but this only opens new creative pathways.[7]

I will now enumerate four problems left from the middle works and the *Parmenides*. Plato explicitly attempts to solve several of these problems in the late dialogues, while others admit of what I think is an adequate solution—constructed from resources in the late works—although Plato's awareness of these results is at best speculative.

(1) The problem of participation is the most memorable *aporia*. As stated in the middle works, the problem is how the spatial, temporal phenomena participate in a nonspatial, separate Form. The most plausible answer is given at *Philebus* 15–18. If, as I hope to show, εἴδη in the *Philebus* are kinds, then when Plato states that we may let the phenomena become indefinite in number only after we thoroughly enumerate the lowest species, we are given an answer in terms of instantiation. The problem of participation is perhaps dissolved rather than solved by changing the ontological status of εἴδη so that they are now related to phenomena as kinds are to their instances.

(2) The most explicit legacy from the *Parmenides* is how a Form can be *F* and not-*F*. The *Sophist* explicitly proposes a framework for solving a similar problem, and this analysis consists in the careful separation of different forms of statement: "—— is the same as ——," "—— is different from ——," "—— is ——," "—— is not ——," and so on. Again I will attempt to show that the entities that commune in the *Sophist* are kinds not Forms, and it is the extensive communication between kinds that forces Plato, consciously or unconsciously, away from separate paradigmatism. As Plato analyzes in greater and greater detail how the εἴδη interconnect, paradigmatism disappears and is replaced by an ontology of kinds. The late dialogues thus complete, but more radically, the development in Plato's theory found in the middle works.

(3) Plato's middle-period εἴδη are self-predicated; *F*-ness is *F*. Self-predication is the backbone of paradigmatism and the individual nature of the Forms. Self-predication is also a necessary premise in the third man arguments. The *Sophist*, I will argue, does not self-predicate Forms. "Sameness is the same ——," and "Difference is different ——," (cf. 258c) do not express the natures of their subjects, but rather relate each

subject to itself or to other kinds; for example, "Sameness is the same as itself" and "Difference is different from, for example, Beauty." "Change changes," and "Rest rests" are only slightly more difficult to interpret. The verbs do express natures but they are not the natures of transcendent individuals. "Change changes," I would interpret as the same type of statement as "The cow is a milk-producing animal," or "The automobile is a conveyance for transportation." These statements tell us something about the natures of certain kinds.[8] Likewise, "Rest rests" would be read "Rest is the absence of locomotion, alteration, quantitative change, or the like," or "Rest is the state of immobility." "Change changes" would then be "Change is the state of locomotion, or alteration, etc." Except for the highest genera, the nature of a kind is displayed or revealed through the *genus* and *differentia*: change is a state, and it is the state of locomotion, or alteration, or the like. Kind talk is in a sense paradigm talk, since it tells you what the typical *x* is, but it does not commit one to an ontology of separate, paradigmatic individuals. For kinds are not separate individuals.

(4) A. Nehamas has recently argued that a name, for Plato, reveals the nature of what it names. Since "name" is a very broad term—including proper names, general terms, predicates, as well as verbs—a thing could have, on this view of a name, only one name, since it has only a single nature.[9] We may see the remnants of this perplexity in the late learners' mistake in the *Sophist* (251b f.), and the naming but not knowing or giving a *logos* of the elements in the *Theaetetus* (201c ff.). The *Sophist* explicitly scuttles such problems, and the view of names that generates them, by showing how through the communion of kinds, a single thing can have many true claims made about it.

Before we turn to specific late dialogues, let me make some comments about the exegesis of these works. The debate between the revisionists and the unitarians is so heated and shows so little sign of amelioration that their debate could not be simply a matter of looking at the text. In fact, I believe, both theories are sometimes underdetermined by the evidence.[10] By this I mean that some key statements in the text, when taken apart from their broader textual environment, are consistent with incompatible ontological theories. A crucial example is the following: Plato frequently, even in the late works, states that an εἶδος or γένος is ungenerated and indestructible as well as unchanging. What does this prove? Unitarians immediately see such claims as references to Forms; revisionists more often than not are silent about them. But both theories are compatible with these claims. For Forms are ungenerated, indestructible, as well as unchanging; but kinds are also. Even if kinds are not separate, but rather are ontologically tied to phenomena, there is no doubt that Plato believes that most, if not all, kinds are always instantiated (cf. *Timaeus* 39e–40a). Just as for Aristotle the species, man, always is because men always are—

the former collectively and the latter distributively—so also for Plato. Note that my position on underdetermination by the evidence does not introduce any radical skeptical implications; for I believe that the broader textual contexts almost invariably allow us to solve interpretative disputes. Frequently it is most informative, for example, to look at Plato's examples. Nevertheless, unrecognized underdetermination by the evidence helps perpetuate deadlocked debate.

Another problem in pinpointing the relationship between the ontological commitments of the middle dialogues and those of the late is what counts as a modification of a theory and what is a repudiation of that theory. This problem is further complicated because there are, as I showed in Chapter 3, at least two variants of the theory of Forms, one where each Form is isolated and the other where they interconnect. The only characteristics Forms have on both versions are: ungenerated, indestructible, unchanging, divine, and separate. (Note that when the Forms lose their isolation and begin to interconnect, they are no longer self-predicated paradigms.) Only the "separate" characteristic need be unique to a theory of Forms as versus a theory of kinds. For kinds can easily be construed in such a manner as to be unchanging and even divine! Thus separation is the key notion in Plato's ontology, and if separation is lost we clearly have a repudiation of the middle-period Forms. A separate Form can exist, even though it is uninstantiated; a kind cannot.

Let us now turn to an analysis of the late dialogues.

The *Philebus*

The topic of the *Philebus*, as well as its ontological commitments, is established very early in the dialogue. At 11d Socrates says:

> Each of us will next try to prove clearly that it is a condition and disposition of the *psyche* (ἕξιν ψυχῆς καὶ διάθεσιν) which can make life happy for all human beings. Is not that what we are going to do? . . . Then you will show that it is the condition of pleasure, and I that it is that of wisdom?

The topic of the *Philebus* is the good life *for man*. This good life is immediately agreed to be a certain condition and disposition of the *psyche*. Protarchus and Philebus claim that this condition is pleasure, while Socrates believes that it is wisdom and the other mental excellences (21b). The *Philebus* is thus focused on the *psyche*, and the greater part of the dialogue is spent in the classification of kinds of pleasure and knowledge. But goodness connotes self-sufficiency, and Socrates soon sees that the good life for man must be self-sufficient; that is, it must contain all of the necessary satisfactions. Hence the good life will be a mixture of intellectual excellences and pleasure (20b ff.). In order to explain how a mixture comes into being, Socrates introduces the notions of limit (πέρας), unlimited (ἄπειρον), and the cause (αἰτία) of the mixture.

First I will discuss the classifications of pleasure and knowledge. I will show that these passages are about the kinds of pleasures and knowledge. Then I will discuss the explanations for a proper mixture. I will argue that these explanations are within the *Cosmos*, and hence none of them can be identified with the middle-period Forms.

Protarchus *ab initio* stoutly maintains that pleasures do not differ in so far as they are pleasures (12e). Protarchus is correct that pleasures *qua* pleasures are alike and that as pleasures they do not differ in kind (γένει). But he incorrectly concludes that since pleasures are one in kind, they are all good. Protarchus fails to see that what is one in kind can yet contain different and even opposite parts (μέρη) or shapes (μορφάς, 12c). Socrates instructs Protarchus with an analogy (12e–13a):

> And so, too, figure is like figure; they are all one in kind; but the parts of the kind are in some instances absolutely opposed to each other (γένει μέν ἐστι πᾶν ἕν, τὰ δὲ μέρη τοῖς μέρεσιν αὐτοῦ τὰ μὲν ἐναντιώτατα ἀλλήλοις), and in other cases there is endless variety of difference; . . . .

Protarchus, as we shall soon see, needs a thorough training in the division of genera into species. Three features of this passage suggest that Socrates is simply concerned with classification into kinds and not separate εἴδη: (1) Classification proceeds by seeing how pleasures are like or unlike one another. 12c–13e repeatedly emphasizes the similarities and dissimilarities between pleasures. This is the correct epistemic approach to kinds,[11] but it is utterly inappropriate for separate Forms. Phenomena in the middle dialogues only recollect the Forms to us, but the phenomena fall short and are deficient. There is not even a hint of this view at *Philebus* 12c f. (2) The γένος, pleasure, which on Protarchus' view makes all pleasures good, is in (ἐν, 13b) those pleasures. I have shown in Chapter 1 that this sort of terminology is not appropriate to express the separate being of a Form. (3) If Forms are at issue in these passages, then Plato has drastically extended the range of his theory. There are now Forms of pleasure, figure, and color (cf. 12e), whereas in the middle works there are primarily Forms corresponding to only incomplete, relational, and attributive predicates. If Plato is classifying the kinds of pleasures, colors, and figures, then this change is quite explicable.

Socrates generalizes Protarchus' error as a quandary about the one and the many: "For the assertions that one is many and many are one are marvelous, and it is easy to dispute with anyone who makes either of them" (14c). Then Socrates distinguishes two different one/many problems.

The first arises where a single subject is *F* and not-*F*. For example, Protarchus is great and small, heavy and light, has many parts and yet is one thing (14d–e). Socrates unexpectedly states that this problem is ". . . common property, and almost everybody is agreed that they [the *F* and the not-*F* predicates] ought to be disregarded because they are childish and easy and great hindrances to speculation; . . ." (14d). One may well wonder why a problem that generated the theory of Forms, and is the focal point of the *Parmenides*, is now reduced to such a low status. A unitarian could answer that it is because of the theory of Forms that this problem is childish and easy. For in the *Parmenides* (129 ff.) the Forms are introduced to explain these contrary predicates. Nevertheless, it is still odd to describe a problem as "childish and easy" when it generates such an extraordinary and thoughtful solution. Are the Forms the unmentioned solutions to this childish perplexity? Not necessarily. The *Sophist*, which is generally considered earlier than the *Philebus*,[12] gives a simpler answer. The late learners believe that we can only correctly say that man is man, dog is dog, and red is red, because one cannot be many (251b f.). Each thing can correctly have one and only one name applied to it, and hence only identity assertions are correct. But most of the commentators on the *Sophist* agree that Plato successfully answers the late learners, and he does this by distinguishing identity and predicative assertions. This is a simple solution to the problem, and Plato could have known of it when he wrote the *Philebus*. Therefore we cannot infer that Plato presupposes the theory of Forms when he dismisses this problem.

The next one/many problem is considerably tougher both in Socrates' estimation and for his interpreters. As generally stated the problem is (15a):

> But when the assertion is made that man is one (ἕνα ἄνθρωπον), or ox is one, or beauty is one (τὸ καλὸν ἕν), or the good is one, the intense interest in these and similar unities becomes disagreement and controversy.

The unities just mentioned are contrasted with the unities of those things that come to be and are destroyed (15a).

Socrates introduces such unities and the problems that they imply as "not yet common property and generally acknowledged" (14e). Of course not everyone in Plato's intellectual milieu would agree that these unities if they are Forms exist, but the problems surrounding their postulation must have been common coin at least since the *Parmenides*. For it is in the *Parmenides* that the unity of each Form is under attack. The problem in the *Parmenides* is how the one Form can remain a ἕν either if it is in the phenomena or if it is separate from them. But perhaps the unities posited here in the *Philebus* are not Forms. This would explain why these unities and their attendant problems are not yet common property.

The henads (ἐνάδων) and monads (μονάδας) that Socrates postulates are unchanging as well as ungenerated and indestructible (15b). They are contrasted with the unities of those things that are generated and destroyed. But what is Socrates' contrast? The juxtaposition of generated and ungenerated unity is compatible with each of the plausible, but mutually exclusive, interpretations of the passage, and therefore *this* textual evidence underdetermines those interpretations. Forms are ungenerated unities, while their participants are generated ones; but kinds are also ungenerated and immutable unities, while their instances are generated, changing ones. All we need now see in this contrast is Aristotle's distinction between "one in form" and "one in number" (*Metaphysics* 999b33 f., 1016b32–34, 1033b31–32, 1034a7–9). Aristotle's species and genera always are because they are always instantiated. Plato, moreover, believes that the bounteous demiurge instantiates all of the εἴδη, and in conjunction with an unawareness of recent (nineteenth-century) theories of evolution, Plato might easily conclude, as did Aristotle, that kinds are unchanging. Nevertheless, from the above contrast alone we cannot be certain what Plato's ontological commitments are.

In Chapter 3 I show that there is scant evidence (with the exception of the late/middle dialogues *Phaedrus* and *Parmenides*) for Forms corresponding to sortal predicates in the middle works. Forms are introduced there to save the phenomena from inconsistency, and hence nonexistence; if *x* is *F* and not-*F*, then these incompatible predicates demand an explanation. But phenomena do not have contrary sortal predicates. The *Philebus*, on the other hand, unhesitatingly posits immutable unities for ox and man, and with the same ease as those for beauty and goodness. The reason for this is not hard to find. The ungenerated unities of the *Philebus* are posited to explain recurrent characteristics. Thus there are εἴδη and γένη of figures, colors, knowledges, pleasures, letters, oxen, men, and so on, as well as the old standards, beauty and goodness. The εἴδη and γένη now classify the phenomena rather than save them from inconsistency. A corollary of this revised (new?) approach is that the phenomena are elevated in status; they are no longer deficient images or ikons of the Forms. Indeed, some characteristics are said to be pure and in themselves *F* by nature (51c–d); moreover, phenomena are generally described as "coming into being" (γένεσιν εἰς οὐσίαν, 26d) or as "generated being" (γεγενημένην οὐσίαν, 27b). This is precisely what we should expect if Plato is classifying phenomena into kinds. Below I will discuss the status of phenomena in greater detail.

Socrates then lists several questions about the monads, and my position is that these questions only make sense if he is asking them about kinds. The first question is whether one should believe that some such monads truly exist (15b). This question is never really answered in the *Philebus*; rather it is assumed that there are such entities. The question, as one about Forms, is moderately puzzling. In the middle dialogues Plato posits Forms, attempts to explain them, and analyzes how we can talk about them. In the *Parmenides*, even after Parmenides' devastating arguments, the Eleatic says that εἴδη must exist if there is to be speech (διαλέγεσθαι, 135b–c). Plato never questions that Forms exist, nor does he doubt that they exist as the real Beings (*Republic* 478c ff.). Why would Socrates now ask in the *Philebus* if separate εἴδη exist?

The second question is how "each [monad] being one, and always the same, and admitting neither generation nor destruction, is permanently this unity?" (15b). The predicates "one," "always the same," "not generated," and "not destructible," are, as I mentioned above, both consistent with a theory of Forms and with one about kinds. But as a question about Forms, the second is considerably more puzzling than the first. Separate εἴδη are "immutable" and "one" precisely because they are apart from the phenomena; in fact, "is one" [unique and incomposite] is a defining feature of the type of Being that a Form is. To ask how a Form is a permanent unity scarcely makes any sense; Forms just are in themselves. But as a question about kinds it is quite important. The question is not so much how a kind is incomposite or unique as how it is the unity of its cases; how are Mary, Frank, and John each a case of man, and yet man is a single unified species?

The third question states precisely this perplexity (15b–c):

> ... and next, whether in (ἐν) those things that come to be and are indefinite in number, either we must assume that it is dispersed and has become many, or that as a whole it is itself separate from itself— which appears to be the most impossible option of all—being the same and one, and is at the same time in (ἐν) one and in many.

This last question is especially interesting because of the "in" terminology. The monads are in the phenomena; this strongly suggests that they are ontologically dependent upon them. But the phenomena come to be and are destroyed; how then can the monads be unchanging and permanent? The phenomena are scattered; how can the monads be unities? As questions about the relationship between kinds and their instances or cases, these are the correct questions to ask. As questions about separate εἴδη, we must suppose that Plato is forcing the εἴδη into the quasi-material model of the *Parmenides* 131a–132c; and this model, it is generally agreed, is inappropriate for separate Forms. But *Philebus* 15b–c raises fundamentally appropriate questions about the entities at issue. Therefore it is reasonable to believe that the monads are kinds not Forms.

Plato is refreshingly optimistic about whether these questions can be solved even though the stakes are high. He says, "If ill solved, they cause the utmost perplexity; but if well solved, they are of the greatest assistance?" (15c). Plato's solutions will prove to be of great assistance to us.

Protarchus, caught up in Socrates' optimism, says that they will thrash the matter out.

The gift of gods to men provides the solution at least to the last question. This gift, division and collection, is that through which "all of the inventions of art have been brought to light" (16b). The practice of this gift is also what distinguishes between the dialectic and disputatious methods of discussion (17a). John McGinley has recently made a good case for the claim that division and collection is the method of each art; each art proceeds through a classification of its own subject matter. The philosopher, on the other hand, also understands the principles that lie behind all art in general; in the *Philebus* these principles are limit, unlimited, and the cause of a mixture.[13] Socrates and Protrachus first establish the theory of division and collection, and then an account of what grounds all mixtures, and finally they apply both methods to the task at hand, the good life for man. But since division and collection is the method of all art, and is also an important element in philosophy, we would not expect division and collection to presuppose an erudite ontology. For cobblers as well as philosophers will practice this method. Kinds are the sorts of entities that can be grasped by all of the different types of artists. We have, then, a very different situation from that found in the *Republic*. There only the philosophers know the Forms, and this knowledge, conjoined with their erotic drive for truth, is what distinguishes them from the military and artisan classes.[14] In the *Philebus*, both philosophers and artisans practice division and collection, and hence they have the same kinds of entities at their command, but the philosopher also tries to understand the principles behind all art—limited, unlimited, and *nous*.

At 16c–e Socrates gives an extensive description of his method:

> ... all things that are ever said to be are sprung from one and many and have inherent in them (ἐν αὐτοῖς) limit (πέρας) and unlimited (ἀπειρίαν). This being the way in which these things are arranged, we must always assume that there is in every case one form (μίαν ἰδέαν) of everything, and must look for it, for we shall find that it is present (ἐνοῦσαν), and if we get a grasp of this, we must look next for two, if there be two, and if not, for three or some other number; and again we must treat each of these units in the same way, until we can see not only that the original unit is one and many and unlimited (ἓν καὶ πολλὰ καὶ ἄπειρα), but just how many it is. And we must not apply the idea of unlimited to plurality until we have a view of its whole number between the unlimited and one; then, and not before, we may let each unit of everything pass on unhindered into infinity.

This passage is of the utmost importance. A careful reading of it reveals that the single generic form is also many and infinite. What this implies is that Plato's ontology has the structure in (I) below. The broken lines represent the fact that a higher genus or species is ἐν αὑτοῖς (in these) things that constitute a lower stage, and this "being-in" (ἐνοῦσαν) relation is transitive. Thus the genera are in the species, and since the species are in the phenomena, so too are the genera. The species of a genus are frequently said to be parts of that genus (μέρη, 12e), and we might schematize this relation as in (II). Moreover, a species has arranged "under" it an indefinite number of phenomena as in (III). Thus since the broken lines do not represent ontological separations, Plato can claim that the single genus *is* both one *and* many *and* an indefinite multitude. For all of the phenomena "under" a single genus are one in genus. Furthermore, the genus is in its cases. At 17b Socrates illustrates these relationships: "Sound, which passes out through the mouth of each and all of us, is one, and yet again it is infinite in number." Socrates is classifying spoken sounds. The genus, sound, is both one and infinite in number. It is infinite in number because it is *in* the infinite spoken sounds; it is one because all of these sounds are sounds. Socrates, at 16c ff., anticipates Aristotle's distinction between individuals that are "one in number," and groups of individuals that are "one in species" or "one in genus" because each possesses, respectively, the same specific or generic εἴδη.

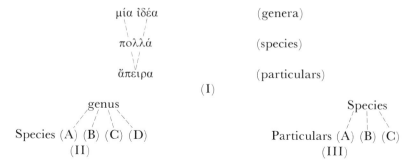

The phrase "let each unit of everything pass on unhindered into infinity" (16e) is Plato's solution to the problem of participation, but within this different ontology. After we enumerate the different types of species, it is permissible to acknowledge that they have an indefinite number of instances. Plato comes very close to expressing, but in a picturesque way, what we now call "instantiation." This relation is basic and unanalyzable, and it consists in some *x* being a case of a sound, or vowel, or pleasure, or the like. Such a solution to participation would, of course, not answer the middle-period problem of participation because the Forms are apart from their deficient instances. But perhaps the old problem can be "solved" only within a new ontological framework.

Socrates' examples of division and collection display his ontological commitments. The sounds that come through the mouth are infinite in number, but they are all one kind of thing, sound (17b–c). An intelligent musician knows the different species of sound that mediate between the single genus and the infinite instances (17b). A failure to grasp the intermediate species is the source of eristic disputation, and it makes one indefinite in thought (17e). Socrates also illustrates his thesis with the letters of the alphabet. The good grammarian knows how to classify the letters into their different species. Thus the classifications of the musician are about sound, and those of the grammarian are about letters. Division and collection does not cut ethereal, separate εἴδη but rather classifies kinds of sounds, pleasures, and the like. It is also worthy of note that in the middle dialogues there are, so far as we know, no Forms for letters, sounds, and pleasures.

Socrates describes correct artistic methodology because Protarchus, who is unskilled in it, has fallen into eristic disputation. Protarchus initially believed that pleasure is pleasure, and hence that all pleasures are alike and thus must be good. All pleasures are generically alike, but since they can be specifically different, they need not all be good. He now comes to see that both wisdom and pleasure are "one and many, and that they are not immediately infinite, but each possesses a definite number before the phenomena become infinite" (18e). Socrates and Protarchus must now investigate how many kinds of pleasure and wisdom there are, and what their natures are (καὶ ὁπόσα ἐστὶ καὶ ὁποῖα, 19b). This investigation classifies phenomena into types, and it is by looking at phenomena that one learns the distinguishing characteristics of each species. This is very unlike the middle dialogues where one looks away at a Form to know, upon return, the phenomena.

We do not need to discuss Plato's lengthy classification of the types of pleasure and knowledge. However, several passages in these discussions are relevant to our investigation.

At 44e Socrates presents an analogy designed to expedite their investigation of pleasure: if one wants to see the nature of a kind (εἴδους τὴν φύσιν ἰδεῖν), the hard for instance, then we are more likely to learn it by looking at the hardest things. So too with pleasures; we should look at those that are most extreme and intense. We are not here dealing with the theory of recollection; the deficient phenomena in recollection are not alone sufficient for a grasp of pure Being. But the nature of a kind is found in the phenomena, and we discover this nature by looking at them. The methodological advice Socrates gives is that we should look at those phenomena that best reveal natures, for example, the hardest things and the most intense pleasures.

At 51c–d Socrates asserts that the straight line, the circle, the plane, and solid figures—all formed by turning lathes, rulers, and patterns of angles—are beautiful not in comparison with other things (πρός τι), but are always beautiful in themselves by nature (ἀεὶ καλὰ καθ᾽ αὑτὰ πεφυκέναι). These forms that are beautiful in themselves are the objects of pleasures that are pure. Socrates also claims that certain colors and sounds meet these purity standards, and are likewise the objects of pure pleasures (51b–e, 53a–b). This passage marks a startling departure from the middle dialogues. There only the Form of Beauty is *F* in itself (καθ᾽ αὑτό), and all phenomenal instances of beauty are *F* and not-*F*. Real beauty is found only in the paradigmatic Form, and pure pleasures primarily attach to the Forms. But 51c–d destroys the need for a separate paradigm of Beauty, since it asserts that an instance of absolute beauty occurs among phenomena. This is precisely what we should expect if Socrates is classifying the phenomena into kinds.

At *Philebus* 53d Socrates divides being into two parts: the first is "itself in itself" (αὐτὸ καθ᾽ αὑτό), and the second is "that which is always striving for something else." The latter portion of being is for the sake of the former (54a–b). But the good is found only in that part of existence that is οὐσία (54c). Pleasure, however, is a form of generation, and hence it is not good. Owen thinks that the phrase "generation is for the sake of being" (γένεσις οὐσίας ἕνεκα γίγνεται) elevates the status of the phenomenal world; within the *Cosmos* are now distinguished "becoming" and "being."[15] Cherniss denies Owen's claim, and says, "This is ... [not] what could be meant, for, if it were, pleasure in coming to be would become the good and the argument would obviously reach a conclusion the opposite to that which is stated and intended."[16] Cherniss' reply has no force. Pleasure as a "becoming" need not come to be pleasure as an οὐσία; for just as medicine is for the sake of health, so too pleasure is for the sake of the good life. Of course medicine is not a sufficient condition for health, any more than pleasure is for the good life. Health and the good life are *cosmoi* of the body and *psyche* respectively. Therefore Plato can argue that pleasure is a becoming that results in phenomenal οὐσία, and not be compelled to admit that pleasure is a good.

Socrates' examples clearly depict phenomenal οὐσίαι. Brave lovers are for the sake of beloved boys, shipbuilding for ships, and drugs for health (53d, 54b–c). Beloved boys, ships, and health are all classified as οὐσίαι— beings (54a,c). Cherniss correctly points out that some statements in the *Timaeus* and middle dialogues also assert that phenomena are. But those that have a clearly doctrinal character also assert that phenomena are not.[17] Phenomena are and are not in contrast with Being (cf. *Republic* 477c ff.). But 26d and 27b clearly describe, in a distinctly theoretical context, the mixture as simply generated being (γένεσιν εἰς οὐσίαν, γεγενημένην οὐσίαν). The end result of limit, unlimited, and the efficient cause of mixing the two is οὐσία. Thus Plato radically upgrades the status of the phenomenal world, so that it is divided into becoming and being. In the middle works there are two worlds: the aspatial world of the Forms, and the spatial domain of phenomena.

Cherniss' ace in the hole is at *Philebus* 58a ff. He claims that even if the *Timaeus* were a middle dialogue, 58a ff. is sufficient to show that Plato continues to believe in separate Forms in the late dialogues.[18] In these passages Plato is describing the highest and most pure type of knowledge, and the objects of such knowledge are, of course, the best things. Plato says:

> ... for I am confident that all men who have any intellect whatsoever believe that the knowledge concerning being (τὸ ὄν), reality (τὸ ὄντως), and what is unchanging (τὸ κατὰ ταὐτὸν ἀεὶ πεφυκός) is the truest kind of knowledge (58a).

and again:

> Such thinkers [bad artists and craftsmen], then, toil to discover, not what always is (τὰ ὄντα ἀεί), but what comes to be, will come to be, and has come to be (τὰ γιγνόμενα καὶ γενησόμενα καὶ γεγονότα, 59a).

Plato repeatedly distinguishes unchanging real being and inferior becoming (cf. 59b–c, 61d–e). This juxtaposition is sufficient for Cherniss to claim that, "the same disjunction between what *really is* and what incessantly *becomes* with which Timaeus begins his account *is* reasserted at the end of the *Philebus* ...."[19] Of course Cherniss believes that the real Beings of the *Timaeus* are the Forms, and these are also, he believes, what is referred to in the *Philebus*.

Does the evidence compel this conclusion? It does not. The juxtaposition of being and becoming, and the relegating of the former to the status of the highest objects of knowledge, is compatible with any number of incompatible explanations. Moreover, a similarity in terminology between 59a ff. and middle-period passages does not imply an identity in doctrine. The same term or phrase can take on very different meanings in different contexts, and we must penetrate to the contextual meaning of Socrates' claims. 59a ff. is consistent with either the distinction between an eternal Form and its deficient participants or with that between an unchanging kind and its generated and destructible instances. The evidence underdetermines either interpretation.

At 59a Socrates accuses the bad craftsmen of operating only at the level of opinion, and with investigating "the things of the world, the manner of their production, their action, and the forces to which they are subjected." Such thinkers do not seek real being, but only becoming (59a). The problem with bad craftsmen is not that they investigate those things concerning the *Cosmos* (τὰ περὶ τὸν κόσμον), but rather that they seek only the mutable aspects of such things. Real artistic production, as we have seen, classifies phenomena into kinds, and division and collection are the good craftsman's real tools. The juxtaposition of generated and ungenerated being occurs in this context. Hence it is probable that kinds are the real beings, while phenomena in their physical generations, destructions, and causal relations are becoming.

Let us now turn to the meta-explanations for being: limit, unlimited, and the efficient cause of the mixture. These explanations are introduced ostensibly to explain the good life, which was just shown to be a mixture of pleasure and wisdom, but they also explain any determination and structure in the *Cosmos*. Plato introduces them as the beings (τὰ ὄντα) that are in the all (ἐν τῷ παντί, 23c), and "the all" clearly refers here to the whole universe (cf. ἐν ὅλῳ τε οὐρανῷ, 30b). Commentators have often attempted to identify one or the other of these explanations with the Forms, usually focusing on the notion of limit.[20] But none of these attempts can succeed; for in the middle dialogues the Forms are outside the *Cosmos* (cf. *Symposium* 211–212), but all of the explanations in the *Philebus* are within it. We are not dealing here with a transcendent metaphysics, but rather with the factors in the *Cosmos* that explain its structure. I will briefly discuss each of these explanations.

The best translation for ἄπειρον is "unlimited." Plato gives a number of examples of what he means by "unlimited": hotter and colder (24a–b), drier and wetter, quicker and slower, greater and smaller (25c), acute and grave (26a). All of these examples, Plato believes, fall into the γένος of the unlimited because they (at least in principle) admit of the more and the less, having unlimited gradations at both ends of their spectra. For example, the quicker can always be quicker and the slower slower, the hotter hotter and the colder colder. But what is Plato driving at with the notion of unlimited? One might attempt to connect the unlimited with the receptacle in the *Timaeus*.[21] But clearly the two are not identical; the receptacle as a molding stuff is composed only of random powers, and is as devoid of characteristics as possible (50b–c). The unlimited, on the other hand, is closely allied with the notion of *genus*. The unlimited is temperature, speed, sound, and quantity before any specific unit of these ranges is marked out. Let me give an analogy from Aristotle: Aristotle sometimes claims that the genus is matter (*Metaphysics* 1024b5–10), but how is this possible? The genus is a commutative universal that is less determinate than its species; but then matter *qua* potentiality is also less determinate than the actualities it can take on. For example, the *genus* animal might be thought of as substance with sensible powers; substance with sensible powers would then be both the *genus* for man, and the matter capable of further specific characterization. In any case, the unlimited functions both as a generic concept and as a material substrate. It is, for example, both temperature *per se* and the substrate for some particular degree of temperature.

Plato describes the limit as follows (25a–b):

> ... first equality and the equal, then the double, and anything which is definite number or measure in relation to such a number or measure, all these might properly be assigned to the class of the finite.

I am not at all certain that Plato ever really unifies limit by stating the characteristics of this *genus* (cf. 25d–e). But the idea is reasonably clear; limit is mathematical ratio or proportion, and when it enters the un-limited it "puts an end to the differences between opposites and makes them commensurable and harmonious by the introduction of number" (25d–e).

There is an ambiguity in Plato's discussion of the mixed class. The characteristic of this class is that it is the offspring of limit and unlimited when they "commune" (κοινωνία, 25e) with each other; it is generation into being (γένεσιν εἰς οὐσίαν, 26d), or generated being (γεγενημένην οὐσίαν, 27b). While it might seem more natural to describe particular phenomena as "generated being," Plato's examples are unclear about whether he is referring to particulars or to specific, determinate universals; his examples are health, the art of music, the seasons, and all the beauties of this world (25e–26b). This ambiguity is, however, of no importance. For since particulars can be classified into kinds, they have specific determination as an aspect of their generated being. The unlimited provides the generic matter, and the limited the specific determination; the offspring are either specifically determined particulars or specific determinations (of particulars). Finally, the limit is depicted as "in the all" and "in the mixture" (25e–26a); hence limit is not a separate εἶδος.

The final kind is intelligence, the efficient cause of the mixture. Plato approaches this explanation by asking where the elements in a man originate; for example, do we feed the fire in the *Cosmos* or does it supply the material for us? The latter is the correct answer. So too the *psyche* in the *Cosmos* (ἐν ὅλῳ τε οὐρανῷ, 30b) is the source of *psyche* in us, and hence there is a plentiful *psyche* in the *Cosmos* (ἐν τῷ παντί, 30c). Moreover, reason and mind are in *psyche* (30c). The efficient cause of the *Philebus* is an enpsyched cosmic intellect, not a demiurge standing outside the *Cosmos*. It is the world *psyche* of the *Timaeus*, and not the demiurge. Nevertheless, a line at 30c–d has sometimes been taken to refer to the demiurge: "Then in the nature of Zeus, you would say that a kingly *psyche* and a kingly *nous* were implanted through the power of the cause, and in the others other noble qualities, from which they derive their favorite epithets." All this obscure saying need mean is that the intellect in world *psyche* is the power behind all intelligence, and that it rules the all, infusing, among others, even the planets with intelligence (30d).

At the end of the *Philebus* Plato presents an encomium on his grand principle—order, harmony, and proportion (64d–e):

> That any compound, however made, which lacks measure and proportion, must necessarily destroy its components and first of all itself: for it is in truth no compound, but an uncompounded jumble, and is always a misfortune to those who possess it.... So now the power of the good has taken refuge in the nature of the beautiful; for measure and proportion are everywhere identified with beauty and virtue.

The good life is the beautiful one, but the good life is also, ontologically, the one displaying proper measure and proportion. Hence the power of the good is found in the nature of the beautiful; that is, in measure and proportion. We see again, as we did in the *Hippias Major*, that Plato's highest ontological principle is the aesthetic one of measure and proportion. Furthermore, just as in the *Hippias Major*, the beautiful is in things; it is a principle in the *Cosmos*. Every mixture, in order to be a mixture, must represent in some at least minimal degree the triumph of cosmic mind over chaos. Hence *in toto* the *Cosmos* is beautiful. Those mixtures that obtain a higher degree of harmony are, relatively speaking, the best.

In conclusion: The *Philebus* is a very important document in support of revisionism in the late dialogues. It depicts a more explicit position than the *Sophist* or *Statesman*; hence I have spent a large section of Chapter 5 on it. I have argued that division and collection, the method of each art, is about kinds. These kinds are grounded in the phenomena because limit is in the phenomena. Hence these kinds are not separate like the Forms. Furthermore, the explanations of all art—limit, unlimited, and *nous*—are all at work in the *Cosmos*. There is no evidence in the *Philebus* that unambiguously commits Plato to separate εἴδη, and when interpreted in its proper context the evidence supports a theory of kinds. A unitarian might reply that the cosmology and metaphysics of the *Timaeus* ultimately explain that of the *Philebus*, and that the *Philebus* is restricted in its ontological commitments only because of the limited question it addresses, that is, the nature of the good life for man. Specifically, Forms would explain limits and the receptacle the unlimited. But the *Philebus* is intelligible without such further explanations; and there are serious difficulties in how the indeterminate receptacle of the *Timaeus* explains the generic determinations of the unlimited and how the paradigmatic Forms explain the mathematical notions of limit. In the *Philebus*, Plato introduces a specific ontological theory to use in investigating a specific problem.

The *Sophist*

> Now most of the hearers, Theaetetus, when they have lived longer
> and grown older, will perforce come closer to realities and will be
> forced by sad experience openly to lay hold on being (ἐφάπτεσθαι τῶν
> ὄντων); they will have to change the opinions which they had at first
> accepted, so that what was great will appear small and what was
> easy, difficult, and all the apparent truths in arguments will be
> turned topsy-turvy by the facts that have come upon them in real life
> (234d–e).

The Stranger's comment is a fitting introduction to the *Sophist*, and it
reveals that the dialogue is not a treatise on how to grasp transcendent
Forms in another world. Sad experience in this life would not teach that!

First I will marshal arguments for the ontological status of the entities
that are discussed in the *Sophist*. Two recent articles, one by J. M. E.
Moravcsik and the other by Richard Ketchum, have already presented
parts of my position.[22] The following discussion is indebted to them,
especially to the Ketchum essay. The evidence for either unitarianism or
revisionism is not as strong as either side would hope. But I will argue that
outside the passage on the battle of the gods and giants, Plato does not
mention the Forms; the entities at issue are kinds. Finally I will show that
a passage that Cherniss claims to be a clear argument for separate Forms
does not provide such evidence. I will then turn to a lengthy discussion of
Plato's use of εἶναι, and in the context of this analysis will interpret several
important passages in the *Sophist*.

What are the entities at issue? I will show that the εἴδη of division and
collection and the five greatest εἴδη are kinds. There is, according to the
Statesman (287c), a kind for every natural articulation of phenomena.
Hence the extension of a kind theory is much broader than that of the
middle-period Forms. Kinds are also ontologically dependent upon particulars; the Sophist, for example, exists only so long as a sophist exists.
This, of course, does not preclude the Sophist from always existing just so
long as there always is some sophist or other. It is not a purpose of this
essay to analyze kinds. It is, however, part of my exegetical task to show
that the statements made about εἴδη in the *Sophist* can all be consistently
and plausibly read as kind assertions, and not as assertions about Forms or
as universally quantified assertions.[23]

J. M. E. Moravcsik has successfully argued the following claims about
division and collection:[24] (1) The bearers of names are single entities, not
pluralities, although pluralities are sometimes named. Thus 223a names a
certain kind of art, and 225a a certain type of combat. (2) What is being
cut in a division or cutting is a kind, and it is cut into parts or kinds. At
219a art is divided into kinds, and at 219c the result of such cutting is said

to be a kind. (3) The criteria of correctness for namings and cuttings is "an undefined, intuitively introduced, notion of naturalness." At *Statesman* 287c we are told to cut "at the natural joints." (4) The instances of the respective art kinds are in many passages more accurately said not to be artists or craftsmen but rather the specific activities, events, and processes of art. At *Sophist* 227b the activities and capacities of purification are instances of the kind sophistry, and at *Statesman* 281d the arts are instanced in activities not agents.

Moravcsik clearly sees that the entities that are divided and collected are not Forms.[25] The middle-period Forms are "themselves in themselves," "pure," and "indivisible." Division, however, cuts through εἴδη, and it shows that εἴδη are related as part to whole. Moreover, from an epistemic perspective, there is no lifting of the mind's eye to another place; nor are the activities and processes of an art thought of as deficient instantiations of a purer commodity. In order to classify the arts one simply looks at their instances; this epistemic model fits well with a theory of kinds. The kinds are kinds of phenomena.

This analysis of division and collection helps illuminate the greatest kinds: Being, Rest, Motion, Sameness, and Difference.[26] At 253b–c dialectic is described as the science that shows which kinds (τῶν γενῶν) harmonize with which, which reject one another, and also if there are some elemental kinds extending through all others and holding them together so that they can mingle and separate. This description of dialectic is a depiction of the interweaving of the five greatest kinds. Hence where Plato describes how the greatest kinds interweave, he is practicing dialectic. But just below 253c Plato gives another account of dialectic. The dialectician "has a clear perception of one form extending entirely through many, each of which lies apart, and of many forms differing from one another, but included in one greater form, and again of one form evolved by the union of many wholes, and of many forms entirely apart and separate" (253d–e). This account of dialectic is a description of division and collection. Therefore, dialectic consists both in division and collection and in the investigation of the more important and ubiquitous εἴδη. But dialectic would not be about two different types of objects; or if it were, Plato would probably have said so. Thus since division and collection is about kinds, I conclude that the other aspect of dialectic, that concerned with the most important εἴδη, is also about kinds.

The battle of the gods and the giants (246a ff.) also provides evidence for the *Sophist's* ontology. I will discuss this passage in detail later when I introduce Cherniss' interpretation of it. For now let me make the following remarks. The gods are the friends of the Forms, and the Forms they believe in are very like the middle-period ones (cf. 246b, 248a). But the Stranger, while sympathetic with the godlike position, is not a friend of the Forms. He distances himself from the gods' position although not as much as from that of the giants. Can we conclude that the author of the *Sophist* also distances himself from the Forms? We do not know, but it seems probable. All we know is that the Eleatic Stranger is not one of the Forms' friends, and that his position in the dispute is to adjudicate between different positions, and show how they all require a solution to the problem of being and nonbeing. We should not, then, be at all surprised if the *Sophist* does not endorse the Forms, since it is narrated from the perspective of the Eleatic Stranger. Of course, we cannot infer from this that Plato ceases to believe in Forms, even if there is no evidence for them in the *Sophist*.

After some rather startling argumentation (discussed below), the Stranger concludes that the friends of the Forms should hold the position that τὸ ὄν (being) and τὸ πᾶν (the all) consist in all things movable (κεκινημένα) and immovable (ἀκίνητα) (249d). This conclusion certainly represents a dramatic departure from the middle dialogues. Both changing things and unchanging ones are called τὸ ὄν (being); this is a dramatic juxtaposition with the earlier view where only the Forms are Beings. Moreover, both the mutable and the immutable are said to be included in τὸ πᾶν (the all). Usually in the late dialogues, as we have seen in the *Philebus*, τὸ πᾶν refers to the whole *Cosmos*. As far as I can tell from the context, τὸ πᾶν has the same reference at 249d. Therefore, both movable and immovable things are in the *Cosmos*; and hence 249d is a denial of separation. The Stranger, by including both movable and immovable things within the all, significantly modifies the position of the friends. The all now has two aspects: a changing and an unchanging one. I suggest that kinds constitute the unchanging aspect of the all, while particulars that are generated and destroyed are the changing aspect.

It is not at all plausible that the five greatest kinds are Forms. To see this we must focus on why Plato discusses how the kinds interweave. The Stranger examines a wide range of his predecessor's views about being in order to show that they are in as much perplexity about being as about not-being. The *physiologoi* claim, for example, that both the hot and the cold are; but what does this mean? Is being to be identified with the hot or the cold, or does it emerge as some third thing? The Eleatic monists are also driven to similar quandaries. Then Plato turns to the materialists and the friends of the Forms. The former are forced to admit that *psyche* and its states are, while the latter are compelled to agree that movable things are. In either case we are left with the *aporia* of what it means to say that *x* and *y* are. Last and least, the exploits of the late learners are described; their position is that we can correctly make only identity assertions about a subject, for the one can be only one and not many. In reference to all of the above Plato says (251c–d):

Then, to include in our discussion all those who have ever engaged in any talk whatsoever about being, let us address our present arguments to these men as well as to those with whom we were conversing before, and let us employ the form of questions.

The interweaving of the greatest kinds is meant to persuade *physiologoi*, late learners, Eleatics, friends of the Forms, and even materialists; moreover, it is meant to remove their combined perplexities about being. If the kinds were theoretically loaded Forms, then they would not be persuasive to those who do not believe in Forms.[27] Furthermore, the interweaving of the greatest kinds does not constitute an argument for their existence; they are assumed to exist. Whatever the kinds are, they must be readily intelligible to all those who have difficulties with being. Kinds are a reasonable candidate for this position, but Forms are not.

At 252d the Stranger asks whether all things have the power to participate in one another. If this were the case, then "Motion itself would be wholly at rest, and Rest in turn would itself be in motion, if these two could be joined with one another. But surely this at least is impossible, that Motion be at rest and Rest be in motion?" (252d, also cf. 255a–b). Rest and Motion are two of the greatest kinds. If these kinds were Forms, then the claim that Motion is at rest would be perfectly correct; for all of the middle-period Forms are ungenerated, indestructible, immutable, and always being: But the Stranger claims that if Motion partakes in Rest, then it rests, and that this is absolutely impossible. It follows that Motion and Rest are not middle-period Forms.[28]

Someone might object that even in the middle dialogues a Form cannot have the quality of its opposite: The Beautiful is beautiful, and does not have any taint of ugliness; Justice is just, and does not have any trace of injustice. Would it not, then, be perfectly reasonable to say of the Form Motion that it cannot rest? A Form excludes the quality of its opposite only when that opposite is not a metapredicate of all the Forms. Even in a sense Injustice and Ugliness (cf. *Republic* 476a) are beautiful just as all of the Forms are beautiful. A Form is beautiful because of its stability and purity. In the *Parmenides* each of the Forms is repeatedly said to be one— unique and incomposite—even Multiplicity (131a–b, by implication). Therefore, Motion, if it were a Form, would be at rest. But the Stranger says without qualification that this is impossible; thus Motion is not a Form. But if Motion is not a Form, then, of course, it is highly unlikely that the other greatest kinds are Forms. For Motion interweaves with all of the greatest kinds in one way or another; for example, it is different from Being, Sameness, Difference, and Rest.

We should also note at this point that the other metapredicates of the Forms are absent from the *Sophist*. We have just seen that "Motion rests" cannot be a Form predication. The Stranger also says that "Being is not at rest" (250c), and this also cannot be a Form predication. Moreover, nowhere in the discussion about the interweaving of the greatest kinds do we find claims of the following sort: "Motion is one," "Being is unchanging," and "Sameness is ungenerated." Arguments from silence are, of course, notoriously weak, unless we have some reason to believe that an author would have said *x* if he had believed it. Think back to the middle dialogues; whenever Plato posited a Form, and was going to make any use of the Form theory, he always surrounded the Form with many signposts of its ontological status. Plato was never reticent to mention that Forms are ungenerated, divine, one, or had other predicates, and these predicates had the important function of telling us what sorts of entities were being posited. So too in the *Sophist* we are told (implicitly) what sorts of entities are posited by what we can and cannot say about them. "Change is eternal," "Difference is divine," "Motion is incomposite," and "Being is immutable" do not appear in the *Sophist*. Is it at all likely, then, that Forms do?

At 258c the Stranger makes the following superficially puzzling claim:

> Just as we found that the Great was great (τὸ μέγα ἦν μέγα) and the Beautiful was beautiful, the not-Great was not-great and the not-Beautiful was not-beautiful, shall we in the same way say that not-Being was and is not-being, to be counted as one class among the many classes of being?

One might be tempted to argue that 258c self-predicates a kind, and hence changes it into a paradigmatic, separate individual.[29] But this interpretation is untenable. First, while there are Forms of opposites in the middle works there are not Forms of negations; such Forms would not have any positive content, and hence there is no good reason for Plato to posit them. Second, "not beautiful," "not great," and "not being" could not function as self-predicates even if there were Forms of negations. In Chapter 3 we discussed the multiple reasons why Plato self-predicates a Form. Among other functions a self-predicate describes what we see a Form as, since it specifies the nature of a Form; negative predicates cannot fulfill this function. Furthermore, a self-predicate specifies the causally relevant feature of a Form (given the Causal Principle); a negative predicate could not have this function. I conclude that the apparent predications at 258c are not self-predications. Third, τὸ καλὸν ἦν καλόν, τὸ μὴ μέγα μὴ μέγα, and the like are not predications. Grammatically it is permissible to understand an implicit τὸ before the last occurrences of καλόν and μέγα. The statements would then translate "The Beautiful was the Beautiful," and "The not-Great was the not-Great." These translations are plausible because the *Sophist* has an explicit analysis of such identities: "The Beautiful in virtue of partaking in Sameness is the same as itself," "The not-Great in virtue of partaking in Sameness is the not-Great." This analysis also holds for negations as long as we remember that negations are parts of Difference (257c–d).[30] Generically, "The Different in virtue of partaking in Sameness is the Different," and specifically "The Different from the Great [the not-Great] by partaking in Sameness is different from the Great [is the not-Great]," and "The Different from Being [not-Being] by partaking in Sameness is the Different from Being [is not-Being]." All of the statements at 258c are explicable as participations in Sameness or Difference. Hence they do not provide any evidence for separate, paradigmatic Forms in the *Sophist*.

Let us return to Plato's discussion of the friends of the Forms. Cherniss makes the following claims about this passage:[31]

> The argument of this notoriously maltreated passage is succinctly but exactly the following: The "friends of the ideas" say that the real being of these ideas, which is always unalterably the same, and not γένεσις, which is incessant in its variation, is the object of knowledge. This assertion, however, implies the existence of the action of knowing and therefore of intelligence and life and so of *psyche*, the requisite vehicle of both; and consequently it implies the existence of vital motion that *is pysche* and so of real motion. This last, of course, is the *idea* of κίνησις, of which the vital motion (i.e. self-motion) is the manifestation.

Cherniss then claims:[32]

> There is in the text no hint of the existence of γένεσις and nothing to suggest that the original disjunction of γένεσις and οὐσία should be rejected or even qualified.

I disagree with each of Cherniss' three positions: (1) that Plato introduces a Form of Change; (2) that Plato provides no hint that generation is; and (3) that Plato does not reject the original two-world disjunction between generation and Being.

The Stranger's interrogation of the friends begins with the disjunction between generation and Being that is familiar from the middle dialogues (248a). Generation is different at different times and it participates in the power of acting and being acted on; Being is unchanging and it has no power for change (248a,c). But Being is known, and in so far as it is known it is moved (κινεῖσθαι, 248e). The Stranger surprisingly concludes: "... shall we be persuaded that motion and life and *psyche* and mind are really not present to absolute Being, and that it neither lives nor thinks, but awful and holy, devoid of mind, is fixed and immovable?" This passage had incalculable influence on Neoplatonic thought; in particular, it influenced Plotinus' second hypostasis where Being and mind are indivisibly unified. In the case of 248e–249a the Neoplatonists are better interpreters than modern scholars who are reticent to admit what is obviously in the text. Plato makes the following invalid moves:

(1) Being is known.
∴ (2) Being is moved (κινεῖσθαι).
∴ (3) Mind is present to (παρεῖναι) Being.
∴ (4) Being lives and thinks.
∴ (5) Being has life and mind and *psyche* (249a).

The Stranger then draws a more reasonable inference: motion and that which is moved exist (249b). Motion is a necessary condition for mind (249b). On the other hand, if all things are in flux, there will be no mind (249c). The philosopher must, then, reject the theory that all is motionless, and the theory that all is in flux; he must "quote the children's prayer, 'all things immovable and in motion,' and must say that being (τὸ ὄν) and the universe (τὸ πᾶν) consist of both" (249d). So concludes the interrogation of the friends.

Nowhere in the whole discussion is there any mention of a Form of Motion. Therefore the point of this passage is not to introduce this Form. The overt conclusion of the passage, and certainly a modification and criticism of the friends' position, is that being and the whole contain all things movable and immovable. To categorize moving things as τὸ ὄν is to elevate their status from the middle dialogues; it claims that generation is real. To categorize both movable and immovable things under τὸ ὄν and τὸ πᾶν is to reject a radical juxtaposition of two worlds, as is found in the middle dialogues—on the one hand the realm of real Being, on the other the domain of deficient phenomena. All things movable and immovable are now real, and contained within a single whole. I conclude that Cherniss' three claims about this passage are false, and especially that the Stranger does not force the friends to posit a Form of Motion. In fact the Stranger tempers the friends' original contrast between Being and becoming. Is Plato in the guise of the Stranger implicitly repudiating his earlier positions? Given the textual evidence in the *Sophist*, an affirmative answer is warranted.

A crucial claim for my position is that the Stranger's interweavings of the greatest kinds as well as his divisions and collections can naturally be read as kind assertions. I have already shown that "Motion rests" and "Being rests," which are emphatically said to be false, cannot be Form predications. Let me sketch the sort of interpretations I intend. My general interpretative scheme is the following: "x is the kind of —— that is F."[33] The variable x could have as its substitution instances the Sophist, the Angler, Sophistry, Motion, Rest, Being, and the like; and the blank, if possible, would be filled with the genus of what instantiates the subject position. If no genus is available, then "thing" may be supplied in the blank. With this schema we can generate reasonable and consistent interpretations of the statements made in the *Sophist*. Below are specimen examples.

(1) The Sophist is a hunter of young men.
(2) The Fisherman is a hunter of animals in water.
(3) Sophistry is the art of persuasion.
(4) Being is the kind of thing that is.
(5) Being is the kind of thing that is not Sameness.
(6) Motion is a kind of state that is not Rest.
(7) Difference is the kind of relation that is not Sameness.
(8) Difference is the kind of relation that is πρός τι.
(9) Sameness is the kind of relation that is.
(10) Sameness is the kind of relation that is not-Being.

(1)–(3) are possible examples of the results of division; (4)–(10) are specimen examples of the interweavings of the greatest kinds. It is a strength of my position that both types of assertions can be read as kind assertions; and, as I argued above, dialectic is about both types of assertions (253b f.). Also (1)–(3) can no more be interpreted as claims about Forms than (4)–(10). For what would it mean to say that, for example, the Form, the Sophist, is a hunter of young men? I can make no sense out of such a claim. Thus neither assertions like (1)–(3) nor those like (4)–(10) can be read as Form predications.

As far as we are told, (1)–(3) do not depend upon and presuppose participation statements. The Sophist, for example, is not what he is because he participates in the hunting of young men, where "participates" has the technical meaning given to it in the *Sophist*. (4)–(10), however, do depend upon and presuppose participation statements; for example, (4) results from "Being participates in Sameness, and therefore is the same as itself (Being)," (6) from "Motion participates in Difference, and thus is different from (Rest)," (9) from "Sameness participates in Being, and therefore is," and (10) from "Sameness participates in Difference, and thus is different from (Being)."

The above difference between kind assertions like (1)–(3) and those like (4)–(10), delineates a further important distinction. Division has the purpose of capturing the nature or essence of what it investigates; division attempts to define the nature of Sophistry or Fishing. The interweavings of the greatest kinds, however, do not attempt to state the nature or essence of a kind. Participation in Being tells us that a kind is or is *F*, while participation in Difference tells us that a kind is not identical with some other kind, but these participation statements do not analyze the nature or essence of their subjects. Plato is aware of this. A careful reading of 254c and 257a reveals that participation is governed by a kind's nature, not that it gives that nature. The nature of a kind obviously regulates whether it is or is *F*, what it is the same as, and what it is different from.

We have already seen that kind assertions cannot be about Forms. But we must still rule out deflationistic interpretations. Can we interpret statements like (1)–(10) as universally quantified statements?[34] "(x) [x is a sophist ⊃ x is a hunter of young men]" is quite likely false even though "The Sophist is a hunter of young men" is true. For some sophists may be in prison or exile, but the Sophist is not. "Change is different from the Same" is true, but "(x) [x is changing ⊃ x is different from anything that is the same (as itself)]" is clearly false. We need not multiply examples beyond necessity; assertions that are clearly thought to be true in the *Sophist* are false if interpreted as universally quantified statements. Hence this sort of deflationistic interpretation fails.

I have not philosophized about what a kind is or whether there are kinds. These are interesting and important questions, but they are not centrally relevant to my exegetical concerns. I have argued that the relevant claims in the *Sophist* can plausibly and consistently be interpreted as kind assertions, and cannot be read as about Forms or as universally quantified statements. Hence it is reasonable to impute to Plato in the *Sophist* an interest in kinds, not Forms.

One might object to my argument that we cannot tell whether the *Sophist* employs an ontology of kinds without having a complete analysis of what a kind is. I would reply that it is certainly possible to know some characteristics of kinds, and to understand talk about kinds, without having a complete analysis of what a kind is. There are numerous philosophical problems about kinds, and they need to be solved for a complete analysis, but they do not prevent us from recognizing talk about kinds. Furthermore, kind talk is common in both ancient Greek and English, and it has its recognizable characteristics. Finally, it should not be assumed that I endorse a theory of kinds; my task is to interpret Plato. My revisionist views of the *Sophist* are, to the best of my knowledge, not based on my present philosophical proclivities.

The interweaving of the greatest kinds also solves, but in a different framework, the *Parmenides*' problem of how *x* can be *F* and not-*F*. At 256a–b the Stranger says:

> Then we must admit that Motion is the same and is not the same, and we must not be disturbed thereby; for when we say it is the same and not the same, we do not use the words alike (ὁμοίως). When we call it the same, we do so because it partakes of the Same in relation to itself, and when we call it not the same, we do so on account of its

participation in Difference, by which it is separated from the Same, and becomes not that but other, so that it is correctly spoken of in turn as not the Same.

The interweavings of the kinds explain how they can be *F* and not-*F*. Being is because it partakes in Sameness and hence is the same as itself, but Being also is not because it partakes in Difference and hence is not (not-Being, Sameness, and the like). Motion is because it partakes in Being and hence is or is *F*, but also Motion is not because it partakes in Difference from (Being, Sameness, Rest, and the like). These two examples provide, whether Plato realized it or not, different analyses of *F* and not-*F* predications. The former contrast is between a statement of self-identity and a nonidentity assertion; the latter contrast is between either a positive existential claim or a positive predication on the one hand, and a statement of nonidentity on the other. Later in the *Sophist* the Stranger also forges an analysis of negative predications (not-being *F*, 257b ff.), and this further enriches the senses in which *x* can be *F* and not-*F*. Joan does not partake in Beauty, and hence is, predicatively, not-beautiful, although there are many things that Joan is predicatively.

Let me speculate about why we find kinds and not Forms in the *Sophist*. The Stranger, when criticizing the position of the friends of the Forms, clearly wants to change their stance so that there are not two worlds related by participation, but one world with changing and unchanging features. A clear impetus for this modification would be Plato's earlier inability, as seen in the *Parmenides*, to successfully relate Forms and phenomena. The Stranger is quite clear that knowledge requires both change and stability, but kinds provide just such stability within the *Cosmos*. As long as a kind is instantiated it exists; and unlike particular phenomena, kinds do not alter their characteristics. A kind for Plato or Aristotle is always instantiated, and it is fixed in the nature of things; it is not the result of quasi-arbitrary classificational schemes. Furthermore, a kind has a strong resemblance to a paradigm; for the definition of a kind states the standard features that make it and its instances what they are. The Whale is a kind of animal that swims, bears its young alive, eats plankton, and so on. It would not be difficult to confuse kind assertions with those about separate, paradigmatic Forms, although I do not see any evidence that Plato made this confusion.

Another impetus for the change from Forms to kinds is the intensified interest in how Forms interrelate. As long as Forms were aloof and isolated no connections were possible. The more Plato analyzes and experiments with such connections, the less separate the Forms become. The changes probably were gradual, but the end results are clearly distinct; in the middle works there are separate Forms, in the *Philebus* and *Sophist* kinds.

At 250b the Stranger makes the following startling claim:

> Being, then, you consider to be something else in the *psyche* (τὸ ὂν ἐν
> τῇ ψυχῇ), a third in addition to these two, inasmuch as you think
> Rest and Motion are embraced by it . . . .

Does Plato really mean to say that Being is in the *psyche*? If not, what other
interpretation could this passage have? Since 250b is a unique and isolated
claim in the *Sophist*, we might write if off as a slip of the tongue or some
mere form of expression. But this would be too hasty. For as I will show
below both the *Timaeus* and the *Theaetetus* make Being, Sameness, and
Difference psychic categories in virtue of which we recognize these kinds in
reality. Plato may well believe, although it is mere speculation for the
Sophist alone, that Being, for example, is both a kind and a psychic
category. Being as a kind does not have a visible appearance as does red,
and our recognition of its instantiation may require psychic capacities
autonomous of visual ones. While this is speculation, Plato might believe
that both the kinds—Being, Sameness, and Difference—and the corresponding psychic categories have the same logical grammar; they are
isomorphically related to each other.[35]

The Verb "to be" in the *Sophist*

Let us now turn to the use of the Greek verb "to be" in the *Sophist*. In
Chapter 3 I argued that Plato uses "to be" primarily in what Kahn calls
the "veridical sense," and that existential and predicative uses are special
cases of this more fundamental sense. I will argue that this is also true in
the *Sophist*, and that participation in Being explains statements like
"Motion is" where "is" has the general veridical sense, but that in the
appropriate contexts the "is" could have the existential, or the predicative, or the identity use. I do not believe that Plato explicitly distinguishes
and gives different analyses for the semantically complete (existential) and
the semantically incomplete (predicative and identity) senses of "to be."
Hence I disagree with Ackrill's interpretation.[36] But the problems and
solutions of the *Sophist* can be read as, in part, existential in nature. Hence
I also disagree with Owen's interpretation.[37] My position is closest to that
held, I believe, by John Malcolm.[38]

First I will outline three interpretations of Plato's use of "to be" in the
Sophist.

(A) J. L. Ackrill boldly argues that Plato recognizes a three-way ambiguity in "to be." In respect to the existential use of "to be" Ackrill
says:[39] "μετέχει τοῦ ὄντος (shares in being) is the philosopher's
equivalent of the existential ἔστι, but, as will be seen, it is not his
analysis of ἔστι in its other uses. So the existential meaning is marked

off." Ackrill goes on to argue that Plato also marks off the predicative and identity uses.

(B) John Malcolm presents a more subtle analysis. Malcolm says,[40] "But if μετέχει τοῦ ὄντος does not mean 'X exists,' what does it mean? I submit that it means 'X is' where 'is' has an undifferentiated sense which covers both existential (complete) and predicative (incomplete) uses." Malcolm criticizes Ackrill for not seeing that at 256e "partaking in Being" implies that the participant *is* many things. The italicized "is" is undifferentiated in use. It could be completed either existentially or predicatively (extended to include the identity sense). Malcolm believes that Plato distinguishes predicative and identity uses of "to be." Finally, Malcolm argues that the Pre-Socratic puzzles about being are most plausibly read as *aporia* about naming and predicating; however, Malcolm admits that the puzzles can be given an existential interpretation.[41]

(C) G. E. L. Owen argues that the *Sophist* "neither contains nor compels any isolation of an existential verb."[42] The problems about not-being only appear to be rooted in existential puzzles; in fact, they are predicative puzzles, and they lead to a study of "... is ...," and "... is not ...". I will list the key elements in Owen's argument:

(1) At 250e–251a the Stranger claims that we will be jointly illumined about both being and not-being. Owen calls this the "parity assumption."[43] But the Stranger nowhere makes sense of "does not exist," hence if we believe the parity assumption, he does not attempt to rescue "exists" as a sense of "to be." Plato does analyze "is not-*F*"; thus he only attempts to explain "is *F*."

(2) At 242a–b Plato states that he will contradict all of the sophist's puzzles about speaking of not-being. If these puzzles are existential in nature, then Plato fails; for he only resuscitates a meaning for "is not-*F*." To be charitable to Plato we should also see the puzzles about not-being as only about incomplete senses of "to be."[44]

(3) Plato's problem is with "not being *F*," not "does not exist." He makes this clear to his readers with an analogy: Not-being is analogous to is not-large (257b–c).[45]

(4) The sophist's paradox equates "What is not" with "Nothing," and commentators immediately assume that "Nothing" is "What does not exist." But we need not accept this imputation. "Nothing" = "What is not anything," a "subject with all the being knocked out of it and so unidentifiable ...."[46]

(5) "Partakes in Being" implies that the participant is many things (256e); hence "partakes in Being" cannot be read existentially.[47]

(6)   Plato distinguishes Being and Otherness by claiming that the former is both αὐτὰ καθ᾽ αὑτά and πρὸς ἄλλα, while the latter is always πρὸς ἄλλα (255c–d). Commentators have argued that Being must be both existential (itself in itself) and predicative, while Difference is always in respect to other things, that is, to difference from something else. Owen argues that identity claims are not πρὸς ἄλλα, and hence "to be" can be αὐτὰ καθ᾽ αὑτά even though it does not have an existential interpretation.[48]

I will first briefly sketch my position, and then reply to each of Owen's points. I believe, following Kahn, that the verb "to be" is primarily veridical with semantically complete and incomplete uses as special cases. Hence John Malcolm's interpretation is, I believe, correct. When the sophist's paradox equates "What is not the case," with "Nothing," Plato is talking about what both predicatively and existentially is not. The *physiologoi* are depicted as naming the hot or the cold when they claim that, for example, "The hot is." What is their problem? It can be viewed in at least two ways: the *physiologoi* need to distinguish either naming and predicating or naming from assertions of existence. This is also true of the gods and the giants. The interweavings of the greatest kinds are, of course, introduced to solve these problems. "Partaking in Being" simply tells us to add "is" to the participant, and this is an undifferentiated "is." Participation in Being when nothing else need be added explains the semantically complete—existential—sense; when a predicate adjective is present or appropriately added, we are given the predicative sense; and when the kinds Sameness and Difference are conjoined to "to be," they create identity and nonidentity statements. It remains that "participating in Being" does not isolate the existential sense, but only tells us to add the undifferentiated "is." Owen is correct that Plato only solves the problem of how to speak about not-being at the predicative and nonidentity levels. Nevertheless, Plato himself admits that he is only going to solve *a version* of the Sophists' paradox (241c,d).

I will now turn to each of Owen's arguments, taking them in reverse order:

(6)   Owen is correct that "to be" could be seen as "itself in itself" in contrast with Difference, if it is the identity sense of "to be." For "to be" would not, then, connect different things. Owen's argument does not show that "to be" cannot *also* be read existentially and hence again be "itself in itself." The evidence of this passage (255c–d) underdetermines either interpretation.

(5)   256e does show that "*x* participates in Being" implies that "*x* is in many ways (πολύ)." Therefore, participation in Being does not isolate an existential sense of "to be." Furthermore, such participation certainly introduces the incomplete sense of "to be." But none of these arguments

imply that "to be" cannot also be read, in part, existentially. Πολὺ μέν ἐστι τὸ ὄν may have as part of its meaning—or as one case of its undifferentiated veridical use—"exists." Plato's point would then be that participation in Being permits us to attach the undifferentiated veridical "to be," and the verb could then be read, depending on context, in any one of its three special senses.

(4) Owen claims that "nothing" in the sophist's paradox about the impossibility of speaking about nothing should be interpreted as an indescribable subject, a subject with all the being (being *F*, *G*, and so on) knocked out of it. I believe that "nothing" is both indescribable and nonexistent. Plato, himself, says that nothing = not any being (τὶ τῶν ὄντων, 237e ff.); but this phrase underdetermines, and hence is compatible with either of the above interpretations. Owen's position, however, has the massive implausibility of equating nothing with the indescribable subject, the receptacle, of the *Timaeus* (cf. 50c ff.). But the receptacle, being an existing subject with all of the descriptive being knocked out of it, is in an odd sense intelligible; it is known by bastard reason. Nothing in the *Sophist*, however, is not intelligible in any way, not even by bastard reason. The reason for this is that unlike the receptacle, nothing does not exist.

The assumption that governs why it is impossible to speak about nothing = what is not in any way *F*, and does not exist, is implied at 228c:

> But if things which partake of motion and aim at some particular mark pass beside the mark and miss it on every occasion when they try to hit it, does this happen through proportion ... or disproportion? ... Now being ignorant is nothing else than the aberration of a *psyche* that aims at truth, when the understanding passes beside the mark.

Thinking and speaking are intentional activities. But Plato does not have any concept of intentional inexistence. Hence he likens thinking, saying, and believing to shooting an arrow out into reality. False believing and speaking, in the only sense Plato can make of it, misses the mark. But nothing does not exist at all; therefore it is absolutely impossible to think or speak about it. The receptacle exists, but it is indescribable; since it exists, it provides a target for thought, but in an odd sense because it is an indescribable target. Hence the receptacle is known by bastard reason, but no such claim is made about nothing.

Let us briefly turn to the *physiologoi's* problems about being, the late learners, and that of the gods and giants. All of these puzzles can be read as, in part, existential. Some *physiologoi* name the hot and the cold "being" (243e f.). But then either being is some third thing or the hot and the cold are identical. Both alternatives are obviously unacceptable. What are the confusions here? We could say either of the following: the *physiologoi* fail to distinguish naming and predicating, or they fail to distinguish naming from assertions of existence. In truth they fail to do both. The same is also true about the gods (250b f.). What do they mean when they say that motion and rest are? Are they the same, or is being some third thing? Now even if we say with Owen that what is known to solve these puzzles is an understanding of "is real," we cannot go on and conclude with Owen that to predicate "is real" is not to say anything about existence. For as I have already argued in Chapter 3, existence is part of the analysis of "is real." In any case it is perfectly possible to read these puzzles equally as about the difference between naming and predicating, between naming and asserting existence, or between naming and asserting reality. The last possibility contains examples of the former two as its components. Finally, the late learners' paradox (251b f.) generally precludes saying that one thing is many, or the many one. The late learners claim that we can make only identity statements correctly. The explicit examples that they rule out are all predications—we may not call a man, "white," "tall," "good," or "just"; we may only say that "Man is man," "Good is good," and the like. Obviously the solution to the late learners' position is to distinguish and explain the difference between predicational and identity assertions. And Plato does just this. But the late learners also, at least implicitly, rule out existential claims, because we cannot say any multiplicity of things about a subject. (For the best discussion I know of all of these problems with asserting "being," cf. John Malcolm's essay.[49])

(2) Let me address (2) before (1) and (3). 242a–b asserts only that the Stranger will attempt to refute father Parmenides; this does not imply that the Stranger will take on the sophist's paradox in all of its forms. It is sufficient to refute Parmenides and to disarm the sophist that not-being makes sense in any sense. Moreover, at 241c and again at 241d the Stranger indicates that he will attack only a part of the sophist's defense; he wants to get hold of not-being in at least some way. The sophist can be unmasked if it can be shown that in some sense we speak of not-being.

(1) and (3) Owen is correct that Plato solves the problem of how to speak about not-being only for incomplete uses of the verb. The parity assumption would then indicate that only positive and negative predications and identities are fully illumined. But this certainly does not show that Plato solves all of the initial problem, and not just part of it. Plato is clear that he only intends to grasp not-being in one sense; furthermore, as long as he continues to assume that thinking and speaking aim at objects, not-being, as nonexistence, will remain intractible.

In conclusion: Against Ackrill I do not see that Plato explicitly marks off the existential sense of "to be." Against Owen I believe that (1) speaking about not-being is *in part* an existential problem, (2) the *aporia* of the *physiologoi*, gods and giants, and late learners can *in part* be interpreted as the inability to distinguish naming from asserting existence, and (3) "participation in Being" is not simply predicative, but rather allows us to add the undifferentiated use of "to be." Existential and predicative senses are special cases of this undifferentiated use, and which is appropriate will depend on the context.

The *Theaetetus*

The *Philebus* and *Sophist* are the strongest documents for revisionism. Hence I have spent a large proportion of this chapter on them. There are, however, two passages in the *Theaetetus* that are of interest to my project, and so I will briefly turn to them. The first passage at 184c ff. is about what the *psyche* discerns in itself, and the second at 201e ff. is about why the elements are unknowable. I will first summarize in detail 184c ff.; then I will discuss whether or not it introduces separate Forms. Finally I will turn my attention to 201e ff. and see what implications for the Forms this passage has.

Socrates asks whether we see by (ᾧ) the eyes or through (δι' οὗ) them, hear by the ears or through them, and so on. It is agreed that we generally perceive through the organs of the body and not by them (184c). Socrates and Theaetetus then agree that there is one power in the *psyche* by which we perceive through the bodily instruments, the senses (184d). It is impossible to perceive through one sense what you perceive through another; you cannot perceive through sight what you perceive through hearing, and the converse (184e–185a). If there is a thought about both what is heard and seen, then it does not come through one sense organ or the other (185a). But in regard to sound and color one thinks about both of them: (1) that they are, (2) that each is different from the other, (3) that each is the same as itself, (4) that both are two and each is one, and (5) that they are like and unlike one another. One cannot grasp these common judgments (τὸ κοινόν) concerning them (περὶ αὐτοῖν) through one organ or the other (185b). There is, then, no organ at all through which we grasp the common characteristics. By a process of elimination Socrates concludes, "The *psyche* views itself through itself those things that are common in respect to all things" (αὐτὴ δι' αὑτῆς ἡ ψυχὴ τὰ κοινά μοι φαίνεται περὶ πάντων ἐπισκοπεῖν, 185d–e). Socrates also claims that beautiful and ugly, good and bad are grasped by the *psyche* in itself (186a). The upshot of this argument is that knowledge is not perception, but rather lies in some function of the *psyche* when, itself in itself, it is engaged concerning being (ὅταν αὐτὴ καθ' αὑτὴν πραγματεύηται περὶ τὰ ὄντα, 187a).

There are two general categories of interpretation for this passage. The first kind of interpretation—as held by Cornford and Cherniss—is that perception is not knowledge because the objects of perception are not separate Forms.⁵⁰ Only the unchanging Forms can be known. The point of the passage is that knowledge is achieved by the *psyche* operating "itself in itself" independent of the senses; the beings that the *psyche* engages in itself are the separate Forms. The *psyche's* independent activity is an acquaintance and grasping of the Forms. The Forms are described in this passage as the τὰ κοινά (the common things). Thus the major distinction in this passage is between the perceptions of sensible objects, that do not constitute knowledge, and the intuitions of Forms, that do. The other kind of interpretation—held by Cooper, Ryle, and Crombie—is that Forms are not introduced in this passage.⁵¹ The point of the passage is to contrast perception through the sense organs with the reflective and judgmental capacities of the *psyche* in itself. The former do not constitute knowledge, at least in this passage, while the latter do. The judgments the *psyche* makes in itself are about the common characteristics of perceptual objects. The *psyche* needs to judge about these characteristics in itself because the characteristics are not, themselves, perceptual objects. We do not see being, unity, difference, or likeness through any sense organ; rather we judge that something "is," "is the same as itself," "is unlike another thing," and so on. I am in complete agreement with the latter interpretation; there is no evidence that separate Forms are introduced in this passage, and the main point of the passage is to contrast perception and judgment.⁵²

Cornford and Cherniss equate the τὰ κοινά with Forms, and the *psyche's* independent activity in grasping these common things with the intuitive grasping of Forms found in the *Phaedo* and *Republic*. Indeed, there is some similarity in terminology between the *Theaetetus* passage and earlier ones; at 185e the *psyche* itself in itself views (ἐπισκοπεῖν) the common things, and at 187a it, in itself, engages the beings (πραγματεύηται περὶ τὰ ὄντα). But as I have often emphasized, a similarity in terminology does not guarantee the same doctrine; a careful analysis of the context is also needed to see if the terms are used in the same way, and about the same things. Let us look at the contexts in which the claims at 185d and 187a are embedded.

For a multiplicity of reasons Forms are not introduced in these passages:⁵³

(1) The τὰ κοινά are features of the perceptual objects, such as sound and color. Περὶ αὐτοῖν 185b, περὶ αὐτῶν 185b, ἐπὶ πᾶσι 185c, περὶ πάντων 185d, and ἐπὶ πάντων at 186a all directly or indirectly refer back to the examples of perceptual objects at 185a. The common things are, then, characteristics of sights, sounds, and the like.

(2) While Plato does talk about our viewing the common characteristics, he also uses a group of verbs that emphasize the judgmental aspects of psychic activity, namely: ἀναλογιζομένη 186a,c, and συλλογισμῷ 186d.

(3) Closely related to (1) and (2), 186d claims that knowledge is not in

the perceptions (ἐν ... τοῖς παθήμασιν), but in the reasoning concerning them (περὶ ἐκείνων).

(4) At 186a Socrates includes being, likeness and unlikeness, identity and difference, beautiful and ugly, and good and bad among the characteristics that the *psyche* views in itself. Socrates, then, claims (186a–b):

> I think that these also are among the things the being of which the *psyche* most certainly views in their relations to one another, reflecting within itself upon the past and present in relation to the future [cf. the next half dozen lines].

The *psyche* does not look away at the supersensible Forms; rather it looks at the perceptual objects; it compares them with one another, and it compares them with past occurrences as well as possible future ones. This description makes no sense, if it were about separate Forms; we do not come to know a Form by comparing it with past, present, and future temporal events. In the recollection of a Form the senses only stimulate us to investigate that Form in itself; beyond that the senses are hindrances to such knowledge. But 186a–b is a reasonably intelligible if brief summary of, for example, judgments about beauty.[54] We compare something with others of its kind, and also make comparisons with past and anticipated future instances; likewise, for judgments about good and evil.

(5) At 186b–c Socrates claims that perceptions that reach the *psyche* through the body can be had both by men and animals from the moment of birth. On the other hand, reflections concerning these (περὶ τούτων ἀναλογίσματα) in respect to their being and benefit (οὐσίαν, ὠφέλειαν) are difficult and are acquired only through time on account of many experiences (πραγμάτων), and through education. The reflections in this passage are about the perceptions; we judge their being and benefit, and experience as well as education are necessary for such judgments. Plato does not talk about our knowledge of the Forms in this way.

I conclude that the *psyche* in itself judges the τὰ κοινά. These characteristics are not given through the five sense organs, but are brought to perception by the *psyche*. On the basis of this passage, then, we see in Plato the "Neo-Kantianism" imputed to him by such commentators as Natorp and Stewart. The main distinction in the passage is, then, between perception that does not yield knowledge and reflection about the perceptions, that does.

At 186c Socrates asserts that it is impossible to attain truth (ἀληθείας) without being (οὐσίας). Also, being repeatedly heads the list of judgments made by the *psyche* (185a, 186a). Why must we grasp being in order to grasp truth; and why is being listed first among all of the judgments? In some contexts in this passage, "being" is naturally read as "exists," but if "being" is employed in its undifferentiated, veridical sense, then it is the ground of all judgments. For a judgment involves some use of the verb "to be"; either *x* exists, or *x* is like *y*, or *x* is different from *y*, or the like. Thus we cannot make a true or a false judgment without a grasp of being. Therefore we cannot attain truth (a true judgment) without being—without a use of "to be."

The second passage of interest to us is Socrates' version of Theaetetus' dream (201c ff.). Theaetetus remembers having heard from someone that knowledge is true opinion plus an account (λόγος), and that matters of which there is not an account are not knowable. Theaetetus does not recall what things are knowable and what unknowable, and so Socrates relates to him a "dream for a dream" (201e). Socrates has heard certain persons say that the primary elements (πρῶτα ... στοιχεῖα) from which we and all other things are composed do not admit of a *logos*, for each element alone, by itself, can only be named (201e). If we were to try to speak of an element alone, and give a *logos* of it, then we cannot say of it that it is or is not, for that would be to add being (οὐσία) or not-being to it; nor can we say "itself" or "that" or "each" or "alone" or "this" or anything else of the sort, for these prevalent terms are added to all things, and they are different from the things to which they are added (202a). If it were possible to explain an element, then it would have to be explained apart from everything else. But the elements can only be named, they do not admit of a *logos*, and thus they are not the objects of reason or knowledge, but only of perception (202b). The compounds, however, that are made out of the elements do admit a *logos*, and thus are objects of knowledge.

Socrates is quick to demolish this theory. Either the compound is constituted of the elements as its parts, and is nothing over and above those parts, in which case it is known by knowing unknowable elements, which is absurd; or the compound is something over and above its constituent elements, in which case it is a single form (μονοειδές) that is without parts (ἀμέριστον, 205d), and hence it is just as unknowable as the elements. Socrates concludes with the observation that we all know the elements before we know how to combine them (206b).

Whose theory of elements is Socrates discussing here? There does not seem to be any satisfactory answer to this question. M. F. Burnyeat argues that Socrates' returning "a dream for a dream" is an instance of Plato's general use of dream motifs, and these motifs:[55]

(1) Introduce a dream as a model for the recalling of an experience for which one is unable to specify a precise time, or which never happened at all, and
(2) Are a natural image for inspiration, for an idea coming to mind, not one that is definitely asserted to be true, but as an inspired idea that one may well wonder whether to accept as true.

When Socrates and Theaetetus dream that they have heard certain persons distinguish the knowable from the unknowable, "certain persons" need not have a reference to any known or unknown historical figures. Both Theaetetus and Socrates may simply have a vague inspiration about what knowledge is, and dreaming is the natural way to introduce such a phenomenon.

The elements, moreover, are broadly characterized. First they are said to be that out of which we and all other things are composed (201e), suggesting that they are the physical elements of nature; then they are likened to the elements in writing, the letters of the alphabet (202e). Plato attributes both positions to proponents of the element theory. Glenn Morrow suggests that Plato is not referring to a single theory, but rather has constructed a model that is applicable to numerous fields.[56] In physical studies, the elements are parts in lexical letters, in grammatical words, in mathematical premises, and the like. The combined effect of Burnyeat and Morrow is to suggest that Plato is nondogmatically entertaining a general *aporia*, contained in the very notions of analysis and giving a *logos*.

What is of interest for our study in this passage is that there is a striking resemblance between the elements and Plato's middle-period Forms as seen through the visual model. Forms are "themselves in themselves," "indivisible," "single-formed," "isolated," and the like, and yet Socrates claims that they are the objects of knowledge . Furthermore, as we have seen in Chapter 3, both intellectual vision and giving an account are necessary conditions for knowledge. But in the middle dialogues Plato never really gives a *logos* of an incomposite Form, and the *Theaetetus* may well explain why this is the case. The elements are described as αὐτὸ καθ᾽ αὑτό (201e), μία τις ἰδέα ἀμέριστος (205c, by implication because of their comparison with a syllable), ἀσύνθετον (205c), and μονοειδές (205d). Because the elements are themselves in themselves, they are isolated from all other things; because they are incomposite, language cannot be used to describe internal differentiation in them, and hence they are uniform. For both reasons we can only give a name and not a *logos* of an element, *if we are to state its nature*. Elements are perceivable, and presumably we perceive them as uniform, but they are not knowable, for knowledge requires a *logos*.

In the early middle dialogues we find a parallel situation. The isolated Forms are "in themselves," "incomposite," and "single-formed"; moreover, Plato emphasizes the intellectual vision of these Beings. But Plato also insists that giving a *logos* is a necessary condition for knowledge (cf. *Phaedo* 76b). However, there is no way to give a *logos* of an elemental Form; the nature of a Form can only be expressed in a "self-predicate" name. The very positing of atomistic Forms is incompatible with the definitional enterprise. To work through this tension Plato first begins to connect the Forms, to show that they form a network of noncontingent relations, and as he engages in this investigation with greater fervor, the Forms lose their isolation, single-formedness, paradigmatic status, and eventually even their separation. The Forms become the kinds of the *Philebus* and *Sophist*.

We cannot be sure that the *Theaetetus* would include among the element theories Plato's own middle-period Forms. But the resemblances between elements and Forms are persuasive, and if Morrow is correct, Plato's target is a broad range of theories that are "in the air," and his own may well be among them. The *Theaetetus*, moreover, never does say how an element is knowable, even though Theaetetus and Socrates agree that they are. Certainly Plato must have thought the problem a serious and puzzling one.

The *Timaeus*

I will assume that the *Timaeus* is a late dialogue, and I will argue for the relatively uncontroversial claim that separate, paradigmatic Forms are in the *Timaeus*. Furthermore, I will argue for the more interesting positions that there is a more radical separation between Forms and phenomena in the *Timaeus* than in any other dialogue, and that Plato desubstantializes phenomena more in the *Timaeus* than elsewhere. I will show that the position of the *Timaeus* is more radical with respect to separation than that of the *Phaedo* and *Republic*.

Before turning to the *Timaeus*, let me briefly restate my overall position on the late dialogues. The unitarians would have a complete victory if both of two conditions are satisfied: the *Timaeus* is late and Forms are found in other late dialogues. The revisionists would have a complete victory if both of two conditions hold: the *Timaeus* antedates the *Parmenides* and there is no evidence for Forms in the late dialogues. I have supported one conjunct of the revisionists' claim, since I have argued that Forms do not occur in the *Philebus*, *Sophist*, and *Theaetetus*. Nevertheless, I am assuming, given the best evidence to date, that the *Timaeus* is late.[57] How, then, does the *Timaeus* affect my interpretation of the other late dialogues?

Let us arrange claims about these dialogues in a decreasing order of strength.

(1) There is direct evidence for Forms in the *Sophist*, *Philebus*, and *Theaetetus*.

(2) The *Sophist*, *Philebus*, and *Theaetetus* cannot be understood, and are not self-contained dramatic or philosophical wholes, without the background assumption that Plato believes in Forms.

(3) It is reasonable to believe that Plato believes in Forms when he

writes the *Sophist, Philebus,* and *Theaetetus,* even though claims (1) and (2) are not true.

(4) It is not plausible to believe that Plato believes in Forms at the time he writes the *Sophist, Philebus,* and *Theaetetus.*

I have already argued that claim (1) is false. To satisfy the *physiologoi,* gods, and giants about what they mean by "to be," Plato could not assume his own ontology of Forms; moreover, the interweavings of the greatest kinds in the *Sophist* cannot be read as Form assertions. The monads of the *Philebus* are kinds—the genus *is* many (the species), and *is* an indefinite multitude (the phenomena)—and the three explanations, limit, unlimited, and the efficient cause are all in the *Cosmos.* I have also discussed the major passage in the *Theaetetus* where commentators see Forms. Claim (2) is also false or unproven. For the *Sophist* and *Philebus* it is the former, for the *Theaetetus* the latter. The *Sophist* provides an answer to the problem of being and not-being without a need to assume or even know anything about the theory of Forms; the *Philebus* answers the question about the good life for man without any need of Forms anywhere in the picture. Commentators often claim that the aporetic structure of the *Theaetetus* requires Forms to solve its epistemic puzzles. The burden of proof is on these commentators, and to date I do not see that their arguments are very persuasive. Claim (3) is the strongest claim a unitarian can cogently make. If the *Timaeus* is a late dialogue, and if separate Forms are endorsed in the *Timaeus,* then there is evidence that Plato, in his late period, believes in Forms. This evidence makes it *prima facie* reasonable to believe that even though (1) and (2) are false, Plato believes in Forms when he writes the *Sophist, Theaetetus,* and *Philebus.* It does not follow that Forms are required to solve the specific problems of those dialogues.

In the introduction to this book I discussed the limits to the interpretive principle of historical charity. A philosopher should be interpreted as consistent and plausible, but only within the limits set by the textual evidence. What is the evidence in this case? To put it in very broad strokes, I have argued that the *Parmenides* sets serious problems for the Forms, and yet admits that some stable entities are necessary for speech; the *Sophist* and *Philebus* work through the difficulties set by the *Parmenides,* and yet so seriously modify the Forms to answer these problems that we must judge that Plato abandons them, at least in the written texts. Then in the late *Timaeus,* in a theological-cosmological context, the Forms reappear. Moreover, the *Timaeus* does not even attempt to answer the problems set in the *Parmenides.* What are we to think? Is the following account implausible when viewed from the perspective of human nature, and its complex motives, rather than sheer philosophical consistency? In the *Sophist, Philebus,* and *Theaetetus* Plato is hot on the trail of how to solve various problems in an intracosmic context; the Forms slip from his attention; perhaps they are stored in a separate compartment, or perhaps he has ceased to be interested in them or even to believe in them. In the *Timaeus*, late in Plato's life, in a context that is cosmological, theological, and self-admittedly storylike, Plato with great nostalgia returns to his great hypothesis, to display its last great power of explanation as the paradigm for demiurgic creativity.

If the above story is at all convincing, then something between claim (3) and claim (4) is the correct account; perhaps (4a): It is plausible to believe that Plato froze his belief in Forms when working through the problems of the *Sophist*, *Philebus* and *Theaetetus*. A frozen belief could be any number of things: the belief is suppressed or repressed; it is set aside and suspended; it is compartmentalized and ignored; and still others. In any case, (3), (4), and (4a) are underdetermined by the evidence as given to us by the texts.

Let us now turn to a brief interpretation of the *Timaeus*. My basic position is the following: In the *Phaedo* Forms always are, and they are always F—F at every time, in every respect, and in every relation. The evidence of the middle dialogues only supports the position that Forms exist through all of time; we do not yet see Plato make the distinction between eternity and everlasting through time. Phenomena in the *Phaedo* (102 ff.) and *Republic* (523 ff.) are essentially characterized particulars; Phaedo is what it is to be a man, although he is not what it is to be tall; a finger is what it is to be a finger, although a finger is not what it is to be large. Only the attributive, relational, and incomplete predicates of phenomena are F and not-F. Hence in the middle dialogues Plato primarily introduces Forms for attributive, relational, and incomplete predicates because he introduces the Forms to save the phenomena from apparent inconsistency. But in the *Timaeus* Plato's position is more radical than that in the middle dialogues. First, Plato distinguishes between what is eternal and outside of time, what exists through all of time, and what is temporally limited in existence. The Forms are eternal, the *Cosmos* and the heavenly gods exist through all of time,[58] and phenomena are limited in temporal existence. Plato's contrast is now between Forms (about which we can accurately say that they atemporally "are") and phenomena (about which we cannot accurately say that they "are" at all, not even that they "are becoming") (38b). Phenomena are *in toto* "becoming," they in no sense "are." Second, in the *Timaeus*, for the first time, Forms of sortals are prominent; in fact, they are the commonest Forms in that dialogue. The Animal itself is a generic Form that contains within itself the Forms of all other genera and species (30c–d, 39e–40a). Concordantly, the phenomena are denatured; they are mere images cast in the receptacle in which images cling to existence as best they may (52c); and there is only one essentially characterized subject in the *Timaeus*, the receptacle, that is by its own nature a receiver of images (49a). Therefore, Plato elevates the status of Forms, and denatures the phenomena; the Forms are eternal, and the phenomena are *in toto* mere images. This is the strongest account of separation and deficiency found in any Platonic dialogue.

I am not at all concerned about whether the *Timaeus* depicts a literal crafting of the *Cosmos* or a genetic myth whose purpose is to display the elements that are and always have been at work in the *Cosmos*. An answer to this important problem will not affect my account of the *Timaeus'* ontology. Timaeus, himself, at 27c is a bit indifferent as to whether the *Cosmos* was literally crafted or not.

At 27d–28a Timaeus says the following:

> What is that which always is, and does not have generation, and what is that which is always becoming, and never is? The former is grasped by reason with a *logos* and it is always the same, the other by opinion with sensation, and it comes to be and is destroyed and never really is.

Similar language occurs in the *Phaedo* (78e, 80b), but the *Phaedo* also has passages that imply that phenomena are essentially characterized particulars. Therefore, as I have argued in Chapter 3, phenomena are deficient in the *Phaedo* because: (1) they have contingent predicates, (2) they have F and not-F predicates, and (3) they come to be—substantially—and cease to be. (3) is the ultimate source of phenomenal deficiency. However, in the *Timaeus* the distinction at 27d–28a has different implications. There are no essentially characterized particulars, and an object of becoming (τὸ γιγνόμενον) is, as we shall see, a mere reflection, cast in the receptacle, whose major features are temporal limitation and complete ontological dependence upon its parents—the Forms and the receptacle.

At 28a–b Timaeus says:

> But when the artificer of any object, in forming its shape and quality, keeps his gaze fixed on that which is uniform, using a model (παραδείγματι) of this kind, that object, executed in this way, must of necessity be beautiful; but whenever he gazes at that which has come into existence and uses a created model, the object thus executed is not beautiful.

The separate Forms recur in the *Timaeus* with their old function as paradigms, but there is a different twist. The paradigms are not only for human sight, but also for divine sight. The demiurge, a divine craftsman, looks at the Forms when he constructs the *Cosmos*. The demiurge is good, and because he is good as well as nonjealous, he wants the *Cosmos* to be the best possible (29a–30b); thus he uses the divine Forms in its construction. The demiurge, as far as I can tell, takes the place, but not the function as a teleological cause, of the Form of the Good in the *Republic*. The demiurge is again and again said to be good, and because of this excellence he makes a *Cosmos* that is the best possible. The demiurge is the primary locus of goodness, although all of the Forms are, of course, excellent.

The divine paradigms are autonomous of the demiurge. The demiurge must look away at them when he constructs the *Cosmos*. The paradigms are analogous to the blueprints or plans that a human craftsman would use in building something. But the paradigms are very unusual sorts of blueprints; they are spoken of as the Animal itself:

> We shall affirm that the *Cosmos*, more than anything else, resembles most closely that Living Creature (τῶν ζῴων) of which all other living creatures individually and generically are parts. For that Living Creature embraces and contains within itself all the intelligible Living Creatures (νοητὰ ζῷα), just as this universe contains us and all the other visible living creatures that have been fashioned (30c–d).

> ... he completed it [the *Cosmos*] by molding it after the nature of the Model. According, then, as Reason perceives Forms existing in the Living Creature (ὃ ἔστι ζῷον), such and so many as exist therein did he deem that this world also should possess. And the Forms are four—one the heavenly kind of gods; another the winged kind which traverses the air; third, the class which inhabits the waters; and fourth, that which goes on foot on dry land (39e–40a).

The Animal itself contains within itself all of the other Intelligible Animals as parts; it is apparently related to them as supreme genus to subordinate genera—land animals, water animals, and so on. Since the Animal itself is the primary paradigmatic blueprint in the *Timaeus*, there is no doubt that Forms corresponding to sortals occur there; in fact, in the *Timaeus*, they are the most important kind of Form, although the more traditional types of Forms are also found in the dialogue (cf. 51b–c). Moreover, at 51c Timaeus states that there is in each case an intelligible Form for each thing (ἑκάστοτε εἶναί τί φαμεν εἶδος ἑκάστου νοητόν), and the ἑκάστου here appears to be very general, including all phenomena—animals, elements, relations, moral qualities, and the like. There are, then, Forms corresponding to sortals in the *Timaeus*, and we should not be surprised to see this affect Plato's position on the nature of phenomena.

The demiurge uses the Animal itself in crafting the *Cosmos*, but how is such crafting accomplished? Timaeus claims that reason persuades necessity, for the most part, to take on order, shape, and harmony; necessity, for the most part, yields to intelligent persuasion (48a). But we still do not learn how reason persuades necessity (I will discuss the nature of necessity below). I believe that world *psyche* is the mediator between the demiurge and the receptacle. The demiurge infuses *psyche* throughout the bodily and wraps *psyche* around the bodily (34b). Moreover, the world *psyche* is the cosmic seat of reason (30b). The world *psyche* mediates between the demiurge and the bodily because it is intelligent; it works from within the bodily and teleologically shapes and forms the bodily as best it may. The world *psyche* is thus very close to Aristotle's notion of "nature" in *Physics* II. But in the *Timaeus* the Forms do not enter the receptacle (52a), whereas in Aristotle the actualities are, of course, in things. Hence the world *psyche*, the bearer of *nous*—a sort of intelligent genetic coding—strives to inform matter from within it, and yet the final goal is transcendent. If my account of crafting is correct, then we have valuable insight into the explanatory nature of the Paradigms: from the perspective of the demiurge the Paradigms are primarily formal causes; they are that in accordance with which the demiurge will shape and form the bodily through the mediation of world *psyche*. From the perspective of world *psyche* and the *Cosmos*, the Paradigms are both formal and final causes; the world *psyche* strives for them, and in so striving it forms or shapes the bodily nature.

The receptacle or nurse of becoming is a crucial notion in the *Timaeus*; as we shall see it is the only real subject for change and the only essentially characterized subject. It is seldom recognized that the receptacle has two diverse but not inconsistent functions. The first is that the receptacle is space (χώρα, 52b), it is the room in which all things come to be and are destroyed. Timaeus insists that "all that is should be in some place and occupying some space, and that which is neither on earth nor anywhere in the heaven is nothing" (52b). As space, the receptacle essentially has the power of being the receiver of all things (δύναμιν κατὰ φύσιν, 49a), and if the receptacle is to receive the images well, then in itself it nowhere and no wise assumes any shape similar to any of the things that enter into it (50c). But the receptacle is not just space; it also has the function of molding stuff (ἐκμαγεῖον, 50c); it is that out of which becoming is formed and crafted (50a–c). This is the point of the gold analogy at 50a–c; just as gold can be molded into all sorts of different figures and yet it is not any of these figures, so too the receptacle can be molded into the copies of the Forms, and yet it is not, in its own nature, any of these images. In fact, to take on these images as best it may, the receptacle must be void of all forms (50e–51a).

But what is this molding stuff constituted of? The molding stuff is made of rudimentary physical powers (52e), and these powers operate according to what we would now call physical laws.[59] Because the powers are organized according to the mechanistic principles of the *physiologoi* they constitute the domain of necessity; necessity for Plato is unintelligent because it does not act for a purpose. Only teleological movement, which is introduced by *nous*, is intelligent. Thus when the demiurge persuades necessity to take on form, shape, and purpose, he is attempting to organize the physical powers teleologically, but his success is only partial. An analogy would be a sculptor who works in marble. As he introduces the figure into the marble, he must work with the natural grain of the stone. If he does not, the stone will crumble. The natural grain also limits the figure's perfection. Finally, the molding stuff is not earth, air, fire, or water, since these characters are introduced into it by reason; nevertheless, the receptacle before formation does have disordered traces of such powers (53a–b). Plato is trying to describe the completely disordered, which, of course, cannot be done; but since the receptacle exists even if it has no determinate characteristics, it can still be known by a sort of bastard reason (52b). For this reason, the receptacle is not the not-being of the *Republic* and the *Sophist*.

C. M. Turbayne argues that the primary model for the *Timaeus* is biological reproduction and not crafting.[60] I am not interested in the general plausibility of Turbayne's interesting position, but in one of the claims it illuminates. Turbayne draws an analogy between the receptacle and a nurse, which, of course, Plato also does (50d). But a nurse has two functions, just as the receptacle does: a nurse can be both wet and dry.[61] A wet nurse nourishes and suckles the child, while a dry nurse embraces and holds it. Likewise, the receptacle as a molding stuff nourishes becoming and provides it with matter, while as space it embraces phenomena and provides them with room.[62]

Let us now turn to Being and becoming. The nature of the Living Creature is eternal (αἰώνιος, 37d), but it is not possible to attach eternity to the created *Cosmos*; thus the demiurge makes a movable image of eternity when he sets in order the heavens (37d–e). This movable image is called "time," and it is necessarily dependent on the movements of the heavens (37e). Timaeus then draws the implications of this new distinction between atemporal eternity and temporality. "Was" and "shall be" are generated forms of time, although we wrongly apply them without noticing to eternal Being (37e). In truth, "is" alone is the only term appropriately applied to eternal Being. Eternal Being, the Animal itself, does not become older or younger through time, while becoming does. Hence we should not apply "was" or "shall be" to Being, or "is" to becoming. We cannot even accurately say that "What is become *is* become, what is becoming *is* becoming, and what is about to become *is* about to become" (38b). The distinction in these passages is not simply between the changeless, frozen Forms and the mutable phenomena; this distinction is found in the middle dialogues where Being and becoming are both, apparently, in time. The Forms always are, phenomena are and are not. For this reason I argued in Chapter 3 that a necessary condition for Being is temporally unlimited existence. But in the *Timaeus* there is a different and stronger distinction; Being is not even in principle susceptible to time, and everything in time is simply becoming. The Forms, then, eternally and atemporally are; the stars, planets, and *Cosmos* as a whole come to be for all of time; and other phenomena are temporally limited in becoming.[63]

The characters that come to be in the receptacle are given an utterly insubstantial status. Timaeus illustrates their condition with the four elements. Since the elements are continuously passing on to one another in an unbroken circle the gift of birth (49c–d)—earth becomes water, water air, and so on—the elements are not stable. Thus we should not refer to them as "these," but rather "suchlikes" (τοιαῦτα). Timaeus goes on to say, "But that wherein they are always, in appearance, coming severally into existence, and wherefrom in turn they perish, in describing that and that alone should we employ the terms 'this' and 'that' ...." Only the receptacle has the requisite stability to be referred to; the characters that enter and leave the receptacle are too evanescent to be fit subjects of reference. One reason these characters are so insubstantial is that there are no longer any essentially characterized particulars. The receptacle is the only subject, and all other characters—attributive, relational, incomplete, and sortal—are treated on a par. An object is, then, simply a bundle of such characters, "suches," temporarily conjoined together. Unlike the middle dialogues, the *Timaeus* does not have many substances with their *F* and not-*F* characters; hence all phenomena are downgraded to the level of "suches," mere insubstantial reflections.

A related reason the characters are so insubstantial is that they are mere reflections. Timaeus says (50c, and 52c):

> And the figures that enter and depart are copies (μιμήματα) of those that are always existent, being stamped from them in a fashion marvelous and hard to describe....

> ... it belongs to a copy—seeing that it has not for its own even that substance for which it came to be, but fleets ever as a phantom (φάντασμα) of something else—to come to be in some other thing, clinging to being as best it may, on pain of being nothing at all.

Not only are the characters insubstantial, but also they are *in toto* copies, or phantoms, or ikons. All of the characters, no matter of what type, are dependencies of the Forms. Moreover, all of the characters are dependent for their being on the receptacle. The domain of becoming is now totally denatured; the reflections are merely becomings whose real being is in the

Forms. The *Philebus*' view of the all as a "coming into being," is the opposite of that stated at *Timaeus* 52c; 52c represents the lowest esteem Plato ever has for phenomena. I conclude that there is no room in the *Timaeus* for essentially characterized particulars, and that all of the characters are mere dependencies of the Forms and the receptacle.

Does this position, which is a considerable modification of that found in the middle dialogues, escape the objections of the *Parmenides*? I believe not. By including sortal predicates in with the others, and denying that there are essentially characterized phenomena, Plato increases the extension of his Form theory, but this does not help him solve the third man arguments of the *Parmenides*. Furthermore, Plato emphasizes in the *Timaeus* that phenomena are mere images or phantoms of the Forms, but this language is precisely what is at issue in the second third man argument of the *Parmenides*. Indeed, phenomena are copies of the paradigms—Plato emphasizes this more in the *Timaeus* than anywhere else—and the copy/paradigm relation is asymmetrical, but we still need a further relation of similarity to determine what paradigm a copy is a copy of. The *Timaeus* provides nothing new to dispel my arguments in Chapter 3 for self-predication.

There is, moreover, an interesting instance in the *Timaeus* of the middle-period tension between a conception of isolated and a conception of interconnected Forms. On the one hand the *Timaeus* depicts the Forms as arranged in genus/species hierarchies, but on the other the Forms are pure paradigms for vision. The former conception has decided preference because the *Timaeus* is about the crafting of an ecology, a group of interrelated parts that make a cosmic whole.

We have now seen two reasons why the separation between Forms and phenomena in the *Timaeus* is more radical than elsewhere. The Forms are placed outside of time, they are eternal rather than temporally unlimited in existence; phenomena are *in toto* mere reflections of the Forms, they are totally dependent on the Forms, and not just for their F and not-F predicates.

One last feature of the *Timaeus* is relevant to our discussion. We have already seen that a single passage in the *Sophist* places Being, Sameness, and Difference in the *psyche*; likewise, we have seen that the *Theaetetus* claims that these notions, among others, are provided by the *psyche*, in itself, to all things. This "Kantian-like" position is reaffirmed on no less than a cosmic level in the *Timaeus*. At 35a Timaeus claims that the world *psyche* is fashioned out of divisible and indivisible Being, Sameness, and Difference. Divisible Being, Sameness, and Difference are related to temporal bodies, and their indivisible counterparts to the Forms. The *psyche* is an intermediate blend between both kinds. Because of its constitution the *psyche* is able to fulfill the following epistemic function:

> Inasmuch, then, as she [the *psyche*] is a compound, blended of the natures of the Same and the Different and Being, these three portions, and is proportionately divided and bound together, and revolves back upon herself, whenever she touches anything which has its substance dispersed or anything which has its substance undivided she is moved throughout her whole being and announces what the object is identical with and from what it is different, and in what relation, where and how and when it comes about that each thing is and is acted upon by others both in the sphere of becoming and in that of the ever uniform (37a–b).

When Plato is concerned about the epistemic recognition of such notions as Being, Sameness, and Difference, he makes them concepts in the *psyche*. Nevertheless, they are also, as we see in the *Sophist*, kinds. Notions are posited in the *psyche* probably because they are not given through the five senses. Plato does not, however, discuss the relationship between these psychic notions and their counterpart kinds that are in the all.

In conclusion: I have argued that Plato is committed only to an ontology of kinds in the *Philebus* and *Sophist*. I have also shown that one major passage, which is often thought to introduce Forms in the *Theaetetus*, does not have this implication at all. Furthermore, the *Sophist* and *Philebus* can plausibly be interpreted as self-sufficient investigations of certain problems that do not presuppose, require, or imply Forms for their solutions. To this extent the revisionists are correct that Plato abandons the Forms in some late dialogues. I have also argued that the presumably late *Timaeus* clearly evidences separate Forms; moreover, the separation is more radical in the *Timaeus* than anywhere else. My own hypothesis to explain these puzzling "facts" is that when Plato "solves" the *aporia* set by the *Parmenides*, as in the *Philebus*, he abandons the Forms—at least in his writing—but when late in his life he returns to the grandeur of cosmology, his love for the Forms is irrepressible. Perhaps in this broad-stroke context, the analytic rigor of the *Parmenides* seems less important.

List of Works Cited

(1) Ackrill, J. L. "Plato and the Copula: *Sophist* 251–259." *Journal of Hellenic Studies*, 77 (part I) (1957), pp. 1–6. Reprinted in *Studies in Plato's Metaphysics*, ed. R. E. Allen, pp. 339–378.

(1) Allen, R. E. *Plato's 'Euthyphro' and the Earlier Theory of Forms*. New York: Humanities Press, 1970.

(2) Allen, R. E. *Studies in Plato's Metaphysics*. New York: Humanities Press, 1965.

(3) Allen, R. E. "Participation and Predication in Plato's Middle Dialogues." *Philosophical Review*, 69 (1960), pp. 147–164. Reprinted in *Studies in Plato's Metaphysics*, ed. R. E. Allen, pp. 43–60.

(4) Allen, R. E. "The Argument from Opposites in *Republic* V." *Review of Metaphysics*, 15 (1961), pp. 325–335. Reprinted in *Essays in Ancient Greek Philosophy*, ed. J. P. Anton and G. L. Kustas. Albany: State University of New York Press, 1971.

(5) Allen, R. E. "The Interpretation of Plato's *Parmenides*: Zeno's Paradox and the Theory of Forms." *Journal of the History of Philosophy*, II (1964), pp. 143–155.

(1) Baldry, H. C. "Plato's Technical Terms." *Classical Quarterly*, 31 (1937), pp. 141–150.

(1) Bambrough, R., ed. *New Essays on Plato and Aristotle*. New York: Humanities Press, 1965.

(1) Barrett, W., and Aiken, H. *Philosophy in the Twentieth Century*. New York: Random House, 1962.

(1) Brentlinger, J. "Incomplete Predicates and the Two-World Theory of the *Phaedo*." *Phronesis*, 17 (1972), pp. 61–80.

(1) Burge, E. L. "The Ideas as Aitiai in the *Phaedo*." *Phronesis*, 16 (1971), pp. 1–13.

(1) Burnyeat, M. F. "Virtues in Action." In *The Philosophy of Socrates*, ed. G. Vlastos, pp. 209–234.

(2) Burnyeat, M. F. "The Material and Sources of Plato's Dream." *Phronesis*, 15 (1970), pp. 101–122.

(1) Bury, R. G. *The Symposium of Plato*. Cambridge: Cambridge University Press, 1932.

(1) Calvert, B. "Forms and Flux in Plato's *Cratylus*." *Phronesis*, 15 (1970), pp. 26–47.

(1) Cherniss, H. *The Riddle of the Early Academy*. 1945; reprinted New York: Russell & Russell, 1962.

(2) Cherniss, H. "The Relation of the *Timaeus* to Plato's Later Dialogues." *American Journal of Philology*, 78 (1957), pp. 225–266. Reprinted in *Studies in Plato's Metaphysics*, ed. R. E. Allen, pp. 339–378.

(3) Cherniss, H. *Aristotle's Criticism of Plato and the Academy*. 1944; reprinted New York: Russell & Russell, 1962.

(4) Cherniss, H. "On Plato's *Republic* X 597B." *American Journal of Philology*, 53 (1932), pp. 233–243.

(5) Cherniss, H. "The Sources of Evil According to Plato." *Proceedings of the American Philosophical Society*, 98 (1954), pp. 23–30.

(1) Cooper, J. M. "Plato on Sense-Perception and Knowledge (*Theaetetus* 184–186)." *Phronesis*, 15 (1970), pp. 123–146.

(1) Cornford, F. M. *Plato's Theory of Knowledge*. Indianapolis: Bobbs-Merrill, 1957. Library of Liberal Arts reprint from the original 1951.

(1) Crombie, I. M. *An Examination of Plato's Doctrines:* Vol. II, *Plato on Knowledge and Reality*. New York: Humanities Press, 1963.

(1) Cross, R. C., and Woozley, A. D. *Plato's Republic: A Philosophical Commentary*. London: 1964.

(1) Devereux, D. "Courage and Wisdom in Plato's *Laches*." *Journal of the History of Philosophy*, 15 (1977), pp. 129–141.

(1) Dodds, E. R. *Plato's Gorgias: A Revised Text with Introduction and Commentary*. Oxford: Clarendon Press, 1959.

(1) Fields, G. C. *Plato and His Contemporaries: A Study in Fourth-Century Life and Thought*. London: Methuen & Co., 1967.

(2) Fields, G. C. *The Philosophy of Plato*. London: Methuen & Co., 1949.

(1) Findlay, J. *Plato: The Written and Unwritten Doctrines*. New York: Humanities Press, 1974.

(1) Forrester, J. W. "Some Perils of Paulinity." *Phronesis*, 20 (1975), pp. 15–21.

(1) Frankena, W. *Ethics*. Englewood Cliffs: Prentice-Hall, 1963.

(1) Friedländer, P. *Plato*, Vol. II, *The Dialogues, First Period*. Trans. from the German by Hans Meyerhoff. New York: Pantheon Books, 1964. Originally published as *Platon*, II: *Die Platonischen Schriften, Erste Periode* (2nd ed.); Berlin: 1957.

(1) Gallop, D. "Justice and Holiness in *Protagoras* 330–331." *Phronesis*, 6 (1961), pp. 86–93.

(2) Gallop, D. "Image and Reality in Plato's *Republic*." *Archiv für Geschichte der Philosophie*, 47 (1965), pp. 113–131.

(1) Garland, W. "Plato's Ontology in the *Timaeus* and *Philebus*." Presented at the Pacific Division of the American Philosophical Association, 1976.

(1) Geach, P. "Plato's *Euthyphro*: An Analysis and Commentary." *Monist*, 50 (1966), pp. 69–82.

(2) Geach, P. "The Third Man Again." *Philosophical Review*, 55 (1956). Reprinted in *Studies in Plato's Metaphysics*, ed. R. E. Allen, pp. 265–277.

(1) Gillespie, C. M. "The Use of Εἶδος and Ἰδέα in Hippocrates." *Classical Quarterly*, 6 (1912), pp. 179–203.

(1) Goodman, N. *Languages of Art*. Indianapolis: Bobbs-Merrill, 1968.

(1) Gosling, J. "*Republic* Book V: τὰ πολλὰ καλά, etc." *Phronesis*, 5 (1960), pp 116–128.

(2) Gosling, J. "Similarity in *Phaedo* 73b seq." *Phronesis*, 10 (1965), pp. 151–161.

(3) Gosling, J. *Plato*. Boston and London: Routledge & Kegan Paul, 1973.

(1) Grote, G. *Plato and the Other Companions of Socrates*. Vol. I. London: 1865.

(1) Grube, G. M. A. "Plato's Theory of Beauty." *Monist*, 37 (1927), pp. 269–288.

(2) Grube, G. M. A. *Plato's Thought*. 1935; reprinted Boston: Beacon Press, 1958.

(1) Gulley, N. "Plato's Theory of Recollection." *Classical Quarterly*, N.S., 4 (1954), pp. 194–213.

(1) Guthrie, W. K. C. *A History of Greek Philosophy*: Vol. 3. Cambridge: Cambridge University Press, 1969.

(2) Guthrie, W. K. C. *A History of Greek Philosophy*: Vol. 4. Cambridge: Cambridge University Press, 1975.

(1) Hackforth, R. *Plato's Phaedo*. Cambridge: Cambridge University Press, 1955.

(1) Hall, R. M. "Plato's Just Man." *New Scholasticism*, 43 (1968), pp. 202–225.

(1) Hay, W. H. "Nicolaus Cusanus: The Structure of His Philosophy." *Philosophical Review*, 61 (1952), pp. 14–25.

(1) Heidegger, M. "Plato's Doctrine of Truth." In *Philosophy in the Twentieth Century*, ed. W. Barrett and H. Aiken, pp. 251–270.

(1) Hintikka, J. "Time, Truth, and Knowledge in Ancient Greek Philosophy." *American Philosophical Quarterly*, 4 (1967), pp. 1–14.

(1) Hoerber, R. G. "Plato's *Greater Hippias*." *Phronesis*, 9 (1964), pp. 143–155.

(2) Hoerber, R. G. "Plato's *Hippias Major*." *Classical Journal*, 50 (1955), pp. 183–186.

(1) Kahn, C. "The Greek Verb 'To Be' and the Concept of Being." *Foundations of Language*, 2 (1966), pp. 245–265.

(1) Ketchum, R. "Participation and Predication in the *Sophist* 251–60." *Phronesis*, 23 (1978), pp. 42–62.

(1) Lee, E. N. "The Second 'Third Man': An Interpretation." In *Patterns in Plato's Thought*, ed. J. M. E. Moravscik, pp. 101–122.

(2) Lee, E. N. "Plato on Negation and Not-Being in the *Sophist*." *Philosophical Review*, 81 (1972), pp. 267–304.

(1) Liddell, H., and Scott, R. *An Intermediate Greek-English Lexicon*. Oxford: Clarendon Press, 1964.

(1) Loeb Classical Library. Cambridge, Mass.

(1) Lovejoy, A. O. *The Great Chain of Being: A Study of the History of an Idea*. 1936; reprinted New York: Harper Torchbooks, 1960.

(1) Luce, J. V. "The Date of the *Cratylus*." *American Journal of Philology*, 85 (1964), pp. 136–154.

(2) Luce, J. V. "The Theory of Ideas in the *Cratylus*." *Phronesis*, 10 (1965), pp. 21–36.

(1) Malcolm, J. "On the Place of the *Hippias Major* in the Development of Plato's Thought." *Archiv für Geschichte der Philosophie*, 50 (1968), pp. 189–195.

(2) Malcolm, J. "Plato's Analysis of *to on* and *to mē on* in the *Sophist*." *Phronesis*, 12 (1967), pp. 130–146.

(1) McGinley, J. "The Doctrine of the Good in the *Philebus*." *Apeiron*, 11 (1977), pp. 29–57.

(1) Moore, J. D. "The Relation between Plato's *Symposium* and *Phaedrus*." In *Patterns in Plato's Thought*, ed. J. M. E. Moravscik, pp. 52–71.

(1) Moravscik, J. M. E. *Patterns in Plato's Thought*. Dordrecht: D. Reidel, 1973.

(2) Moravscik, J. M. E. "The 'Third Man' Argument and Plato's Theory of Forms." *Phronesis*, 8 (1963), pp. 50–62.

(3) Moravscik, J. M. E. "Plato's Method of Division." In *Patterns in Plato's Thought*, ed. J. M. E. Moravscik, pp. 158–180.

(1) Morrow, G. R. "Plato and the Mathematicians: An Interpretation of Socrates' Dream in the *Theaetetus*." *Philosophical Review*, 79 (1970), pp. 309–333.

(2) Morrow, G. R. "Necessity and Persuasion in Plato's *Timaeus*." *Philosophical Review*, 59 (1950), pp. 147–164. Reprinted in *Studies in Plato's Metaphysics*, ed. R. E. Allen, pp. 421–437.

(1) Mourelatos, A. *The Route of Parmenides*. New Haven: Yale University Press, 1970.

(1) Natorp, P. *Platos Ideenlehre*. Zweite Auflage. Leipzig, 1921.

(1) Nehamas, A. "Confusing Universals and Particulars in Plato's Early Dialogues." *Review of Metaphysics*, 29 (1975), pp. 287–306.

(2) Nehamas, A. "Predication and Forms of Opposites in the *Phaedo*." *Review of Metaphysics*, 26 (1973), pp. 461–491.

(3) Nehamas, A. "Plato on the Imperfection of the Sensible World." *American Philosophical Quarterly*, 12 (1975).

(4) Nehamas, A. "Self-Predication and Plato's Theory of Forms." *American Philosophical Quarterly*, 16 (1979), pp. 93–103.

(1) Owen, G. E. L. "The Place of the *Timaeus* in Plato's Dialogues." *Classical Quarterly*, N.S., 2 (1953), pp. 79–95. Reprinted in *Studies in Plato's Metaphysics*, ed. R. E. Allen, pp. 313–338.

(2) Owen, G. E. L. "A Proof in the 'Peri Ideon'." *Journal of Hellenic Studies*, 57, part 1 (1957). Reprinted in *Studies in Plato's Metaphysics*, ed. R. E. Allen, pp. 293–312.

(3) Owen, G. E. L. "Plato on Not-Being." In *Plato*, ed. G. Vlastos, Vol. 1, pp. 223–267.

(1) Panagiotou, S. "Vlastos on *Parmenides* 132 A1–B2: Some of His Text and Logic." *Philosophical Quarterly*, 21 (1971), pp. 255–259.

(2) Panagiotou, S. "A Note on the Translation and Interpretation of Plato's *Parmenides*." *Classical Philology*, 69 (1974), pp. 50–55.

(1) Penner, T. "The Unity of Virtue." *Philosophical Review*, 82 (1973), pp. 35–68.

(2) Penner, T. "Thought and Desire in Plato." In *Plato*, ed. by G. Vlastos, Vol. 2,

pp. 96–118.

(1) Quine, W. V. O. "On the Reasons for Indeterminacy of Translation." *Journal of Philosophy*, 67 (1970), pp. 178–183.

(2) Quine, W. V. O. *Ontological Relativity and Other Essays*. New York: Columbia University Press, 1969.

(1) Robinson, R. *Plato's Earlier Dialectic*. 2nd ed. 1941; reprinted Oxford: Clarendon Press, 1962.

(1) Ross, W. D. *Plato's Theory of Ideas*. 1951; reprinted Oxford: Clarendon Press, 1953.

(1) Ryle, G. "Plato's *Parmenides*." *Mind*, 48 (1939), pp. 129–151, 302–325. Reprinted in *Studies in Plato's Metaphysics*, ed. R. E. Allen, pp. 97–147.

(1) Sachs, D. "A Fallacy in Plato's *Republic*." *Philosophical Review*, 72 (1963). Reprinted in *Plato*, ed. G. Vlastos, Vol. 2, pp. 141–158.

(1) Santas, G. "The Socratic Fallacy." *Journal of the History of Philosophy*, 10 (1972), pp. 127–141.

(2) Santas, G. "Socrates at Work on Virtue and Knowledge in Plato's *Laches*." *Review of Metaphysics*, 22 (1969), pp. 433–460. Reprinted in *The Philosophy of Socrates*, ed. G. Vlastos, pp. 175–208.

(1) Savan, D. "Self-Predication in *Protagoras* 330–331." *Phronesis*, 9 (1964), pp. 130–135.

(1) Sellars, W. "Vlastos and the 'Third Man'." *Philosophical Review*, 64 (1955), pp. 405–437.

(1) Shiner, R. "Self-Predication and the 'Third Man' Argument." *Journal of the History of Philosophy*, 8 (1970), pp. 371–386.

(1) Shorey, P. *What Plato Said*. Chicago: University of Chicago Press, 1933.

(1) Solmsen, F. "Parmenides and the Description of Perfect Beauty in Plato's *Symposium*." *American Journal of Philology*, 92 (1971), pp. 62–70.

(2) Solmsen, F. "The 'Eleatic One' in Melissus." *Mededelingen Nederlandse Akad.*, 32 (1969), pp. 3–15.

(1) Sprague, R. K. *Plato's Use of Fallacy: A Study of the Euthydemus and Some Other Dialogues*. London: Routledge and Kegan Paul, 1962.

(2) Sprague, R. K. "Parmenides' Sail and Dionysodorus' Ox." *Phronesis*, 12 (1967), pp. 91–98.

(1) Stewart, J. *Plato's Doctrine of Ideas*. Oxford: Clarendon Press, 1909.

(1) Stough, C. "Forms and Explanations in the *Phaedo*." *Phronesis*, 21 (1976), pp. 1–30.

(1) Tarán, L. *Parmenides*. Princeton: Princeton University Press, 1965.

(1) Tarrant, D. "The Pseudo-Platonic Socrates." *Classical Quarterly*, 33 (1939), pp. 167–175.

(2) Tarrant, D. *The Hippias Major, Attributed to Plato*. Cambridge: Cambridge University Press, 1928.

(1) Teloh, H. "The Isolation and Connection of the Forms in Plato's Middle Dialogues." *Apeiron*, 10 (1976), pp. 20–34.

(2) Teloh, H. "Parmenides and Plato's *Parmenides* 131a–132c." *Journal of the History of Philosophy*, 14 (1976), pp. 125–130.

(3) Teloh, H. "Human Nature, Psychic Energy, and Self-Actualization in Plato's *Republic*." *Southern Journal of Philosophy*, 14 (1976), pp. 345–358.

(4) Teloh, H. "A Vulgar and a Philosophical Test for Justice in Plato's *Republic*." *Southern Journal of Philosophy*, 13 (1975), pp. 499–510.

(5) Teloh, H. "Aristotle's *Metaphysics* Z 13." Forthcoming in *Canadian Journal of Philosophy*.

(6) Teloh, H. "Self-Predication or Anaxagorean Causation in Plato." *Apeiron*, 9 (1975), pp. 15–23.

(1) Teloh, H., and Louzecky, D. "Plato's Third Man Argument." *Phronesis*, 17 (1972), pp. 80–94.

(1) Turbayne, C. M. "Plato's 'Fantastic' Appendix: The Procreation Model of the *Timaeus*." *Paideia: Special Plato Issue*, 5 (1976), pp. 125–140.

(1) Turnbull, R. G. "Aristotle's Debt to the 'Natural Philosophy' of the *Phaedo*." *Philosophical Quarterly*, 8 (1958), pp. 131–146.

(1) Vlastos, G. "The Third Man Argument in the *Parmenides*." *Philosophical Review*, 63 (1954), pp. 319–349. Reprinted with an addendum in *Studies in Plato's Metaphysics*, ed. R. E. Allen, pp. 231–263.

(2) Vlastos, G. "Plato's 'Third Man' Argument (*Parm.* 132A1–B2): Text and Logic." *Philosophical Quarterly*, 19 (1969), pp. 289–301.

(3) Vlastos, G. "Degrees of Reality in Plato." In *New Essays on Plato and Aristotle*, ed. Renford Bambrough, pp. 1–19. Reprinted in *Platonic Studies*, ed. G. Vlastos, pp. 58–75.

(4) Vlastos, G. *Plato's Protagoras.* Trans. by B. Jowett, trans. revised by M. Ostwald, ed. with an introduction by G. Vlastos. New York: Bobbs-Merrill, 1956.

(5) Vlastos, G. "Postscript to the Third Man: A Reply to Mr. Geach." *Philosophical Review*, 69 (1960). Reprinted in *Studies in Plato's Metaphysics*, ed. R. E. Allen, pp. 279–291.

(6) Vlastos, G., ed. *The Philosophy of Socrates.* New York: Doubleday Anchor Books, 1971.

(7) Vlastos, G. "Introduction: The Paradox of Socrates." In *The Philosophy of Socrates*, ed. G. Vlastos, pp. 1–21.

(8) Vlastos, G. *Platonic Studies.* Princeton: Princeton University Press, 1975.

(9) Vlastos, G. "The Unity of the Virtues in the *Protagoras*." *Review of Metaphysics*, 25 (1972), pp. 415–458. Reprinted in *Platonic Studies*, ed. G. Vlastos, pp. 221–269.

(10) Vlastos, G., ed. *Plato.* Vol. 1, *Metaphysics, Epistemology.* Vol. 2, *Ethics, Politics, and the Philosophy of Art and Religion.* Garden City, N.Y.: Doubleday Anchor Books, 1970.

(11) Vlastos, G. "A Metaphysical Paradox." In *Proceedings of the American Philosophical Association*, 39 (1966), pp. 5–19. Reprinted in *Platonic Studies*, ed. G. Vlastos, pp. 43–57.

(12) Vlastos, G. "Pauline Predications in Plato." *Phronesis*, 19 (1974), pp. 95–101.

(13) Vlastos, G. "Reasons and Causes in the *Phaedo*." In *Plato*, ed. G. Vlastos, Vol. I, pp. 132–166.

(1) White, F. C. "Plato's Middle Dialogues and the Independence of Particulars." *Philosophical Quarterly*, 27 (1977), pp. 193–213.

(2) White, F. C. "Particulars in *Phaedo*, 95e–107a." In *New Essays on Plato and the Pre-Socratics*, ed. Roger Shiner and John King-Farlow. *Canadian Journal of Philosophy*, Supplementary Volume 2, pp. 129–147.

(1) Zeller, E. *Philosophie der Griechen*. 5th. ed. Leipzig: 1922.

Supplementary Bibliography

These works, which are relevant to my study, came to my attention too late for inclusion and explicit discussion.

1. Cresswell, M. J. "Essence and Existence in Plato and Aristotle." *Theoria*, 37 (1971), pp. 91–113.

2. Gold, J. "The Ambiguity of 'Name' in Plato's *Cratylus*." *Philosophical Studies*, 34 (1978), pp. 223–246.

3. Gold, J. "The Soul's Relation to the Forms: Plato's Account of Knowledge." Forthcoming.

4. Goldstein, L., and Mannick, P. "The Form of the Third Man Argument." *Apeiron*, 12 (1978), pp. 6–13.

5. Irwin, T. *Plato's Moral Theory*. Oxford: Oxford University Press, 1979.

6. Ketchum, R. "Knowledge and Recollection in the *Phaedo*: An Interpretation of 74a–75b." *Journal of the History of Philosophy*, 17 (1979), pp. 243–253.

7. Parry, R. D. "The Unique World of the *Timaeus*." *Journal of the History of Philosophy*, 17 (1979), pp. 1–10.

8. Santas, G. *Socrates*. London: Routledge and Kegan Paul, 1979.

9. Shiner, R. *Knowledge and Reality in Plato's Philebus*. Assen: Van Gorcum, 1974.

10. Skipper, E. *Forms in Plato's Later Dialogues*. The Hague: Martinus Nijhoff, 1965.

11. Smith, N. "Knowledge by Acquaintance and 'Knowing What' in Plato's *Republic*." *Dialogue*, 18 (1979), pp. 281–288.

12. Smith, N. "The Various Equals at Plato's *Phaedo* 74b–c." Forthcoming in *Journal of the History of Philosophy*.

13. Smith, N. "The Objects of *Dianoia* in Plato's Divided Line." Forthcoming in *Apeiron*.

14. Smith, R. "Mass Terms, Generic Expressions, and Plato's Theory of Forms." *Journal of the History of Philosophy*, 16 (1978), pp. 141–153.

15. Turnbull, R. "Plato: The Soul and Its Place in Nature." Forthcoming.

Notes

Introduction (*pages 1–17*)

1. Cherniss (1), p. 4; Cherniss (2), p. 362 in the reprint; Friedländer (1), p. 85; and Allen (1), p. 136. On the other hand, Ross (1), pp. 11–21, 228–231; Grube (1), pp. 272–273; and Dodds (1), pp. 20–21, 328 n. on 503e1—all of these claim that in the early dialogues the Forms are not separate.

2. Cherniss (2), pp. 339–349 in the reprint.

3. "*F*-ness" is the name of a single Form; "*F*" is the name of the predicate that corresponds to the Form *F*-ness: for example, "Largeness" and "is large," "Justice" and "is just." In using this terminology I am following the practice of Vlastos (1) and many of the commentators who follow him. This terminology does not assume self-predication, that is, that the predicate *F* can be said of *F*-ness. When I refer to the separate Forms, or what are thought by other commentators to be the separate Forms, I use capitals, for instance Justice, Holiness, Form; but when I refer to the "immanent" form, or a form whose status is undetermined, I use lower case letters, for instance justice, holiness, form.

4. Cherniss (2), pp. 369–374; Allen (1), p. 71; Allen (3), pp. 46, 49–50 in the reprint.

5. The pagination numbers are from the Loeb editions of Plato, as is the Greek. The translations are either from these editions, based upon them, or in some cases are my own.

6. I prefer "*psyche*" to "soul" because "*psyche*" has fewer metaphysical, especially Christian, connotations. "*Psyche*" more than "soul" suggests what vivifies a body, and is not separate from it. I wish to convey this impression.

7. Cf. Penner (1), pp. 35 ff.

8. Allen (1), p. 6; Grote (1), pp. 322–323.

9. The following commentators either explicitly state that the *Hippias Major* is genuine, or they cite passages from it in such a way as to presuppose its authenticity: Hoerber (1), pp. 143–144; Hoerber (2), p. 183; Ross (1), p. 3; Malcolm (1), p. 189; Friedländer (1), p. 105; Dodds (1), p. 22; Allen (1), p. 1 n. 1; Crombie (1), p. 256; Guthrie (1), p. 281; Robinson (1), pp. 33, 49; Vlastos (1), p. 249 n. 2 in the reprint. Many of these commentators also believe that the *Hippias Major* is early in date of composition.

10. Again I refer to the separate εἶδος with capitals, e.g. The Beautiful.

11. The *Hippias Major* opens with a reference to Hippias' beautiful speech, and the speech is beautiful because it has *cosmos*.

12. On the use of this expression for such a change see Solmsen (1), p. 64.

13. See Solmsen (1), pp. 62–70; Teloh (1), pp. 23–25; Teloh (2), pp. 125–130.

14. For a negative opinion on this issue see Moore (1), pp. 52–71. I tend to believe that the *Symposium* is an early middle dialogue.

15. Cherniss (2), p. 350.

16. Kahn (1).

17. See Quine (1). The evidence underdetermines a position when incompatible

theories are consistent with the evidence. For example, the textual claim "Φ is unchanging" could be about either a Form or a kind. For the late dialogues especially, much of the evidence underdetermines the interpretations of them. I do not, however, draw Quine's skeptical conclusions from underdetermination. Often the larger context will help us decide Plato's intent.

18. See Vlastos (4), p. liii, n. 10, who uses this anachronistic terminology.

19. See Ross (1), pp. 11–21, 228–231, who argues for the obscure notion of an "immanent universal" in the early dialogues. Ross never really says what an immanent universal is.

20. Robinson (1).

Chapter 1 (pages 18–66)

1. The text is from the Loeb editions of Plato, and the translations are based upon the same editions. I use capital letters, as Form, Justice, when I refer to the separate Forms, and lower case letters when I do not.

2. Allen (1); Shorey (1), pp. 67–69; Cherniss (1), pp. 4–5; Cherniss (2), p. 362 in the reprint; Friedländer (1), p. 85.

3. See Penner (1), for a recent example.

4. I will assume throughout this essay that evidence from dialogues closer in date of composition to the *Euthyphro* is better than that from more distant ones. I will assume the following: *Republic* I is an early dialogue, and the *Meno, Gorgias,* and *Hippias Major* are late/early dialogues; otherwise, I accept the received distinction between early, middle, and late periods, and do not attempt to chronologically order dialogues within a period.

5. For commentators who make this objection see Geach (1), pp. 69–82; and Robinson (1), p. 53. G. Santas also argues against this objection, and for the view that Plato uses examples to determine a paradigm. See Santas (1), pp. 127–141.

6. Guthrie (1), p. 117.

7. See Guthrie (1), p. 120.

8. My summarization of this position attempts to stay as close as possible to Guthrie, but in some cases I will have to develop the position beyond what Guthrie explicitly says.

9. For a defense of this point see Nehamas (1), pp. 287–306.

10. See Allen (1).

11. Allen (1), p. 113.

12. Allen (1), p. 123.

13. Allen (1), p. 132, n. 3.

14. Allen (1), p. 71; also see Allen (3).

15. Again I attempt to stay as close as possible to Allen but sometimes I expand the position along more traditional lines than Allen employs, and fill *lacunae.*

16. Allen (1), pp. 69–70.

17. Allen (1), pp. 69–70. Ross (1), p. 12, apparently contradicts himself when he states that εἶδος and ἰδέα at *Euthyphro* 5d and 6d–e have their "special Platonic sense." Ross usually claims that Forms are immanent in the early dialogues.

18. Allen (1), p. 71; Allen (3), pp. 46, 49–50 in the reprint; and Allen (4), p. 170 in the reprint.

19. The Pauline interpretation is shown to be mistaken because (1) I show that "Justice is δίκαιον" is predicational in form, and (2) I show that "Justice" refers to a psychic state. I accomplish (2) below. For the Pauline interpretation see Vlastos (12) and (9).

20. This phrase is Vlastos'; see Vlastos (1), p. 249 in the reprint.

21. See Allen (4), p. 171 in the reprint; and (3), p. 46 in the reprint. Allen does not always characterize his view as an uninformative identity, but also uses these other formulations. Allen presumably tries to capture phrases such as "what each is" (ὅ ἔστιν ἕκαστον) with the interpretation "Justice is what Justice really is," but he does not argue that "what each is" is equivalent to a self-predicational assertion.

22. See D. Gallop's excellent analysis of this argument. Gallop (1), pp. 86–93. I agree with Gallop on the form and purpose of this argument.

23. In Teloh (6) I also argue that *Euthydemus* 300e–301c, and *Lysis* 217c are "self-predications."

24. This formulation appears to beg the question against Allen, but I will show that attempts to understand paradigmatism without resemblance fail. See N. Goodman (1), pp. 52–57.

25. See Vlastos (5), pp. 284–286 in the reprint.

26. Likewise modal operators do not change the meaning of a predicate, nor do adverbial qualifications. To be necessarily, contingently, humdrumly, and superbly beautiful are all ways of being beautiful.

27. Allen (1), p. 71.

28. Allen (3), pp. 46, 49–50 in the reprint.

29. I agree with those commentators who argue that even in the middle dialogues Plato tends not to posit Forms for sortal predicates, but only for incomplete, relational, and attributive ones. The reason for this is that the dominant argument for Forms starts from the F and not-F characteristics of phenomena, but a sortal predicate is not juxtaposed with a contrary. See Turnbull (1), pp. 131–146; Nehamas (2), pp. 461–491; and Owen (2), pp. 293–312 in the reprint.

30. See on this point White (1), p. 208. White's excellent essay appeared after I wrote this chapter. I am in substantial agreement with his arguments for univocal predication.

31. Shorey (1), pp. 67–69; Cherniss (1), pp. 4–5; Cherniss (2), p. 362 in the reprint; Friedländer (1), p. 85.

32. See the entries under τοιοῦτος in Liddell and Scott.

33. Penner (1), and Burnyeat (1) also argue that the virtues are motive forces or states of *psyche*. Neither commentator, however, attempts to interpret *Euthyphro* 6d–e. Penner also argues that the virtues are identical with each other and with the knowledge of good and evil. I accept these conclusions, and will argue for them below.

34. In the *Euthyphro*, 6d–e, piety is also called an εἶδος and ἰδέα. For Pre-Socratic uses of these terms see C. M. Gillespie (1), pp. 179–203, and H. C. Baldry (1), pp. 141–150. These terms can mean "shape," "structure," "nature," "appearance," "essence," "kind," and "species" among other things. At *Republic* 435b and 434d they are also applied to psychic states. To call piety a form does not, in any case, ascribe any particular ontological status to it.

35. I argue for this position in Teloh (4), pp. 502–504.

36. See Dodds (1), pp. 20–21.

37. See Cherniss (5), pp. 23–30.

38. Teloh (6), pp. 15–23. I argue that the (CP) explains numerous passages in both the early and the middle dialogues.

39. Several commentators argue that Plato presupposes the (CP), although they do not address this topic in any depth. Sellars (1), p. 435, claims that the (CP) explains some of the self-predicational passages, but he does not provide any

evidence for the (CP). Burge (1), pp. 4–5, argues that the (CP) is implied by *Phaedo* 100b ff., where Plato says that it is absurd for a small thing to be the cause of a large thing's being large. Burge goes on to say: "Some such view as this [CP] may be a factor in the notorious 'self-predication' of the ideas in so far as they are considered *aitiai* (100b ff.)."

40. Brentlinger (1), pp. 66 ff., argues that Plato accepts an Anaxagorean account of the elements and causation in the early and middle dialogues.

41. I am indebted for this translation and for these examples to Hay (1), pp. 22–23.

42. Sprague (1), p. 27.

43. Savan (1), pp. 132–133.

44. In Teloh (6) I also argue that *Lysis* 217c, *Republic* I 335d–e, and *Euthydemus* 301a f. also presuppose the (CP).

45. See Penner (1), pp. 35 ff.

46. On Socrates' nondogmatic credo in the early dialogues, see Vlastos (7), 9 ff. The early dialogues are sometimes thought to be tentative and exploratory. But we must separate appearance and reality. The dramatic appearance is of tentative aporetic discussion, but, as I will show, the early dialogues have very carefully planned structures and conclusions which reveal the didactic nature of the man who wrote them.

47. A recent, and one of the best, attempts to support this position is found in Devereux (1), pp. 129–141.

48. There is, I believe, no difference for Plato between a teacher of virtue and a true statesman; both have as their aim the production of psychic virtue.

49. See Vlastos (7), pp. 12–14, for a similar comment about the *Euthyphro*, although Vlastos states that Socrates invariably attempts to get an interlocutor to "see for himself" what the truth is.

50. My analysis of this argument is substantially in agreement with that of Penner (1).

51. See Santas (2), pp. 189–193 in the reprint.

52. For arguments against this interpretation see Devereux (1), pp. 138–140; and Vlastos (9), 266 ff. I am in obvious disagreement with both Devereux and Vlastos. Steps (2)–(7) may in fact be unsound, but there is no evidence that Plato recognizes this.

53. See Vlastos (7), p. 14. Vlastos, of course, does not embrace the identity interpretation, but he does go so far as to say that Socrates tries to get Euthyphro to see that piety is care for the *psyche*.

54. Plato's moral regeneration of the gods occurs very early: see *Apology* 21b, 23a, 30d, 31a, 41c—d, *Gorgias* 507e–508a, 523a ff.

55. In the *Phaedo* we are in the service of the gods who are good rulers (62d–63a), and in the *Apology* Socrates' service to the gods is to urge people to care for their *psyches* (30a–b). *Charmides* 163e suggests both that temperance is the doing of good things, and that some sort of knowledge is necessary for this.

56. Vlastos (7), pp. 9–10, is much too generous to Plato when he interprets a number of such passages as a genuine request for information.

57. I am obviously in considerable disagreement with the purely negative interpretation of the early dialogues, that is, that early dialectic simply destroys dogmatically held beliefs, and has no positive thrust to it.

58. See Vlastos (7), pp. 1–21.

59. See Devereux (1), who argues that Laches represents the endurance aspect of courage and Nicias the intellectual. Of course both generals represent to a greater or lesser extent vulgar interpretations of these components.

60. For an excellent analysis of the difference between Plato's early and middle psychological views see Penner (2), pp. 96 ff.

61. See Hall (1), pp. 202–225.

62. Frankena (1), p. 53.

63. I have argued this criticism for *Republic* IV and V in Teloh (4), pp. 502–504, and I attempt to answer the criticism at 504–508.

64. See Sachs (1), pp. 35–51 in the reprint. In Teloh (4) I argue *contra* Sachs that 442c–443b is not a vulgar account of virtue, but a vulgar test for psychic justice. Plato does not attempt in the *Republic*, nor is he challenged by Glaucon or Adeimantus, to show that vulgar and psychic justice are coimplicants. Rather the vulgar tests are an attempt to identify the presence of psychic justice.

Chapter 2 (*pages 67–99*)

1. Tarrant (1), p. 171; Tarrant (2); Grube (1), pp. 269 ff.

2. See n. 9 in the Introduction.

3. Dodds (1), pp. 22, 249–250 n. on 474d4, places the *Gorgias* just after the *Hippias Major* in date of composition, and believes that the *Gorgias* presupposes the discussion of beauty in the *Hippias Major*.

4. Again I use capitals to indicate the separate εἶδος, and lowercase letters for the immanent one.

5. The phrase τῷ ὄντι would, of course, be primarily reserved in the middle dialogues for the separate εἶδος.

6. Nowhere in the early dialogues does Plato assert that a virtue or the beautiful "always is," or "is ungenerated and indestructible." Indeed, Plato would not make such an assertion because such entities can be generated in *psyches* or other phenomenal objects. Being temporally unlimited in existence occurs only with the advent of the middle-period separate Forms.

7. See above, pp. 29–32, 42–46. My arguments that other self-predications are indeed predications also imply that *Hippias Major* 292d–e should be understood as a predication.

8. See above pp. 42–46.

9. Thus my account satisfies the condition, mentioned above (p. 26), that a cause must be distinct from its effect.

10. 286a certainly seems to hint that the beauty of something lies in its compositional features.

11. This dramatic aspect of the dialogue, where Socrates pretends to question Hippias in the same way that an intimate friend has questioned him, has been thought to be a clumsy dramatic device unworthy of Plato's literary abilities. This intimate friend is slowly revealed to be a member of Socrates' household, and finally to be Socrates himself, although Hippias probably never grasps this fact. This dramatic device is developed with great subtlety, and a humor that appears to me to be typically Plato's. In fact, I rate the *Hippias Major* to be one of the most dramatic and well constructed dialogues. On this point see Hoerber (1), pp. 143–155. There is good reason why Socrates in his own *persona* does not address Hippias: the refutations are so pointed and so devastating that Hippias would certainly leave the discussion.

12. Grube (1), pp. 75–76.

13. Sellars (1), pp. 429–430 in the reprint.

14. Grube (2), p. 220; Sellars (1), pp. 429–430 in the reprint; and also see Gallop (1), p. 88 n. 2. See above pp. 29–32.

15. This grammatical device is also mentioned by Hoerber in support of his

"straw man" interpretation of 297c, but he neither defends nor elaborates upon it. Hoerber (1), p. 135; Hoerber (2), p. 184.

16. Socrates is certainly not above such tactics; see in the *Protagoras* his playful, sophistical interpretation of Simonides' poem (340e ff.).

17. Hoerber advises us to accept the disjunct "hearing or sight" so that we will receive "a clue to the third facet of τὸ καλόν, conceived aesthetically." Hoeber does see that harmony produces such pleasures, but I do not see any point in accepting a disjunct that Socrates explicitly rejects, nor do I see how this provides a clue to the interpretation of the beautiful. See Hoerber (1), p. 154.

18. Also see *Philebus* 64d–e.

19. Dodds (1), pp. 22, 244–245 n. on 474d4.

20. See Dodds (1), p. 329 n. on 504a1.

21. See Dodds (1), pp. 334–335 n. on 506e1. Dodds appropriately quotes Santayana's dictum that "Reason adds to the natural materials only the perfect order which it introduces into them (*Reason in Religion*, Chapter 1)." But Dodds does not follow up the insight, nor does he connect order with aesthetic and utilitarian excellence.

22. See Fields (1), pp. 102–103, for the close connection between ἀγαθός, καλός, and ἀρετή.

23. Of course some degree of excellence must be present for the type form to be successfully instantiated at all. But it is only when the creative act is successful that the beautiful is present.

24. Ross (1), pp. 11–21, 228–231; Grube (2), p. 9; Grube (1), pp. 272–273; Dodds (1), pp. 20–21, 328 n. on 503e1.

25. Cherniss (1), p. 4.

26. Cherniss (2), p. 362 in the reprint.

27. Ross, for example, does not include the instrumental dative in his list of terms that imply immanence or transcendence. Although the dative is not a term but a grammatical construction, if Ross thinks that it has any particular ontological implications, he certainly would have mentioned it. See Ross (1), pp. 11–22, 228–230.

28. Allen (1), p. 146 n. 2, 122–123. Allen uses the phrase "ontological priority" instead of "transcendent" or "separate," but all three mean the same thing. However, while Allen thinks that the Forms are separate in the early dialogues, he does not believe that they are more real than their instances (pp. 132–133). But in a puzzling note Allen claims that as a "matter of economy in the universe" all of the Forms may well be instantiated (p. 132 n. 3). Probably Allen means the following: a Form of itself does not presuppose an instantiation of that Form, but the demiurge because of his goodness instantiates all of the Forms. On the tension between the self-sufficient and complete nature of the demiurge, and the necessity that he create phenomena and instantiate all of the patterns, see Lovejoy (1), pp. 49–52.

29. Questions and answers have been transposed into declarative statements.

30. Ross (1), pp. 228–230. There are, however, serious problems with Ross' analysis. See Cherniss (2), pp. 362–363 in the reprint.

31. Allen (1), p. 146.

32. See Turnbull (1).

33. See Calvert (1), p. 34, who holds this view.

34. There is considerable disagreement about where to place the *Cratylus*. I find Luce's arguments persuasive. He believes that the *Cratylus* is a pre-*Republic* dialogue, but is undogmatic about where in the late/early or early/middle periods it should be placed. See Luce (1), p. 154.

35. Calvert (1), p. 34.

36. See Luce (2), pp. 22–24. Luce displays numerous dissimilarities between this passage and *Republic* 597b ff.

37. See Baldry (1); Gillespie (1).

38. Crombie makes the interesting suggestion that the forms of name and shuttle are designs or specifications that a client gives to the architect. Crombie (1), pp. 273–274. I agree with this suggestion as long as we remember that such designs can be embodied in mental images as well as on paper.

39. We may even speculate with Grube that in the early dialogues Plato asks for what something looks like, and then in the middle dialogues for what it is that phenomena look like, thus supposing the existence of something beyond that the phenomena resemble. Grube (2), p. 10.

40. Malcolm (1), pp. 193–194.

41. Gosling (1), p. 127, states, "It seems to me quite mistaken to pass from similarity of terminology in Plato to similarity of problem: the terminology should be interpreted in terms of relevance to the particular argument." I am in complete agreement with this claim.

42. See Vlastos (4), p. liii, n. 10; Vlastos (1), p. 250 in the reprint. In the latter work Vlastos says, "Is it possible that a man should say, and with the greatest emphasis, 'Justice is just,' yet not realize that this is as good as saying that a Form which *is* a character *has* that character?" (his emphasis). It is anachronistic and erroneous to describe either the virtues or the separate paradigms as "characters," and Vlastos compounds this mistake by thinking of one and the same type of thing, characters, as being either in things or apart from them.

43. Vlastos (1), pp. 248–249 in the reprint.

44. See n. 42.

45. Ross (1), pp. 20–21, claims that this passage is "the first distinct appearance in Plato of the argument from the existence of knowledge to the existence of unchangeable, nonsensible objects."

46. On the Eleatic legacy to the Forms see Solmsen (1), pp. 62–70; Friedländer (1), pp. 23–26; Hackforth (1), p. 84; and Teloh (2), pp. 125–130.

47. There are a number of alternative texts for οὖλον μουνογενές, but "whole, unique" is a commonly accepted reading.

48. Solmsen (2), p. 221 n. 1, correctly connects ἕν with συνεχές, and takes it to mean the "intrinsic unity" of Being, while μουνογενές "emphasizes the uniqueness of Being." I disagree on this point with both Tarán (1), pp. 189–190, and Mourelatos (1), pp. 95, 113–114. Tarán takes both words to mean "unique," while Mourelatos thinks that they both indicate indivisibility.

49. "Being" is the subject and "one" a predicate for both Parmenides and Melissus; the "Eleatic One" is, in fact, a Platonic creation. See Solmsen (2); and Tarán (1), pp. 269 ff.

50. Friendländer (1), p. 24.

51. Hackforth (1), p. 84.

52. See Bury (1), p. 128.

53. See Solmsen (1), pp. 62–70.

54. I am, in part, indebted to Solmsen (1) for the comparisons that follow.

55. Those commentators who deny self-predication would also deny that the beautiful is beautiful. For arguments that the beautiful in the *Symposium* is beautiful, see White (1), pp. 210–211.

56. See Gosling (2), pp. 151–161, and Nehamas (3), pp. 105–117. They argue that Forms and phenomena are not related on the model of bright red to pale red, or being exactly a yard long and being only approximately a yard long; rather,

Forms are always *F*, in every respect, relation, at every time, and so on, while particular phenomena and types of actions are *F* and not-*F* at different times, in different relations, or in different respects.

57. The burden of proof is on those who claim that such adverbial qualifications change the meaning of a predicate. But I know of no plausible arguments to this effect.

58. Malcolm (1), pp. 193–194.

59. In Chapter 3 I will extensively defend this predicative and existential interpretation of types of reality.

60. See Ross (1), p. 21.

61. See Cherniss (3), pp. 206, 208, 210 n. 125. Cherniss lists a considerable number of other passages that he claims imply or assert transcendence. Certainly Cherniss is correct about many of these passages, especially those from the middle dialogues, although I do not accept his unitarian thesis that separate Forms occur in dialogues of all periods.

62. Malcolm (1), pp. 193–194.

63. See pp. 108–109 below.

64. I should, to some extent, qualify this claim. Plato claims that phenomena are *F* and not-*F* in both early and middle dialogues; moreover, both the beautiful and The Beautiful are always beautiful. Nevertheless, these claims support very different theories, so that the resemblances between the early and middle dialogues are far fewer than is generally supposed.

Chapter 3 (*pages 100–146*)

1. I am unconvinced by attempts to reduce both the Forms and mental-vision language to more mundane, if plausible, views. For a recent attempt see Gosling (3), Chapter 8, who interprets the Forms simply as teleological principles and the visual language as mere metaphor.

2. See: *Republic* 430b, 443b, where both the virtues and knowledge are called "powers"; *Charmides* 168d–e, where sight, hearing, and knowledge are all treated as powers; and *Cratylus* 420b–d, where Plato relates οἴησις and δόξα to the shooting or aiming of a bow.

3. This is certainly a common nontechnical use of these terms. See Baldry (1); and Gillespie (1).

4. Gulley (1), pp. 194–213, argues that *Phaedo* 74–76 implies an immediate transition from the sensible to the intelligible world, and that such a direct transition is inconsistent with what Plato says elsewhere about how we acquire knowledge of the Forms. I do not believe, however, that we need see such an immediate transition in this passage; Plato simply cannot be expected to make every point when he makes any point. It is quite possible that *logoi* mediate between the perception of phenomena and the vision of the Forms, although at both beginning and end there is a visual acquaintance with an object.

5. The precise translation of τῷ is in doubt; it either means "in one respect," or "to one person." This ambiguity is irrelevant to the argument since Equality appears equal in every respect and to everyone.

6. See below, pp. 108–109.

7. Bury (1), p. 128.

8. See Solmsen (1), pp. 62–70; Hackforth (1), p. 84; Friedländer (1), pp. 23–26.

9. By "early stage of development" I do not mean the early dialogues where the eparate Forms do not occur; rather I mean the first appearances of the Forms in the middle works.

10. Parmenides uses a physical language that is the only one available to him, but it is clear that he means to deny that Being has either physical or conceptual parts. At DK B8.38–41 he denies that Being has any qualitative distinctions: "Coming to be and perishing, being and not being, change of place and mixture of bright colors" are only "the mere names of mortals."

11. Polar opposites are not logical contraries or contradictions; rather they are extremes on the same spectrum, instances being white and black, tall and short, and the like.

12. There have been numerous attempts to show that the neuter plurals do not refer to a Form, but I do not see that any of these attempts are at all plausible.

13. See Heidegger (1), pp. 251–270.

14. See Stough (1), pp. 1–30. Stough argues that in the *Phaedo* Socrates tries to see his way clear of the following type of Pre-Socratic analysis: if x is F and not-F, then x is partially identical with F and partially identical with not-F (we are to understand polar opposites and not contradictories here) which may well appear to be a contradiction or "strife of opposites." The introduction of separate Forms, according to Stough, explains relational and incomplete predicates.

15. See Turnbull (1), pp. 136–137.

16. See White (1), pp. 195–196.

17. See Nehamas (2), pp. 482–491; and White (2), pp. 140–145.

18. See Cherniss (4), pp. 239–242.

19. For a comparison and analysis of these two claims see Solmsen (1), pp. 67–68; also see DK B8.45–50.

20. At *Symposium* 204c Diotima states that the object of love, not the lover, is really beautiful, tender, perfect (τέλεον), and blessed; Parmenides' Being, likewise, is without need (B8.33), and perfect or complete (τελεστόν, B8.4).

21. There are a number of alternative texts for οὖλον μουνογενές, but "whole, unique" is a commonly accepted reading.

22. Vlastos (1), p. 252 in the reprint.

23. See Aristotle's *Metaphysics* 999b33–1000a2, 1016b32–34, 1033b31–32, 1034a7–9 and 1052a32–b2. For Aristotle what is "one in number" is individual, and what is "one in form or species" is universal.

24. Teloh (5).

25. Hintikka (1), pp. 1–14.

26. This is the analysis of Allen (3).

27. See Allen (3), pp. 43 ff. in the reprint.

28. Lee (1), pp. 108–109.

29. See Nehamas (2), pp. 461–491.

30. See DK 59 B10, A4, A46.

31. Vlastos (1), pp. 249–250 in the reprint.

32. See Nehamas (2).

33. See Moravscik (2), pp. 50–62, and Shiner (1), p. 362. Shiner argues against commentators like Moravscik who deny self-predication on the basis of a "focal meaning" view. Shiner claims, "It is, rather, quite sufficient for the Self-Predication Assumption (SPA) to be vicious, if 'F' is predicated of both Form and particular *not equivocally*" (his emphasis). Shiner also purports to show that Plato may not employ focal meaning between Forms and phenomena, although I believe him to be mistaken about this.

34. Owen (2), pp. 293–312 in the reprint.

35. Cross and Woozley (1), p. 145.

36. Cross and Woozley (1), p. 175. For the same view see Fields (2), p. 52.

37. See Vlastos (3) and (11).

38. Kahn (1), pp. 245–265.

39. See Vlastos (11), pp. 46–47 in the reprint.

40. See Malcolm (2), pp. 130, 144; Owen (3), pp. 223–267; and Kahn (1).

41. The phrase "temporally unlimited in existence" is designed to exclude eternity. In the *Timaeus* Plato claims that the Forms are eternal, but in earlier dialogues he says only that they always exist. I will show that the cognitive reliability of a Form requires only the weaker claim that the Form be temporally unlimited in existence.

42. Thus I agree with the existence interpretation on the analysis of nonbeing. Later I will show that an implication of the predication interpretation is that nonbeing is not-being or indescribable existence, and hence that nonbeing in the *Republic*, on this view, should be identified with the receptacle in the *Timaeus*. But as I will show, this identification is false.

43. Vlastos (11), p. 48 in the reprint.

44. In the other sense of "real" the word functions as a value predicate; see Vlastos (3), p. 7. I will frequently switch between epistemological and ontological deficiency. These types of deficiency, however, are equivalent.

45. Vlastos (11), pp. 44–45 in the reprint. The only role that existence plays in Vlastos' interpretation is that it is presupposed in statements about deficient phenomena. See Vlastos (3), p. 9. Of course I do not deny that Vlastos may well believe that Forms are temporally unlimited and phenomena temporally limited in existence; but I do deny that these existential claims have a role in Vlastos' analysis of "degrees of reality."

46. Vlastos (3), p. 10; also see Vlastos (11), p. 50 in the reprint.

47. Vlastos (3), p. 17; also see Vlastos (11), p. 50 in the reprint.

48. Vlastos does not explicitly state either that the purity and modal tests are equivalent, or that phenomena have all their predicates contingently. I attribute these claims to Vlastos because he does say that our "best clue" to why phenomena are deficient is that their impure predicates are had contingently, and Vlastos does not appear to believe that phenomena have any pure predicates. Vlastos then uses both tests interchangeably in both essays. He also says that "Simmias is taller than Socrates" is in the "domain of contingent truth," while "Three is Odd" takes us "into that of logical necessity," and Vlastos seems to believe that phenomena are *in toto* members of the "domain of contingent truth." See Vlastos (3), pp. 11–12. Phenomena must have all their predicates contingently for Vlastos, or otherwise he could not show with the modal test that Being and becoming are mutually exclusive.

49. See Vlastos (3), pp. 11–13. Vlastos misapplies the modal account because he focuses exclusively upon predicates like "large" when talking about phenomena.

50. See Hintikka (1), p. 8.

51. For a discussion of these different types of predicates see Owen (2), pp. 305–307 in the reprint. Late in the middle period, in the *Phaedrus*, Plato employs a general one-over-many argument that would generate Forms for sortals.

52. See Turnbull (1), pp. 131 ff.

53. See Allen (3).

54. See Vlastos (11), p. 50 in the reprint, for the interesting but mistaken claim that Plato believes that every predicate of a phenomenal object is juxtaposed with a polar opposite. Certainly this is not true of sortal predicates, but Vlastos is correct about other types of predicates.

55. Empedocles, Anaxagoras, Democritus, and Plato predicate of their basic entities the Parmenidean predicates of Being. They also believe that these entities are neither generated nor destroyed.

56. On variant texts for this passage see Tarán (1), pp. 82 ff.

57. See Forrester (1), pp. 11–21, on the distinction between formal and non-formal predicates of the Forms.

58. Plato also believes that Forms "analytically connect" with each other; see Vlastos (3), pp. 12–13.

59. This is not a necessary condition since the receptacle in the *Timaeus* might be temporally unlimited in existence, but is itself unknowable because it does not have either an intelligible nature or characteristics. Thus condition (4) below is also only a sufficient condition.

60. Vlastos (3), p. 6 n.4; Vlastos (11), pp. 48–49 in the reprint.

61. See Vlastos (13), pp. 134–137.

62. Vlastos (13), pp. 135, 143–144.

63. Zeller (1), Vol. 2, p. 687 n. 1; and in my conversations with Findlay.

64. White (1), p. 212.

65. See Turnbull (1); Lee (1).

66. See Hoerber (1), pp. 154–155; Grube (1), pp. 269–288.

67. Also see *Phaedo* 74b αὐτὰ τὰ ἴσα, and *Parmenides* 129b αὐτὰ τὰ ὅμοια. These neuter plurals apparently refer to the Forms Equality and Likeness respectively. Definitions of these Forms would immediately imply that they are complex, since they embody relational "notions" requiring two or more relata. Plato's use of the plurals suggests that he was vaguely aware of this, although he does not explicitly investigate the matter.

68. For an excellent discussion of these points see Gallop (2), pp. 113–131.

69. Plato is equally vague in the *Phaedo* (101d–e): "And when you had to give an explanation (λόγον) of the principle [the hypothesis originally posited], you would give it in the same way by assuming some other principle, that seemed to you the best of the higher ones, and so on until you reached one that was adequate (τι ἱκανόν)."

70. Brief references are made to division, or at least the value of making distinctions, prior to the *Phaedrus* at *Euthyphro* 11e ff., and *Republic* 454a, but it is not until the late dialogues that this method gains prominence, and begins to influence Plato's conception of a Form.

71. Moravscik (3), pp. 159 ff., argues that Plato, in division, divides through "Forms" and not just according to them. Furthermore, Moravscik sees that this destroys the incomposite nature of the middle-period Forms.

Chapter 4 (pages 147–170)

1. See DK 28 B6.8–9.

2. See Tarán (1), pp. 269 ff.; Solmsen (2).

3. See Sprague (2), pp. 91–98.

4. Plato must have thought that his theory of Forms was a rationalists' posit much as the Eleatic Being, and that it would not be dramatically inappropriate to portray Parmenides as sympathetic to the Forms.

5. A number of recent essays have analyzed the logic and metaphysics behind the failure to separate substances and attributes. If attributes are conceived of as component elements in substances, then to say, for example, that John is tall and short (in different comparisons), or white and black (in different respects), can be quite puzzling. These claims may be analyzed as the "partial identities," "John is the tall and the short," or "John is the white and the black." Since there is not a distinction between substances and attributes, it may well appear that John is, in virtue of himself, the tall and the short. In this way we generate Heraclitus'

"identity of opposites," and ultimately the Eleatic denial that phenomena exist. See Stough (1), pp. 1–30.

6. These "logical" puzzles are of a piece with the "late-learners" belief in the *Sophist* that we can only correctly make identity assertions, and not predications. For John is John, but he is not good because he is not the good, or as it would be ambiguously put in Greek with the article, he is not what is good. The phrase "what is good" (τὸ ἀγαθόν) could mean "the good," "what is [predicatively] good," or "what has [the nature of] good." If one reads it in the last way, then it may well appear that only identity statements are logically correct.

7. Thus I believe that the *Parmenides* is not an *ignoratio* against the middle-period Forms.

8. Allen (5), pp. 143–155, is an important exception. Allen captures much of the dramatic tension in the first part of the *Parmenides*, and he emphasizes Socrates' challenge, but I disagree with him about how Parmenides answers the challenge. Allen argues that only certain Forms of unrestricted generality, such as Likeness, are qualified by their opposites, while Forms such as Largeness, of restricted generality, are not affected by Parmenides' arguments. I will argue that Parmenides intends to show that all the Forms suffer contrary predicates, since they all are one and many.

9. This point is easier to see when we remember that Socrates explicitly introduces the Forms to show how phenomena can be both one and many (129c–d; also see *Republic* 525a). Also at *Phaedrus* 261d Plato states that the Eleatic Palamedes (Zeno) has the art of speaking which makes the same things appear to be like and unlike, one and many, stationary and in motion.

10. If Forms are meanings, then there would be a Form corresponding to every general term.

11. See Sprague (2), pp. 91–98.

12. Vlastos (1), pp. 256–257 in the reprint.

13. Vlastos (3), pp. 14–15.

14. For a justification of this translation of the first step of the third man argument, as well as the last step, see Teloh and Louzecky (1), pp. 82–85.

15. Vlastos (1), pp. 232–233 in the reprint. Also see Sellars (1), pp. 415–419; and Geach (2), pp. 271 ff. in the reprint.

16. Vlastos (1), p. 236 in the reprint.

17. Vlastos (1), pp. 236–237 in the reprint.

18. Vlastos (1), pp. 233–234 in the reprint. Vlastos adds that he presumes no more information than can be extracted from the text, that he raises no questions about the Theory of Forms, and that he is not looking at other texts to see what Plato's suppressed premises may have been (p. 236). What he is looking for are the simplest formally adequate premises (p. 236). He poses this task because he sees the second step as an inference from the first and a horrible *non sequitur*, the avoidance of which requires further premises (p. 239).

19. The infinite series of different sets with which the third man argument is concerned is an ordered series: particulars; particulars and *F*-ness; particulars, *F*-ness, and *F*-ness$_1$, and so on.

20. It should be noted that (T) precludes there being one and only one Form for every set of *F* things—Forms or phenomena—in the T.M.A. Also it is unclear whether (T) is restricted to impure predicates or has a broader extension.

21. There is an indefinite number of specifically identical, but not numerically identical, Largenesses, one for each of the newly emerging sets of large things. The result of the T.M.A is, then, similar to the earlier argument (129b f.) that generates a multiplicity of "whole" Forms in different participants.

22. See n. 5 above. If we revert to the position where attributes and substances are not distinguished, then we can see the problem for the Forms. If a Form is F and not-F, then it has contradictory natures: what is F is also what is not-F, and thus the Forms cannot exist.

23. Vlastos (1), pp. 237–241 in the reprint.

24. Vlastos (1), pp. 254–255 in the reprint.

25. Cherniss (2), pp. 366 ff. in the reprint.

26. Teloh and Louzecky (1).

27. Vlastos (1), p. 234 n. 1 in the reprint.

28. Cherniss (2), p. 366 in the reprint.

29. See Panagiotou (1), pp. 255–259, for excellent arguments for this point.

30. Vlastos (2), pp. 290, 294.

31. See Panagiotou (2), pp. 50–55, for arguments for this position.

32. Vlastos (2), p. 290.

33. In the next chapter we will see whether or not the εἴδη in the *Sophist* "self-participate." We will also investigate how the εἴδη participate in each other.

34. Cherniss (2), pp. 366 ff. in the reprint.

35. Cherniss (2), pp. 371–373 in the reprint.

36. Ross (1), pp. 87, 230–231.

37. One might attempt to unite Forms and phenomena by claiming that the latter strive to instantiate the former. Nevertheless, unless the striver successfully obtains the quality striven for, we cannot tell what Form is related to what particular.

38. Cherniss (2), pp. 365, 374–375.

39. Ross (1), p. 99.

40. Ross (1), pp. 100–101.

41. Ryle (1), pp. 106–110 in the reprint.

Chapter 5 (*pages 171–218*)

1. See Cherniss (2).

2. See Owen (1).

3. As I will show, my interpretation is inconsistent with that of Owen (3).

4. I am thinking particularly of Natorp and Stewart.

5. See Ross (1), pp. 1–10.

6. As we shall see, we cannot accurately say of anything in the domain of becoming that it is, not even that it *is* becoming.

7. As least the Forms are found to be no longer necessary to solve the *aporia* of the *Sophist* and *Philebus*.

8. See Ketchum (1), pp. 42–62, for an analysis of εἴδη in the *Sophist* as kinds. Ketchum also argues that division and collection seek the nature of kinds, but the communion of the greatest kinds does not have this function.

9. Nehamas (4), pp. 100–103.

10. My terminology is obviously borrowed from Quine, among others. I do not, however, accept or employ the skeptical implications Quine draws from underdetermination, at least as it applies to ancient texts. It would, however, be fruitful for scholars in ancient philosophy to read Quine on underdetermination. See Quine (1), pp. 178–183.

11. See Quine (2), pp. 114–138.

12. See Ross (1), pp. 2, 10.

13. McGinley (1), pp. 29–30.

14. See Teloh (3), pp. 349–350.

15. Owen (1), pp. 322–333 in the reprint.

16. Cherniss (2), p. 351 in the reprint.

17. Cherniss (2), pp. 354–355. Oddly, Cherniss sees that the *Republic* only claims that generation "is and is not," but he does not think that this phrase is different and even incompatible with the *Philebus* statements. Of course in many informal contexts Plato calls many things, including becoming, "being," but these offhand assertions do not prove anything.

18. Cherniss (2), p. 350.

19. Cherniss (2), p. 350.

20. See Ross (1), pp. 132–135.

21. See Garland (1).

22. Ketchum (1); Moravcsik (3).

23. See Ketchum (1). Ketchum makes both of these points in his excellent essay.

24. Moravcsik (3), pp. 160 ff.

25. Moravcsik (3), pp. 159–160.

26. I will use capital letters for the greatest kinds and for certain other kinds, for example the Sophist, but this, of course, will not imply that the kinds are separate Forms.

27. See Ketchum (1), p. 57.

28. See Ketchum (1), pp. 43–44.

29. Kinds are paradigms only in that the statements we can correctly make about them specify the criteria for their instances, but if they were self-predicated, then they would also be separate individuals.

30. See Lee (2), pp. 269 ff.

31. Cherniss (2), p. 352.

32. Cherniss (2), p. 352.

33. I have borrowed this scheme from Ketchum (1), p. 49.

34. See Ketchum (1), pp. 47–48.

35. The interconnections between the greatest kinds in the *Sophist* would also, then, be mirrored by the interconnections between psychic categories.

36. See Ackrill (1).

37. See Owen (3).

38. See Malcolm (2).

39. Ackrill (1), p. 212 in the reprint.

40. Malcolm (2), p. 130.

41. Malcolm (2), pp. 133–134.

42. Owen (3), p. 225 in the reprint.

43. Owen (3), pp. 229–231 in the reprint.

44. Owen (3), p. 259 in the reprint.

45. Owen (3), pp. 331–332 in the reprint.

46. Owen (3), p. 247 in the reprint.

47. Owen (3), pp. 253–255 in the reprint.

48. Owen (3), pp. 256–258 in the reprint.

49. Malcolm (2).

50. See Cornford (1), pp. 102–109; Cherniss (3), p. 236 n. 141.

51. See Cooper (1); Ryle (1), p. 317 in the reprint; Crombie (1), p. 14. I am greatly indebted to the Cooper essay in what follows.

52. For different interpretations of this contrast see Cooper (1).

53. See Cooper (1), pp. 135–138.

54. See Cooper (1), p. 137.

55. Burnyeat (2), pp. 103–104.

56. Morrow (1), pp. 327–329.

57. See Ross (1), pp. 1–10; Cherniss (2), pp. 339 ff. in the reprint.

58. This claim is consistent either with time having literally come to be with the *Cosmos*, or with time always existing.

59. See Morrow (2).

60. See Turbayne (1).

61. See Turbayne (1), p. 131.

62. The irrational mechanistic nature of necessity is also a source of evil and deficiency in Plato. See Cherniss (5). The receptacle ultimately accounts for the defective nature of the copies, as well as the overthrow of instantiated form. Plato also depicts necessity as a wild, untamed energy (52d–53a), but it is hotly debated whether necessity has its own source of mechanistic motion, or whether all motion is introduced into the receptacle by *psyche*. See Morrow (2).

63. I am indebted to Richard Patterson (Columbia University), who forcefully brought this view of the *Timaeus* to my attention.

General Index

accidental predicates, 111, 129
Ackrill, J. L., 12, 199–204, 219, 240n
add; be added to something: 79, 81–82, 92, 96
aesthetics. *See* beautiful, the
Aiken, H., 219
Allen, R. E., 38–39, 81, 167, 219, 227n, 228n, 229n, 232n, 235n, 236n, 238n; on phenomena as resemblances of Forms, 129; on self-predication, 3, 28–30; on separate essences in the early dialogues, 3, 27–32, 79, 81; unitarian position, 1, 32, 85
American Philosophical Association, xii
anachronism in interpretation, 14, 86, 233n
Anaxagoras, 42, 99, 121–122, 230n, 236n
Anaximander, 135
Anaximenes, 110, 135
Animal; The Animal itself in the *Timaeus*: 142, 145, 213, 215
aporia (perplexity), 4, 55, 75, 100, 174, 191, 200, 203, 208, 218, 230n, 239n
Aristotelian genera, 145
Aristotle, 14, 16, 42, 111, 116–117, 118, 124, 133–135, 175, 186, 198, 214
art and craft. *See* beautiful, the

Baldry, H. C., 84, 219, 229n, 233n, 234n
Bambrough, R., 219
Barrett, W., 219
bastard reason: in the *Timaeus*, 133, 202, 215
battle of the gods and giants: in the *Sophist*, 189, 190
beautiful, the; beauty; and The Beautiful: art and craft production, 54–55, 76–78, 82–84, 181, 185–186;

fine and mechanical arts, 5, 71–72, 74–75; in the *Gorgias*, 5, 67–68, 70, 75–79, 84–85, 91–93; in the *Hippias Major*, 4–6, 67–75, 84–85, 91–93, 96–99; in the *Symposium*, 4–6, 68, 84, 91–99, 104–105; the Greek word "beautiful," 72; as the harmony of the Form-world, 141; as harmony and proportion, 5, 43, 76–79, 82, 86, 89, 92, 97, 141, 188; the separate Form of, 88, 93–96; best sensible manifestation of, 172
Brentlinger, J., 219, 230n
Burge, E. L., 219, 230n
Burnyeat, M. F., 207–208, 219, 229n, 240n
Bury, R. G., 219, 233n

Calvert, B., 83, 219, 232n, 233n
Campbell, E., xiii
causal principle (CP), 4, 16–17, 42–46, 65, 70, 121–123, 156–158, 193, 229n–230n
causal terms and constructions: in the *Hippias Major*, 79–82
cause; causation; explanation: 44–45, 70, 96, 121–125, 133–138
"cause," the Greek word, 133–134
cause of mixture: in the *Philebus*, 177, 181, 186–188
characteristic account. *See* virtues, in the early dialogues
Cherniss, H., 114, 219–220, 227n, 228n, 229n, 234n, 235n, 239n, 240n, 241n; on self-predication, 3, 28–29, 164–165, 167; on separate Forms in the early dialogues, 3, 32; on the chronology of the dialogues, 2; on the Form of Motion in the *Sophist*, 189, 190, 194–195; on Forms in the *Theaetetus*, 204–205; on Forms in the *Philebus*, 12, 184–185; on the third

sites in, 7, 9, 10, 99, 105, 110, 113,
147, 149, 161, 237n–238n; influence
on the Forms, 110–111, 113
Hintikka, J., 117–118, 130, 221, 235n,
236n
Hippias Major: authenticity of, 67, 227n
historical charity: in interpretation,
13–14, 210
Hoerber, R. G., 221, 227n, 231n, 232n,
237n
holiness. *See* piety
Homeric belief systems: and divinities,
59–60
Hume, D., 42
hypotheses, 140, 143–144, 237n

Ideal City: Form of, 141–142
identity of opposites. *See* Heraclitus
identity statements, 73–74, 110, 149,
178, 198, 238n. *See also einai*
imitations. *See* resemblance
immanent characters and universals,
14, 81–82, 111–112, 114–115, 121,
137, 151, 156, 227n, 228n
immutability. *See* Forms; Parmenides,
Being
incomplete predicates, 107–109,
111–113, 123, 128–130, 157. *See also*
Forms, explanatory nature of;
phenomena, ontological status of
incorrigibility. *See* Forms
indivisibility. *See* Forms; Parmenides,
Being
instantiation, 174, 182
instrumental dative. *See* dative of
instrument
intentional inexistence, 202
interlocutors. *See* Socratic teaching
irony. *See* Socratic teaching
Irwin, T., 226
isolation. *See* Forms; Parmenides, Being

justice, 8, 40, 139–141

Kahn, C., 12, 126, 133, 199, 221, 227n,
236n
Kant, I., 65
Katchi, Y., xii
Ketchum, R., 189, 221, 226, 239n,
240n
kinds: in the late dialogues, 11–12, 172,
174–199, 210; greatest kinds in the

Sophist, 171, 190, 210; as paradigms,
12, 175, 198; interconnections
between, 174, 190, 192–194, 198;
philosophical analysis of, 197; deflationistic interpretations of, 12,
172, 197
knowledge, 98, 102–103, 117–119, 145,
167, 176–177, 183, 185, 198; discursive account of, 6–7, 139–146, 147;
immutability of, 117–119, 145;
visual account of, 6–7, 100–105;
about unchanging objects, 117–119,
130, 145, 198; of good and evil, *see*
wisdom

Larisa: road to, 102
late learners: in the *Sophist*, 175, 178,
192, 202–203, 238n
law of noncontradiction, 111
Lee, E. N., 121, 138, 221, 235n, 240n
Leue, W. H., xiii
Liddell and Scott, Greek-English
Lexicon, 81, 221, 229n
limit: in the *Philebus*, 11–12, 173, 177,
181, 186–188, 210
linguistic turn in philosophy, 14
Loeb editions of Plato, 221, 227n, 228n
logical contrariety, 53, 130
logical grammar of a term, 15–16, 38
logos (statement, account, definition):
29, 36, 40, 51, 52, 100, 104, 117, 120,
139–146, 164, 169, 175, 207–208,
234n
Louzecky, D., xii, xiii, 162, 238n, 239n
Lovejoy, A. O., 221, 232n
Luce, J. V., 221, 232n, 233n

madness: Platonic, 93
Malcolm, J., 222, 227n, 233n, 234n,
236n, 240n; on the relation between
the *Hippias Major* and *Phaedo*, 85–86,
97–98; on "to be" in the *Sophist*,
199–204
Mannick, P., 226
materialists: in the *Sophist*, 191–192
McGinley, J., 181, 222, 239n
mechanical arts. *See* beautiful, the
medical writers (ancient Greek), 15
Melissus, 90, 94, 233n
memory, 104
Milesian philosophers, 9, 110. *See also*
Anaximander; Anaximenes

Index Locorum

I. Plato